C000254170

THE ILLUSTRATED
ENCYCLOPEDIA OF
TREES & SHRUBS

THE ILLUSTRATED ENCYCLOPEDIA OF
TREES & SHRUBS

ALLEN J. COOMBES

PHOTOGRAPHS BY JUSTYN WILLSMORE

PUBLISHED BY
SALAMANDER BOOKS LIMITED
LONDON

A Salamander Book

Published by Salamander Books Ltd
8 Blenheim Court
Brewery Road
London N7 9NY
United Kingdom

1 3 5 7 9 8 6 4 2
Text © Salamander Books 2001

A member of the Chrysalis Group plc

ISBN 1 84065 162 8

Designed, edited and produced by Hilton/Sadler
Art Director: John Heritage Production: Phillip Chamberlain
Indexer Kathie Gill

Produced by Toppan (HK) Ltd
Printed in China

Author's Acknowledgements

I would like to thank all at Salamander, particularly Charlotte Davies for asking
me to work on this project. Special thanks go to Jonathan Hilton and Margaret
Sadler, with whom it was a pleasure to work, for their thorough and professional
work on the layouts and for keeping me on target. Finally I am indebted to both
Justyn Willsmore and David Brown for their fine photography.

Picture Credits

All pictures by Justyn Willsmore except:
David Brown: p. 54tr; p. 58tl; p. 72bl; p. 95tl; p. 98b; p. 123br; p. 136; p. 138ml; p. 159mr; p. 168b; p. 169b; p. 175;
p. 177bl; p. 179b; p. 180t; p. 195t; p. 221b; p. 227tr; p. 229b; p. 238t; p. 243t; p. 247; p. 275tl
Salamander Picture Library: half title; artworks on pp. 10–13; p. 26b; p. 27b; p. 31tl; p. 36b; p. 38b; p. 42t; p. 46tl; p. 52b; p. 57; p. 58b;
p. 61; p. 65t; p. 66br; p. 68b; p. 75; p. 77br; p. 78tr; p. 79ml; p. 82; p. 83bl; p. 87tr; p. 88ml, mr; p. 91m; p. 96; p. 103bl; p. 117tl; p. 118; p. 133ml; p. 137;
p. 138tl; p. 142br; p. 143; p. 144; p. 145t; p. 149tr; p. 153; p. 158tl, ml; p. 159tl; p. 169t; p. 173b; p. 174; p. 183; p. 187t; p. 188b; p. 198b; p. 208; p. 214b;
p. 225m; p. 232t; p. 241; p. 243b; p. 245t; pp. 270–3; p. 274br; p. 275br; p. 276; p. 277tr, mr; pp. 278–80; pp. 282–94; p. 295tr; p. 297tl, b; p. 298
Joy Stirling Images: p. 179t; p. 216; p. 251; p. 252tl
Garden & Wildlife Matters Photo Library/J Feltwell: p. 213t; p. 267; p. 268tr
Allen Coombes: p. 109
Gardens used in the book: pp. 16, 17t Hampton Court Palace flower show
p. 17b Mr and Mrs J Willsmore, Southampton
pp. 9, 14 Mr and Mrs Ward
All others from: The Sir Harold Hillier Gardens and Arboretum, RHS Wisley, Westonbirt Aboretum, Kew Gardens

Contents

Introduction

The trees, shrubs, climbers and conifers described in this book are all woody plants, so they do not die back into the soil in winter. They may, however, be deciduous, meaning they lose their leaves in winter, or evergreen, and they are also normally long-lived and permanent garden features.

The wide range of ornamental features displayed by woody plants makes them ideal for providing a design structure for your garden, a backbone of planting around which you can add annuals, herbaceous perennials, and the like. From upright to spreading, pendulous or creeping, woody plants can be found for virtually any situation or size of garden, perhaps as striking specimens in a lawn or woodland setting or as attractive screens and hedges, ground cover, or as plants for a mixed border. If combined thoughtfully, they can produce flowers throughout the year, while additional features, such as ornamental foliage or bark, can give additional autumn colour and winter interest.

Decoding plant names

Plants are referred to in the following chapters by their scientific names. Although many people often refer to plants by common names, this is often a source of confusion. Many plants do not have common names, for example, and many common names apply to more than one plant. In addition, different countries or even different regions, will often have their own common name for a particular plant. In fact, the scientific name is the only internationally recognized method of plant naming.

Plants are listed alphabetically by genus, after which the family name is given. There follows a description of that genus including any cultivation requirements, after which individual species in the genus are listed. As an example, the genus *Abelia* contains about 30 species. It is placed in the family Caprifoliaceae, which includes related genera (the plural of genus) such as *Lonicera* and *Viburnum*.

Within the genus *Abelia* several species are listed, such as *A. chinensis*. This is a species that is grown in gardens but occurs naturally in China. Some species are hybrids between two others, denoted by an x between the name of the genus and the species epithet. An example of this is *Abelia* x *grandiflora* – a hybrid that occurs only in gardens. Both naturally occurring species and garden hybrids can have named selections or cultivars. These have been selected for a particular feature. In the case of *A.* x *grandiflora*, several cultivars have been selected. The cultivar epithet is placed in inverted commas – for example *Abelia* x *grandiflora* 'Confetti'.

Sometimes a cultivar is not placed under any species, particularly if it has a complicated or unknown parentage. *Abelia*

'Edward Goucher' is an example of this. The purpose of naming a cultivar is that plants grown under that name are relatively uniform. When a selection is not uniform but is based on a variable feature, it may be referred to as a Group. For example *Abeliophyllum distichum* Roseum Group includes all plants with pink flowers and no specific selection. Some plants are most commonly sold under selling or trademark names. This is particularly common in roses. In this case, the selling name is given first without inverted commas, followed by the accepted cultivar epithet, such as *Rosa* Blue Moon ('Tannacht').

Choosing a plant

As woody plants are intended to be long-lived in the garden, it is particularly important to choose healthy specimens. Reputable garden centres will normally sell plants only when they are ready for planting. With plants grown in containers, this is throughout the year. Don't necessarily choose the largest plant, instead look for one that is growing strongly and has no obvious signs of damage or disease. Pot-bound plants, those with a mass of roots circling the pot or emerging from the base, should be avoided.

Trees may also be sold bare root – with no or little soil and usually wrapped in hessian. Check that the roots are healthy and not congested and have not dried out. Root-balled trees are sold with a ball of soil wrapped in hessian. Check that the root ball is firm and has not dried out. Both bare root and root-balled trees are generally available only between autumn and early spring.

Planting

After choosing a plant it is important to ensure that it does not dry out before it is planted. Keep the plant in a sheltered place and keep the root ball or roots moist until it is safely in the ground. Those in containers should be soaked in water for about 30 minutes before planting. Avoid planting in frosty or very dry conditions. The planting hole should be two to three times the width of the root ball and deep enough so that the soil level in the pot matches that of the ground. Refill the hole with soil mixed with organic matter. Most trees should be staked on planting. Water well after planting and frequently in the first year. Applying a mulch at the base of a plant will help to conserve water around the roots and prevent desiccation.

Opposite: Traditional climbers, in this case Clematis 'Jackmanii' and Boston ivy (Parthenocissus tricuspidata) around a doorway create a welcoming, cottage-garden effect. The raised bed, with its mixture of small shrubs and herbaceous perennials sloping to a stone pathway, brings the planting visually close to the house without actually encroaching on it.

Hardiness zones

Throughout the following chapters, plant entries have been given a hardiness rating. Hardiness is a measure of a plant's ability to resist low winter temperatures. Plants that will survive winters in a particular area are often termed 'hardy', while those that will not are referred to as 'tender'. Hardiness, however, is a relative term, and a plant that is tender in one area or region may well be perfectly hardy in a slightly warmer one. The hardiness zones used here are based on those developed by the United States Department of Agriculture, and are shown on the maps below and opposite. If the hardiness rating for a plant is given as Zone 7, for example, it will survive winters in Zones 7 and above, but is likely to be damaged by typical winter conditions in Zones 6 and below.

In spite of this, it is often well worth trying plants that should only be hardy in a warmer area – for example, Zone 8 plants in Zone 7. Within a typical garden, even a small one, there is likely to be a limited range of 'microclimates' – sheltered areas that will often be slightly warmer during winter than a more exposed site lying just a little distance away. A planting position against a wall or under tree cover are just two examples where the worst effects of winter conditions may be lessened, and in such places many plants regarded as tender can be tried.

Winter temperature, however, is not the only factor that influences hardiness. Some plants require very hot summers in order to ripen their growth, and without this heat they will not survive a cold winter. Other plants are successful only if the winters are dry rather than mild, and if it is wet they are likely to succumb to the unfavourable conditions. In yet other situations, plants that grow naturally in high northerly or southerly latitudes may not thrive in warmer regions. Some of these plants may require a permanently moist soil, which may be difficult to provide in areas with a long, dry season, or they may come into growth very early and then fall victim to late spring frosts.

Minimum winter temperature

Zone 1: Below -45° C (Below -50° F)
Zone 2: -45 to -37° C (-50 to -35° F)
Zone 3: -37 to -29° C (-35 to -20° F)
Zone 4: -29 to -23° C (-20 to -10° F)
Zone 5: -23 to -21° C (-10 to -5° F)
Zone 6: -21 to -15° C (-5 to 5° F)
Zone 7: -15 to -12° C (5 to 10° F)
Zone 8: -12 to -7° C (10 to 20° F)
Zone 9: -7 to -1° C (20 to 30° F)
Zone 10: -1 to 4° C (30 to 40° F)
Zone 11: Above +5° C (Above +40° F)

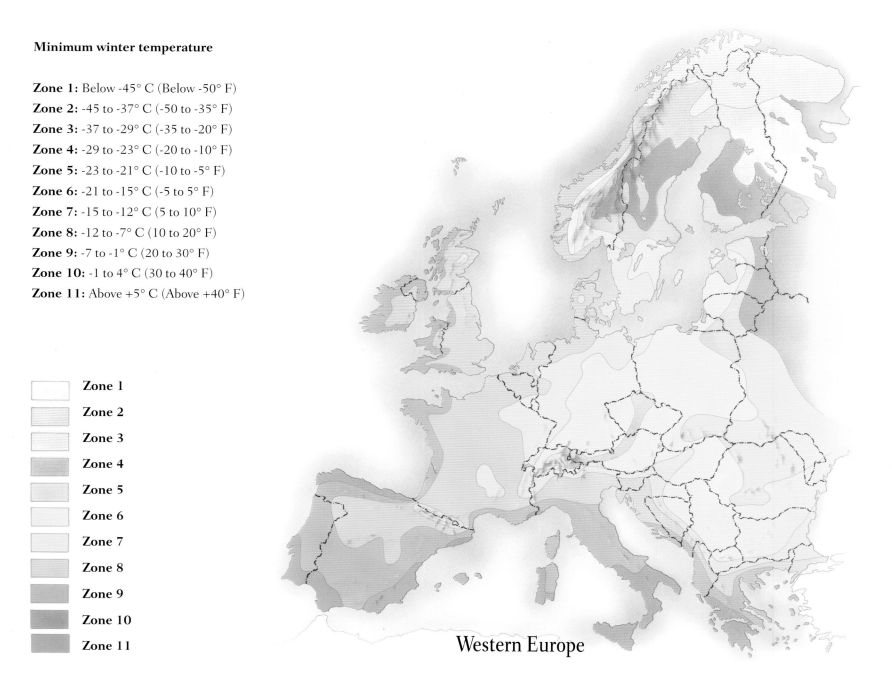

Zone 1
Zone 2
Zone 3
Zone 4
Zone 5
Zone 6
Zone 7
Zone 8
Zone 9
Zone 10
Zone 11

Western Europe

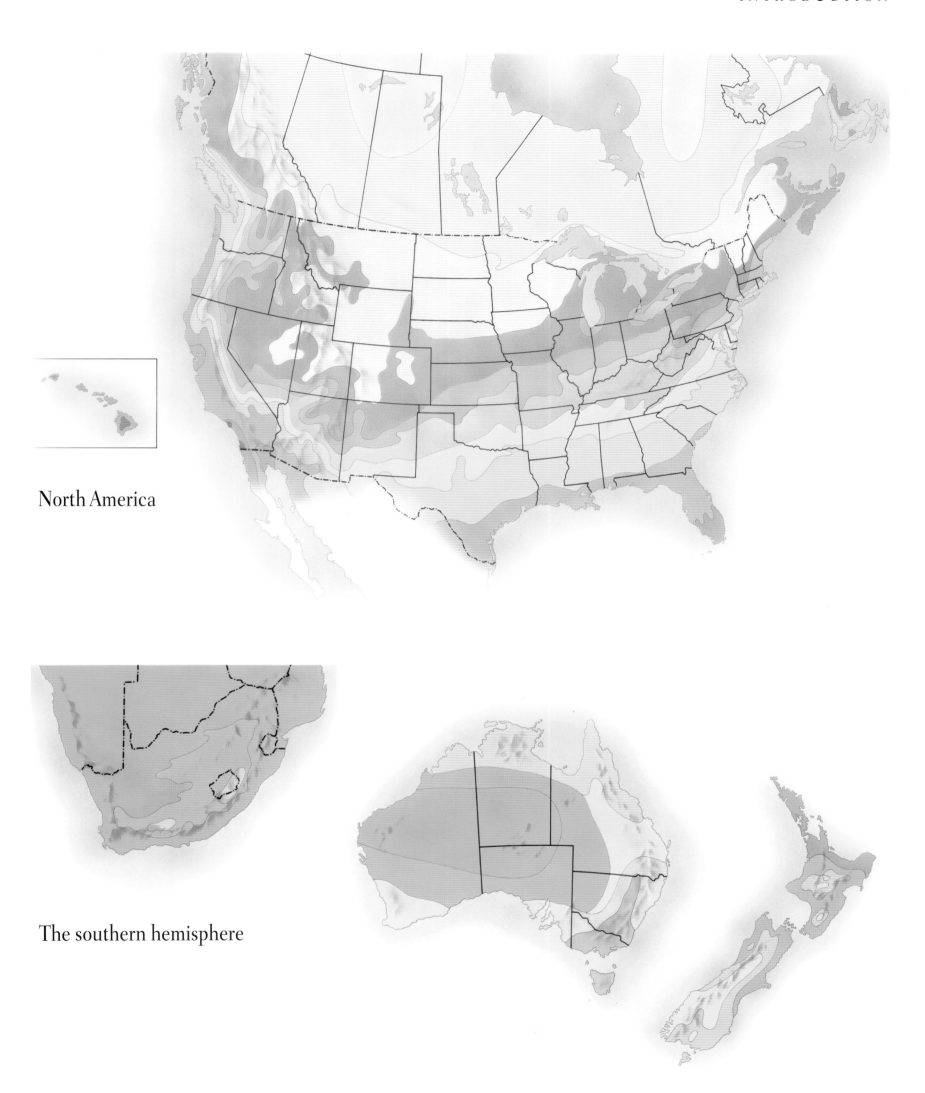

North America

The southern hemisphere

Leaf and tree shapes

Trees are extremely varied in many of their most obvious features, such as their leaves and growth habit. The shape of their leaves and how they are arranged can be very useful guides to identification. When leaves are said to be opposite they are arranged in pairs, one opposite the other. Some trees with superficially similar leaves can be distinguished in this way – for example the opposite-leaved *Liquidambar* from the alternate-leaved maples (*Acer*). Unless otherwise stated, plants described in the working chapters of the book have alternate leaves.

Compound leaves

When a leaf is divided into several leaflets it is said to be 'compound'. There are different types of compound leaves, however, for example, the ashes (*Fraxinus*) with their pinnately (leaflets growing opposite each other in pairs either side of the leaf stalk) compound leaves, and the horse chestnuts (*Aesculus*) with their palmately (hand-shaped) compound leaves.

Types of growth

While the shape of a tree's leaves will affect its appearance, the shape of the tree itself is vital in aiding its placement in the garden, and especially its relationship with other garden plants. Thus, shape is an important feature to consider when choosing a tree to buy. For example, a very narrow, columnar tree will not be effective for use as a screen – perhaps to provide privacy from neighbouring gardens or to help divide a garden up into different areas, or 'rooms' – but it may be excellent as a focal point if the available space is restricted – perhaps at the end of a well-planted mixed border. While a wide-spreading or weeping tree may create just the desired effect, remember that it will cast a good deal of shade and will need plenty of space.

Tree shapes

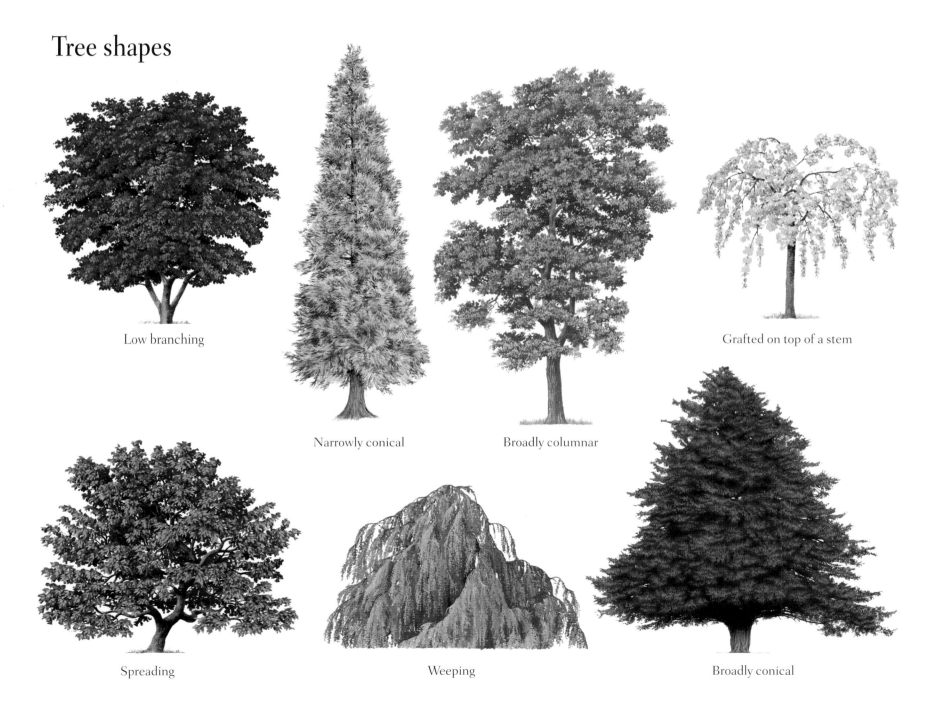

Low branching

Narrowly conical

Broadly columnar

Grafted on top of a stem

Spreading

Weeping

Broadly conical

Leaf shapes

Alternate leaves

Toothed

Juniperus chinensis with adult and juvenile foliage on same plant

Chamaecyparis – scale-like leaves of forms with adult (*above left*) and juvenile foliage (*above right*)

Pinnate

Untoothed, unlobed

Ovate

Opposite leaves

Cordate (heart-shaped)

Palmately lobed

Pendulous cones

Upright cones

Trifoliolate (with three leaflets)

Toothed and lobed

Male and female catkins on same plant

Male and female flowers

Palmately compound

Fern-leaved and copper beech showing variation in foliage in same species

Pruning

While many plants will grow happily without intervention, there are several reasons why a plant may need to be pruned. In each case it is important to understand why the pruning is necessary, what it achieves and how best to go about it. The object of pruning may be to remove damaged or diseased wood, remove suckers from grafted plants, encourage a bushy habit, stimulate fresh growth, restrict overall size, balance a misshapen plant, renovate old plants, or to create special effects, such as coppicing, hedging or topiary.

In each case, you will minimize damage to the plant if you use sharp, clean tools. Plants that are pruned regularly should also be given regular doses of a balanced fertilizer. Where relevant, pruning recommendations are given under each genus.

Pruning trees

Trees do not normally need a great deal of pruning. Most formative pruning is carried out in the nursery, but small trees may need to be trained by gradually removing the lower shoots. If you purchase what is known as a 'feathered' tree, it will be a young plant with branches almost to the base. If a standard tree is required, one with a clear stem, you will have to remove the lower branches over a period of a few years.

Pruning is normally carried out when the tree is dormant. In the first year, remove any shoots growing from the lower third of the stem. Cut back by about a half the shoots arising from the middle one-third of the stem, pruning to an outward-facing bud. In the second and third years, remove the shoots shortened in the previous year, cutting them back to the main stem, and cut back by two-thirds the shoots arising from the middle third of the stem. The following year, remove all side shoots to the desired height. Any pruning of the upper part of the tree is restricted to removing congested, diseased or damaged wood.

Once the tree is established, continue removing congested, diseased or damaged wood, reverting shoots on variegated plants, and any shoots that arise from the base or the trunk. Any work on large trees should be carried out by professionals.

Pruning shrubs

Shrubs vary tremendously in their pruning requirements. Many benefit from regular pruning to encourage new growth from the base or to remove older shoots that often do not flower or fruit as effectively as younger growth. Old shrubs that have become tall and leggy can often be renovated by cutting them back hard to

Left: The association of stonework and rock garden plants is made more intimate by the seclusion created by shrubs and trees in the background. Shrubs, which have been sensitively pruned, also hide the destination of the path, inviting further exploration.

the base. When pruning shrubs, the time of pruning is often a crucial factor. Shrubs that flower late in the year, for example, should often be pruned in the early spring. This then promotes young growth that will bear flowers later in that same year. For shrubs that flower early in the year, however, such a pruning regime would result in the loss of an entire season's flowers, and for this reason these shrubs should be pruned after flowering has finished. The resulting growth then bears flowers in the following year. Shrubs grown for their attractively coloured winter shoots can be hard pruned in spring, just before the new season's growth starts. How often you prune, however, depends largely on a shrub's vigour and the eventual size you want it to reach in the garden.

Bamboos usually require very little attention in the garden, but well-established clumps will benefit if you cut some of the old or dead culms right back to the base in spring. Some bamboos can be invasive, however, and the spread of these may need to be checked by removing unwanted culms.

Pruning climbers

The pruning of climbers depends on how they are to be grown. While those that are encouraged to scramble into a tree can be left unpruned, those that are grown on a wall or over a trellis will probably require pruning at some time to restrict their growth.

Climbers that produce several shoots from the base can have the older growths removed if necessary while some, such as *Clematis* and *Wisteria*, have specific pruning requirements designed to promote flowering. If you wish to train a climber to grow in a particular direction, make your pruning cuts to buds facing in the desired direction.

Pruning conifers

Conifers mostly need very little pruning if given the space they need. Allowed to reach their full size in an open situation, those that make large trees can look magnificent when fully clothed with branches sweeping right down to the ground. As trees mature, however, it often becomes necessary to remove some of the lower branches as they become shaded, either by the upper canopy or by surrounding trees. Dwarf conifers occasionally produce reverting shoots, which can grow strongly and quickly dominate the plant. These you should cut back to their point of origin as soon as you notice them.

Conifers that are used for hedging require the most pruning. Their dense habit and vigorous growth, as well as their tolerance of frequent pruning, make conifers such as *Chamaecyparis*, *Thuja* and x *Cupressocyparis* popular subjects for hedging . These plants should be pruned regularly from an early age – in this way you avoid the necessity of cutting into old wood, which will not generate new growth. This is the best way to ensure that a conifer hedge remains dense and well clothed with foliage.

Designing a garden

Whether you are remodelling an existing garden or merely adding to it, or if you are about to start work on an entirely new site, the design stage can be an exciting and rewarding process. Many gardens simply evolve through the acquisition and loss of plants over a period of years. While the gradual development of a garden has its advantages and rewards – for example, it allows for frequent changes of mind regarding the content of the garden and its use – it is the planning of a completely new garden or a major development of an existing one that presents the greatest challenge.

The initial design

When planting a new garden, there is always a temptation to rush to the garden centre, choose from the many attractive plants on sale, and get them into the ground as soon as possible. However, a better effect usually results from first thinking carefully about how the garden will be used. Will it be mainly for recreation, or as a showcase for your plant collection? How much of it will be lawn? Is any hard landscaping needed, such as

decking or stonework? Will screening be required, such as that provided by hedges? Make a rough plan to scale showing the position of any important features – lawns, paths, where hedges are needed, and the places where trees will be planted – and then add in the positions of any special plants you intend to grow, borders, raised beds, screes and so on. Once you have worked out the structure of the garden, then you can think about choosing specific plants.

Garden conditions

To be able to choose plants suitable for your garden, first you need to know the conditions that prevail there. How cold does it get in winter? Is it susceptible to late spring frosts? Which areas are in shade and which in full sun? What is the pH of the soil? Does the soil dry out very quickly? A look at other gardens in the same area will give you a very good idea of how local conditions will affect your choice of plants. If rhododendrons and camellias are common locally, then the soil is likely to be acid and not too dry.

Below: *A clever use of colour and of hard landscaping make the link between living area and garden in this water garden. The intimate association created effectively makes the garden part of the house, and the house part of the garden.*

Above: Don't be afraid to mix hard landscaping with associated plantings. Here, a rustic wooden walkway is softened with closely planted foliage plants. In this way, any structure can be linked to the rest of the garden and close contact with the plants around it increase overall enjoyment of the garden.

If common hydrangeas are lush, then conditions are likely to be moist, without too many late frosts. Hedges of escallonias or fuchsias indicate relatively mild conditions. Above all, talk to local gardeners about what they grow, and why.

Placing trees

Since trees are the largest and most permanent plants in a garden, the most careful thought needs to be given to their selection and position. Never be tempted to rely on pruning to restrict a tree's growth – this is simply not practical. Instead, choose one with an eventual size and spread suitable for its intended position. Exceptions to this include the forms of *Salix alba*, which can be cut back regularly to a short stem for their coloured young shoots. Where space is tight, trees of narrow or upright habit are useful, while spreading or weeping trees can create microclimates in which shade-loving plants will thrive.

Trees can be used to frame a view or to hide it, to enclose a garden or to provide a window on to the landscape outside. As well, a tree can highlight an area rather than dominate it.

Specimen plants

Depending on the size of your garden, choose specimen trees and shrubs for focal positions. These plants should have several ornamental qualities so that they remain interesting over more than a single season. They may, for example, combine an upright habit with ornamental foliage, as in *Taxus baccata* 'Standishii', or a weeping habit with silvery leaves, as in *Pyrus salicifolia* 'Pendula'. Trees with ornamental bark, such as the snake bark maples (*Acer*), are particularly useful as specimens as the bark is visible throughout the year. Specimen plants need not be at the centre of a garden; they could become the focal point of a side border or draw the eye to a more secluded part of the garden.

Borders

Borders are ideal situations for combining a wide range of plants. Choose plants according to the size and aspect of the area under cultivation and look for examples that can be combined to give contrasts of shape, foliage colour and texture, and flowering times. In this way, a border of shrubs and herbaceous perennials can be attractive throughout the year. Large shrubs, combined according to taste, at the back of a border can create an effective and ornamental screen, in colours ranging from shades of muted green to striking contrasts – such as that between purple-leaved *Cotinus* and *Philadelphus coronarius* 'Aureus'. Smaller shrubs can be accommodated towards the front, perhaps using a selection of aromatic plants here. There is always the danger in a border that plants will become too large and grow into adjacent ones. For this reason, those shrubs that tolerate, or even welcome, hard pruning are useful for providing ground cover, such as *Cornus*, *Hypericum* and *Caryopteris*.

Below: Climbers are very effective at hiding or softening hard structures in the garden. In this case, Virginia creeper (Parthenocissus quinquefolia) scrambles over stonework to provide an effective contrast with its striking autumn colour. Sticky pads on the tendrils enable this useful plant to cling to almost any surface.

Trees, shrubs and bamboos

The great variation in habit, foliage, stems and flowers shown by woody plants provides an almost endless choice of ornamental features to be used either singly or in combination. Although many plants are selected for their flowers, it is wise not to rely on this feature alone for ornamental effect in the garden. Many trees and shrubs also have attractive young foliage, such as the red new leaves of many *Pieris* and *Photinia*, while others have coloured or variegated foliage. Variegated evergreens can be particularly valuable, especially if they have other desirable assets. For example, the holly *Ilex* x *altaclerensis* 'Lawsoniana' not only has boldly variegated leaves, but also red berries in the autumn and winter seasons.

Don't be tempted to use too many trees and shrubs with coloured or variegated foliage: use just a few well-chosen examples to highlight or draw attention to particular areas, contrasting them with green foliage from, for example, a clump of bamboo. Variegated plants will usually not flower as freely as their green-leaved counterparts, and they usually grow more slowly – a factor that may well be an advantage in small gardens.

Trees and shrubs can be used in combination to provide a succession of flower colour throughout the year, but other qualities can also be used to extend the seasonal attractions of your planting scheme. Fruiting shrubs, such as *Pyracantha* and *Cotoneaster*, provide autumn displays, while striking autumn colour can be provided by such plants as *Euonymus alatus*. The winged shoots of the *Euonymus* also provide an extra winter attraction, and this can be supplemented by winter-flowering plants such as the witch hazels (*Hamamelis*) and *Daphne*.

Abelia
Caprifoliaceae

The 30 species in this genus of shrubs include evergreen as well as deciduous specimens with opposite leaves grown for their attractive foliage and their usually small, but profusely borne, tubular- or funnel-shaped, sometimes fragrant flowers. In some forms the foliage is variegated. Additional attractions of this genus include the young foliage, which is often coloured, and the sepals, which can be tinted and enlarged after flowering is over.

They are generally easy-to-grow shrubs and tend to do best if planted in a sunny position in a border. Prune as necessary to control growth, depending on the space available, and established plants can be cut back hard in early spring.

In particularly cold areas, it is best to grow them against a sunny wall, but even if they are cut down by severe winter frosts they will often regrow from the base. They are native plants of East Asia, from the Himalayas to Japan, and Mexico.

Abelia 'Edward Goucher'

Abelia chinensis

A deciduous shrub of spreading habit with glossy dark green leaves to 4 cm (1½ in) long, sometimes bronzy when young. The small, white or pink-tinged and fragrant, funnel-shaped flowers are borne in dense clusters over a long period during summer and autumn. As the flowers fade, the sepals around them turn from green to pink.

Native range: China
Height: 1.5 m (5 ft)
Spread: 2 m (6 ft)
Hardiness: Zone 7

Abelia 'Edward Goucher'

This semi-evergreen shrub is a hybrid between *A.* x *grandiflora* and *A. schumannii*. It has a vigorous, spreading habit with arching branches bearing glossy green leaves to 5 cm (2 in) long, bronze-coloured when young. The clusters of funnel-shaped, lilac-pink flowers open over a long period through summer and autumn.

Height: 1.5 m (5 ft)
Spread: 2 m (6 ft)
Hardiness: Zone 6

Abelia floribunda

This striking species is among the most attractive of the entire genus, but it is also the most tender. It makes a large, vigorous evergreen shrub with arching branches and glossy dark green leaves up to 5 cm (2 in) long. The tubular, bright magenta-pink flowers are 5 cm (2 in) long and hang in small clusters from the shoots during summer and through to autumn. It can be grown to good effect if trained against a wall.

Common name: Mexican Abelia
Native range: Mexico
Height: 2 m (6 ft) or more
Spread: 3 m (10 ft) or more
Hardiness: Zone 8

Abelia x grandiflora

The most popular plant in the genus, this semi-evergreen shrub is a hybrid between *A. chinensis* and *A. uniflora*. It makes a vigorous bush with attractive arching branches. The glossy dark green leaves are about 5 cm (2 in) long and often turn bronze in the cold weather. The small, funnel-shaped, white or pink-tinged and slightly fragrant flowers are borne in clusters over a long period during summer and autumn. As the flowers fade, the sepals turn to a pink hue, thus extending the long period of colour this shrub brings to the garden.

Common name: Glossy Abelia
Height: 3 m (10 ft)
Spread: 4 m (13 ft)
Hardiness: Zone 6
Variants: *Abelia* x *grandiflora* has given rise to several forms, often with variegated foliage, that do not tend to be as striking in flower as those with

Abelia x *grandiflora*

green leaves. 'Confetti' is a smaller shrub, reaching a height of about 1 m (3 ft) and a spread of 1.5 m (5 ft), with slender leaves that are narrowly edged with white or pink. 'Francis Mason' has yellow-green leaves edged with yellow and reaches a height and spread of 1.5 m (5 ft). Some plants under this name include 'Goldsport', which is a little less vigorous, with completely yellow leaves. 'Sunrise' is low growing, to 1 m (3 ft) tall and 1.5 m (5 ft) across, with dark green leaves edged with bright yellow.

Abelia schumannii

A vigorous and particularly hardy deciduous species with purple young shoots and arching branches. The mid-green leaves are about 3 cm (1 in) long and are bronze when young. The funnel-shaped flowers are slightly fragrant and lilac-pink, with a conspicuous orange blotch in the throat. They are borne in clusters during summer and autumn, and the sepals turn pink with age.

Native range: China
Height: 2 m (6 ft)
Spread: 3 m (10 ft)
Hardiness: Zone 6

Abelia triflora

This less commonly seen species is a very distinct tree-like shrub with a vigorous, upright habit, developing a stout trunk with ridged bark. The branches arch with age and the large, hairy leaves, to 8 cm (3 in) long, are occasionally lobed. The fragrant, white or pink-tinged tubular flowers have red sepals and are borne in clusters during summer.

Native range: W Himalayas
Height: 4 m (13 ft)
Spread: 2.5 m (8 ft)
Hardiness: Zone 6

Abelia x *grandiflora* 'Francis Mason'

Abeliophyllum distichum
Oleaceae

The single species in this genus is native to Korea and is related to *Forsythia*. Being a winter-flowering shrub, it makes a valuable addition to the garden at a time of year when colour is usually at a premium.

The shrub is easy to cultivate in any reasonable soil, but it prefers a sunny position in a border if it is to flower at its best. In areas that experience relatively cool summers, *Abeliophyllum distichum* will benefit from the additional warmth that comes from being grown against a wall. Old plants that have become straggly do better if they are cut back hard after flowering.

This deciduous, spreading shrub has opposite leaves that grow up to 8 cm (3 in) long. They are matt dark green in colour but often turn a deep red-purple in autumn before falling. The young shoots in winter are also a deep red-purple colour, as are the buds, which open in late winter to early spring. The flowers are white, four-lobed and fragrant – sometimes pink-tinged as they emerge.

Common name: White Forsythia
Native range: Korea
Height: 1.5 m (5 ft)
Spread: 2 m (6 ft)
Hardiness: Zone 5
Variants: Roseum Group includes plants that have pink flowers.

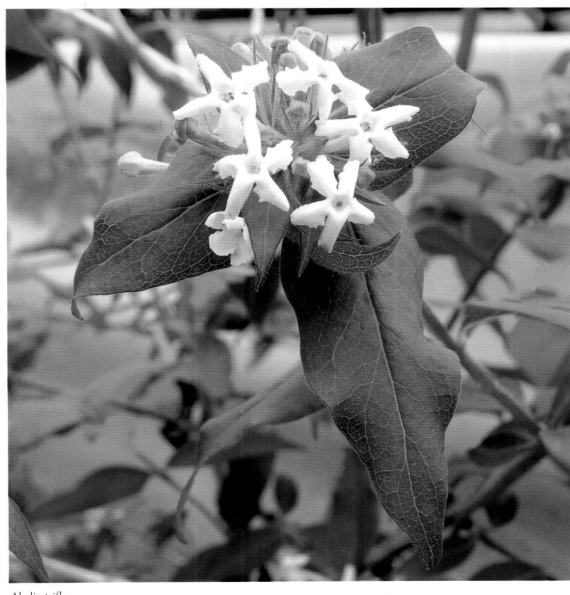

Abelia triflora

Abutilon
Malvaceae

This large and varied genus contains some 150 different species of annual and perennial herbaceous plants. In addition, the genus encompasses deciduous and evergreen trees and shrubs that are widely distributed throughout the tropical and subtropical regions of the world.

The often lobed leaves of *Abutilon* species are variegated in some forms. They are valued for their showy, bell- or saucer-shaped flowers, which are borne in a variety of colours. They are suitable only for milder garden temperatures, however, and while they will survive in any reasonable soil they prefer a site that is sheltered from any strong winds – either in a border or against a wall in a sunny position.

Prune these plants in early spring before growth starts, either by trimming as required to restrict growth or by cutting back hard to create a low framework of branches. Many tender *Abutilon* species not described here are grown as conservatory plants or for summer bedding.

Abutilon 'Kentish Belle'

This semi-evergreen shrub has slender shoots and dark green, slightly lobed leaves that grow to 4 cm (1½ in) long. The pendulous bell-shaped flowers, which are also about 4 cm (1½ in) long, are borne from the growing shoots over a long period during summer and autumn. Each flower has red sepals and pale apricot petals from which protrudes a cluster of purple stamens. It is best trained against a wall as it grows.

Height: 2.5 m (8 ft)
Spread: 2.5 m (8 ft)
Hardiness: Zone 8

Abutilon megapotamicum

A vigorous semi-evergreen shrub with slender shoots and dark green unlobed leaves to 12 cm (5 in) long. The pendulous bell-shaped flowers, 4 cm (1½ in) long, hang from arching shoots during summer and autumn. The flowers have conspicuous, bright red sepals, from the mouths of which appear yellow petals and clusters of purple stamens. It is best grown trained against a wall.

Common name: Trailing Abutilon
Native range: Brazil
Height: 2 m (6 ft)
Spread: 2 m (6 ft)
Hardiness: Zone 8
Variants: 'Variegatum' has leaves that are densely mottled with yellow.

Abutilon megapotamicum

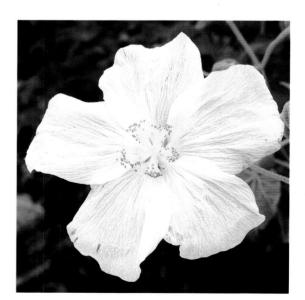

Abutilon vitifolium 'Veronica Tennant'

Abutilon x suntense

This hybrid is a cross between *A. ochsenii* and *A. vitifolium*. It makes a vigorous, tree-like deciduous shrub with bold, heart-shaped, lobed and toothed, green to grey-green leaves that grow to a length of about 12 cm (5 in). The colour of the saucer-shaped flowers, which are up to 6 cm (2½ in) across, varies from white to deep violet. The shrub comes into flower in late spring or early summer, depending on conditions.

Height: 5 m (16 ft)
Spread: 2.5 m (8 ft)
Hardiness: Zone 8
Variants: Selections of this hybrid include 'Gorer's White', which has white flowers; 'Jermyns', a shrub with deep mauve flowers; 'Ralph Gould', which has strikingly large violet-coloured flowers; and 'Violetta', with deep violet-blue flowers.

Abutilon vitifolium

This vigorous, tree-like deciduous shrub has stout, felted shoots and large, grey-haired leaves that are markedly lobed and toothed. The leaves grow up to 15 cm (6 in) in length. The saucer-shaped flowers of *Abutilon vitifolium*, which grow up to 8 cm (3 in) across, vary in colour from white to mauve, and they are profusely borne in the late spring and summer.

Native range: Chile
Height: 5 m (16 ft)
Spread: 2.5 m (8 ft)
Hardiness: Zone 8
Variants: var. *album* has white-coloured flowers; 'Tennant's White' is another white-flowering form of *Abutilon*, but it has particularly large flowers; and 'Veronica Tennant' has large and attractive mauve-coloured flowers.

Acacia

Leguminosae

A very large genus of more than 1,000 species of mainly evergreen trees and shrubs, with some herbaceous species, widely distributed in tropical and subtropical regions of Australia, Africa and South and Central America. They are mainly grown for their attractive, often fragrant flowers, which, although individually tiny, are borne in dense clusters. Many also have attractive foliage, which in some is composed of leaves with numerous leaflets, while in the mature plants of others the leaves are reduced to an expanded leaf stalk (phyllode).

Acacias are suitable for growing outside only in mild or nearly frost-free areas. They prefer a sunny position and make specimen plants in such locations. In areas with cooler winters they can be grown if afforded the protection of a wall. Ideally sited in a neutral to acidic soil, Acacias can show signs of chlorosis on shallow alkaline soils. Cut back lightly after flowering if necessary, and remove any damaged or dead wood in early spring.

Acacia baileyana

This is a small evergreen tree, sometimes shrubby, with a spreading habit, and with blue-green leaves

Acacia dealbata

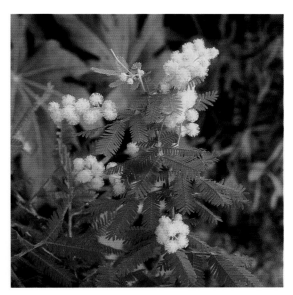

Acacia baileyana

up to 5 cm (2 in) long, finely divided into numerous tiny leaflets. Small rounded heads of bright yellow flowers open in large clusters, up to 10 cm (4 in), long during the late winter and early spring.

Common name: Cootamundra wattle
Native range: New South Wales (Australia)
Height: 6 m (20 ft)
Spread: 6 m (20 ft)
Hardiness: Zone 8

Variants: 'Purpurea' is a very attractive form in which the young leaves are deep purple, later turning to blue-green.

Acacia dealbata

This is a fast-growing evergreen tree with fern-like, blue-green leaves, reaching up to about 12 cm (5 in) long, finely divided into small leaflets. The large clusters, about 20 cm (8 in) long, of small, rounded heads of fragrant yellow flowers open during late winter and early spring.

Common names: Mimosa, silver wattle
Native range: SE Australia, Tasmania
Height: 15 m (50 ft) or more
Spread: 10 m (33 ft)
Hardiness: Zone 8

Acacia pravissima

This is an unusual and large-growing evergreen shrub featuring slender, arching branches. The leaves have been reduced to densely arranged blue-green, triangular, spine-tipped phyllodes, growing up to about 2 cm (¾ in) in length. Clusters of small, bright yellow, fragrant flowerheads, up to about 10 cm (4in) long, open

during the late winter and early spring. This species looks particularly effective when it is grown against a wall.

Common name: Ovens wattle
Native range: SE Australia
Height: 6 m (20 ft)
Spread: 8 m (26 ft)
Hardiness: Zone 8

Acacia retinodes

This species can be grown as a small evergreen tree or as a large shrub with arching shoots and willow-like foliage. The leaves have been reduced to slender, slightly curved, blue-green phyllodes that grow up to about 20 cm (8 in) in length. The small rounded heads of yellow flowers are borne in clusters up to about 4 cm (1½ in) long during the summer, and then intermittently throughout the year.

Native range: SE Australia, Tasmania
Height: 8 m (26 ft)
Spread: 7 m (23 ft)
Hardiness: Zone 8

Acca sellowiana

Acca
Myrtaceae

Of the two or three species in this small genus of South American evergreen shrubs, only the following example is commonly cultivated. Grown for its unusual flowers, it is suitable for any reasonable soil as long as it has a sunny position. In cold areas, it should be grown with a wall for protection, while in mild regions it can be used as a free-standing specimen shrub or planted as hedging. In warm climates it is cultivated for its edible fruit and some forms selected for their fruits are grown. Pruning is not usually required; however, a light trimming back in spring will help to retain a compact habit.

Acca sellowiana

This evergreen shrub has opposite, grey-green, untoothed leaves that grow up to about 7 cm (3 in) long. The leaves have a dense felt of grey hairs beneath. The showy flowers are about 4 cm (1½ in) across and are borne in the summer months. The flowers have four rather fleshy petals, deep red above and curling upwards at their edges to show a starkly contrasting white undersurface. At the centre of each bloom is found a dense brush of conspicuous red stamens. In warm climates edible, egg-shaped green fruits, up to about 5 cm (2 in), long are produced.

Synonym: *Feijoa sellowiana*
Common name: Pineapple guava
Native range: Brazil, Uruguay
Height: 2 m (6 ft)
Spread: 2.5 m (8 ft)
Hardiness: Zone 8
Variants: 'Variegata' is a form in which the leaves are narrowly edged with creamy white.

Acer
Aceraceae

The maples are an important and very varied genus of plants consisting of more than 120 species of mainly deciduous trees, with some shrubs, that are widely distributed throughout the northern hemisphere. All maples have opposite-growing leaves, which, in most species, are palmately (hand-shaped) lobed, occasionally unlobed, and sometimes divided into separate leaflets. The flowers are small and usually green in colour, but they can be an attractive feature when they open in spring and are then followed by the familiar winged fruits.

While maples are grown principally for their striking foliage, which can provide a spectacular autumn display, some species – such as the snakebark maples – have attractively striped bark to recommend them. Such species include *A. capillipes*, *A. davidii*, *A. grosseri* var. *hersii*, *A. pensylvanicum* and *A. rufinerve*.

Maples are generally easy to grow in any good garden soil. The Japanese maples (*A. palmatum* and *A. japonicum*) are subject to damage by late frosts and cold winds in spring, and so they are best planted in a sheltered position. Those following are all deciduous.

Acer buergerianum

This is a rather slow-growing tree for small gardens. It has glossy dark green leaves to 9 cm (3½ in) long, blue-green beneath and three-lobed at the tip. Late in autumn or early winter the leaves turn yellow, orange and red before falling. Its small yellow-green flowers are rather inconspicuous among the foliage as it emerges in spring. Mature trees develop attractive, flaking red-brown bark.

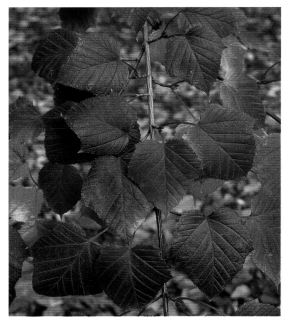

Acer capillipes

Common name: Trident maple
Native range: E China, Korea
Height: 10 m (33 ft)
Spread: 9m (30 ft)
Hardiness: Zone 5

Acer campestre

This is a densely branched, spreading or rounded tree with dark green, slender-stalked leaves, three- to five-lobed, turning butter-yellow in autumn. Small greenish flowers are inconspicuous as the leaves emerge. This is a tough, small tree for a variety of situations, from streets to small gardens. It also responds well to pruning and makes a very effective dense hedge.

Common names: Field maple, hedge maple
Native range: Europe, N Africa, W Asia
Height: 10 m (33 ft) or more
Spread: 10 m (33 ft)
Hardiness: Zone 5
Variants: 'Carnival' is a form in which the leaves are broadly edged in creamy white.

Acer capillipes

This snakebark maple is a small tree. The young shoots are red and the main trunk and branches streaked with white. The dark green leaves, 12 cm (5 in) long, are prominently three-lobed with slender tapering tips, and turn striking shades of red in autumn. The green flowers appear in drooping clusters in spring as the leaves emerge.

Native range: Japan
Height: 10 m (33 ft)
Spread: 10 m (33 ft)
Hardiness: Zone 5

Acer cappadocicum 'Rubrum'

Acer cappadocium 'Aureum'

Acer davidii

Perhaps the best known of the snakebark maples, this small tree has arching branches and green bark on the main trunk attractively streaked with white. The oval, mid- to dark green leaves are up to 15 cm (6 in) long, unlobed or with two small lobes, with taper-pointed tips. Leaves often turn orange and yellow in autumn. Pale green flowers open in drooping clusters in the spring.

Common name: Père David's maple
Native range: China
Height: 15 m (50 ft)
Spread: 12 m (40 ft)
Hardiness: Zone 5
Variants: 'Ernest Wilson' has pale green leaves turning orange-yellow in autumn. 'George Forrest' has bold, dark green, unlobed leaves, up to 20 cm (8 in) long, that usually fall without colouring. 'Serpentine' has small dark green leaves, up to 10 cm (4 in) long, and purple shoots.

Acer cappadocicum

This is a vigorous tree of a spreading habit with bold, bright green leaves up to 15 cm (6 in) across, each with five to seven lobes ending in slender, tapering points. Often bronzy or red when young, the leaves turn to an attractive butter-yellow colour in autumn. The tree bears small clusters of yellow flowers in spring.

Common names: Cappadocian maple, Caucasian maple
Native range: Turkey to China
Height: 20 m (65 ft)
Spread: 15 m (50 ft)
Hardiness: Zone 5
Variants: 'Aureum' is a smaller tree that grows up to about 15 m (50 ft) tall. It has bright yellow young foliage that turns green in summer and then back to yellow in autumn. The young foliage of 'Rubrum' is deep blackish-red in colour.

Acer circinatum

A close relative of the Japanese maples, *A. palmatum* and *A. japonicum*, *A. circinatum* makes a small shrubby tree with a spreading habit. The rounded leaves are up to 12 cm (5 in) across and have seven to nine toothed lobes. Leaves turn to shades of orange, yellow and red in autumn. Small purple and white flowers are borne in clusters in spring. A useful tree that thrives well in dry, shady positions.

Common name: Vine maple
Native range: W North America
Height: 5 m (16 ft)
Spread: 5 m (16 ft)
Hardiness: Zone 5

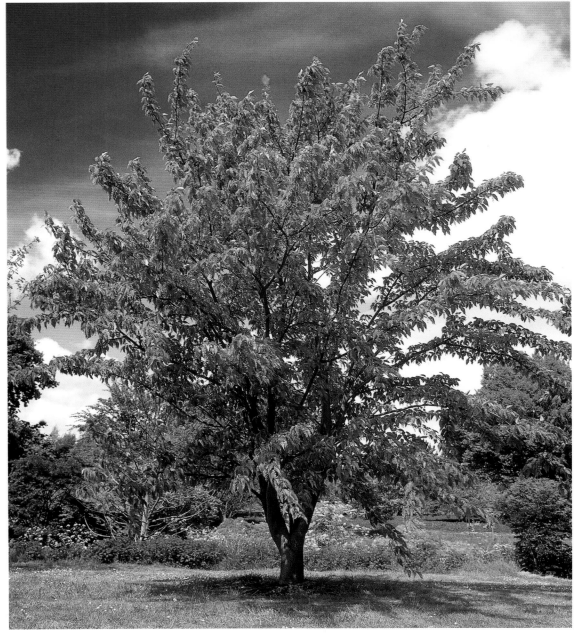

Acer davidii 'George Forrest'

Acer griseum

This species is among the most striking and most sought after of all trees for its bark. *Acer griseum* is slow growing but, once they are mature, trees develop a spreading habit and their attractive cinnamon-brown bark starts to peel in thin flakes on the main trunk and even the smallest branches. The dark green leaves have three leaflets growing up to 10 cm (4 in) long and these can turn orange and red in autumn, when the tree is often laden with contrasting pale green fruits.

Common name: Paperbark maple
Native range: China
Height: 10 m (33 ft)
Spread: 10 m (33 ft)
Hardiness: Zone 5

Acer grosseri var. hersii

A vigorous snakebark maple with arching branches, which, like the main trunk, are green and attractively marked with white streaks. The broadly oval, glossy green leaves are taper-pointed at the tip and have two small lobes at the base, turning bright yellow to orange-yellow in autumn.

Native range: China
Height: 15 m (50 ft)
Spread: 12 m (40 ft)
Hardiness: Zone 5

Acer japonicum

A bushy, spreading tree, often branching low and shrubby, with rounded leaves, up to 13 cm (5 in) long, edged with up to 11 sharply toothed lobes. Silky hairy when young, leaves become dark green then turn to shades of orange and red in autumn. Pendulous clusters of small red and purple flowers open in spring with the emerging leaves.

Common name: Fullmoon maple
Native range: Japan
Height: 10 m (33 ft)
Spread: 10 m (33 ft)
Hardiness: Zone 5
Variants: 'Aconitifolium' has leaves that are deeply cut, nearly to the centre, into sharply toothed lobes, turning deep crimson in autumn. 'Vitifolium' has very large leaves that turn brilliant orange, red and purple in autumn.

Acer maximowiczianum

This is a spreading tree, the leaves of which are divided into three stalked leaflets that have few, if any, teeth. Leaves are up to 10 cm (4 in) long, dark

Acer japonicum 'Aconitifolium'

Acer griseum

green above, blue-green beneath with a layer of soft hairs. The leaves take on bright autumn colours at the end of the season. Drooping clusters of small yellow flowers open with the young leaves in spring.

Synonym: *A. nikoense*
Common name: Nikko maple
Native range: Japan, China
Height: 10 m (33 ft)
Spread: 8 m (26 ft)
Hardiness: Zone 5

Acer negundo

A very fast-growing tree of broadly columnar habit with leaves up to 20 cm (8 in) long, each with from three to seven separate, sometimes lobed, leaflets. Leaves can turn yellow in autumn, but they can also fall without colouring. Male and female flowers are borne on separate plants in pendulous tassel-like clusters before the leaves appear in the spring. It is normally grown only as one of the forms listed below. Those with variegated leaves often produce green-leaved reversions, which must be removed as soon as possible.

Acer maximowiczianum

Spread: 10 m (33 ft)
Hardiness: Zone 5
Variants: Numerous garden selections have been made varying in size, leaf shape and colour. 'Atropurpureum' has red-purple leaves that turn bright red in autumn. 'Bloodgood' has deeply cut, deep red-purple leaves, turning red in autumn. 'Butterfly' is a dainty, slow-growing, upright form reaching a height of 2 m (6 ft) or more, and its small leaves have margins of pink and cream. 'Chitoseyama' is shrubby, up to about 2 m (6 ft) tall, with arching branches and deeply cut, bronze-coloured leaves that turn deep red in autumn. 'Crimson Queen' grows to about 3 m (10 ft) with pendulous shoots and finely cut, deep red-purple foliage, turning red in autumn. 'Dissectum' is similar to 'Crimson Queen', but with green foliage turning orange-yellow in autumn, while 'Garnet' has rich garnet-red foliage turning red in autumn. 'Inaba-shidare' has large red-purple leaves deeply cut into slender lobes, turning red in autumn. 'Osakazuki' has dark green, seven-lobed leaves turning a brilliant deep red in autumn. 'Red Pygmy' is slow growing and bushy, up to about 1.5 m (5 ft) tall, and its deep red-purple leaves are deeply cut into narrow lobes. 'Sangokaku' ('Senkaki'), known as the coral-bark maple, has pale green leaves, turning orange-yellow in autumn, and young shoots are bright pink in winter. 'Seiryu' resembles 'Dissectum' with its finely cut leaves, but it is upright, reaching about 4 m (13 ft) or more. 'Trompenburg' has deep red-purple leaves, but the margins of the lobes are rolled under making them appear narrow.

Common names: Box elder, ash-leaved maple
Native range: North America
Height: 20 m (65 ft) or more
Spread: 15 m (50 ft)
Hardiness: Zone 3
Variants: 'Elegans' has leaflets that are broadly edged with yellow and grows to a height of about 10 m (33 ft). 'Flamingo' is similar, but the margin of its leaves are pink at first and later turn to white. The leaves of 'Variegatum' have a white margin from the outset.

Acer palmatum

This is among the most popular of all the maples and grows into a rounded tree, usually branching low down, with slender shoots. The dark green leaves are deeply cut into five or seven taper-pointed and toothed lobes, and leaves turn various shades of orange, yellow and red in the autumn. The drooping clusters of red-purple flowers open with the young leaves in spring.

Common name: Japanese maple
Native range: Japan, China, Korea
Height: 8 m (26 ft)

Acer palmatum

Acer palmatum 'Bloodgood'

Acer palmatum 'Osakazuki'

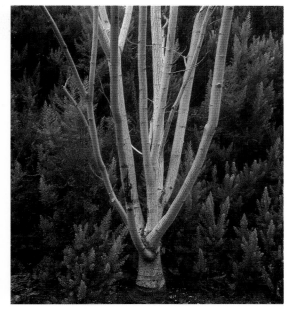

Acer pensylvanicum 'Erythrocladum'

Acer pseudoplatanus

A large, vigorous and very tough tree of rounded habit. The dark green leaves are blue-grey beneath, up to 15 cm (6 in) or more long, with five, toothed lobes. Leaves do not usually colour in autumn. Dense, pendulous clusters of small yellow-green flowers without petals open with the young leaves. Useful in exposed and coastal positions.

Common name: Sycamore
Native range: Europe, SW Asia
Height: 30 m (100 ft)
Spread: 25 m (80 ft)
Hardiness: Zone 4
Variants: The leaves of 'Atropurpureum' are deep red-purple beneath. 'Brilliantissimum' is useful in small gardens, reaching about 6 m (20 ft) in height. Its young leaves are bright pink in spring, turning yellow-green. 'Leopoldii' has leaves mottled with creamy yellow, pink when young. 'Prinz Handjéry' is similar to 'Brilliantissimum', but its leaves are purple beneath. 'Simon-Louis Frères' has pink young leaves, later turning green blotched with creamy white. 'Worley' ('Worleei') has pale yellow young leaves on red stalks, later turning green.

Acer pensylvanicum

This is the only snakebark maple that is native outside of East Asia. It is a vigorous tree and its green bark is attractively marked with white stripes. The bold, rather pale green leaves grow to a length of 15 cm (6 in) or more, and have three conspicuous, taper-pointed lobes at the tip. Leaves turn a striking butter-yellow in autumn. Its slender, drooping clusters of pale green flowers open as the leaves are emerging in spring.

Common name: Moosewood
Native range: E North America
Height: 8 m (26 ft)
Spread: 7 m (23 ft)
Hardiness: Zone 3
Variants: 'Erythrocladum' has yellow-green foliage and yellow bark. The young shoots are brilliant pink in winter. It is best grown as a shrub rather than trained as a single stem.

Acer platanoides

A vigorous large tree that is normally taller than it is wide – suited only to large gardens. The bold, bright green leaves are up to 15 cm (6 in) long and are divided into five lobes edged with taper-pointed teeth. Leaves turn yellow, occasionally red, in autumn. Among the best of the maples for flowers, the conspicuous clusters of yellow blooms open in spring before the leaves emerge.

Common name: Norway maple
Native range: Europe, SW Asia
Height: 25 m (80 ft) or more
Spread: 15 m (50 ft)
Hardiness: Zone 5
Variants: 'Crimson King' has deep red-purple foliage and red-tinged flowers. 'Crimson Sentry' is compact and upright in habit, reaching 12 m

(40 ft) tall, with leaves that are red when young, becoming deep purple-green. 'Drummondii' has leaves with a broad, creamy yellow margin when young, turning to creamy white, but often produces reverting shoots with all-green leaves. It reaches a height of about 12 m (40 ft).

Acer platanoides 'Crimson King'

Acer platanoides 'Drummondii'

Acer rubrum

This is a fast-growing member of the maple family with a broadly columnar to rounded habit when mature. The glossy dark green leaves have between three and five lobes each, and grow up to about 10 cm (4 in) long. The leaves are coloured blue-white on their undersurfaces and often turn a brilliant red in autumn, but sometimes yellow. Dense clusters of deep red flowers open on the bare shoots in early spring. If *Acer rubrum* is grown on dry, alkaline soils, it may not develop the type of autumn colour for which it is valued.

Common name: Red maple
Native range: E North America
Height: 25 m (80 ft)
Spread: 15 m (50 ft)
Hardiness: Zone 4
Variants: 'October Glory' has reliably good, bright red autumn colour. 'Scanlon' exhibits a compact form of columnar habit and grows to about 15 m (50 ft) in height and with a 5-m (16-ft) spread. It, too, has good red autumn colour.

Acer rufinerve

This striking snakebark maple makes a compact tree suitable for most small gardens. It has arching branches and green bark conspicuously streaked with white. The dark green leaves grow up to about 13 cm (5 in) in length and are sharply toothed and shallowly three-lobed. In autumn, its foliage turns from green to orange-yellow and red-purple. The small yellow-green flowers produced in spring are followed by fruits which often have distinctly red-flushed wings.

Native range: Japan
Height: 10 m (33 ft)
Spread: 8 m (26 ft)
Hardiness: Zone 5

Acer pseudoplatanus 'Brilliantissimum'

Acer rufinerve

Acer saccharinum

A. saccharinum is a vigorous tree with a broadly columnar to spreading habit. Its large leaves grow up to 15 cm (6 in) long and they are deeply cut into usually five lobes. These, in turn, are lobed and toothed. Rather a pale green colour above, the leaves have a distinct blue-white tint to their undersurfaces and they turn yellow or orange in autumn. Like *A. rubrum*, the small flowers open on the bare shoots in early spring, but they are less conspicuous as they are yellow-green.

Common name: Silver maple
Native range: E North America
Height: 25 m (80 ft)
Spread: 15 m (50 ft)
Hardiness: Zone 3

Acer saccharum

Probably best known as the tree from which maple syrup is obtained, this species is also one of the

Acer shirasawanum 'Aureum'

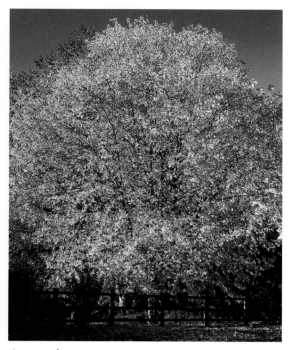

Acer saccharinum

Spread: 10 m (33 ft)
Hardiness: Zone 5
Variants: The most commonly found form of this tree in garden cultivation is 'Aureum' (*A. japonicum* 'Aureum'). This is a slower growing tree and attains a maximum height of up to about 6 m (20 ft). As implied by its name, it produces bright yellow foliage.

Acer tataricum

Due to its extreme hardiness, *A. tataricum* is an extremely useful tree to grow in areas that experience cold winters. This tough tree is also a fast-growing and small specimen, features that makes it an extra bonus for small gardens. It has a spreading habit, and its bright green, toothed, but usually unlobed leaves are up to about 10 cm (4 in) long. The leaves break through early in the spring season, turning yellow or red before falling in the autumn. Fragrant white flowers are borne in small clusters in the late spring after the leaves have emerged, and these are followed by red-winged fruits.

Common name: Tatarian maple
Native range: SE Europe, SW Asia
Height: 6 m (20 ft) or more
Spread: 5 m (16 ft)
Hardiness: Zone 3
Variants: The most commonly seen form is subsp. *ginnala* (*A. ginnala*), Amur maple, which differs from *A. tataricum* in that it has distinctly three-lobed leaves. This tree is native to China and Japan.

best for autumn colour. It is a large tree of normally broadly columnar habit, whose five-lobed leaves grow up to 15 cm (6 in) long and the same size across. Mid- to dark green above, the leaves are blue-green beneath, and they turn striking shades of orange, yellow and red in autumn. Many selections have been made of this species for their habit and autumn colour.

Common name: Sugar maple
Native range: E North America
Height: 25 m (80 ft)
Spread: 15 m (50 ft)
Hardiness: Zone 4

Acer shirasawanum

This is a rather bushy tree with a rounded habit, closely related to *A. japonicum*. In fact, these maple species are sometimes confused with each other in gardens. The bright green, rounded leaves grow up to about 12 cm (5 in) in length and they are edged with, usually, 11 toothed lobes. The leaves turn to colours of orange and red in autumn. Small, upright clusters of pink and cream flowers open with the leaves in spring.

Native range: Japan
Height: 10 m (33 ft)

Acradenia frankliniae

Acradenia
Rutaceae

The two species that make up this small genus are evergreen shrubs native of Australia. Only the following, however, is commonly cultivated, and it is grown principally for its aromatic foliage and small white flowers.

This species is best planted in soil that is not too dry, and in cold regions it should be given a position where it is sheltered from the effects of strong winds. Apart from the removal of any damaged, diseased, or unwanted growth, pruning is not usually necessary.

Acradenia frankliniae

This evergreen shrub has an upright habit and is broadly columnar. The dark green, opposite, leathery leaves have three leaflets, up to 5 cm (2 in) long, and are pleasantly aromatic when crushed. Small clusters of starry white flowers are produced in late spring and sometimes again in autumn.

Common name: Whitey wood
Native range: Tasmania
Height: 3 m (10 ft)
Spread: 1.5 m (5 ft)
Hardiness: Zone 8

Aesculus
Hippocastanaceae

The horse chestnuts and buckeyes comprise a small genus of about 15 species of deciduous trees and shrubs that are native to North America, south-east Europe and East Asia. They all have opposite leaves divided into several leaflets. They are mainly grown for their flowers, which are borne in conical clusters at the ends of the shoots in spring or summer. They prefer a good, but not too dry soil and are mainly planted as specimen trees.

Aesculus x carnea

This deciduous tree is a hybrid between *A. hippocastanum* and *A. pavia* and is known only in cultivation. It is most often planted as a street tree and in parks, and it has a rounded habit when mature. Its dark green leaves have between five and seven leaflets, growing to a length of up to 25 cm (10 in), and they can turn orange-red in autumn. Large clusters of pink flowers, blotched yellow, open in late spring, followed by rounded, slightly prickly fruits.

Common name: Red horse chestnut
Height: 20 m (65 ft)
Spread: 15 m (50 ft)
Hardiness: Zone 4
Variants: 'Briotii' is a good selection to consider with its particularly glossy green leaves and deep red-coloured flowers.

Aesculus flava

This broadly conical-to-rounded deciduous tree is a particularly good choice for autumn colour. The dark green leaves usually have five leaflets and grow up to 15 cm (6 in) long; leaves turn a bright

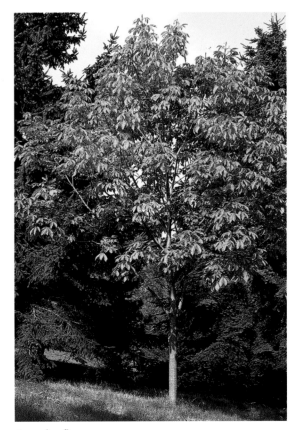

Aesculus flava

orange-red in autumn. In late spring to early summer it produces large clusters of pale yellow flowers tinged with pink, followed by smooth, rounded-to-pear-shaped fruits.

Synonym: *A. octandra*
Common names: Sweet buckeye, yellow buckeye
Native range: E United States of America
Height: 25 m (80 ft) or more
Spread: 15 m (50 ft)
Hardiness: Zone 4

Aesculus hippocastanum

A fast-growing deciduous tree with stout shoots and large sticky buds. The long-stalked leaves have between five and seven leaflets, each growing up to 30 cm (12 in) long, and leaves can turn yellow in autumn. The large clusters, up to 30 cm (12 in) long, of white flowers are blotched with red and open in late spring. These are followed by rounded, very spiny fruits.

Common name: Common horse chestnut
Native range: SE Europe
Height: 30 m (100 ft)
Spread: 25 m (80 ft)
Hardiness: Zone 4
Variants: 'Baumannii' is a form that has double flowers but it produces no fruit.

Aesculus indica

This very elegant species of tree provides a welcome change from the more commonly seen members of the genus, in that it flowers much later in the year. It has a broadly columnar-to-rounded habit and is of a large size. The leaves of *A. indica* are large, dark green in colour and bear five to seven leaflets up to 25 cm (10 in) long. Leaves are bronze when young and turn orange and yellow in autumn. White and pink flowers with a yellow blotch open in clusters up to 30 cm (12 in) long in mid-summer, and these are followed by smooth, pear-shaped fruits.

Common name: Indian horse chestnut
Native range: NW Himalayas
Height: 20 m (65 ft)
Spread: 15 m (50 ft)
Hardiness: Zone 7

Aesculus x neglecta 'Erythroblastos'

This striking-looking tree is a garden selection of a naturally occurring hybrid between *A. flava* and *A. sylvatica*. It is a slow-growing, medium-sized tree of essentially columnar habit with leaves

Aesculus hippocastanum

that are divided into five leaflets. When the leaves first emerge in the spring they are a brilliant pink colour and they then slowly turn whitish as the season advances. Finally the leaves become green flushed with yellow. The small flowers are creamy white with a pink flush, but they are relatively inconspicuous when they open in the early summer.

Common name: Sunrise horse chestnut
Height: 10 m (33 ft)

Spread: 5 m (16 ft)
Hardiness: Zone 6

Aesculus parviflora

This deciduous shrub forms dense mounds and spreads by producing suckers. The dark green leaves have between five and seven leaflets, and grow up to 20 cm (8 in) long. Leaves are bronze when young, turning yellow in autumn. The long,

slender clusters of flowers that appear in mid-summer reach 30 cm (12 in), and their most striking feature is the long white stamens with red anthers that project from each flower. An excellent plant as a lawn specimen or in a shrub border.

Common name: Bottlebrush buckeye
Native range: SE United States of America
Height: 3 m (10 ft)
Spread: 5 m (16 ft) or more
Hardiness: Zone 4

Ailanthus
Simaroubaceae

This small genus of five species of deciduous trees, all of which are natives of the region from China to Australia, is mainly represented in cultivation by the following species. It is extremely fast growing and is able to flourish almost anywhere. It also suckers extensively and has become naturalized and is considered as being a weed in many parts of the world. Flowering and fruiting are best given hot summers, but some trees may be all male and produce no fruit.

Ailanthus altissima

A very vigorous, large deciduous tree of broadly columnar-to-spreading habit with stout shoots. The leaves are truly impressive, being up to 60 cm (24 in) long, and are divided into numerous leaflets. They are bronze when young, becoming dark green, but show no autumnal change of colour. Large clusters of small, yellow-green flowers open in mid- to late summer, and these are followed by small, pale green winged fruits that turn red as they ripen.

Common name: Tree of heaven
Native range: China
Height: 25 m (80 ft)
Spread: 15 m (50 ft)
Hardiness: Zone 4

Ailanthus altissima

Albizia julibrissin f. *rosea*

Albizia
Leguminosae

The 150 or so species in this genus of deciduous trees, shrubs and climbers are widely distributed throughout the warm regions of the world. The elegant leaves are finely cut into numerous small leaflets and the showy part of the flowers are the long stamens. Only the following is commonly grown. It thrives in any well-drained soil and does best when planted in full sun. Although it is hardy in all but the coldest areas, it requires hot summer temperatures to ripen the growth, and without this summer heat it can suffer from frost damage during the winter months.

Albizia julibrissin f. rosea

An elegant, spreading deciduous tree with fern-like, dark green leaves growing up to 50 cm (20 in) long cut into many small leaflets. The individual flowers are small but are borne in clusters made conspicuous by long pink stamens. Flowers open in early summer in warm climates, but in late summer to early autumn where summers are cool, followed by flattened pods up to 15 cm (6 in) long.

Common name: Silk tree
Native range: Iran to E Asia
Height: 8 m (26 ft)
Spread: 10 m (33 ft)
Hardiness: Zone 6

Alnus
Betulaceae

The alders are a genus of some 35 species of deciduous, catkin-bearing trees and shrubs widely distributed in the northern hemisphere and extending into the Andes of South America. Male and female catkins are borne separately on the same tree: the male catkins are long and pendulous, opening, in most of the cultivated species, in early spring before the leaves appear; the female catkins mature into persistent, woody, cone-like fruits. Alders are useful for growing in very poor, even wet soils, and through bacteria in their roots they are able to enrich soils with nitrogen. They are best planted in full sun.

Alnus cordata

This handsome and vigorous, large-growing tree is among the finest of all the cultivated alders. It has a conical form and glossy dark green leaves growing up to 10 cm (4 in) in length with a heart-shaped base. The yellow male catkins are up to

Alnus cordata

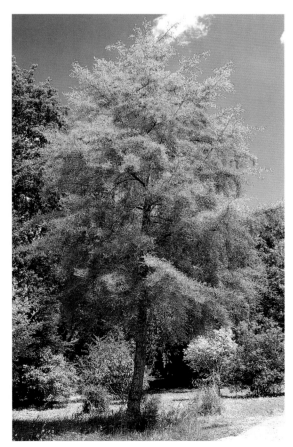

Alnus glutinosa 'Imperialis'

Variants: 'Aurea' is a smaller tree growing up to about 12 m (40 ft) with golden yellow young foliage. 'Imperialis' is smaller again and its leaves are deeply cut into slender lobes. It reaches a height of 10 m (33 ft).

Alnus incana

A good choice for poor, dry or wet soils, it is a broadly conical-shaped tree, very tough and hardy. The dark green leaves grow up to 10 cm (4 in) long and are blue-green beneath, pointed at the tip, and edged with small, sharp teeth. The yellow-brown catkins are 10 cm (4 in) long and open in late winter or early spring. They are tinged red at first.

Common name: Grey alder
Native range: Europe, Caucasus
Height: 20 m (65 ft)
Spread: 12 m (40 ft)
Hardiness: Zone 2
Variants: 'Aurea' is a smaller tree, reaching a height of about 10 m (33 ft). Its young leaves are flushed with yellow and the shoots and catkins are coloured orange-pink during winter.

Aloysia
Verbenaceae

The 35 or so species in this genus comprise both deciduous and evergreen shrubs that are native from the southwest of the United States of America to Central and South America. Only the following is commonly grown – primarily for its aromatic foliage. It requires a well-drained soil in full sun and is suitable for growing or training against a sunny wall. The long shoots produced in summer are best cut back hard in spring before growth starts to a suitable bud just above the base.

Aloysia triphylla

A. triphylla is a deciduous shrub that is capable of reaching a large size. It is normally restricted to about 1.5–2 m (5–6 ft), however, by being cut back annually. The glossy green leaves grow to 10 cm (4 in) long and are normally borne in whorls of three. Leaves are rough to the touch and are very strongly lemon-scented. Large, open clusters of tiny pale lilac flowers open in late summer.

Synonym: *Lippia citriodora*
Common name: Lemon verbena
Native range: Chile, Argentina
Height: 3 m (10 ft)
Spread: 3 m (10 ft)
Hardiness: Zone 8

7.5 cm (3 in) long and open in late winter or early spring before the leaves emerge.

Common name: Italian alder
Native range: Corsica, S Italy
Height: 25 m (80 ft)
Spread: 8 m (26 ft)
Hardiness: Zone 5

Alnus glutinosa

This is a vigorous tree that is extremely tolerant of poor-quality and wet soils. It is mainly planted in gardens as one of the selected forms, but it is also useful in wet soil by riverbanks, where it is frequently seen. The dark green leaves grow up to 10 cm (4 in) long and they are broadest towards the tip. The leaves are edged with small teeth or lobes. The yellow-brown male catkins open in late winter or early spring.

Common name: Common alder
Native range: Europe, N Africa, W Asia
Height: 25 m (80 ft)
Spread: 10 m (33 ft)
Hardiness: Zone 4

Amelanchier
Rosaceae

Variously known as serviceberries, Juneberries and snowy mespilus, this genus of about 25 species of deciduous trees and shrubs is widely distributed in North America, Europe and Asia. Grown for their foliage, which is ornamental in spring and autumn, as well as for their flowers and fruits, they require a lime-free soil and are an excellent choice for providing spring interest in the garden among other trees and shrubs, or in a shrub border.

Amelanchier canadensis

This is a deciduous shrub that forms thickets of upright stems. The silky, hairy young leaves, up to 5 cm (2 in) long, mature to a dark green colour and then turn orange-yellow in autumn. Slender, upright clusters of white flowers open as the leaves begin to unfold, and these are followed by edible blue-black fruits. Some plants grown under this name are *A. lamarckii*.

Common name: Shadbush
Height: 5 m (16 ft)
Spread: 2.5 m (8 ft)
Hardiness: Zone 3

Amelanchier x grandiflora

Many forms of this hybrid, between *A. arborea* and *A. laevis*, have originated in gardens. It is a vigorous deciduous tree of spreading habit, sometimes

shrubby, with dark green leaves up to 7.5 cm (3 in) long, silky and bronze when young, turning orange and red in autumn. White flowers in drooping clusters open in spring as the leaves unfold, and these are followed by edible blue-black fruits.

Height: 12 m (40 ft)
Spread: 12 m (40 ft)
Hardiness: Zone 4
Variants: Many selections have been made, including 'Ballerina', with profusely borne, large white flowers and red and purple autumn colour. 'Rubescens' has pale pink flowers, deeper in bud.

Amelanchier lamarckii

A spreading, shrubby deciduous tree, often with several main stems. Silky hairy young leaves, up to 7.5 cm (3 in) long, become bronzy and then dark green, turning orange and red in autumn. Arching clusters of white flowers appear as the leaves open, followed by edible purple-black fruits.

Native range: Europe
Height: 10 m (33 ft)
Spread: 10 m (33 ft)
Hardiness: Zone 4

Andromeda
Ericaceae

This small genus, comprising just two species of evergreen shrubs, is native over a wide area of the

Aralia elata

northern hemisphere, where it is found in northerly latitudes and on mountains further south. The following species is the most commonly seen in garden cultivation and requires a cool, moist position in a peaty, lime-free soil. It is suitable for the peat garden among plants requiring similar conditions. It does best in full sun, but it needs to be grown in the shade where summers or soil conditions are dry.

Andromeda polifolia

This is a dwarf and extremely hardy evergreen shrub with slender, glossy, dark green or blue-green, leathery leaves up to 4 cm (1½ in) long, blue-white beneath. Clusters of small, nodding, urn-shaped pale pink or white flowers open during the late spring and early summer.

Common name: Bog rosemary
Native range: North temperate regions
Height: 45 cm (18 in)
Spread: 60 cm (24 in)
Hardiness: Zone 2
Variants: 'Alba' is compact, up to 15 cm (6 in) tall, with white flowers. 'Compacta' reaches 30 cm (12 in), with blue-green foliage and bright pink-coloured flowers.

Aralia
Araliaceae

Containing about 40 species of herbaceous perennials and climbers as well as trees and shrubs, Aralias are widely distributed in East and South Asia, as well as in North and South America. The following woody species is grown for its bold foliage, autumn colour and flowers. It does best in a good, not too dry, soil and should be given some

Amelanchier lamarckii

Arbutus x andrachnoides

shelter from strong winds, which can damage its large leaves. It may be necessary to remove suckers if they become invasive.

Aralia elata

A vigorous deciduous shrub that spreads by suckers. It has stout, erect, sparsely branched and spiny shoots, and sometimes forms a spreading tree. The very large leaves can be 1 m (3 ft) or more long and are divided into numerous leaflets. In late summer and early autumn large clusters of small white flowers open at the ends of the shoots as the huge leaves turn to orange, yellow and purple. This is followed by small black fruits. It is sometimes grown as *A. chinensis*.

Common name: Japanese angelica tree
Native range: E Asia
Height: 10 m (33 ft)
Spread: 10 m (33 ft)
Hardiness: Zone 4
Variants: The following variegated forms are slower growing and smaller, only reaching about 5 m (16 ft) or less. Any shoots with green leaves that arise at the base should be removed. 'Aureovariegata' has the leaflets edged with yellow when young, becoming similar to 'Variegata', which has leaflets edged with creamy white.

Arbutus
Ericaceae

These valuable evergreens provide a range of ornamental features, from attractive bark to winter flowers and fruits. There are about 15 species of trees and shrubs found in Europe and the west of North America, Mexico and Central America. The following will grow on any well-drained soil,

Arbutus x andrachnoides

including chalky soils. In cold areas they should be protected from the effects of strong winds.

Arbutus x andrachnoides

This naturally occurring hybrid of *A. andrachne* and *A. unedo* is among the finest in the genus. A large evergreen shrub or spreading tree with glossy dark green leaves, up to 10 cm (4 in) long, it bears nodding clusters of small, urn-shaped, white flowers in autumn and sporadically during winter, sometimes followed by warty red fruits. The warm reddish-brown bark peels attractively in thin strips.

Native range: Greece
Height: 10 m (33 ft)
Spread: 10 m (33 ft)
Hardiness: Zone 7

Arbutus 'Marina'

This small-to-medium-sized spreading tree is of uncertain origin but is proving to be a handsome addition to gardens. It has cinnamon-brown peeling bark and glossy dark green leaves to 12 cm

(5 in) long, bronze when young. The drooping urn-shaped flowers are white flushed with deep pink and open in large, upright panicles during summer and autumn, followed by yellow then red fruits.

Height: 10 m (33 ft)
Spread: 10 m (33 ft)
Hardiness: Zone 8

Arbutus unedo

This well known plant makes a spreading evergreen tree with rough, red-brown bark and smooth, glossy dark green leaves to 10 cm (4 in) long. Drooping clusters of small, urn-shaped, white or pink-tinged flowers open at the ends of the shoots in autumn – the warty red fruits, about 2 cm (1 in) across, ripening at the same time from the previous year's flowers.

Common name: Strawberry tree
Native range: Mediterranean region, SW Ireland
Height: 10 m (33 ft)
Spread: 10 m (33 ft)
Hardiness: Zone 7
Variants: Deep pink flowers are found on f. *rubra*.

Arctostaphylos uva-ursi

Arctostaphylos
Ericaceae

This genus, which contains about 50 species of evergreen shrubs and small trees, is mainly confined to California, with the exception of the following, which is probably the most commonly cultivated of all the species. Given a lime-free soil it is easy to grow, and it prefers a position where it receives full sun. It is an excellent plant for providing dense ground cover and it is a good choice for a large rock garden.

Arctostaphylos uva-ursi

This is a vigorous, creeping evergreen shrub that, unless checked, forms an extensive carpet, with small, leathery, glossy dark green leaves growing up to 4 cm (1½ in) in length. It bears clusters of small, urn-shaped, white or pink-tinged flowers that open in late spring and summer. The flowers are followed by small, glossy red fruits.

Common name: Bearberry
Native range: North temperate regions
Height: 30 cm (12 in)
Spread: 3 m (10 ft) or more
Hardiness: Zone 2
Variants: Several selections have been made, the most popular of which are 'Massachusetts', which has small, glossy green leaves and pink-tinged flowers, and 'Vancouver Jade', which has attractive red shoots, bright green leaves, which turn to shades of bronze in winter, and pink-coloured flowers.

Aronia
Rosaceae

The chokeberries are a genus of two species of deciduous shrubs native to eastern North America. Valued in gardens for their toughness as well as their flowers, autumn colour and fruits, they will grow in almost any soil, but they may become chlorotic in shallow, dry, alkaline soils. They do best in full sun but they will tolerate shade.

Aronia arbutifolia

A deciduous shrub with upright branches, forming thickets by producing basal suckers. Glossy dark green leaves, to 10 cm (4 in) long, are grey-felted beneath and turn brilliant red to purple in autumn. In mid- to late spring, small clusters of white flowers open, followed by bright red fruits.

Common name: Red chokeberry
Native range: E North America
Height: 2.5 m (8 ft)
Spread: 1.5 m (5 ft)
Hardiness: Zone 4

Aronia melanocarpa

This is a vigorous, upright deciduous shrub with smooth, glossy dark green leaves up to 10 cm (4 in) long. Its clusters of small white flowers in spring are followed by glossy black fruits.

Common name: Black chokeberry
Native range: E North America
Height: 2.5 m (8 ft)
Spread: 2 m (6 ft)
Hardiness: Zone 3

Atriplex
Chenopodiaceae

The 100 or so species in this genus are annual and perennial herbs as well as shrubs, and are widely distributed. The following is useful for its ability to withstand full coastal exposure, thriving on sea cliffs and similar situations. In colder inland areas it may need more shelter. It does best in a not-too-rich, well-drained soil in full sun.

Atriplex halimus

An evergreen or semi-evergreen shrub of compact habit with arching branches and diamond-shaped, silvery grey, scaly leaves up to 6 cm (2½ in) long. The tiny yellow-green flowers in long clusters at the ends of the shoots in late summer are relatively inconspicuous and are not always produced.

Common name: Tree purslane
Native range: S Europe
Height: 2 m (6 ft)
Spread: 2 m (6 ft)
Hardiness: Zone 7

Aucuba japonica 'Variegata'

Aronia arbutifolia

Aucuba
Aucubaceae

This is a genus made up of three or four species of evergreen shrubs, all native from the Himalayas to East Asia. Only the following species is commonly grown, principally for its bold, often variegated leaves and fruits. It will thrive in almost any situation, except very wet soils, and is very shade-tolerant. Male and female flowers are borne on separate plants and both are needed to produce fruits. Overgrown or leggy plants can be cut back hard in early spring before growth starts.

Aucuba japonica

A strong-growing and compact evergreen shrub with stout green shoots and glossy green leathery leaves to 20 cm (8 in) long, usually edged with a few teeth. Tiny flowers open in clusters at the ends of the shoots in spring, followed, on females, by glossy red fruits. Usually grown as one of many selected forms, often with variegated foliage.

Common name: Spotted laurel
Native range: Japan
Height: 3 m (10 ft)

Spread: 3 m (10 ft)
Hardiness: Zone 7
Variants: 'Crotonifolia' is a female form, the leaves of which are heavily speckled with golden yellow. 'Golden King' is male with leaves heavily blotched yellow. 'Rozannie' is a compact female and free-fruiting form up to 1.5 m (5 ft) tall, with dark green leaves. 'Sulphurea Marginata' is female and its leaves have a broad, pale yellow margin. 'Variegata' is female with yellow-spotted leaves.

Azara
Flacourtiaceae

The ten species in this genus of evergreen trees and shrubs are all natives of South America and are grown for their handsome foliage as well as their yellow flowers – the prominent feature of which are their long, yellow stamens. They prefer a moist but well-drained soil in a position sheltered from strong winds.

Azara microphylla

This is an evergreen tree with slender shoots and small, glossy dark green leaves that grow only up to about 2.5 cm (1 in) long. The small clusters of vanilla-scented yellow flowers open on the undersides of the shoots in the late winter or early spring, and these are sometimes followed by small orange-red berries.

Native range: Argentina, Chile
Height: 10 m (33 ft)
Spread: 5 m (16 ft)
Hardiness: Zone 8
Variants: 'Variegata' is much slower growing and usually only about half the size. Its leaves have a yellow margin.

Azara serrata

A vigorous evergreen shrub with upright branches and glossy dark green leaves that grow up to 6 cm (2½ in) in length. The most striking species of the genus in flower, its clusters of fragrant golden yellow flowers, which are about 2 cm (¾ in) across, open in late spring and are followed by small, blue-tinged white berries. In cold areas it benefits from the protection of being trained against a wall.

Native range: Chile
Height: 4 m (13 ft)
Spread: 3 m (10 ft)
Hardiness: Zone 8

Ballota
Labiatae

In this genus there are about 35 species of perennial herbs and subshrubs that are all natives of Europe, mainly in the Mediterranean region, North Africa and Southwest Asia. The following low-growing species is cultivated principally for its attractive foliage, and the plant does best in soil that is not too rich. It also prefers a position in full sun. The plant needs to be cut back hard in spring before growth starts in order to maintain a compact habit.

Ballota pseudodictamnus

An evergreen, mound-forming subshrub that has thickly woolly shoots and rounded grey-green leaves up to 3 cm (1 in) long. The small, two-lipped flowers, borne in whorls in the leaf axils in late spring and early summer, are white with a pink tinge, but are relatively inconspicuous compared with the surrounding large, shield-shaped calyx.

Native range: E Mediterranean region
Height: 60 cm (24 in)
Spread: 1 m (3 ft)
Hardiness: Zone 8

Berberis
Berberidaceae

The barberries are a large genus comprising about 450 species of both deciduous and evergreen spiny shrubs that are widely distributed in the northern hemisphere and throughout South America. The species are vary variable in terms of foliage – their leaves range from those that are untoothed to others that are edged with spiny teeth, while the deciduous species often provide good autumn colour as well as including many selections that have coloured leaves. Purple-leaved forms colour best if they are planted in full sun.

The flowers of the barberries are usually small and yellow and are followed by small fruits that range in colour from red to black. They are not demanding plants in cultivation and will grow in most types of soil, except those that are very wet. Little pruning is required, except the removal of stray branches to maintain shape, and this should be carried out when flowering has finished.

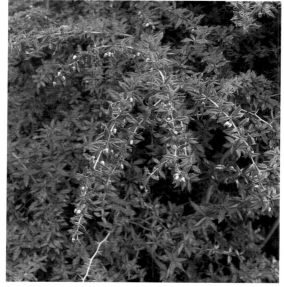

Berberis x frikartii 'Amstelveen'

Berberis candidula

A very dense, mound-forming evergreen shrub useful for ground cover. The narrow leaves, to 3 cm (1 in) long, end in a spiny tip and are glossy dark green above and blue-white beneath. Leaves can turn bronze in cold weather. Bright yellow flowers open singly in the leaf axils in spring followed by egg-shaped, blue-black, bloomy berries.

Native range: China
Height: 60 cm (24 in)
Spread: 1.5 m (5ft)
Hardiness: Zone 6

Berberis darwinii

This is a vigorous evergreen shrub with arching shoots and sharply toothed, glossy dark green leaves up to 4 cm (1½ in) long. The dense, drooping clusters of rich orange flowers hang from the shoots in mid- to late spring, followed by spherical, blue-black, bloomy berries.

Native range: Chile, Argentina
Height: 3 m (10 ft)
Spread: 3 m (10 ft)
Hardiness: Zone 7

Berberis x frikartii 'Amstelveen'

A vigorous evergreen hybrid between *B. candidula* and *B. verruculosa*, making a dense shrub with arching shoots. The glossy green leaves, up to 3 cm (1 in) long, are white beneath and edged with spiny teeth. Small clusters of yellow flowers open in late spring followed by blue-black berries.

Height: 1 m (3 ft)
Spread: 1.5 m (5 ft)
Hardiness: Zone 6

Berberis darwinii

Berberis julianae

This vigorous evergreen shrub forms a large, dense mound with glossy green leathery leaves, up to 8 cm (3 in) long, edged with numerous spiny teeth. Dense clusters of yellow flowers wreath the shoots in late spring, followed by blue-black, bloomy, egg-shaped fruits. A good species for hedging.

Native range: China
Height: 3 m (10 ft)
Spread: 3.5 m (11–12 ft)
Hardiness: Zone 6

Berberis x lologensis

This is a naturally occurring hybrid between *B. darwinii* and *B. linearifolia*. It makes a large evergreen shrub with arching shoots and with glossy dark green, spine-toothed leaves up to 5 cm (2 in) long. In late spring it bears dense clusters of rich orange-coloured flowers, and often periodically at other times of the year, followed by spherical blue-black berries.

Native range: Argentina
Height: 4 m (13 ft)
Spread: 4 m (13 ft)
Hardiness: Zone 6
Variants: 'Apricot Queen' is more upright with large, bright orange flowers, 'Mystery Fire' has profuse orange-yellow flowers, deeper in bud. 'Stapehill' has profuse, rich orange flowers.

Berberis x media

A hybrid that originated in cultivation between *B.* 'Chenaultii' and *B. thunbergii* making a small semi-evergreen shrub. The leaves are up to 3 cm (1 in) long and are untoothed or edged with a few spines. Small clusters of yellow flowers open in late spring followed by dull red fruits. It is only grown in the two forms noted below.

Height: 2 m (6 ft)
Spread: 2.5 m (8 ft)
Hardiness: Zone 5
Variants: 'Parkjuweel' has dark green leaves, some of which turn bright red in autumn. 'Red Jewel' has bronze-purple young foliage becoming dark green.

Berberis x mentorensis

This garden-raised hybrid shrub is a cross between *B. julianae* and *B. thunbergii*. It is semi-evergreen with a rounded habit and is useful for hedging, with long-persistent dark green leaves that are either untoothed or have a few teeth towards the tip. Leaves turn orange-yellow before they fall.

Berberis x *ottawensis* 'Superba'

Berberis x *stenophylla* 'Corallina Compacta'

Clusters of yellow flowers tinged with red are followed by dull red-brown fruits.

Common name: Mentor barberry
Height: 1.5 m (5 ft)
Spread: 2 m (6 ft)
Hardiness: Zone 5

Berberis x ottawensis

This is a vigorous and very hardy hybrid of garden origin between *B. vulgaris* and *B. thunbergii*. It is a large, rounded deciduous shrub with arching shoots and usually untoothed leaves up to 3 cm (1 in) long. The shrub is commonly grown only as forms with purple leaves, which have small clusters of pale yellow flowers tinged with red in spring, followed by egg-shaped red berries.

Height: 2.5 m (8 ft)
Spread: 3 m (10 ft)
Hardiness: Zone 3
Variants: 'Silver Miles' has leaves flushed with silvery grey. The most commonly seen form is 'Superba' ('Purpurea'), which has deep red-purple foliage turning red in autumn.

Berberis x stenophylla

This vigorous garden hybrid between *B. darwinii* and *B. empetrifolia* makes a dense, wide-spreading evergreen shrub with long, slender, arching shoots. bearing slender, spine-tipped, glossy dark green leaves up to 2.5 cm (1 in). In mid-spring the shoots are wreathed in dense clusters of deep yellow flowers followed by bloomy blue-black berries.

Height: 3 m (10 ft)
Spread: 5 m (16 ft)
Hardiness: Zone 5
Variants: 'Claret Cascade' has rich orange flowers flushed red, and purple-tinged young foliage. 'Corallina Compacta' is very compact, up to 60 cm (24 in) tall, with orange flowers from red buds.

Berberis wilsoniae

'Irwinii' is compact, up to 2 m (6 ft) tall, with orange-yellow flowers. 'Lemon Queen' ('Cream Showers') has creamy white flowers. '

Berberis thunbergii

A very hardy deciduous shrub of dense, rounded habit. Untoothed leaves to 3 cm (1 in) are bronzy when young, becoming bright green and turning bright orange and red in autumn. Small clusters of pale yellow flowers tinged with red open in mid- to late spring followed by glossy red, persistent berries. There are numerous and varying selections.

Native range: Japan
Height: 1.5 m (5 ft)
Spread: 2.5 m (8 ft)
Hardiness: Zone 4
Variants: For deep red-purple foliage there is f. *atropurpurea*. 'Atropurpurea Nana' ('Crimson Pygmy') is compact to 60 cm (24 in), also with red-purple foliage. 'Aurea' has bright yellow young foliage and does best in semi-shade. 'Bagatelle' is similar to 'Atropurpurea Nana' but more compact. 'Harlequin' has red-purple leaves heavily blotched with white and pink. 'Rose Glow' has red-purple foliage mottled with white and pink.

Berberis verruculosa

A dense, mound-forming evergreen shrub with rough shoots and small, glossy dark green, spine-toothed leaves up to 4 cm (1½ in) long, blue-white beneath. Golden yellow flowers in late spring are followed by small blue-black fruits, which are covered with a white bloom when young.

Native range: China
Height: 1.5 m (5 ft)
Spread: 1.5 m (5 ft)
Hardiness: Zone 6

Berberis wilsoniae

A deciduous or semi-evergreen shrub with arching shoots and small blue-green leaves up to 2.5 cm (1 in) long. Leaves are untoothed or have few teeth and turn orange and red in autumn. Clusters of pale yellow flowers in late spring and summer are followed by brilliant coral-red fruits.

Native range: China
Height: 1 m (3 ft)
Spread: 1.5 m (5 ft)
Hardiness: Zone 6

Berberis thunbergii 'Aurea'

Betula
Betulaceae

The birches are a genus of some 60 species of catkin-bearing deciduous trees and shrubs widely distributed in north temperate regions. The separate male and female catkins open on the same tree in spring before or as the leaves are emerging. The male catkins are pendulous. Birches are useful in gardens for their fast growth, graceful habit, attractive, sometimes peeling bark, their foliage, which colours in autumn, and their catkins.

These trees are easy to grow in most soils and do best in full sun, although they will tolerate light shade. The typical bark colour is not usually shown by trees until they are a few years old. If any pruning is needed, carry it out in summer as birches bleed sap if their stems are cut in spring.

Betula albosinensis

A conical tree with attractive, orange-red to coppery red bark peeling in horizontal strips to reveal creamy white bark beneath. The glossy green, sharply toothed leaves, 7.5 cm (3 in) long, end in a tapered point and turn yellow in autumn. In spring it bears pendulous male catkins 6 cm (2½ in) long.

Common name: Chinese red birch
Native range: China
Height: 25 m (80 ft)

Betula nigra

Betula albosinensis

Spread: 10 m (33 ft)
Hardiness: Zone 5
Variants: var. *septentrionalis* has less glossy leaves and buff-pink bark.

Betula alleghaniensis

When young this is a conical tree, but it spreads as it matures. Young shoots are scented with

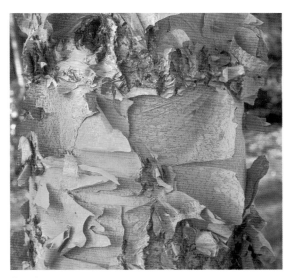
Betula nigra

wintergreen when they are scratched and it has yellow-brown peeling bark. This is among the best species for autumn colour, when the deep green, finely toothed leaves up to 10 cm (4 in) long turn to a beautiful butter-yellow colour. Pendulous male catkins 10 cm (4 in) long open in spring.

Synonym: *Betula lutea*
Common name: Yellow birch
Native range: E North America

Height: 20 m (65 ft)
Spread: 15 m (50 ft)
Hardiness: Zone 3

Betula ermanii

This is a broadly conical tree with rough shoots and striking white bark. The bark is conspicuously marked with horizontal grey-brown bands that are creamy when freshly exposed. Glossy green, finely toothed leaves, 7.5 cm (3 in) long, turn yellow in autumn. Male catkins open in spring.

Native range: NE Asia, Japan
Height: 20 m (65 ft)
Spread: 10 m (33 ft)
Hardiness: Zone 5

Betula nigra

A vigorous tree, conical when young and spreading with age. The striking bark varies from cream to pink, grey and brown, and on young trees it peels conspicuously in numerous thin, shaggy layers. Older trees have ridged, grey-brown bark. The sharply toothed rather blue-green leaves, up to

Betula ermanii

10 cm (4in) long, turn yellow in autumn and pendulous male catkins, about 7.5 cm (3 in) in length, open in spring.

Common name: River birch
Native range: E United States of America
Height: 20 m (65 ft)
Spread: 15 m (50 ft)
Hardiness: Zone 4
Variants: 'Heritage' is a form selected for its vigorous growth and excellent bark.

Betula papyrifera

A vigorous and very tough conical tree. It has white bark that peels in thin strips, pinkish orange when freshly exposed, becoming marked with black on old trees. Taper-pointed and sharply toothed dark green leaves, up to 10 cm (4 in) long, turn yellow to orange-yellow in autumn. It bears pendulous male catkins 10 cm (4 in) long in spring.

Common name: Paper birch, canoe birch
Native range: North America
Height: 20 m (65 ft)
Spread: 12m (40 ft)
Hardiness: Zone 2

Betula pendula

A fast-growing conical tree with distinctive slender, pendulous branches, which give it a very graceful appearance. The white bark does not peel and develops conspicuous blackish cracks towards the base of mature trees. Taper-pointed, glossy dark green and sharply toothed leaves up to 6 cm (2½ in)

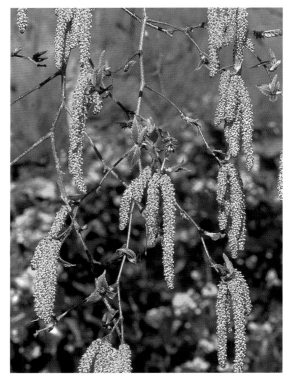

Betula ermanii (catkins)

long turn yellow in autumn, and pendulous male catkins up to 6 cm (2½ in) long open in spring.

Common name: Silver birch
Native range: Europe, N Asia

Height: 25 m (80 ft)
Spread: 10 m (33 ft)
Hardiness: Zone 2
Variants: 'Laciniata' (often grown as 'Dalecarlica') has finely cut leaves. 'Tristis' has slender, very pendulous shoots, hanging vertically. 'Youngii' (Young's weeping birch) is a mop-headed, small, spreading tree, to about 8 m (26 ft) or less, with pendulous shoots.

Betula utilis

This variable and widely distributed species contains some of the best birches for their bark. It is a broadly conical tree with dark green leaves up to 10 cm (4 in) long that turn a rich yellow in autumn. The bark is variable in colour, from coppery brown to pure white, and the striking male catkins can be up to 18 cm (7 in) in length.

Common name: Himalayan birch
Native range: Himalayas, China
Height: 25 m (80 ft)
Spread: 15 m (50 ft)
Hardiness: Zone 5
Variants: var. *jacquemontii* has white bark and good selections of this form include 'Grayswood Ghost', 'Jermyns' and 'Silver Shadow'.

Betula pendula 'Tristis'

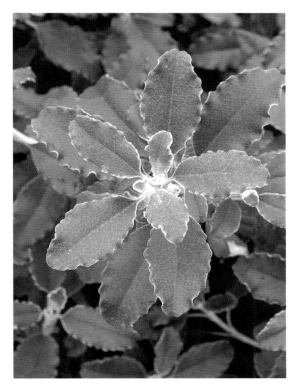

Brachyglottis monroi

Brachyglottis
Compositae

This genus contains approximately 30 species of evergreen trees and shrubs, as well as herbaceous perennials, and all are natives of New Zealand and Tasmania. Many of the species now listed here were previously listed under *Senecio*, to which they are closely related.

The most frequently cultivated members of the genus are the evergreen shrubs, which are commonly grown in borders for their foliage and flower interest. They are easy to grow in any well-drained soil, preferring a position in full sun, and although they are not hardy in the coldest areas they will withstand full coastal exposure. Pruning is not usually necessary, but they can be cut back lightly after flowering.

Brachyglottis monroi

Making a compact, mound-forming evergreen shrub, *B. monroi* has small, leathery, wavy edged leaves that grow up to 4 cm (1½ in) long. The leaves are deep green above and are covered beneath with a dense layer of white hairs. The bright yellow, daisy-like flowerheads are 2 cm (¾ in) across and they open in clusters throughout the summer.

Synonym: *Senecio monroi*
Native range: New Zealand
Height: 75 cm (30 in)
Spread: 1.5 m (5 ft)
Hardiness: Zone 8

Brachyglottis 'Sunshine'

This is an evergreen shrub that develops into a spreading mound. It has leathery dark green leaves, up to about 7 cm (3 in) long, grey and hairy above when young and covered with white hairs beneath. Large clusters of bright yellow, daisy-like flowerheads open over a long period during the summer season and early autumn. This shrub can be used for hedging.

Synonym: *Senecio* 'Sunshine' (sometimes grown as *Senecio greyi*)
Height: 1.5 m (5 ft)
Spread: 2.5 m (8 ft)
Hardiness: Zone 8

Broussonetia
Moraceae

This small genus of just seven species contains deciduous trees and shrubs that are native from East Asia to Polynesia. Only the following is commonly cultivated, however, principally for its handsome foliage as well as its unusual flowers and fruits.

Male and female flowers are borne on separate plants and both are needed to produce fruits. It can be grown in any well-drained soil in full sun, but it is more likely to reach tree-like proportions if it is given hot summers. In cooler areas, growth may not ripen sufficiently and young shoots can then be damaged by winter frosts.

Broussonetia papyrifera

A small and fast-growing deciduous tree or large shrub, *B. papyrifera* has stout shoots and large, dark green leaves that can reach up to 15 cm (6 in) across. The leaves are roughly hairy above and have soft hairs on their undersurfaces. The leaves are also very variable in shape and are often deeply three-lobed. Male plants bear stout, drooping clusters of white flowers in the spring or early summer, while female plants bear spherical clusters of purple flowers. The female flowers are followed by heads of small red fruits.

Common name: Paper mulberry
Native range: China, Japan
Height: 6 m (20 ft) or more
Spread: 6 m (20 ft)
Hardiness: Zone 6

Broussonetia papyrifera (female)

Buddleja
Buddlejaceae

The 100 or so widely distributed species that make up this genus are deciduous and evergreen shrubs and trees. The plants are native to Africa and Asia, as well as from the southern United States of America to Mexico, and Central and South America.

Most species in this genus have opposite leaves and small, often fragrant, flowers borne in large conical clusters at the ends of their shoots. The flowers can be highly attractive to butterflies. They will grow in most good soils but they do best if positioned in full sun. It may be necessary to train less-hardy species against a sunny wall. *B. davidii* is best if it is cut back hard to create a low framework of branches in early spring, before the new season's growth starts.

Buddleja alternifolia

A graceful deciduous shrub with slender, arching shoots and slender, alternate, dark green leaves, growing up to 10 cm (4 in) in length, with grey-white undersurfaces. In early summer, dense clusters of fragrant, lilac-purple flowers open along the shoots that grew in the previous year. Cut branches back after flowering if necessary to maintain shape or to restrict growth.

Native range: China
Height: 3 m (10 ft)
Spread: 3 m (10 ft)
Hardiness: Zone 5
Variants: 'Argentea' has very silvery foliage.

Buddleja crispa

This is a choice garden species, with the double appeal of attractive foliage and extravagant flowers. *B. crispa* is a deciduous shrub with graceful, arching shoots. The soft, grey-green leaves, up to 12 cm (4–5 in) long, have scalloped margins, are hairy white when young and are borne on white downy shoots. Large clusters of fragrant lilac flowers open over a long period during summer. This is a good species for training against a wall.

Native range: Himalayas, China
Height: 3 m (10 ft)
Spread: 3 m (10 ft)
Hardiness: Zone 7

Buddleja davidii

The most popular species in the genus, *B. davidii* makes a deciduous shrub of vigorous growth with

Buddleja alternifolia

Buddleja crispa

Buddleja davidii 'White Profusion'

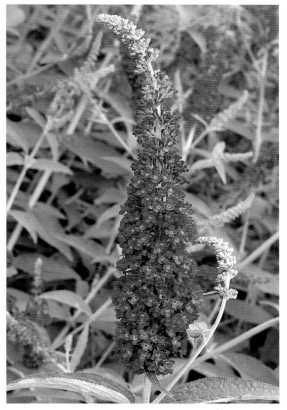

Buddleja davidii 'Empire Blue'

long, arching branches bearing slender, pointed leaves. The large leaves grow up to 25 cm (10 in) in length and are dark green to grey-green above with a layer of white hairs on their undersurfaces. The large, dense terminal clusters of fragrant flowers can be up to 30 cm (12 in) long and they open over a long period during the summer and autumn. It is grown mainly as selected forms, which vary in colour from white, pink, red to blue and purple.

Common name: Butterfly bush
Native range: China
Height: 4 m (13 ft)
Spread: 5 m (16 ft)
Hardiness: Zone 5
Variants: The flower colour of 'Black Knight' is very deep purple, while 'Dartmoor' has large, branched clusters of flowers red-purple in colour. 'Empire Blue' has violet-blue flowers. 'Harlequin' has deep red-purple flowers and its leaves have margins coloured an attractive creamy white. 'Nanho Blue' makes a compact plant, up to 2 m (6 ft) tall, with very slender leaves and small clusters of lilac-blue flowers. 'Nanho Purple' is

similar to 'Nanho Blue', but with strikingly coloured magenta-purple flowers. 'Royal Red' has rich red-purple flowers. For a cooler colour theme consider 'White Bouquet', which produces large clusters of white flowers, each with a distinctive orange eye. 'White Profusion' is another option that also makes very large clusters of white flowers, but here with a yellow eye.

Buddleja fallowiana

This deciduous shrub is somewhat like a refined and more compact version of *B. davidii*, and it makes a particularly desirable addition to the garden because of its attractive foliage, which maintains interest even when the flowers are spent. The young leaves of *B. fallowiana* emerge covered in white down from white woolly shoots before becoming grey-green in colour and growing up to 12 cm (5 in) in length. It may require shelter in exposed sites. The conical clusters of fragrant, lavender flowers, each with an orange eye, reach about 15 cm (6 in) in length and open in the summer and autumn. Like *B. davidii*, it can be cut back hard in the spring.

Native range: China
Height: 3 m (10 ft)
Spread: 3 m (10 ft)
Hardiness: Zone 7
Variants: var. *alba* has creamy white flowers and silvery grey foliage.

Buddleja globosa

This very distinct species makes a large, semi-evergreen, tree-like shrub with dark green, prominently veined leaves that grow up to 20 cm (8 in) in length. The striking orange-yellow fragrant flowers are borne in dense, spherical clusters in early summer. This species does best if it is not pruned.

Common name: Orange ball tree
Native range: Chile, Argentina
Height: 5 m (16 ft)
Spread: 3 m (10 ft)
Hardiness: Zone 7

Buddleja lindleyana

This unusual deciduous or semi-evergreen shrub species makes a thicket of upright and arching shoots bearing glossy, dark green leaves up to 10 cm (4 in) long. The particularly large, deep violet-purple flowers are borne in long, arching clusters up to 20 cm (8 in) long during summer and autumn. Remove spent flowerheads to promote further flowering.

Buddleja davidii 'Dartmoor'

Buddleja globosa

Buddleja lindleyana

Native range: China
Height: 2 m (6 ft)
Spread: 2 m (6 ft)
Hardiness: Zone 7

Buddleja 'Lochinch'

This vigorous deciduous shrub is a garden-raised hybrid between *B. davidii* and *B. fallowiana*. The arching shoots bear grey-green leaves up to 20 cm (8 in) in length. The leaves are covered in white hairs when they are young. During late summer and autumn the shrub produces large clusters of fragrant lavender-blue flowers, up to 20 cm (8 in) long, each with an orange eye. Like *B. davidii*, *B.* 'Lochinch' can be cut back hard in the spring to maintain its shape or to restrict height and spread.

Height: 2.5 m (8 ft)
Spread: 3 m (10 ft)
Hardiness: Zone 6

Buddleja x weyeriana

These vigorous deciduous shrubs are garden hybrids between *B. davidii* and *B. globosa* with dark green leaves growing up to 20 cm (8 in) in length. The rounded heads of usually yellow-coloured flowers are grouped into large clusters, up to 30 cm (12 in) long, at the ends of the shoots. It is normally grown as one of the selected forms listed below.

Height: 4 m (13 ft)
Spread: 3 m (10 ft)
Hardiness: Zone 7
Variants: 'Golden Glow' has orange-yellow flowers flushed with lilac, while 'Sungold' has deep orange-coloured flowers.

Bupleurum
Umbelliferae

The members of this genus, which number about 100 or so species, are mainly annual and perennial herbs and are widely distributed throughout the north temperate regions, as well as South Africa.

The following shrubby species is grown for its attractive foliage and unusual flowers and is suitable for the garden border or, where it is of questionable hardiness, it can be grown against a wall for additional protection from the elements. It is best given a well-drained soil in full sun and will thrive in exposed coastal positions. No pruning is usually needed but it can be cut back in spring if necessary to improve its habit or to remove stray, crossing or unwanted shoots.

Bupleurum fruticosum

This is an evergreen, sparsely branched shrub with a naturally compact habit, with glossy blue-green leaves that grow up to 8 cm (3 in) in length. Open, rounded heads of small, starry shaped, mustard-yellow flowers open over a long period during summer and early autumn.

Common name: Shrubby hare's ear
Native range: Mediterranean region
Height: 1.5 m (5 ft)
Spread: 2 m (6 ft)
Hardiness: Zone 7

Buxus
Buxaceae

The boxes are a genus of some 30 species of evergreen shrubs and trees widely distributed in Europe, Asia, Africa, Mexico and Central America. All have opposite, rather leathery leaves and very small flowers that are borne in clusters in the leaf axils. The only conspicuous part of the male flowers are the yellow anthers.

In gardens, box plants are grown for their neat habit and attractive foliage and, especially, for their tolerance of hard pruning, which makes them suitable for hedging, topiary and ground cover. These very adaptable plants thrive in most conditions, as long as the soil is well drained, and although they will tolerate being positioned in either sun or shade, box does particularly well in partial shade.

Prune hedges and edging box in summer as necessary to maintain their size and shape, while old plants – or those that have become neglected – can be renovated by cutting them back to the base before the new growth starts in spring.

Buxus microphylla

The plant grown under this name is probably a Japanese garden selection of a species widely distributed in several forms in East Asia. It is an evergreen shrub of a dense habit forming a low, spreading mound. The small dark green leaves, growing up to about 2 cm (¾ in) long, are narrow and oblong in shape and can turn bronze in very cold weather.

Height: 1 m (3 ft)
Spread: 1 m (3 ft)
Hardiness: Zone 6
Variants: A variable species with several geographical variants and numerous garden selections. The very hardy var. *koreana* is good for cold areas, while var. *japonica* can reach 2 m (6 ft).

Buxus sempervirens 'Elegantissima'

Buxus sempervirens 'Suffruticosa'

Buxus sempervirens

This species of box develops into an evergreen shrub or small tree with mature leaves that are glossy and very dark green in colour. When they are young, the leaves are usually more blue-green. The leaves, which form a dense mass, grow up to about 2.5 cm (1 in) in length, and are often notched at their tips. The small, but numerous, yellow-green, fragrant flowers add interest and attract insects in spring. *B. sempervirens*, which is much valued by topiarists, makes an excellent dense hedge and is commonly seen clipped into a wide variety of animal, geometric or other unusual shapes.

Common name: Common box
Native range: Europe, North Africa, SW Asia
Height: 5 m (16 ft)
Spread: 5 m (16 ft)
Hardiness: Zone 5
Variants: 'Aureovariegata' has a very compact growth habit, reaching up to about 2.5 m (8 ft) in height, and with leaves that are conspicuously blotched and streaked a creamy yellow colour. 'Elegantissima' is a very dense form. It is slow growing, however, eventually reaching a height of up to about 1.5 m (5 ft). It produces tiny leaves that are narrowly edged with white. 'Suffruticosa' is dwarf and upright in habit, reaching up to 1 m (3 ft) in height, but in gardens it is usually cut back to form low edging to paths or borders.

Callicarpa
Verbenaceae

There are approximately 140 species of shrubs and trees in this genus and although they are largely tropical in origin they also include some very hardy species providing striking displays of brilliantly coloured fruits. Known as the beautyberries, they have opposite leaves and clusters of small flowers in summer. They can be grown in any well-drained soil, preferably in a sunny position such as a shrub border, where they can add valuable autumn interest. Pruning is not essential, but in order to restrict growth or renovate old plants they can be cut back hard before growth starts in spring.

Callicarpa bodinieri

A deciduous shrub of upright growth with dark green, taper-pointed leaves. In summer, clusters of small pink flowers open in the axils of the leaves, followed in autumn by glowing violet fruits.

Native range: China
Height: 3 m (10 ft)
Spread: 2.5 m (8 ft)
Hardiness: Zone 6
Variants: var. *giraldii* 'Profusion' is the best form of this species, with young, bronze-tinged foliage and dense clusters of deep violet fruits.

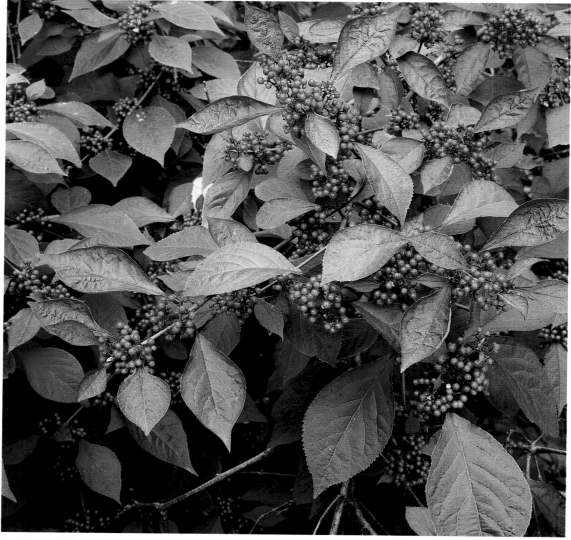

Callicarpa bodinieri var. giraldii 'Profusion'

Callicarpa dichotoma

This elegant deciduous shrub has slender shoots that become arched with age, and bright green, slender-pointed leaves. Pale pink flowers open in small, dense clusters during summer and these are followed by violet-coloured fruits. Given hot summers, this is the hardiest species of the genus.

Native range: China, Korea, Japan
Height: 1.5 m (5 ft)
Spread: 1.5 m (5 ft)
Hardiness: Zone 5

Callistemon
Myrtaceae

The bottlebrushes are a group of very showy evergreen shrubs and trees, related to the myrtles, and are best known for their flower clusters, which are likened to bottlebrushes. With about 30 species in Australia, they have slender, sometimes aromatic leaves, often attractively tinted as they emerge. The flowers are arranged in dense, cylindrical clusters on the shoots and are made

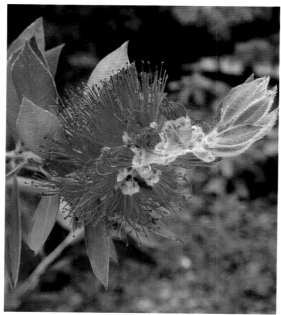

Callistemon citrinus 'Splendens'

conspicuous by their long, colourful and showy stamens. Bottlebrushes are mostly suitable for milder areas but even where they are borderline hardy, they can still be grown if they are given the protection of a wall. They prefer a lime-free soil in a sunny position and are suitable for coastal positions. Cut back after flowering if necessary.

Callistemon citrinus

This popular species makes a large shrub, tree-like in mild areas, with dark green, pointed leaves that are bronze when young and strongly lemon-scented when crushed. The dense, showy clusters of crimson flowers open during spring or summer, and sometimes at other times of the year as well.

Common name: Crimson bottlebrush
Native range: SE Australia
Height: 2 m (6 ft) or more
Spread: 3 m (10 ft)
Hardiness: Zone 8
Variants: 'Splendens' has profuse clusters of bright crimson-coloured flowers.

Callistemon rigidus

This relatively hardy species makes a rigidly branched shrub with long, narrow, sharply pointed, grey-green leaves. The dense, short clusters of red flowers open during the late spring or early summer.

Common name: Stiff bottlebrush
Native range: E Australia

Height: 2 m (6 ft)
Spread: 2.5 m (8 ft)
Hardiness: Zone 8

Callistemon salignus

A striking but tender species reaching tree size in suitable locations, with narrow, willow-like leaves that are bronze or pink when young. The flowers vary in colour from white, green and pale yellow to pink, red and mauve, and are borne in dense clusters in spring or summer.

Common name: Willow bottlebrush
Native range: SE Australia
Height: 5 m (16 ft) or more
Spread: 5 m (16 ft)
Hardiness: Zone 9

Calluna vulgaris
Ericaceae

The single species in this genus is an evergreen shrub widely distributed across northern Europe and Asia, occurring on mountains in the south. The tiny scale-like leaves densely clothe the shoots in opposite pairs, and small urn-shaped flowers, varying in colour from white to pink and purple, are produced in long spikes during late summer

Calluna vulgaris 'Wickwar Flame'

and autumn. It needs a well-drained, acidic, peaty or sandy soil in full sun. Cut back lightly in spring to maintain its compact habit.

Common names: Heather, ling
Native range: Europe, W Asia
Height: 60 cm (24 in)
Spread: 1 m (3 ft)
Hardiness: Zone 4
Variants: 'Beoley Gold' has bright yellow foliage and white flowers. 'County Wicklow' is dwarf, to 25 cm (10 in), with pale pink double flowers. 'Darkness' is compact, to 30 cm (12 in), with dark green foliage and deep purple-pink flowers. 'Gold Haze' has yellow foliage and white flowers. 'H E Beale' has long spikes of bright pink double flowers. 'J H Hamilton' is compact, to 25 cm (10 in), with deep pink double flowers. 'Kinlochruel' has bright green foliage and white double flowers. 'Robert Chapman' has golden yellow foliage, red in winter, and purple flowers. 'Silver Queen' has silvery grey foliage and pale mauve flowers. 'Sir John Charrington' has yellow foliage, turning orange and red in winter, and lilac-mauve flowers. 'Spring Cream' is vigorous with dark green foliage, tipped cream in spring, and long spikes of white flowers. 'Wickwar Flame' has orange-yellow foliage, turning red in winter, and mauve-pink flowers.

Calluna vulgaris 'Darkness'

Calycanthus
Calycanthaceae

This small genus of three species of deciduous shrubs is restricted to North America. Species have opposite, aromatic leaves. As well as handsome foliage, they also have unusual, often fragrant, flowers, which are composed of numerous strap-shaped petals. These shrubs are suitable for a large border or woodland clearing and they prefer a moist, humus-rich soil.

Calycanthus floridus

This bushy spreading shrub has bold, dark green leaves, aromatic when crushed, that sometimes turn yellow in autumn. The flowers, which can be spicily aromatic, open in late spring and sporadically through summer, and they have many strap-like red or red-brown petals.

Common name: Carolina allspice
Native range: SE United States of America
Height: 2.5 m (8 ft)
Spread: 4 m (13 ft)
Hardiness: Zone 5

Calycanthus floridus

Camellia x *williamsii* 'Donation'

Camellia
Theaceae

Containing some 250 named species, this genus of evergreen shrubs and trees originates in East and Southeast Asia. A small number of the total available species provides most garden selections and hybrids. These are all characterized by having dark green leathery leaves and showy flowers, which vary in colour from white to pink and red, with some having yellow centres. While most garden species of camellia flower in the spring, the forms of *C. sasanqua* are unusual in that they bloom in the autumn and winter seasons.

Ideally, camellias should be sited in a border or among other shrubs and trees, and to thrive they require a well-drained, moist, lime-free soil bulked out with abundant organic matter. The buds of camellias are susceptible to damage by early-morning frosts late in the spring season and so may need some protection until the danger period has passed.

The flowers of camellias vary considerably in both shape and in the number of their petals, and the central cluster of stamens often forms a conspicuous and distinguishing feature of the bloom. In the species descriptions on the following pages, the flower terms used are defined as meaning:

Single Flowers with up to eight petals arranged in a single row, and with a conspicuous central cluster of stamens.
Semi-double Flowers with the petals arranged in two or more rows, and with the centre of the flower usually having a conspicuous cluster of stamens.
Double Flowers with numerous overlapping petals and a concave centre of stamens when the bloom is fully open.
Formal double Flowers with numerous overlapping petals and no stamens.
Anemone-form Flowers with the outer petals in one or more rows, with a dense central cluster of stamens mixed with stamen-like petals.
Peony-form A rounded flower composed of mixed petals and stamen-like petals, often with some stamens in the centre.

Camellia 'Inspiration'

Camellia 'Cornish Snow'

This garden-raised hybrid makes a fast-growing, medium-sized, rounded evergreen shrub. It has an essentially open, upright, bushy habit, arching shoots and taper-pointed leaves sometimes described as lance-like. When young, the leaves are bronze in colour, turning dark green as they mature. Small, cup-shaped, single, white or pink-tinged flowers open during spring. Pruning is not usually necessary, but dead, damaged or unwanted branches can be removed in late spring, after flowering has finished.

Height: 2.5 m (8 ft)
Spread: 3 m (10 ft)
Hardiness: Zone 7

Camellia japonica 'Elegans'

Camellia sasanqua 'Crimson King'

Camellia japonica

This is by far the most popular species in garden cultivation, and has given rise to many selections and hybrids with plants varying enormously in terms of flower size, form and colour. Making a dense, usually rounded shrub with glossy dark green foliage, *C. japonica* bears flowers during the spring, and blooms can be single, semi-double or fully double, ranging in colour from white to pink or red, sometimes variegated.

Common name: Japanese camellia
Native range: China, Korea, Japan
Height: 3 m (10 ft) or more
Spread: 5 m (16 ft) or more
Hardiness: Zone 7
Variants: 'Adolphe Audusson' has large, semi-double, deep red flowers, while 'Akashigata' ('Lady Clare') has large, deep pink, semi-double flowers. 'Alba Simplex' has large, white, single flowers with a conspicuous centre of bright yellow stamens. 'Apollo' is a vigorous shrub with small, red, semi-double flowers. 'Betty Sheffield' has large, white, semi-double flowers attractively blotched pink. 'Blood of China' is a vigorous and compact plant with large, deep red, semi-double flowers. 'Debutante' is vigorous and upright in habit with pale pink, peony-form flowers. 'Drama Girl' benefits from having very large, deep salmon-pink, semi-double flowers, while 'Elegans' has a spreading habit and bears large, peach-pink, anemone-form flowers. 'Guilio Nuccio' has vigorous growth and an upright habit, with large, rose-pink, semi-double flowers. 'Hagoromo' ('Magnoliiflora') has pale pink, semi-double flowers. 'Hakurakuten' is vigorous and upright with large, white, semi-double flowers. 'Jupiter' is vigorous with single to semi-double, deep pink flowers with conspicuous stamens. 'Kramer's Supreme' is a compact shrub with an upright habit with very large, peony-form, slightly fragrant red blooms. 'Lady Vansittart' bears white, semi-double flowers that are striped pink or red, while 'Lavinia

Camellia japonica 'Adolphe Audusson'

Camellia 'Inspiration'

This is a medium-sized shrub, vigorous, large-growing, frost-hardy and evergreen. It has an upright habit and dark green, oval-shaped, leathery leaves. The flowers of *C.* 'Inspiration' are large and semi-double in form. They are a rich deep pink colour, and are profusely borne during the spring season. Pruning is not usually necessary, but dead, damaged or unwanted branches can be removed in late spring, after flowering has finished.

Height: 4 m (13 ft)
Spread: 3 m (10 ft)
Hardiness: Zone 7

Maggi' has large, white, formal double flowers striped in deep pink. 'Mars' has large, red, semi-double flowers. 'Nobilissima' flowers very early in the season and has white, peony-form blooms. 'RL Wheeler' is vigorous and has large, semi-double, rose-pink flowers. 'Silver Anniversary' is vigorous and upright in growth and bears large, semi-double, white flowers. 'Tricolor' has single to semi-double flowers that are streaked with white, pink and red.

Camellia 'Leonard Messel'

This garden-raised hybrid has an open, rounded habit with large, oval-shaped, dark green, leathery leaves. Its striking, semi-double, rich clear pink flowers open during the spring season. Flower shape can be flattish to cup-shaped.

Height: 2.5 m (8 ft)
Spread: 3 m (10 ft)
Hardiness: Zone 8

Camellia sasanqua

A rather elegant species with glossy dark green leaves, varying in habit from spreading and shrubby to upright and tree-like. The normally white flowers can be pink or red in garden selections. They are fragrantly scented and open in autumn and early winter.

Native range: Japan
Height: 3 m (10 ft) or more
Spread: 3 m (10 ft)
Hardiness: Zone 7
Variants: 'Crimson King' has single red flowers, while 'Narumigata' has large white flowers.

Camellia 'Spring Festival'

This is a very distinct garden-raised hybrid, a seedling of *C. cuspidata*, which makes an evergreen shrub of compact, narrowly upright habit and with glossy dark green leaves. The small, formal double, pink flowers fade in mid- to late spring to pale pink after opening.

Height: 3 m (10 ft)
Spread: 1 m (3 ft)
Hardiness: Zone 8

Camellia x williamsii

These garden-raised hybrids between *C. japonica* and *C. saluenensis* have provided some of the finest camellias for garden cultivation. They are normally very vigorous and most selections grow into large shrubs with glossy dark green leaves. The flowers vary in form and colour from single to formal double and from white to deep pink. Blooms are produced in spring.

Height: 3 m (10 ft) or more
Spread: 3 m (10 ft) or more
Hardiness: Zone 8
Variants: 'Anticipation' is upright in habit with large, deep pink, peony-form flowers. 'Bow Bells' has single, bright pink, funnel-shaped flowers over a long period. 'Brigadoon' has a compact and upright habit with semi-double, rose-pink flowers. 'China Clay' bears semi-double, white flowers, while 'Debbie' has large, rich pink, peony-form flowers. 'Donation' is among the most popular of all, with large, semi-double, pink flowers and an upright habit. 'E G Waterhouse' has pale pink, formal double flowers and 'Elegant Beauty' has large, deep rose-pink, anemone-form flowers. 'Elsie Jury' bears large, clear pink, peony-form flowers and 'E T R Carlyon' is vigorous with arching shoots and semi-double to double white flowers. 'Francis Hanger' has an upright shape with single white flowers and wavy edged leaves. 'Golden Spangles' has small, single, pink flowers and leaves that are blotched yellow-green in their centres. 'J C Williams' has single pink flowers and 'Jury's Yellow' has anemone-form white flowers, the centres of which contain many yellow petal-like stamens. 'Saint Ewe' has large, single, rich pink flowers and 'Water Lily' has large, fully double, rich pink flowers.

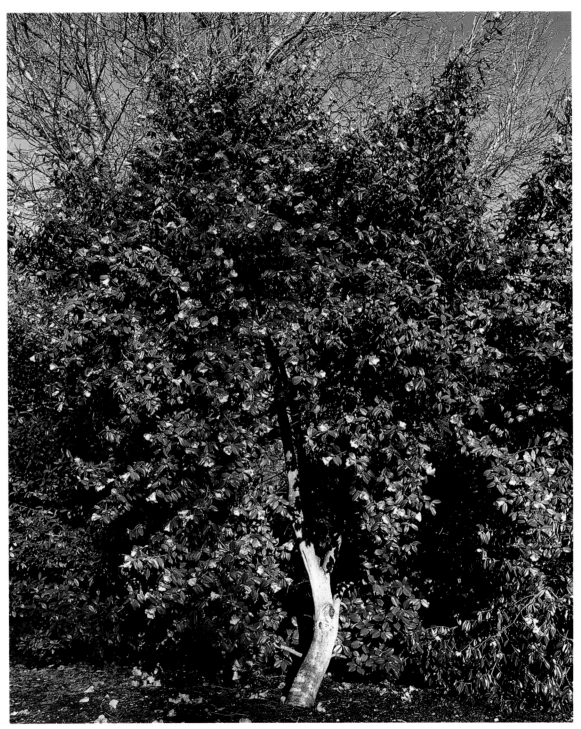

Camellia x *williamsii* 'Bow Bells'

Caragana
Leguminosae

These deciduous and often spiny shrubs and small trees make up a genus comprising some 80 species that are native in Eastern Europe and Asia. They have leaves that are divided into several leaflets and they bear small, pea-like, usually yellow, flowers. The following plant is the only commonly grown species and it is valued for its extreme hardiness and its ability to grow in poor soils. For best results, grow it in any well-drained soil in full sun; it will also tolerate exposed positions. Little pruning is required but selected forms are usually grafted and so it may sometimes be necessary to remove suckers from the base, below the graft point.

Caragana arborescens

A fast-growing deciduous and spiny shrub, whose upright branches bear bright green leaves, each divided up into 12 small leaflets. Small, pea-like, bright yellow flowers open singly or in clusters in spring and these are followed by slender brown seed pods.

Common name: Pea tree
Native range: Siberia, N China
Height: 5 m (16 ft)
Spread: 4 m (13 ft)
Hardiness: Zone 2
Variants: 'Lorbergii' is a very graceful shrub with slender shoots, narrow leaflets and smaller flowers. 'Pendula' is a weeping form, grafted on the top of a stem, usually about 1–1.5 m (3–5 ft) tall. 'Walker' is similar to 'Pendula', but it has foliage that is more like 'Lorbergii'.

Carpenteria
Hydrangeaceae

The single species in this genus is an evergreen shrub with opposite leaves, native to California, USA, and is grown in gardens for its handsome flowers. It should be given well-drained soil and a sunny position, where it will be suitable for a shrub border or, in cooler areas, a sunny wall. Cut back lightly in spring if necessary, removing any dead or crossing wood at the same time.

Carpenteria californica

This is an evergreen shrub with opposite, glossy dark green leaves. The showy white, anemone-like flowers have a conspicuous centre of yellow

Carpinus betulus

stamens and the attractive blooms open in clusters towards the ends of the shoots in the summer months.

Common name: Tree anemone
Native range: California, USA
Height: 2 m (6 ft)
Spread: 1.5 m (5 ft)
Hardiness: Zone 8

Carpinus
Carpinaceae

The hornbeams comprise a genus of about 35 species of deciduous, catkin-bearing trees, mainly found in China, but also widely distributed throughout Europe, Asia and North America.

The following species is useful both as a specimen tree and as hedging. It will grow on any well-drained soil, even shallow chalk soils. Hedges can be cut in late summer.

Carpinus betulus

This is a deciduous tree that has a broadly conical-to-rounded habit with a smooth, grey, fluted trunk and sharply toothed, conspicuously veined leaves turning yellow in autumn. Separate male and

Carpenteria californica

female catkins are borne on the same tree in spring: the males yellow and drooping; the females green and forming attractive, green fruit clusters, later turning yellow-brown in colour.

Common name: Common hornbeam
Native range: Europe, SW Asia
Height: 25 m (80 ft)
Spread: 20 m (65 ft)
Hardiness: Zone 5
Variants: 'Fastigiata' is dense and narrowly upright when young, later rounded, to 15 m (50 ft) tall.

Carya
Juglandaceae

The hickories are a genus of some 20 species of generally fast-growing deciduous trees that are related to the walnuts (*Juglans*). Hickories are natives of North America and Southeast Asia. Suitable for larger gardens only or parks, hickories are mainly large trees grown for their stately habit and bold foliage, which colours in autumn, often turning a clear yellow. Several species produce edible nuts, including the pecan (*Carya illinoinensis*). They require a good, fertile, well-drained soil, and they should also be planted when they are small in order to prevent any possible damage to the tap root.

Carya ovata

A deciduous tree with grey-brown bark, which, on mature trees, peels in long, vertical strips. The leaves are deep green and are usually made up of five individual leaflets. In autumn, leaves turn golden yellow. Male and female flowers are borne separately on the same tree: the male flowers in pendulous catkins growing in clusters of three; the small female flowers developing into thick-shelled edible nuts.

Common name: Shagbark hickory
Native range: E North America
Height: 25 m (80 ft)
Spread: 15 m (50 ft)
Hardiness: Zone 4

Caryopteris
Verbenaceae

This small genus consists of only about six species of deciduous shrubs and herbaceous perennials, all of which are native to East Asia. The following is the most commonly seen shrubby representative of the genus in cultivation and it is grown for its blue flowers.

In order to do well it needs to be grown in a well-drained, but not overly rich soil, and it requires a position where it receives full sun. The shrub is suitable for the front of a garden border or for growing against a sunny wall. Cut it back hard in spring before growth starts.

Caryopteris x clandonensis

This is a garden-raised hybrid between *C. incana* and *C. mongolica* that makes a deciduous, mound-forming shrub with aromatic, grey-green leaves

Caryopteris x *clandonensis* 'Heavenly Blue'

that are silvery white beneath. Clusters of blue flowers open during the late summer and autumn seasons. Several selections have been raised varying in flower colour. In particularly cold areas, it may be treated as a herbaceous perennial and be cut down to soil level in autumn.

Height: 90 cm (35 in)
Spread: 1 m (3 ft)
Hardiness: Zone 6
Variants: 'Arthur Simmonds' has purple-blue flowers. 'Ferndown' has deep blue-violet flowers. 'Heavenly Blue' has very dark blue flowers. 'Kew Blue' has dark blue flowers. 'Worcester Gold' has yellow to yellow-green foliage and lavender blue-coloured flowers.

Cassiope
Ericaceae

In this genus there are about 12 species of unusual heather-like, evergreen shrubs with a restricted native range taking in the arctic and alpine regions of the northern hemisphere. They have small, densely overlapping leaves and bear small, white, nodding flowers in late spring and early summer. They require a moist, acidic, peaty soil and are at their best in cooler climates, where they are suitable for a rock or peat garden.

Cassiope 'Edinburgh'

This garden-raised hybrid grows into an attractive, dwarf, evergreen shrub ideal for a rock garden. It has sparsely branched, upright shoots bearing slender, dark green leaves, and its small, pendulous white flowers, which open in the late spring, are notable for having contrasting red-edged sepals.

Height: 20 cm (8 in)
Spread: 20 cm (8 in)
Hardiness: Zone 3

Cassiope lycopodioides

This is a low-growing and mat-forming evergreen shrub. It spreads by sending out slender, creeping or ascending shoots that have tiny, dark green leaves. In late spring *C. lycopodioides* bears small, nodding, white, bell-shaped flowers with attractively contrasting red sepals and stalks.

Native range: Japan, Alaska
Height: 10 cm (4 in)
Spread: 25 cm (10 in)
Hardiness: Zone 3
Variants: 'Beatrice Lilley' is a compact form and bears profuse flowers.

Castanea
Fagaceae

This small genus of 12 species, which encompasses the sweet chestnut, contains deciduous trees and shrubs that are natives of north temperate regions. They all have sharply toothed leaves and bear their fragrant flowers in upright, slender catkins that are followed by fruits enclosed in conspicuous spiny husks.

The following species is the most commonly grown of the genus. It does best if planted in a good, acidic soil and it is also suitable for planting where soils are very sandy.

Castanea sativa

This is a fast-growing, large deciduous tree with smooth grey bark when young. The bark becomes brown and spirally furrowed with age. The bold, glossy, dark green leaves are edged with numerous bristle-tipped teeth. Masses of creamy, fragrant catkins appear in summer and these are followed by very spiny fruits containing large, brown and edible seeds.

Common names: Spanish chestnut, sweet chestnut
Native range: S Europe, SW Asia, North Africa
Height: 30 m (100 ft)
Spread: 20 m (65 ft)
Hardiness: Zone 5
Variants: 'Albomarginata' has its leaf margins coloured creamy yellow when foliage is young, becoming creamy white with age.

Castanea sativa 'Albomarginata'

Catalpa
Bignoniaceae

The 11 species that make up this genus are all deciduous trees and their native range is North America and East Asia. They make wide-spreading trees with bold leaves that are opposite or borne in whorls of three. Large clusters of white, foxglove-like flowers, variously spotted with purple, are conspicuously borne in summer at the ends of the shoots of older trees, and these are followed by long, pendulous, bean-like seed pods.

These trees will grow in any good soil, as long as it is well-drained, and they do best where they receive full sun. They make striking specimen trees if given adequate room to spread, but they can also be grown as shrubs. In this case, they

Catalpa x *erubescens* 'Purpurea'

need to be cut back annually to just above the base before the new growth starts in spring. If treated as a shrub, they will produce vigorous shoots and very large leaves, but no flowers.

Catalpa bignonioides

This is a vigorous, deciduous, spreading tree that has large, rounded, taper-pointed leaves emerging in late spring. The large, upright, conical clusters of white, bell-shaped flowers are heavily spotted with purple and yellow and open in summer. The flowers are followed by slender, pendulous pods, which persist on the tree. It requires an open site to be seen at its best.

Common name: Indian bean tree
Native range: SE United States of America
Height: 15 m (50 ft)
Spread: 15 m (50 ft)
Hardiness: Zone 5
Variants: 'Aurea' is a smaller-growing tree, attaining a maximum height of about 10 m (33 ft), and has bright yellow foliage.

Catalpa x erubescens

This garden-raised hybrid makes a deciduous tree of spreading habit with large, angularly three-lobed, dark green leaves. Conical clusters of white, bell-shaped, fragrant flowers are heavily spotted with yellow and purple. The flowers open in late summer and these are followed by long, slender, pendulous pods.

Height: 15 m (50 ft)
Spread: 15 m (50 ft)
Hardiness: Zone 5
Variants: 'Purpurea' has particularly attractive foliage. The young leaves are deep blackish-purple, maturing to a purple-green colour before turning dark green.

Catalpa bignonioides 'Aurea'

Ceanothus

Rhamnaceae

Sometimes known as the California lilacs, this genus contains about 55 species of evergreen and deciduous trees and shrubs. They can have opposite or alternate leaves and are found mainly in California, USA, although some do occur in other parts of North and Central America. Showing a wide variation in both habit and foliage, they are valued for their small, but profusely borne, clustered flowers. The flowers are usually blue, but they can also be pink or white.

The plants in this genus all require a well-drained soil and a sunny position. They can be used as specimen plants, grown against a wall, or the low-growing specimens are suitable for ground cover. The deciduous plants can be cut back hard in spring, while the evergreens should be only lightly pruned.

Ceanothus arboreus

This vigorous species makes a large, spreading evergreen shrub or small tree with glossy dark green leaves densely covered with grey hairs beneath. The blue flowers open in large, showy, conical clusters in late spring and early summer.

Common name: Feltleaf ceanothus
Native range: California, USA
Height: 5 m (16 ft)
Spread: 6 m (20 ft)
Hardiness: Zone 8
Variants: 'Trewithen Blue' is a form that has particularly rich-blue flowers.

Ceanothus 'Autumnal Blue'

This garden-raised hybrid is one of the hardiest of the evergreen forms and it makes an outstanding plant for the border. The shrub is of an essentially upright habit and has glossy, dark green, distinctly three-veined leaves. A profusion of conical clusters of sky-blue flowers open in late spring and often there is a repeat flowering in the late summer and autumn.

Height: 3 m (10 ft)
Spread: 2.5 m (8 ft)
Hardiness: Zone 8

Ceanothus 'Blue Mound'

This fast-growing and very tough garden hybrid makes a dense evergreen mound of spreading habit with small, glossy dark green, wavy edged and finely toothed leaves. Clusters of deep blue

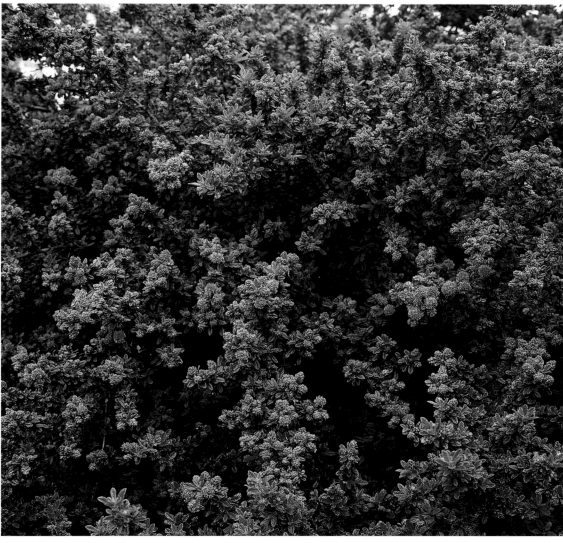

Ceanothus 'Blue Mound'

flowers open in late spring and often there is a repeat flowering in late summer and early autumn.

Height: 2.5 m (8 ft)
Spread: 4 m (13 ft)
Hardiness: Zone 8

Ceanothus 'Cascade'

This large, vigorous shrub of spreading habit has arching branches bearing glossy, dark green, finely toothed leaves. The dense, rounded clusters of powder-blue flowers are profusely borne over a long period in late summer and early autumn.

Height: 4 m (13 ft)
Spread: 5 m (16 ft)
Hardiness: Zone 8

Ceanothus 'Concha'

This is a vigorous garden-raised hybrid making a spreading evergreen shrub with arching shoots bearing narrow, glossy dark green leaves. Dense clusters of deep blue flowers open from red buds during spring.

Height: 2.5 m (8 ft)
Spread: 4 m (13 ft)
Hardiness: Zone 8

Ceanothus x delileanus

This group of garden hybrids between *C. americanus* and *C. coeruleus* contains some of the finest deciduous *Ceanothus*. Vigorous and upright, they bear dark green leaves and large clusters of blue flowers during summer and autumn.

Height: 2 m (6 ft)
Spread: 1.5 m (5 ft)
Hardiness: Zone 7
Variants: Several of the most popular garden forms belong here. 'Gloire de Versailles' bears large clusters of powder-blue flowers. 'Henri Desfossé' has deep blue flowers. 'Topaze' has indigo-blue flowers.

Ceanothus griseus

This vigorous, spreading evergreen shrub has glossy green, toothed and wavy edged leaves covered with grey hairs on their undersurfaces.

The flowers of *C. griseus* vary in colour from lilac to deep blue, and open in large, rounded clusters during the late spring and early summer.

Common name: Carmel ceanothus
Native range: California
Height: 3 m (10 ft)
Spread: 5 m (16 ft)
Hardiness: Zone 8
Variants: var. *horizontalis* 'Yankee Point' is a low-growing selection of compact habit, growing to 60 cm (24 in) tall, with deep blue flowers.

Ceanothus impressus

This species is popular in gardens, as well as being the parent of several hybrids. It makes a compact, rounded evergreen bush with small, dark green, deeply veined leaves. Small, dense, rounded clusters of deep blue flowers open in late spring.

Common name: Santa Barbara ceanothus
Native range: California
Height: 2 m (6 ft)
Spread: 2.5 m (8 ft)
Hardiness: Zone 8

Ceanothus x pallidus

These are garden hybrids between *C.* x *delileanus* and *C. ovatus*. Like the forms of *C.* x *delileanus*, they make deciduous shrubs of upright growth and bear large flower clusters at the ends of their shoots in summer and autumn. They can be cut back in spring before growth starts. There are several selections varying in flower colour.

Height: 1.5 m (5 ft)
Spread: 1 m (3 ft)
Hardiness: Zone 7
Variants: 'Marie Simon' has pale pink flowers, while 'Perle Rose' has carmine-pink flowers.

Ceanothus thyrsiflorus

A vigorous, spreading evergreen shrub, sometimes tree-like, with glossy dark green, finely toothed and three-veined leaves. Among the most striking and hardy of the evergreens, it produces large clusters of bright blue flowers during spring.

Common name: Blue blossom
Native range: California
Height: 5 m (16 ft)
Spread: 6 m (20 ft)
Hardiness: Zone 7
Variants: var. *repens* (creeping blue blossom) is the most commonly grown form. It makes a dense bush of low, spreading habit about 1 m (3 ft) tall.

Ceanothus 'Concha'

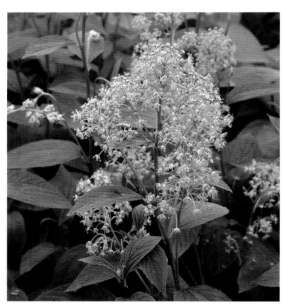

Ceanothus x *pallidus* 'Perle Rose'

Ceratostigma
Plumbaginaceae

This is a genus of about eight species of herbaceous perennials and subshrubs that are natives of Africa and from the Himalayas to East Asia. The few species in cultivation are valued for their unusual blue flowers, which are borne late in the season.

The following is the most popular and easiest species to grow. It is suitable for a garden border or for planting against a wall, and prefers a well-drained soil in full sun. It does best if cut back hard in spring before growth starts or it may behave as a herbaceous perennial in cold areas.

Ceratostigma willmottianum

Ceratostigma willmottianum

This is a small-growing, compact and deciduous subshrub with slender, upright, sparsely branched red shoots and bristly red-edged leaves. The leaves turn red in autumn. Clusters of attractive blue flowers open over a long period during the late summer and autumn.

Native range: China
Height: 1 m (3 ft)
Spread: 1 m (3 ft)
Hardiness: Zone 7

Cercidiphyllum
Cercidiphyllaceae

The two species of trees in this genus are both deciduous and are native to Japan and China. Having very distinctive foliage, they are grown mainly for their autumn leaf colour.

These trees do best in a good, moist, neutral or acidic soil, and they also benefit from the shelter offered by other nearby trees. The foliage emerges very early in the year and can be damaged by late frosts. Established plants can survive this but young plants can be killed.

Cercidiphyllum japonicum

This is a strongly growing deciduous tree. When young, it is essentially conical in shape, but as it ages it becomes more spreading in habit. Its leaves are opposite or alternate, rounded and shallowly toothed, bronze when young and becoming green to blue-green. The very small red flowers – males and females are borne on separate trees – open before the leaves emerge. The leaves turn startling hues in autumn, ranging from yellow to orange and red, and colours are more striking if the tree is grown on acid soils. Unusually, the leaves smell of burned sugar after they have fallen.

Common name: Katsura tree
Native range: Japan, China
Height: 20 m (65 ft)
Spread: 20 m (65 ft)
Hardiness: Zone 4
Variants: 'Pendulum' forms a mound of arching shoots up to 6 m (20 ft) tall. 'Rotfuchs' is upright in habit, with deep red-purple foliage.

Cercis
Leguminosae

The redbuds are a small genus of some seven species of very distinct deciduous trees native from the eastern Mediterranean region to Central and East Asia, and North America, with untoothed, rounded leaves that are distinctly heart-shaped at the base.

Popular in gardens for their small but profuse flowers, borne before or as the leaves emerge, they are suitable for all well-drained soils, including chalk, and they do best in a warm, sunny position.

Cercis canadensis

This is a deciduous tree that has a rounded-to-spreading habit. It bears heart-shaped, bright

Cercis siliquastrum

green leaves, which are bronze when young, ending in short, tapered points. The pea-like flowers vary in colour from white to pale or deep pink, and open in clusters on the shoots before the leaves emerge in the spring. The flowers are followed by flattened seed pods that are green coloured when young and turn red and then brown as they ripen.

Common name: Eastern redbud
Native range: North America
Height: 8 m (26 ft)
Spread: 10 m (33 ft)
Hardiness: Zone 4
Variants: 'Forest Pansy' produces leaves that are deep red-purple in colour.

Cercis siliquastrum

A spreading deciduous tree, often branching low down, with broad, rounded leaves deeply heart-shaped at their bases. Pea-like flowers, pink to deep pink or sometimes white, open in clusters before or as the leaves emerge in the spring. The flowers are occasionally seen in dense bunches on the main trunks, and these are followed by flattened pods that turn from pink to brown.

Common name: Judas tree
Native range: E Mediterranean region
Height: 10 m (33 ft)
Spread: 10 m (33 ft)
Hardiness: Zone 7

Cestrum
Solanaceae

A genus of some 175 New World species of both deciduous and evergreen shrubs. They are characterized by their mostly narrow, simple leaves and are natives of the warm regions from Mexico to South America.

The main attraction of these species is their striking tubular, sometimes fragrant flowers, commonly seen in colours of yellow, red, white or greenish. These plants are suitable for any reasonable soil in a sunny position, but they will grow in an open situation – as a specimen shrub, perhaps – only in mild, nearly frost-free gardens. In colder climates, however, they can be trained on a warm, sun-facing wall. Alternatively, they can be grown in containers and moved to the glasshouse or conservatory during winter.

Chaenomeles speciosa 'Nivalis'

Cestrum aurantiacum

This is an evergreen shrub, sometimes tree-like or with a tendency to develop somewhat climbing shoots when mature. Its leaves are wavy edged, taper-pointed and aromatic. Large, conical clusters of bright orange, tubular flowers open during late

spring and summer followed by white berries.

Native range: Guatemala
Height: 3 m (10 ft) or more
Spread: 3 m (10 ft)
Hardiness: Zone 9

Cestrum elegans

This is a vigorous evergreen shrub with stout, arching shoots and taper-pointed, deep green leaves. The drooping clusters of bright red to purple-red tubular flowers open over a long period during summer and autumn.

Synonym: *Cestrum purpureum*
Native range: Mexico
Height: 3 m (10 ft)
Spread: 3 m (10 ft)
Hardiness: Zone 9

Cestrum 'Newellii'

A garden selection of uncertain origin making a vigorous, evergreen shrub with slender, arching shoots. Large clusters of deep crimson, tubular flowers open at the ends of the shoots in spring.

Height: 2 m (6 ft)
Spread: 3 m (10 ft)
Hardiness: Zone 9

Cestrum parqui

This deciduous shrub is the hardiest of the genus, and has slender, pointed leaves. The large, conical clusters of bright yellow-green flowers open during summer and are fragrant at night. In cold areas it may behave as a herbaceous perennial.

Native range: Chile
Height: 1.5 m (5 ft)
Spread: 2 m (6 ft)
Hardiness: Zone 8

Cestrum elegans

Chaenomeles
Rosaceae

The ornamental flowering quinces are a small genus consisting of just three species, all bearing alternate, toothed leaves. These sometimes spiny deciduous shrubs are East Asian natives, found in China and Japan.

Valuable in gardens for their dense habit and profuse, early flowers, as well as their apple-like ornamental fruits, they are easy to grow in any soil and can be used as specimen shrubs, in the border, for growing against a wall or for hedging. They can be cut back as required to maintain their shape or size in spring. To rejuvenate old or neglected plants, cut back hard in spring. The fruits of some types can be used for making preserves.

Chaenomeles speciosa

A vigorous, deciduous, spreading shrub with spiny shoots and glossy dark green leaves, usually bronze when young. The variously coloured, single or double, white, pink or red flowers open in showy clusters in the spring, the first ones before the leaves emerge. Flowering is followed by aromatic, spherical-shaped fruits.

Native range: China
Height: 2.5 m (8 ft)
Spread: 3 m (10 ft)
Hardiness: Zone 4
Variants: 'Geisha Girl' is a variety that bears double, apricot-peach flowers. 'Moerloosei' ('Apple Blossom') has apple-blossom pink and white flowers. 'Nivalis' has white flowers. 'Simonii' has double, deep red flowers.

Chaenomeles x superba

This garden-raised hybrid between C. *japonica* and C. *speciosa* makes a dense, bushy deciduous shrub with spiny shoots and glossy green leaves. Showy clusters of single or double, white to pink, orange or red flowers open in spring, and these are followed by aromatic fruits.

Height: 1.5 m (5 ft)
Spread: 2.5 m (8 ft)
Hardiness: Zone 4
Variants: 'Crimson and Gold' is low and spreading, growing to 1 m (3 ft) tall, and its deep red flowers have conspicuous yellow stamens. 'Knap Hill Scarlet' is vigorous and compact in habit, with large, deep orange-red flowers. 'Pink Lady' has profusely borne deep pink flowers.

Chamaecytisus
Leguminosae

The 30 species that make up this genus include both deciduous and evergreen shrubs. They are all natives of Europe and bear leaves that are divided into three distinct leaflets.

The following is the most popular species of the genus and is still often listed as being a species of *Cytisus*, to which it is related. It requires a well-drained soil in a sunny position in order to thrive. It is particularly suited to growing in a rock garden, as long as the drainage is good.

Chamaecytisus purpureus

This dwarf deciduous shrub has a compact habit with arching shoots bearing small, dark green leaves, each divided into three leaflets. The small, pea-like, pink flowers open during the late spring or early summer.

Synonym: *Cytisus purpureus*
Common name: Purple broom
Native range: SE Europe
Height: 60 cm (24 in)
Spread: 90 cm (35 in)
Hardiness: Zone 6
Variants: 'Atropurpureus' has attractive deep purple-pink flowers.

Chamaerops
Palmae

The single species, C. *humilis*, that makes up this genus is an evergreen shrubby palm, that grows into a dense mound of foliage. The plant sometimes develops a stem and becomes more tree-like in form.

Chamaerops humilis

The bold, long-stalked, fan-shaped, deep green to blue-green leaves of this evergreen palm are deeply cut into numerous segments and are very striking in appearance. Clusters of small, yellow flowers emerge from near the base of the plant in the late spring or summer. C. *humilis* is one of only two palms that are native in Europe.

Common name: Dwarf fan palm
Native range: Mediterranean region
Height: 2 m (6 ft)
Spread: 3 m (10 ft)
Hardiness: Zone 9

Chaenomeles x superba 'Crimson and Gold'

Chimonanthus
Calycanthaceae

This is a small genus comprising six species of both deciduous and evergreen shrubs, all with opposite leaves, and all natives of China. Only the following species, however, is commonly found in garden cultivation.

Its unusual and very fragrant flowers, which are borne in winter, make it particularly valuable in gardens at a time of year when colour and scent are often largely absent. The shrub can be grown as a free-standing specimen or, in colder climates, it benefits from the protection afforded by being trained against a sunny wall.

It is suitable for any reasonably good soil but will flower best if given a position in full sun. Wall-grown plants can be cut back as necessary just after flowering to maintain their shape or restrict their size. At the same time, remove any damaged, dead or crossing wood.

Chimonanthus praecox

This is a large and vigorous deciduous shrub of upright habit. The plant has glossy dark green leaves that are rough to the touch. The very fragrant, nodding, bell-shaped flowers are yellow and conspicuously marked with purple inside. They open to startling effect on the bare shoots during the winter. Flowers can sometimes be damaged by hard frosts.

Common name: Wintersweet
Native range: China
Height: 5 m (16 ft)
Spread: 3 m (10 ft)
Hardiness: Zone 7
Variants: 'Grandiflorus' has large leaves and flowers; 'Luteus' has large pure yellow flowers.

Chionanthus
Oleaceae

This is a large genus consisting of approximately 100 species of deciduous and evergreen shrubs and trees. All species have opposite-growing leaves and they are widely distributed throughout the tropical regions.

The following is the most commonly grown garden species and its popularity is down to its showy and fragrant white flowers. It is suitable for any good, well-drained soil but flowers best in regions with hot summers – even so, it will still benefit from being positioned in full sun. The similar native Chinese species, *C. retusus*, is also sometimes grown.

Chimonanthus praecox

Chionanthus virginicus

Chionanthus virginicus

This is a deciduous shrub, sometimes grown on a single stem as a tree, with a habit ranging from conical to spreading. The plant has bold, dark green, oblong-shaped leaves, growing up to 20 cm (8 in) long, turning yellow in autumn. The fragrant, slender-petalled flowers are individually small but they open in impressively large clusters, about 20 cm (8 in) in length, during the late spring or summer. The flowers are followed by egg-shaped, blue-black fruits.

Common name: Fringe tree
Native range: E United States of America
Height: 4 m (13 ft)
Spread: 4 m (13 ft)
Hardiness: Zone 4

Choisya
Rutaceae

The five species in this genus are evergreen, aromatic shrubs native to the southwest of the United States of America and Mexico. They all have opposite leaves that are divided, fan-like, into several leaflets.

These species are grown for their attractive foliage as well as their showy, fragrant, white flowers and they are suitable for any fertile, well-drained soil, where they can be planted either in a shrub border or against a wall. They will tolerate shade but prefer a sunny position, and to produce their best display of flowers, full sun is essential. They can be pruned after flowering if necessary to maintain their shape or restrict their size.

Choisya 'Aztec Pearl'

This garden-raised hybrid makes a compact bush, and its elegant and attractively aromatic leaves are

Choisya ternata

Choisya 'Aztec Pearl'

divided into three to five slender leaflets. Its especially prolific clusters of fragrant, pink-tinged, white flowers open at the ends of the shoots in late spring, and usually there is a second flowering in autumn.

Height: 1.5 m (5 ft)
Spread: 2 m (6 ft)
Hardiness: Zone 7

Choisya ternata

This bushy evergreen shrub, which is grown for its foliage and flowers, has a compact habit and provides year-round garden interest. The glossy dark green, aromatic leaves are divided into three untoothed leaflets. Clusters of fragrant, white flowers open in late spring and again in autumn. It can be affected by severe frosts.

Common name: Mexican orange blossom
Native range: Mexico
Height: 2 m (6 ft)
Spread: 2.5 m (8 ft)
Hardiness: Zone 7
Variants: 'Sundance' has golden yellow young foliage when it is positioned in full sun; foliage turns yellow-green if it is planted in the shade, and it is less free-flowering as a result.

Chusquea culeou

Cistus albidus

A dense, mound-forming, bushy shrub with grey, hairy shoots and felted, oblong-shaped leaves. The contrasting lilac-pink, saucer-shaped flowers have a conspicuous yellow centre and are abundantly produced in summer.

Native range: SW Europe, North Africa
Height: 60 cm (24 in)
Spread: 90 cm (35 in)
Hardiness: Zone 8

Chusquea culeou

Chusquea
Gramineae

This is a large genus of about 100 species of evergreen bamboos native to Mexico and central America and the Andes of South America. Only the following species is commonly found in garden cultivation, however, and it is grown principally for its densely leafy, graceful habit. Plant in a good, moist but well-drained soil that is rich in humus. It requires a sheltered position that offers it protection from strong winds.

Chusquea culeou

This is a vigorous, clump-forming bamboo with upright, arching shoots and stout, solid, yellow-green to green culms made more attractive by the presence of persistent white-coloured leaf sheaths. The long, slender and taper-pointed leaves are borne in dense clusters.

Common name: Chilean bamboo
Native range: Chile
Height: 5 m (16 ft)
Spread: 5 m (16 ft)
Hardiness: Zone 7

Cistus
Cistaceae

These evergreen shrubs, known as sun roses or rock roses, comprise a genus of some 20 species found throughout the Mediterranean region, from Turkey to the Canary Islands and North Africa. They are easy to grow in any well-drained soil, as long as it is not too rich, and they need full sun to thrive. They are ideally suited to a border, rock garden, or against a sunny wall. Individual flowers are short-lived but are profusely borne. Light pruning after flowering helps to retain their compact habit.

Cistus x *aguilarii*

A naturally occurring hybrid that makes a spreading shrub with bright green, wavy edged, sticky leaves. Large white flowers with centres of golden yellow stamens are freely borne in summer.

Native range: SW Europe, North Africa
Height: 1 m (3 ft)
Spread: 1.5 m (5 ft)
Hardiness: Zone 8
Variants: 'Maculatus' produces flowers that are blotched in the centre with deep red.

Cistus x *cyprius*

This is a naturally occurring hybrid that makes a rounded, bushy shrub with taper-pointed, grey-green, wavy edged and sticky leaves borne on sticky shoots. The large, white flowers open in

Cistus albidus

succession during summer and are conspicuously blotched with red with a centre of yellow stamens.

Native range: France, Spain
Height: 1.5 m (5 ft)
Spread: 2 m (6 ft)
Hardiness: Zone 8

Cistus x dansereaui

This naturally occurring hybrid forms an upright shrub with sticky shoots and dark green, wavy edged, sticky leaves. Its large, white flowers, which are borne during summer, are conspicuously blotched with red in their centres.

Synonym: *Cistus x lusitanicus* of gardens
Native range: SW Europe
Height: 1 m (3 ft)
Spread: 1.5 m (5 ft)
Hardiness: Zone 8
Variants: 'Decumbens' is a low-growing form with a wide, spreading habit, about 60 cm (24 in) tall.

Cistus x hybridus

A bushy shrub of dense, rounded habit with small, dark green, wavy edged leaves. Masses of small, white flowers, yellow in the centre, open from red buds during late spring and summer.

Synonym: *Cistus x corbariensis*
Native range: S Europe
Height: 1 m (3 ft)
Spread: 1.5 m (5 ft)
Hardiness: Zone 8

Cistus x purpureus

Cistus ladanifer

This is a strongly growing shrub with an upright habit and lance-like, dark green, sticky leaves, aromatic when bruised. Its very large, white flowers have attractively frilled petals, and each

Cistus x aguilarii 'Maculatus'

flower is blotched with deep red at its centre. The flowers open at the ends of the shoots during the summer and the shrub requires a position in full sun in order to thrive.

Common name: Gum cistus
Native range: SW Europe, North Africa
Height: 2 m (6 ft)
Spread: 1.5 m (5 ft)
Hardiness: Zone 8
Variants: var. *albiflorus* bears white flowers with no central blotches.

Cistus laurifolius

This is a stoutly branched and vigorous shrub. When young it has an upright habit, but its shape changes to a more rounded form as the plant matures. Its dark green leaves, with white undersurfaces, are leathery, sticky and wavy edged. Clusters of large, white flowers, coloured yellow in their centres, open throughout the summer. This is a particularly hardy species that looks its best when positioned in full sun.

Native range: SW Europe, North Africa
Height: 1.5 m (5 ft)
Spread: 2 m (6 ft)
Hardiness: Zone 8

Cistus x skanbergii

Cistus x pulverulentus

A naturally occurring hybrid that makes a compact, low shrub with a spreading habit and with wavy edged, grey, hairy leaves. The profusely borne, showy pink flowers open during summer.

Native range: SW Europe
Height: 60 cm (24 in)
Spread: 1 m (3 ft)
Hardiness: Zone 8
Variants: 'Sunset' has deep cerise-pink flowers.

Cistus x purpureus

This is a naturally occurring hybrid making a rounded shrub with sticky red shoots and slender, pointed and slightly wavy edged, dark green leaves. The deep pink flowers have yellow stamens and crinkled petals marked with deep red at the base.

Native range: SW Europe
Height: 1 m (3 ft)
Spread: 1.5 m (5 ft)
Hardiness: Zone 8
Variants: 'Alan Fradd' has white flowers that are blotched with red.

Cistus x skanbergii

This is a naturally occurring hybrid that makes a low-growing, compact shrub with white, hairy shoots and narrow, grey-green leaves. Clusters of delicate, soft pink flowers with yellow stamens at their centres open during summer.

Native range: Greece
Height: 60 cm (24 in)
Spread: 75 cm (30 in)
Hardiness: Zone 8

Cladrastis
Leguminosae

The five species in this genus are deciduous trees mainly natives of China, but only the following – the most commonly grown – is found in North America. The leaves are divided into several leaflets and the pea-like flowers are borne in large clusters. It is suitable for any well-drained soil and flowers best in climates with hot summers.

Cladrastis kentukea

A deciduous tree with bold, bright green leaves, divided into 11 untoothed leaflets that turn yellow in autumn. The white, slightly fragrant, pea-like flowers open in summer in large drooping clusters from the ends of the shoots, and the flowers are followed by flattened pods.

Synonym: *Cladrastis lutea*
Common name: Yellow wood
Native range: SE United States of America
Height: 15 m (50 ft)
Spread: 12 m (40 ft)
Hardiness: Zone 4

Clerodendrum trichotomum var. fargesii

Clerodendrum bungei

Clerodendrum
Verbenaceae

This is a large genus of plants encompassing approximately 400 species of trees, shrubs and climbers, both deciduous and evergreen, native mainly to the tropical regions.

While several species are commonly found growing in conservatories and outside in tropical regions, two species are hardy enough to be planted outside in temperate regions. They are cultivated for their showy clusters of flowers rather than their individual blooms, and they are more likely to thrive if provided with a good, well-drained soil and a position in full sun.

Clerodendrum bungei

A vigorous deciduous shrub that spreads by suckers. It has upright shoots and bold, heart-shaped, dark green leaves, flushed with purple when young. The large, dense, dome-shaped clusters of deep pink, very fragrant flowers open at the ends of the shoots in the late summer and autumn. It can be treated like a herbaceous perennial in cold areas.

Common name: Glory flower
Native range: China
Height: 1.5 m (5 ft)
Spread: 2 m (6 ft)
Hardiness: Zone 8

Clerodendrum trichotomum

This is a deciduous tree of upright habit, often shrubby with several stems, and with broad, dark green, softly hairy leaves. The very fragrant, white

flowers have contrasting red sepals and they open in broad clusters during the late summer and autumn. The flowers are followed by fruits coloured a bright metallic blue.

Common name: Harlequin glorybower
Native range: China, Japan
Height: 6 m (20 ft)
Spread: 5 m (16 ft)
Hardiness: Zone 7
Variants: 'Carnival' has blue-green and grey-green leaves that are irregularly margined with creamy white. var. *fargesii* has smooth leaves that are coloured bronze when young, and it usually fruits more freely.

Clethra
Clethraceae

The 60 or so species that make up this genus comprise both deciduous and evergreen shrubs and trees. They have a very wide distribution, occurring from North through Central and South America, East Asia and Madeira. The following species is the most commonly found one in

cultivation and it requires a moist, humus-rich, acidic soil in order to thrive. Despite this, it is not a difficult plant to grow, but it does benefit from being provided with more shade in areas that experience dry summers.

Clethra alnifolia

This is a deciduous shrub that spreads by producing suckers. It is upright when young but becomes progressively more rounded as it matures. It has glossy green leaves that often turn yellow in autumn. *C. alnifolia* produces slender, upright spikes of very fragrant, small, creamy white clusters of flowers that open over a long period in late summer and early autumn. Pruning is not normally necessary, but damaged or unwanted branches can be removed in early spring.

Common name: Sweet pepper bush
Native range: E United States of America
Height: 2.5 m (8 ft)
Spread: 2 m (6 ft)
Hardiness: Zone 4
Variants: 'Hummingbird' has very dark green leaves, yellow in autumn, and large, profusely borne flower spikes. 'Pink Spires' has pink flowers.

Clethra alnifolia

Clianthus puniceus 'Roseus'

Clianthus
Leguminosae

The two species that make up this genus are southern hemisphere evergreen shrubs, natives of Australia and New Zealand. Their leaves are divided into numerous leaflets and they bear flowers with an unusual appearance – they have been likened in shape to a lobster's claw. The following species is usually grown trained against a sunny wall in more temperate regions and it is suitable for any good, well-drained soil, as long as it receives sun and shelter. Cut back long shoots by about one-third after flowering.

Clianthus puniceus

This is a vigorous evergreen or semi-evergreen shrub with long scandent, or climbing, shoots bearing dark green leaves made up of as many as 25 leaflets. The showy, drooping clusters of large, bright red flowers open over a long period during the summer months.

Common names: Lobster's claw, parrot's bill
Native range: New Zealand (North Island)
Height: 3 m (10 ft)
Spread: 3 m (10 ft)
Hardiness: Zone 8
Variants: 'Albus' has white flowers, while 'Roseus' has deep pink flowers.

Colletia hystrix 'Rosea'

Colletia
Rhamnaceae

This is a small genus of plants comprising five species of very unusual, spiny and distinct deciduous shrubs that are native to South America. The branches often have a thickened and flattened appearance.

These shrubs are leafless, or very sparsely leafy, but they have prominent opposite thorns. Small, fragrant flowers are profusely borne in late summer or autumn, in clusters from below the thorns. They are easy to grow and are suitable for any well-drained soil in a sunny position. Little pruning is usually required.

Colletia hystrix

Deciduous and nearly leafless, this shrub has rigid shoots and stiff, sharply pointed, dark green spines. Flowers are tubular, white and fragrant and open in clusters during late summer and autumn.

Synonym: *Colletia armata*
Native range: Chile
Height: 2.5 m (8 ft)
Spread: 3 m (10 ft)
Hardiness: Zone 8
Variants: 'Rosea' produces pink-coloured flowers.

Colquhounia
Labiatae

The three species in this small genus are evergreen shrubs with bold, opposite leaves, and are natives of the Himalayas and China. The following is the most commonly seen and is cultivated for its striking flowers. It can be grown in any good, well-drained soil in full sun. In cold areas it can behave almost like a herbaceous perennial, regrowing from the base in spring. Cut back any dead shoots to the base as the new growth appears.

Colquhounia coccinea

This is a vigorous, upright evergreen or semi-evergreen shrub with stout, square, felted shoots and aromatic, sage-green leaves. It produces upright clusters of showy, bright orange-red flowers, which open at the ends of the shoots in late summer.

Native range: Himalayas, China
Height: 2.5 m (8 ft)
Spread: 2 m (6 ft)
Hardiness: Zone 8

Colutea
Leguminosae

This widely distributed genus of 25 species of deciduous shrubs can be found throughout Europe, as well as North Africa to the Himalayas. Plants have leaves that are divided into several leaflets, and their pea-like, usually yellow flowers are followed by conspicuous bladder-like pods.

These shrubs are easy to grow in any well-drained soil. They are particularly tolerant of poor, dry soils and are useful in a shrub border due to their long flowering and fruiting season. Little pruning is usually necessary, but to restrict their size they can be cut back hard if required. They are best pruned in early spring, before the new season's growth starts.

Colutea arborescens

This tough, vigorous deciduous shrub has bright green leaves divided into as many as 13 leaflets. Clusters of yellow, pea-like flowers, marked with orange in their centres, are followed by pale green, later grey, inflated, bladder-like pods.

Common name: Bladder senna
Native range: S Europe, North Africa
Height: 3 m (10 ft)
Spread: 2.5 m (8 ft)
Hardiness: Zone 5

Convolvulus
Convolvulaceae

A genus of about 250 species of mainly annual and perennial herbs, with some shrubs, widely distributed mainly in temperate regions. The following is the most popular shrubby species and is grown for its attractive foliage and flowers. It needs a well-drained, not too rich soil in full sun and is suitable for the front of a sheltered border, a rock garden or a sunny wall. Prune lightly after flowering to retain its compact habit.

Convolvulus cneorum

This is a dense, mound-forming evergreen shrub with slender, silky haired, silvery grey leaves. The contrasting funnel-shaped flowers are pink in bud opening white, and are profusely borne in the late spring and early summer.

Native range: Mediterranean region
Height: 60 cm (24 in)
Spread: 1 m (3 ft)
Hardiness: Zone 8

Cordyline
Agavaceae

This genus comprises some 15 species of evergreen, palm-like trees and shrubs that are natives of Southeast Asia, Australasia and the Pacific Islands. All species are characterized by their densely clustered, sword-like leaves. While many are grown as conservatory plants in temperate regions, the following species is hardy in mild areas, although it may require some frost protection. It is suitable for any good, well-drained soil and does best if given a sunny position.

Cordyline australis

This upright evergreen tree has a single trunk until it is mature and then it branches sparsely. The bold, sword-like leaves are borne in large tufts towards the ends of the shoots. The leaves are upright at first, but later become more arching. Mature trees bear large clusters of small, white flowers during the summer season.

Common name: Cabbage palm
Native range: New Zealand
Height: 10 m (33 ft)
Spread: 3 m (10 ft)
Hardiness: Zone 9
Variants: Several variegated forms are also grown, including 'Albertii', with leaves striped green and pink, and 'Purpurea', which has purple leaves.

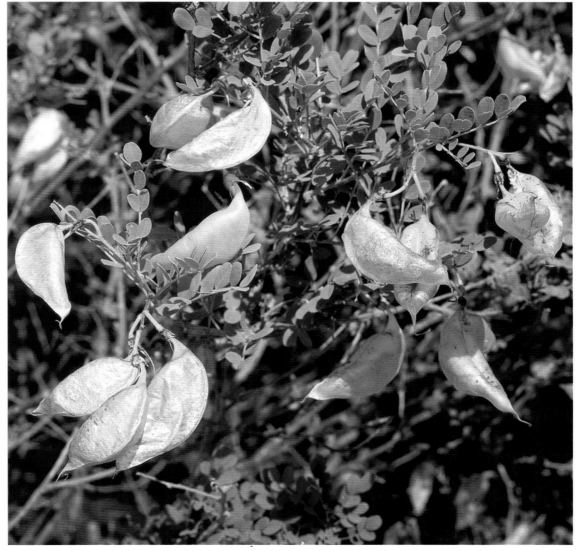

Colutea arborescens

Cornus

Cornaceae

The dogwoods comprise a genus of some 45 species of usually deciduous shrubs and trees, usually with opposite leaves, that are widely distributed in north temperate regions. The genus also includes examples of herbaceous perennials.

The individual flowers are small but are usually borne in dense clusters, which, in some species, are surrounded by conspicuous bracts. They have a variety of ornamental features, some being grown for their coloured winter shoots, some for their foliage, with many variegated selections, and others for their showy flowerheads. Forms of *C. alba*, *C. sanguinea* and *C. stolonifera* grown for their winter shoots can be cut back hard in early spring, before the new growth starts.

Cornus alba

A vigorous, thicket-forming shrub with upright shoots turning bright red in winter. Dark green leaves show autumn colours of orange to red and purple. Flattened heads of small white flowers in late spring to early summer are followed by small white fruits.

Common name: Red-barked dogwood
Native range: N Asia
Height: 3 m (10 ft)
Spread: 3 m (10 ft)
Hardiness: Zone 3
Variants: 'Aurea' has golden yellow foliage. 'Elegantissima' has leaves with irregular white margins. 'Ivory Halo' is compact with white-edged

Cornus alba 'Sibirica'

Cornus alba 'Aurea'

leaves. 'Sibirica' has brilliant red shoots in winter. 'Sibirica Variegata' has leaves with broad, irregular white margins. 'Spaethii' has yellow-margined leaves.

Cornus alternifolia

A conical-to-spreading, large deciduous shrub or small tree, often multi-stemmed, with alternate leaves usually clustered at the ends of the shoots and turning red and purple in autumn. Flattened heads of white flowers appear in early summer and are followed by small blue-black fruits.

Common name: Pagoda dogwood
Native range: E North America
Height: 6 m (20 ft)
Spread: 6 m (20 ft)
Hardiness: Zone 3
Variants: 'Argentea' is a beautiful form. Its small leaves are strikingly margined with creamy white. It is a compact bush to about 3 m (10 ft).

Cornus controversa

This is a spreading deciduous tree with characteristically layered branches and alternate, glossy dark green leaves that turn purple in

autumn. Broad, flattened heads of creamy white flowers appear between early to mid-summer and these are followed by small blue-black fruits.

Native range: E Asia
Height: 15 m (50 ft)
Spread: 15 m (50 ft)
Hardiness: Zone 5
Variants: 'Variegata' is a smaller-growing tree, the leaves of which have a broad creamy yellow margin when young. Margins turn creamy white as the leaves mature.

Cornus 'Eddie's White Wonder'

This is a garden-raised hybrid that makes a conical deciduous tree with dark green, taper-pointed leaves. In autumn, the leaves turn to brilliant orange, red and purple. The dense, button-like heads of small greenish-coloured flowers that open in late spring are surrounded by four large and conspicuous white or pink-tinged bracts.

Height: 6 m (20 ft)
Spread: 4 m (13 ft)
Hardiness: Zone 6

Cornus controversa

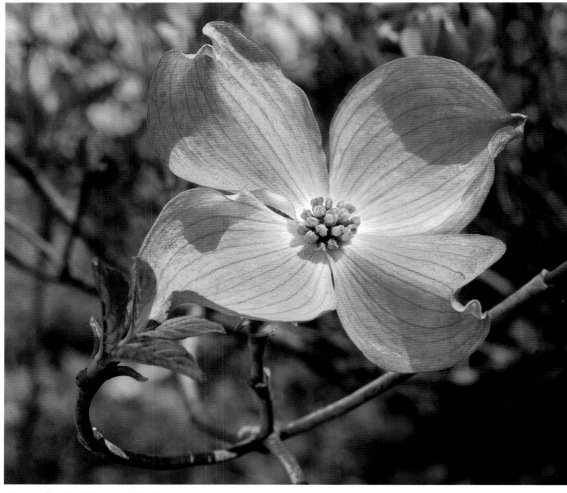

Cornus florida 'Cherokee Chief'

Cornus florida

The dark green leaves of this deciduous, spreading tree turn red to red-purple in autumn. Dense clusters of small, greenish-coloured flowers in spring are surrounded by four conspicuous bracts, which are usually white but can occasionally be various shades of pink.

Common name: Flowering dogwood
Native range: E North America
Height: 8 m (26 ft)
Spread: 10 m (33 ft)
Hardiness: Zone 5
Variants: There are numerous selections, such as 'Cherokee Chief', with deep pink bracts. 'Rainbow' has leaves with yellow margins, the margins turning to red-purple and edged in scarlet in autumn. Its bracts are white.

Cornus kousa

This is a deciduous tree that is conical when young but takes on a spreading habit as it matures. It has peeling, pale and dark brown bark and dark green, wavy edged leaves that turn red-purple in autumn. The small green flowers open in dense heads in early summer surrounded by four large, taper-pointed, creamy white bracts. These are followed by pendulous, strawberry-like red fruits.

Cornus kousa

Native range: Japan
Height: 8 m (26 ft)
Spread: 6 m (20 ft)
Hardiness: Zone 5
Variants: var. *chinensis* is similar but its leaf margins are not wavy. It generally performs better in gardens and many of the selected forms belong here. 'China Girl' has large flowerheads that are

borne profusely, even on young, small plants. 'Gold Star' has leaves that are attractively blotched in their centres with golden yellow, turning red, edged with purple in the autumn. 'Satomi' has deep pink-coloured bracts.

Cornus mas

This vigorous, deciduous, spreading shrub has dark green leaves that sometime turn red-purple in autumn. The small, yellow flowers open in clusters on the bare shoots in late winter, and these are followed by glossy red, edible, fleshy fruits that mature in late summer.

Common name: Cornelian cherry
Native range: Europe, W Asia
Height: 5 m (16 ft)
Spread: 6 m (20 ft)
Hardiness: Zone 4
Variants: 'Aurea' is a form that has golden yellow foliage. 'Aureoelegantissima' is smaller, reaching a height of about 2.5 m (8 ft), and its leaves are edged with yellow and tinged pink. 'Golden Glory' is upright in habit with handsome, glossy foliage and dense clusters of bright yellow flowers followed by freely borne fruits. 'Variegata' is a compact shrub, up to 2 m (6 ft) high, and its leaves are margined with creamy white.

Cornus 'Norman Hadden'

This garden-raised hybrid between *C. capitata* and *C. kousa* makes a semi-evergreen, spreading tree – some of its pale-coloured green leaves turn pink in autumn before dropping; others remain over winter. The dense heads of small, creamy white flowers that appear in early summer are surrounded by

Cornus mas

conspicuous bracts. These open creamy white, then turn white, and finally change to deep pink in mid-summer. In autumn, the strawberry-like fruits ripen to deep red and hang on long stalks. 'Porlock' is similar and has been distributed under this name.

Height: 8 m (26 ft)
Spread: 8 m (26 ft)
Hardiness: Zone 7

Cornus nuttallii

A vigorous, deciduous tree with a conical habit and dark green leaves that can turn red in autumn. Dense heads of small creamy flowers open at the ends of the shoots in late spring surrounded by creamy white bracts. This striking species does best in good, deep soil in a woodland situation.

Common name: Pacific dogwood
Native range: W North America
Height: 12 m (40 ft)
Spread: 8 m (26 ft)
Hardiness: Zone 7
Variants: Selected forms with large flowerheads include 'Colrigo Giant' and 'Portlemouth'

Cornus sanguinea

This is a vigorous, fast-growing deciduous shrub, fully frost hardy, with an essentially upright habit. The young shoots of *C. sanguinea* are flushed with

Cornus mas

red and its dark green leaves turn to red or purple-red in the autumn. Small white flowers open in flattened heads in early summer and these are followed by small, blue-black fruits. This shrub is dense enough to make successful hedging. Apart from the removal of unwanted, dead or crossing branches, no pruning is usually necessary. Any pruning that does occur is best done in spring.

Common name: Common dogwood
Native range: Europe
Height: 5 m (16 ft)
Spread: 4 m (13 ft)
Hardiness: Zone 4
Variants: 'Midwinter Fire' and the similar 'Winter Beauty' ('Winter Flame') are lower growing, with bright orange-red and yellow shoots in winter.

Cornus nuttallii 'Colrigo Giant'

Cornus nuttallii 'Portlemouth'

Cornus stolonifera 'Flaviramea'

Cornus stolonifera

This is a vigorous, thicket-forming deciduous shrub, fully hardy, that is valuable in the garden because of its bright red winter shoots. It is similar to *C. alba*, except that it spreads by suckers. The taper-pointed dark green leaves turn red to purple-red in autumn. Flattened heads of small white flowers appear in late spring and early summer, and these are followed by small white fruits.

Synonym: *Cornus sericea*
Common name: Red osier dogwood
Native range: North America
Height: 2.5 m (8 ft)
Spread: 3 m (10 ft)
Hardiness: Zone 2
Variants: 'Flaviramea' has yellow-green winter shoots and looks very effective when grown in association with *C. alba*. 'Kelseyi' is a dwarf, growing to a maximum height of about 90 cm (35 in), with slender shoots, red-tipped in winter. 'White Gold' has leaves that are edged with creamy white, and yellow winter shoots.

Cornus stolonifera 'Flaviramea'

Coronilla valentina subsp. *glauca*

Corokia
Rhamnaceae

The three species that make up this genus of plants are all evergreen shrubs native to New Zealand. Due to their attractive habit, flowers, fruits and foliage, they can make versatile additions to the garden.

Species have small yellow flowers followed by orange, yellow or red fruits. Suitable for any fertile, well-drained soil, they are best given shelter from strong winds. They also appreciate a position in full sun or they can be planted against a wall for protection. Pruning to restrict their size can be carried out after flowering has finished.

Corokia cotoneaster

This is an intricately branched evergreen shrub with slender, wiry shoots and spoon-shaped, bronze-green leaves that are silvery beneath. Small, star-shaped, yellow, fragrant flowers open in late spring, followed by small yellow or red fruits.

Common name: Wire netting bush
Native range: New Zealand
Height: 2 m (6 ft)
Spread: 2 m (6 ft)
Hardiness: Zone 7

Coronilla
Leguminosae

This is a genus comprising about 20 species of deciduous and evergreen shrubs, as well as annual and perennial herbaceous plants. They are natives mainly of Europe and the Mediterranean region and they are grown principally for their flowers and foliage.

The leaves of the species are usually divided into several leaflets and they bear clusters of yellow, pea-like flowers. They should be grown in well-drained soil that is not too rich, and where they will receive full sun. Plant against a sunny wall in regions where they are not fully hardy.

Coronilla valentina

A bushy evergreen shrub with bright green leaves divided into 13 wedge-shaped leaflets. Long-stalked clusters of small, golden yellow, pea-like flowers open over a long period during spring.

Native range: Mediterranean region
Height: 1.5 m (5 ft)
Spread: 1.5 m (5 ft)
Hardiness: Zone 8
Variants: The most commonly seen is subsp. *glauca*. It has blue-green leaves with up to seven leaflets. Selected forms of this are 'Citrina', with pale yellow flowers, and 'Variegata', in which the leaflets are edged with white.

Corylopsis
Hamamelidaceae

This is a genus of about seven species of deciduous shrubs, all closely related to the witch hazels (*Hamamelis*), and popular in gardens for their early-opening flowers.

These plants are natives of East Asia and bear hazel-like leaves and pendulous clusters of fragrant yellow flowers. They need to be grown in a good, moist but well-drained, lime-free soil. Frost damage is possible, so they are best planted in a sheltered site. Pruning is not normally necessary; however, to restrict growth or to remove dead or damaged wood, branches can be removed after flowering.

Corylopsis pauciflora

This is the most popular species of the genus, making a bushy, spreading shrub with leaves that are bronze when they first open but then turn bright green. The small, but profusely borne, nodding clusters of pale yellow, fragrant flowers open in early to mid-spring.

Native range: Japan, Taiwan
Height: 1.5 m (5 ft)
Spread: 2 m (6 ft)
Hardiness: Zone 6

Corylopsis spicata

A rounded-to-spreading deciduous shrub with blue-green leaves, bronze-purple when young, and bluish white beneath. Drooping spikes of fragrant yellow flowers tipped with orange open on the bare shoots in early spring.

Native range: Japan
Height: 3 m (10 ft)
Spread: 3 m (10 ft)
Hardiness: Zone 5

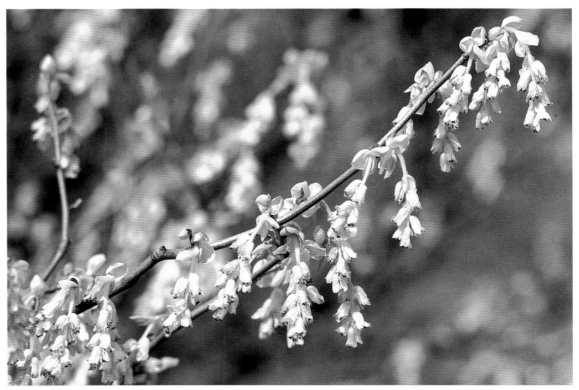

Corylopsis spicata

Corylus
Corylaceae

The hazels comprise some ten species of northern hemisphere deciduous shrubs and trees. They bear separate male and female flowers on the same plant – the males in drooping catkins. They are grown as specimen shrubs and as trees for their foliage, early catkins and edible fruits. They are suitable for any well-drained soil. Forms with coloured foliage do best in a sunny position.

Corylus avellana

A large deciduous shrub or small tree with broad, roughly hairy leaves. The pendulous, pale yellow male catkins are a familiar sight in late winter and early spring, while the tiny, red female flowers give rise to edible hazelnuts. It is mainly grown in gardens as one of the cultivars listed below.

Common name: Common hazel
Native range: Europe, North Africa, W Asia
Height: 5 m (16 ft)
Spread: 5 m (16 ft)

Corylus maxima 'Purpurea'

Corylus avellana 'Contorta'

Hardiness: Zone 4
Variants: 'Aurea' has bright yellow young foliage, turning yellow-green. 'Contorta' (corkscrew hazel, Harry Lauder's walking stick) has contorted shoots and makes a striking winter feature plant.

Corylus colurna

This is a medium-sized, vigorously growing deciduous tree with a compact, conical head and dark green, coarsely toothed leaves, that sometimes turn yellow in the autumn. The male flowers are borne in small, pale yellow, pendulous catkins in the late winter, while the nuts, which ripen as the leaves are falling, are surrounded by a husk that is deeply divided into numerous slender, rigid lobes.

Common name: Turkish hazel
Native range: SE Europe, W Asia
Height: 20 m (65 ft)
Spread: 10 m (33 ft)
Hardiness: Zone 4

Corylus maxima

A large, vigorous deciduous shrub – sometimes tree-like in habit – with broad, dark green leaves. Pendulous male catkins open on the bare shoots in late winter. The large, edible nuts are enclosed in a long, tubular husk.

Common name: Filbert
Native range: SE Europe, W Asia
Height: 6 m (20 ft)
Spread: 5 m (16 ft)
Hardiness: Zone 4

Variants: The most commonly grown form is 'Purpurea', which has deep red-purple leaves and fruit husks. The catkins are also tinged with purple. Other forms are also grown for their edible, autumn-ripening fruits.

Cotinus
Anacardiaceae

This small genus consisting of three species of deciduous shrubs and trees has produced some striking and extremely popular garden plants, which are grown principally for their foliage and conspicuous autumn colour. Individually the flowers are tiny but as the small fruits ripen they develop into large, plume-like clusters, which can then remain attractive well into winter.

The trees and shrubs of this genus are all suitable for any reasonably good, well-drained soil, as long as it is not too dry, but the foliage colour is seen at its best only in full sun. They can be grown in the border or positioned together as a group specimen planting. If it is necessary to restrict their size, they can be cut back, hard if required, in the early spring before the new season's growth commences.

Cotinus 'Grace'

Cotinus coggygria

This bushy, deciduous shrub grows vigorously and its smooth, untoothed blue-green leaves turn shades of yellow to orange-red in autumn. The large, persistent, conical fruit clusters range in colour from pale brown to pink.

Common name: Smoke tree, Venetian sumach
Native range: S Europe to China
Height: 5 m (16 ft)
Spread: 5 m (16 ft)
Hardiness: Zone 4
Variants: There are several selected forms of this species with deep red-purple foliage turning red in autumn, as well as purple-pink fruit clusters. Notable examples include 'Notcutt's Variety' and 'Velvet Cloak'.

Cotinus 'Flame'

A garden hybrid making a large, vigorous, tree-like deciduous shrub with scaly bark and pale blue-green leaves. Foliage turns a brilliant orange-red in autumn. Its conspicuously large fruiting clusters are purple-pink in colour.

Height: 6 m (20 ft)
Spread: 5 m (16 ft)
Hardiness: Zone 4

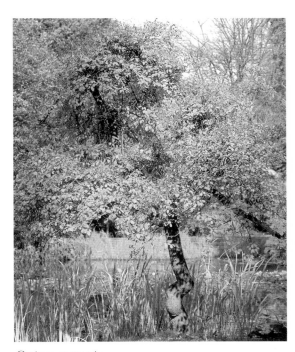

Cotinus coggygria

Cotinus 'Grace'

This is a vigorous deciduous garden hybrid that makes a large shrub, sometimes tree-like in habit, with attractive scaly bark and bold, deep red-purple leaves that turn a bright red in autumn. It bears large, conical-shaped, purple-pink fruit clusters in autumn.

Height: 6 m (20 ft)
Spread: 5 m (16 ft)
Hardiness: Zone 4

Cotinus obovatus

Cotinus obovatus

A deciduous, upright tree with striking scaly bark when mature. The bold, thin, untoothed leaves are bronze at first, becoming blue-green and then shades of orange, yellow, red and purple in autumn.

Common name: Chittamwood
Native range: C and S United States of America
Height: 10 m (33 ft)
Spread: 8 m (26 ft)
Hardiness: Zone 4

Cotoneaster
Rosaceae

This large genus, made up of several hundred species of deciduous and evergreen trees and shrubs, is widely distributed throughout Europe, Asia and North Africa. By far the largest number of species is found in China.

All species have small, white or pink-tinged flowers and they usually bear red fruits in autumn. The larger examples can be used as specimen shrubs, while smaller ones can be grown in the shrub border. Some sorts are used for hedging, while dwarf species are useful either in the rock garden or for ground cover.

Cotoneaster atropurpureus

This is a low, spreading deciduous shrub that makes a broad, dense mound with small, rounded, glossy dark green leaves that turn deep red-purple in autumn. Small, white flowers, flushed with red, are borne singly on the shoots, and these are followed by small orange-red fruits.

Native range: China
Height: 75 cm (30 in)
Spread: 2 m (6 ft)

Cotoneaster atropurpureus 'Variegatus'

Hardiness: Zone 4
Variants: 'Variegatus' (*C. horizontalis* 'Variegatus') has leaves edged with white.

Cotoneaster bullatus

A large deciduous shrub with bold, dark green, conspicuously and deeply veined leaves turning red in autumn. Small clusters of white flowers, tinged with pink in early summer, are followed by showy, bright glossy red fruits.

Native range: China
Height: 4 m (13 ft)
Spread: 3 m (10 ft)
Hardiness: Zone 5

Cotoneaster congestus

This is a dense, creeping evergreen shrub forming a wide mound with tiny, deep matt-green leaves. Its small, white flowers in early summer are followed by bright red fruits. It makes good ground cover in a rock garden.

Native range: Himalayas
Height: 30 cm (12 in)
Spread: 2m (6 ft) or more
Hardiness: Zone 6

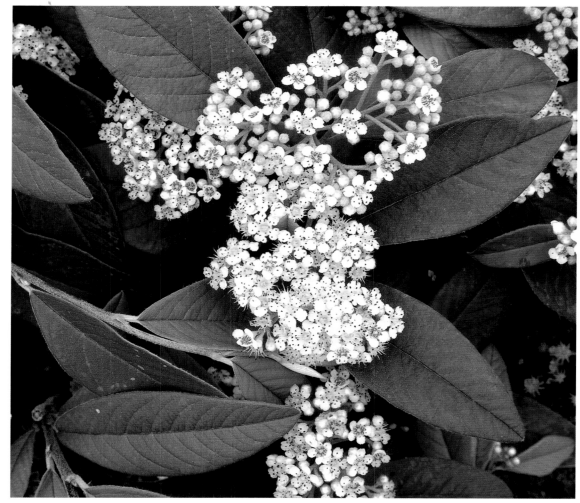

Cotoneaster 'Cornubia'

Cotoneaster conspicuus

This is an evergreen shrub with a compact, rounded habit with stiff, arching shoots and small, glossy dark green leaves. Small, white flowers are borne singly or in clusters in early summer, and these are followed by bright orange-red fruits in autumn. These attractive fruits can persist for several months. It is most commonly grown under the name *C. conspicuus* 'Decorus'. Apart from removing unwanted, dead or damaged branches in spring, pruning is not usually necessary.

Native range: SE Tibet
Height: 2 m (6 ft)
Spread: 2.5 m (8 ft)
Hardiness: Zone 6

Cotoneaster 'Cornubia'

A garden-raised hybrid making a vigorous, large semi-evergreen shrub with arching branches and bold dark green leaves. Foliage can turn bronze-purple in winter. Clusters of white flowers in summer are followed by profuse, bright red fruits.

Height: 5 m (16 ft)
Spread: 6 m (20 ft)
Hardiness: Zone 6

Cotoneaster x suecicus 'Erlinda'

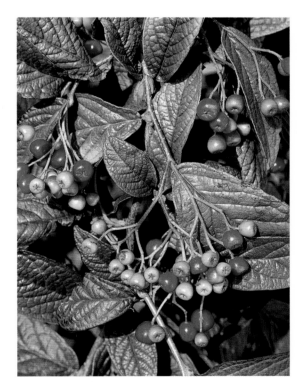

Cotoneaster bullatus

Cotoneaster dammeri

This is a creeping evergreen shrub with glossy dark green leaves that sometimes turn bronze-purple in cold weather. Small, white flowers in early summer are followed by bright red fruits. This is an excellent and vigorous species for ground cover.

Cotoneaster sternianus

Native range: China
Height: 20 cm (8 in)
Spread: 2.5 m (8 ft) or more
Hardiness: Zone 5
Variants: 'Major' is a commonly grown form producing large leaves.

Cotoneaster franchetii

This is a vigorous evergreen shrub with arching shoots bearing attractive grey-green leaves. The leaves later turn glossy and dark green, with the undersurfaces becoming white with hairs. Clusters of white flowers, tinged with pink in early summer, are followed by fruits turning orange-red. *C. sternianus* has larger leaves and fruit.

Native range: China
Height: 3 m (10 ft)
Spread: 3 m (10 ft)
Hardiness: Zone 6

Cotoneaster horizontalis

This wide-spreading deciduous shrub develops with a characteristic flattened, 'herring-bone' pattern of branches, growing largely horizontal with the ground and bearing rounded, glossy dark green leaves that turn red-purple in autumn. The small, white and pink-tinged flowers stud the branches in late spring and these are followed by bright red fruits.

Native range: China
Height: 1 m (3 ft)
Spread: 2 m (6 ft)
Hardiness: Zone 5

Cotoneaster horizontalis

Cotoneaster 'Hybridus Pendulus'

This garden-raised hybrid is usually grafted on top of a stem to make a small, weeping semi-evergreen tree with branches arching gracefully to the ground and deep matt-green leaves. Clusters of small, white flowers in early summer are followed by a profusion of bright red fruits. Apart from the removal of dead, damaged or crossing wood, pruning is not usually required.

Height: 2 m (6 ft)
Spread: 3 m (10 ft)
Hardiness: Zone 6

Cotoneaster integrifolius

A rigidly branched, mound-forming evergreen shrub with small, narrow, glossy dark green leaves. The white flowers are borne singly on the shoots in early summer and these are followed by deep pink fruits in autumn. This species is commonly grown as *C. microphyllus*.

Native range: Himalayas
Height: 1 m (3 ft)
Spread: 2 m (6 ft)
Hardiness: Zone 5

Cotoneaster lacteus

A compact evergreen shrub popular for its handsome foliage, flowers and fruits. The arching branches bear dark green, deeply veined leaves, while conspicuous clusters of creamy white flowers in summer are followed by long-lasting, red fruits.

Native range: China
Height: 2.5 m (8 ft)
Spread: 4 m (13 ft)
Hardiness: Zone 6

Cotoneaster salicifolius

A wide-spreading evergreen shrub with arching branches and long, slender, dark green and deeply veined leaves. Large clusters of white flowers in early summer are followed by glossy red fruits.

Native range: China
Height: 5 m (16 ft)
Spread: 5 m (16 ft)
Hardiness: Zone 6
Variants: 'Exburiensis' has yellow fruits. 'Gnom' is low growing, to 30 cm (12 in) and is good ground cover. 'Rothschildianus' has creamy yellow fruits.

Cotoneaster simonsii

This vigorous, upright deciduous or semi-evergreen shrub is often used for hedging, and its glossy dark green leaves turn red in autumn. Small clusters of white, pink-tinged flowers in early summer are followed by glossy orange-red fruits.

Native range: Himalayas
Height: 3 m (10 ft)
Spread: 2 m (6 ft)
Hardiness: Zone 5

Cotoneaster x suecicus

A group of garden-raised hybrids between *C. conspicuus* and *C. dammeri* making evergreen, creeping or mound-forming shrubs. They have glossy green leaves and white flowers in late spring, followed by orange-red to red fruits.

Height: Variable
Spread: 2 m (6 ft) or more
Hardiness: Zone 5
Variants: 'Coral Beauty' makes a mound to 1 m (3 ft), with orange-red fruits. 'Erlinda' has leaves edged with creamy white and is usually top-grafted to make a small, weeping standard.

Crataegus crus-galli

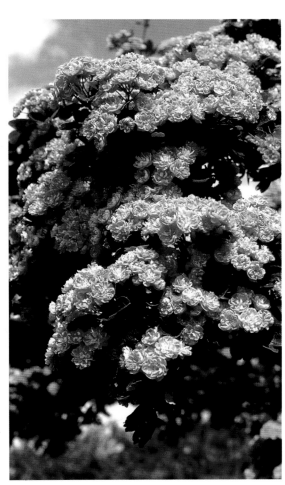

Crataegus laevigata 'Rosea Flore Pleno'

Crataegus
Rosaceae

The hawthorns make a genus of about 200 species of mainly deciduous, often spiny trees and shrubs that are widely distributed in the northern hemisphere. They bear clustered, usually white, flowers sometimes followed by edible fruits that vary in colour from yellow and red to blue, purple or black. Hawthorns will grow in most soils and are generally very tough trees, standing up to exposed positions. Grow as specimen trees or for hedging.

Crataegus crus-galli

This is a spreading, flat-topped deciduous tree with distinctly curved thorns. The glossy dark green leaves turn attractive shades of orange and red in autumn. Clusters of white flowers in early summer are followed by long-persistent, glossy red fruits.

Common name: Cockspur thorn
Native range: E United States of America
Height: 8 m (26 ft)
Spread: 10 m (33 ft)
Hardiness: Zone 4

Crataegus laevigata

This densely branched deciduous tree has a rounded habit with spiny shoots and shallowly lobed and toothed, glossy dark green leaves. Clusters of white flowers in late spring are followed by small, glossy red fruits. It is normally seen in cultivation as one of the selected forms listed below.

Synonym: *Crataegus oxyacantha*
Common name: Midland hawthorn
Native range: Europe, North Africa
Height: 10 m (33 ft)
Spread: 10 m (33 ft)
Hardiness: Zone 4
Variants: 'Crimson Cloud' has large, deep pink flowers, white in the centre. 'Paul's Scarlet' has deep pink, double flowers. 'Plena' has white double flowers turning pink. 'Rosea Flore Pleno' has pink double flowers.

Crataegus x *lavallei* 'Carrièrei'

This popular garden-raised hybrid between *C. crus-galli* and *C. mexicana* is interesting for its late-ripening fruits, which are ornamental during winter. It makes a spreading deciduous tree with bold, glossy dark green, long-persistent leaves, which turn red in late autumn and winter. Clusters of white flowers in early summer are followed by bright orange-red fruits ripening in late autumn.

Height: 10 m (33 ft)
Spread: 10 m (33 ft)
Hardiness: Zone 4

Crataegus monogyna

This is a deciduous tree, rounded-to-spreading in habit, with thorny shoots and deeply lobed and toothed, glossy dark green leaves. Clusters of fragrant white flowers in late spring are followed by small, glossy red fruits. This species is often used for hedging.

Common names: Common hawthorn, Quickthorn
Native range: Europe
Height: 10 m (33 ft)
Spread: 10 m (33 ft)
Hardiness: Zone 4
Variants: 'Biflora' (Glastonbury thorn) has two periods of interest: it comes into leaf and flower during winter and again in spring.

Crataegus x persimilis 'Prunifolia'

This garden hybrid makes a deciduous tree with a rounded habit. It has thorny shoots and glossy dark green, sharply toothed leaves that turn brilliant orange and red in autumn. Clusters of white flowers in early summer are followed by bright red fruits.

Synonym: *Crataegus x prunifolia*
Height: 6 m (20 ft)
Spread: 8 m (26 ft)
Hardiness: Zone 4

Crataegus viridis

A rounded deciduous tree of dense habit with spiny shoots and glossy dark green, sharply toothed and shallowly lobed leaves that sometimes turn red and purple in autumn. Clusters of white flowers in late spring are followed by persistent bright red fruits.

Native range: E United States of America
Height: 10 m (33 ft)
Spread: 10 m (33 ft)
Hardiness: Zone 4
Variants: 'Winter King' has particularly large, long-persistent fruits.

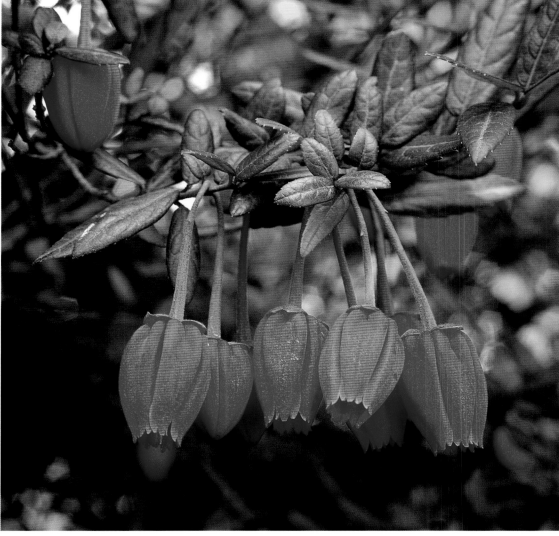

Crinodendron hookerianum

Crinodendron
Elaeocarpaceae

This is a small genus comprising just two species of evergreen trees or shrubs. They are native of Chile and are grown for their unusual flowers.

The following is the most commonly seen in cultivation and it requires a moist, well-drained, acidic soil with abundant organic matter. It does best when planted in areas that experience cool, moist summers and mild winters.

Crinodendron hookerianum

This evergreen shrub has an upright habit, sometimes tree-like, with narrow, dark green leaves. The striking, pendulous, lantern-like, deep pink flowers open in late spring and early summer from buds formed in the previous year.

Common name: Lantern tree
Native range: Chile
Height: 6 m (20 ft)
Spread: 4 m (13 ft)
Hardiness: Zone 8

Cydonia
Rosaceae

The single species in this small genus is a deciduous tree, native to Central and Southwest Asia, and is grown for its flowers and edible fruits. It will grow in any fertile, well-drained soil in full sun. In cooler areas it can be grown near to a warm wall or it can be fan-trained against it.

Cydonia oblonga

A wide-spreading deciduous tree with dark green leaves, grey with down beneath. Pale pink or white flowers open singly in late spring, followed by fragrant, pear-shaped, edible yellow fruits.

Common name: Quince
Native range: C and SW Asia
Height: 6 m (20 ft)
Spread: 6 m (20 ft)
Hardiness: Zone 4
Variants: 'Vranja' is the most popular of several fruiting selections. It bears very fragrant, golden yellow fruits.

Cytisus battandieri

Cytisus
Leguminosae

Grown for their foliage and also popular for their usually yellow, pea-like flowers, the brooms are a genus of some 35 species of widely distributed deciduous and evergreen shrubs and, more rarely, trees. The brooms are natives of Europe, North Africa and West Asia.

The brooms are suitable for the shrub border while the dwarf sorts make excellent additions to a rock garden. They prefer a not-too-rich, even poor or starved, well-drained soil and they should be planted where they will receive full sun.

Pruning lightly after flowering has finished encourages a compact habit. The stems that have borne flowers can be cut back to about half their original length, but care must be taken not to cut into the old wood, since it will not produce new growing stems.

Cytisus battandieri

This vigorous deciduous shrub of upright, tree-like habit has bold, silvery-grey leaves divided into three leaflets. The pineapple-scented yellow flowers open in dense cylindrical clusters in summer.

Common name: Pineapple broom
Native range: Morocco
Height: 4 m (13 ft)
Spread: 4 m (13 ft)
Hardiness: Zone 7

Cytisus x beanii

Making a low, spreading deciduous shrub, this garden-raised hybrid between *C. ardoinoi* and *C. purgans* produces slender, green, arching shoots and small, downy leaves that are divided into three leaflets. Small clusters of bright yellow, pea-like flowers are profusely borne in late spring or early summer on the previous year's growth. Prune lightly after flowering to maintain its shape.

Height: 45 cm (18 in)
Spread: 1 m (3 ft)
Hardiness: Zone 5

Cytisus x kewensis

This garden-raised hybrid between *C. ardoinoi* and *C. multiflorus* is suitable for a large rock garden or a sloping site. It makes a low-growing, spreading deciduous shrub with slender, arching shoots and small, downy leaves that are divided into three very small leaflets. Small clusters of pale creamy yellow to white pea-like flowers open in late spring. It is fully hardy and should be pruned lightly after flowering to maintain its shape.

Height: 30 cm (12 in)
Spread: 1 m (3 ft)
Hardiness: Zone 6
Variants: 'Niki' has golden yellow flowers.

Cytisus x praecox 'Allgold'

Cytisus x praecox

This garden-raised hybrid between *C. multiflorus* and *C. purgans* makes a deciduous shrub with a dense, mound-forming habit. It has slender, upright, later arching, green shoots bearing small, grey-green leaves that are divided into three leaflets. Creamy yellow flowers are profusely borne in small clusters from mid- to late spring. It is normally grown as selected forms listed below.

Height: 1.2 m (4 ft)
Spread: 1.5 m (5 ft)
Hardiness: Zone 5
Variants: 'Albus' has white flowers. 'Allgold' has golden yellow flowers. 'Warminster' (Warminster broom) is sometimes grown as *Cytisus x praecox* and has creamy yellow flowers. Hybrids of this include 'Hollandia', which has cream and deep pink flowers, and 'Zeelandia', which has lilac-pink flowers flushed with cream.

Cytisus scoparius

A deciduous shrub that produces slender, green, arching shoots and small leaves divided into three leaflets. Clusters of showy, deep yellow, pea-like flowers open in late spring. This species, together with its many forms and hybrids, is not at its best if grown on shallow, chalky soils.

Common name: Common broom
Native range: Europe
Height: 1.5 m (5 ft)
Spread: 1.5 m (5 ft)
Hardiness: Zone 5
Variants: There are numerous selections and hybrids in garden cultivation with variously coloured flowers. These include f. *andreanus*, which has dark green leaves and yellow flowers marked with red; 'Burkwoodii', with deep crimson and yellow flowers; and 'Lena', which is compact and has deep yellow flowers marked with red.

Cytisus x beanii

Daboecia
Ericaceae

A genus of a single species – an evergreen shrub – related to the heathers. Native of western Europe and popular for its variously coloured, urn-shaped flowers, it is suitable for the heather garden or a similar situation. It needs a neutral to acidic soil and does best in full sun. Cut back lightly before growth starts in spring to retain a compact habit.

Daboecia cantabrica

A heath-like evergreen shrub with small, glossy green, pointed leaves. The nodding, urn-shaped flowers, which are usually purple-pink, open in long, upright, spike-like clusters over a long period during summer and autumn.

Common names: Connemara heath, St Dabeoc's heath
Native range: W Europe (W Ireland to Portugal), Azores
Height: 45 cm (18 in)
Spread: 60 cm (24 in)
Hardiness: Zone 6
Variants: 'Alba' has white flowers. 'Atropurpurea' has deep purple-pink flowers. 'Praegerae' has rich pink flowers. 'William Buchanan' has crimson-purple flowers.

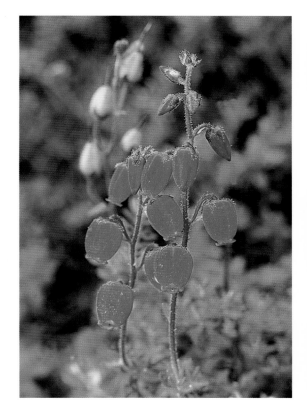

Daboecia cantabrica 'William Buchanan'

Danae
Ruscaceae

The single species in this genus is a remarkable evergreen, related to the butcher's broom, and

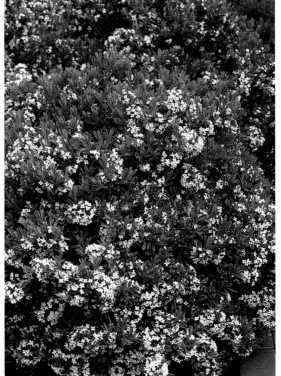

Daphne x burkwoodii 'Somerset'

sends up new shoots from the base each year. It is easy to grow in sun or shade and it is suitable for any not-too-dry, well-drained soil. The apparent leaves are really flattened stems. Any dead shoots can be cut back to the base in spring.

Danae racemosa

An evergreen shrub forming a clump of upright, later arching, green stems with glossy dark green 'leaves'. Sprays of small, pale green flowers in early summer are followed by red berries.

Common name: Alexandrian laurel
Native range: Turkey, N Iran
Height: 1 m (3 ft)
Spread: 1.2 m (4 ft)
Hardiness: Zone 7

Daphne
Thymelaeaceae

This is a remarkable genus comprising about 50 species of both deciduous and evergreen shrubs widely distributed throughout Europe, North Africa and Asia. They are popular in gardens for their often very fragrant four-lobed flowers. They can be grown in a good, moist but well-drained soil in a sunny position: the smaller sorts are suitable for a rock garden. *D. bholua*, *D. laureola* and *D. pontica* are very shade tolerant plants and will thrive in woodland conditions. They are all very poisonous if eaten.

Daboecia cantabrica 'Alba'

Daphne bholua

This is a very beautiful deciduous or evergreen shrub of upright growth with dark green leaves. Clusters of extremely fragrant usually pink and white flowers open at the ends of the shoots during late winter and early spring. Apart from removing dead or damaged wood after flowering, pruning is not usually recommended.

Native range: Himalayas
Height: 2.5 m (8 ft)
Spread: 1.5 m (5 ft)
Hardiness: Zone 8
Variants: 'Gurkha' is deciduous with purple-pink and white flowers. 'Jacqueline Postill' is evergreen or semi-evergreen with particularly large, deep purple-pink and white flowers.

Daphne blagayana

This low-growing evergreen shrub has long, trailing shoots with dark green leathery leaves growing mainly at the tips. In spring, the clusters of richly fragrant creamy flowers open mainly at

Daphne bholua 'Jacqueline Postill'

Daphne mezereum

the ends of the shoots, and these are sometimes followed by fleshy white fruits. *D. blagayana* is equally successful in a semi-shaded woodland situation or in a scree bed.

Native range: SE Europe
Height: 45 cm (18 in)
Spread: 1 m (3 ft)
Hardiness: Zone 5

Daphne odora 'Aureomarginata'

Daphne x burkwoodii

This popular garden-raised hybrid between *D. caucasica* and *D. cneorum* makes an upright semi-evergreen shrub, becoming more rounded as it matures, with bright green foliage. The dense clusters of extremely fragrant pink flowers, fading to white, open over a long period during spring, and often there is a repeat flowering in autumn.

Height: 1 m (3 ft)
Spread: 1 m (3 ft)
Hardiness: Zone 4
Variants: Several forms are grown, including 'Albert Burkwood' and the more upright 'Somerset'. Variegated forms include 'Carol Mackie', which has leaves edged with yellow that later turn creamy white.

Daphne caucasica

This is a rounded deciduous shrub with slender, pale green leaves. The fragrant white flowers open in dense clusters during late spring and early summer, and often there is a repeat flowering in the autumn.

Native range: Caucasus, W Asia
Height: 1.5 m (5 ft)
Spread: 1.5 m (5 ft)
Hardiness: Zone 5

Daphne cneorum

This dwarf evergreen shrub makes a low mound of spreading shoots with densely arranged, narrow, dark green leaves. Thick clusters of very fragrant pink flowers open at the ends of the shoots in spring, often flowering again in summer.

Common name: Garland flower
Native range: Europe
Height: 20 cm (8 in)

Daphne cneorum

Daphne laureola subsp. *philippi*

Spread: 1 m (3 ft)
Hardiness: Zone 4
Variants: 'Eximia' has deep pink flowers. 'Variegata' has leaves that are edged with cream.

Daphne laureola

An evergreen shrub with stout shoots and glossy, dark green, leathery leaves. Pale green slightly fragrant flowers open during late winter and early spring in dense clusters under the leaves, followed by glossy black fruits. Suitable for sun or shade.

Common name: Spurge laurel
Native range: S and W Europe, N Africa

Height: 1.2 m (4 ft)
Spread: 1.5 m (5 ft)
Hardiness: Zone 7
Variants: subsp. *philippi* from the Pyrenees region makes a compact mound, up to 60 cm (24 in) tall, with smaller leaves and flowers.

Daphne mezereum

This deciduous shrub has an open habit with upright shoots and slender, grey-green leaves. The fragrant deep pink flowers are borne profusely clustered on the bare shoots in the late winter and early spring, either before or as the leaves emerge. The flowers are followed by red fruits.

Common name: Mezereon
Native range: Europe, W Asia
Height: 1 m (3 ft)
Spread: 1 m (3 ft)
Hardiness: Zone 4

Daphne odora

A dense, rounded evergreen shrub with glossy dark green, leathery leaves. The large, dense heads of very fragrant purple-pink flowers open at the ends of the shoots in late winter and early spring, and these are sometimes followed by red fruits.

Native range: China, Japan
Height: 1.2 m (4 ft)
Spread: 1.2 m (4 ft)

Hardiness: Zone 7
Variants: f. *alba* produces white flowers, while 'Aureomarginata' has leaf margins that are edged with yellow.

Daphne pontica

An evergreen shrub that makes a wide, spreading mound with glossy dark green leaves. Its slightly fragrant pale yellow-green flowers open in clusters during the spring, and these are followed by glossy black fruits. This is a useful shrub for growing in a shady garden site.

Native range: SE Europe, Caucasus, N Turkey
Height: 1 m (3 ft)
Spread: 1.5 m (5 ft)
Hardiness: Zone 6

Daphne tangutica

This is a handsome and an adaptable species that is suitable for growing in a border or a rock garden. It has matt-green, leathery leaves and makes a rounded evergreen shrub. Clusters of fragrant pink flowers flushed with white open in the late spring and early summer, and these are followed by orange-red fruits.

Native range: China
Height: 1 m (3 ft)
Spread: 1 m (3 ft)
Hardiness: Zone 6

Davidia involucrata

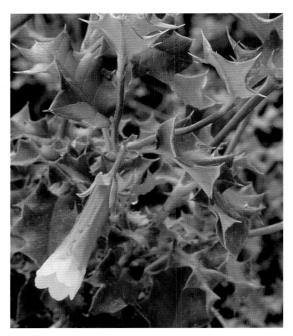

Desfontainia spinosa

green leaves. The leaves are coloured blue-green beneath and are divided up into as many as 25 individual leaflets. The drooping, pale green, bell-shaped flowers open in large, pendulous sprays in late spring to early summer, and these are followed by large blue fruits covered in a white bloom. These fruits are filled with a thick white pulp that contains the seeds.

Native range: W China
Height: 5 m (16 ft)
Spread: 5 m (16 ft)
Hardiness: Zone 5

Davidia
Cornaceae

The single species in this genus is a deciduous tree native to China. It has very distinctive large white bracts surrounding the flowerheads. It prefers a good, moist and well-drained soil and it is ideally suited to a position among other trees, where it can receive some protection from strong winds.

Davidia involucrata

A deciduous tree, conical when young but later spreading, with broadly heart-shaped leaves ending in a tapered point. Leaves are bright green above, densely covered in soft hairs beneath on mature trees. The rounded heads of small flowers in late spring have purple anthers and are surrounded by two large and conspicuous, unequal white bracts.

Common names: Dove tree, ghost tree, handkerchief tree
Native range: China

Height: 15 m (50 ft)
Spread: 12 m (40 ft)
Hardiness: Zone 6
Variants: var. *vilmoriniana* is the most commonly seen form, differing only in having leaves that have smooth undersurfaces.

Decaisnea
Lardizabalaceae

The two species in this genus are deciduous shrubs, natives of the Himalayas and China, with leaves divided into many leaflets and unusual flowers and fruits. The following species is the only example commonly found in cultivation and it does best in good, well-drained, not-too-dry soil in a position sheltered by trees or other large shrubs.

Decaisnea fargesii

This is a vigorous deciduous shrub that has stout, sparsely branched, upright shoots and bold, dark

Desfontainia
Loganiaceae

The single species that makes up this genus is a South American evergreen shrub with foliage very similar to that of a holly, except that the leaves are borne opposite on the shoots. It requires a moist, peaty, lime-free soil, and is suitable for a sunny position. In dry areas, however, it needs more shade. Pruning is rarely necessary.

Desfontainia spinosa

An evergreen shrub of a dense, upright habit with spiny toothed, glossy dark green, opposite-growing leaves. The showy tubular flowers are bright red and tipped with orange-yellow. The flowers open during summer and early autumn.

Native range: Andes of South America
Height: 2 m (6 ft)
Spread: 1.5 m (5 ft)
Hardiness: Zone 7

Deutzia
Hydrangeaceae

A genus of about 60 species of mainly deciduous shrubs with opposite leaves and white to pink, starry flowers, native from the Himalayas to East Asia. They are suitable for a shrub border, but old plants can become rather leggy and look best if they are regularly pruned. Either cut them back lightly after flowering or cut some of the older shoots right down to the base. Old plants can be rejuvenated by cutting them back to the base in early spring, before the new season's growth starts, but that year's flowers will then be lost.

Deutzia gracilis

A mound-forming deciduous shrub of spreading habit with slender shoots and bright green, toothed leaves. Small, slightly fragrant, white flowers open in clusters during late spring and early summer.

Native range: Japan
Height: 1.2 m (4 ft)
Spread: 1.2 m (4 ft)
Hardiness: Zone 4
Variants: 'Nikko' is a compact dwarf form that makes a low, dense mound only 60 cm (24 in) tall.

Deutzia x elegantissima

This group of garden-raised hybrids makes upright to rounded deciduous shrubs with matt-green, toothed leaves that are rough to the touch. The rounded heads of pink or white flowers open during the late spring and early summer.

Height: 1.5 m (5 ft)
Spread: 1.5 m (5 ft)
Hardiness: Zone 6
Variants: 'Fasciculata' has bright rose-pink flowers. 'Rosealind' has deep carmine-pink flowers.

Deutzia x hybrida

Garden-raised hybrids between D. *discolor* and D. *longifolia* making deciduous, upright shrubs with dark green, toothed leaves that are slightly rough to the touch. Large sprays of starry shaped flowers in various shades of pink are produced in early summer. Normally grown as selected forms.

Height: 1.5 m (5 ft)
Spread: 1.5 m (5 ft)
Hardiness: Zone 6
Variants: 'Mont Rose' has profuse, rose-pink flowers. 'Magicien' has large, pink flowers that are banded deep purple-pink on the outside.

Deutzia x *rosea* 'Carminea'

Deutzia x *rosea* 'Carminea'

Deutzia x rosea

Garden-raised deciduous hybrids between D. *gracilis* and D. *purpurascens* with a compact, rounded habit. They all have arching shoots and dark green leaves. The open, bell-shaped, white flowers, flushed pink outside, are borne in large clusters in the late spring and early summer.

Height: 1.2 m (4 ft)
Spread: 1.5 m (5 ft)
Hardiness: Zone 5
Variants: 'Carminea' produces attractive flowers that are carmine-pink on the outside.

Deutzia scabra

This is a vigorous deciduous shrub of a dense, upright habit, with pale brown, peeling bark and deep matt-green leaves rough to the touch on both sides. Large, conical clusters of white or pink-tinged flowers open in early summer.

Native range: Japan
Height: 3 m (10 ft)
Spread: 2.5 m (8 ft)
Hardiness: Zone 5
Variants: 'Candidissima' has double white flowers. 'Plena' has double white flowers that are flushed purple-pink outside. 'Pride of Rochester' has double white flowers that are pink outside.

Dipelta floribunda

taper-pointed leaves that are bronze when young, red-purple in autumn. Slender, tubular, pale yellow flowers open in small clusters during summer.

Height: 1.5 m (5 ft)
Spread: 1.5 m (5 ft)
Hardiness: Zone 4

Dipelta
Caprifoliaceae

Four species of deciduous shrubs, natives of China and all with opposite leaves, make up this genus. Species are grown for their large flowers.

The following is the most commonly grown species and is suitable for any well-drained soil. It can be planted either in a shrub border or as a specimen among trees and other large shrubs.

Dipelta floribunda

This is a large, vigorous deciduous shrub with stout, upright shoots and bold, taper-pointed leaves with, on mature plants, pale brown, peeling bark. The large, funnel-shaped, fragrant flowers are white flushed with pink and marked with yellow in the throat. Flowers open in clusters during the late spring and early summer. As the flowers fade, large, pale green, later brown, persistent bracts expand around them.

Native range: China
Height: 4 m (13 ft)
Spread: 3 m (10 ft)
Hardiness: Zone 6

Dicksonia
Dicksoniaceae

This is a genus consisting of some 25 species of widely distributed evergreen or semi-evergreen ferns that are native to Australasia, the Pacific islands, Southeast Asia and South America. These tree-like ferns have creeping or upright rhizomes and large fronds. They are often used to provide a variety of heights in a fern bed.

When grown outside, the following species needs a moist, humus-rich, acid soil in a shady or partially shaded position. These plants are at their best in areas that experience mild winters and cool, moist summers. Dead fronds need to be regularly removed.

Dicksonia antarctica

This impressively large, tree-like evergreen or semi-evergreen fern has a sturdy trunk-like, unbranched rhizome that is densely covered in fibrous roots. The large, arching, palm-like fronds are deeply divided and dark green in colour when mature. In areas that experience cold winters *D. antarctica* may lose its foliage.

Common name: Soft tree fern
Native range: E Australia, Tasmania
Height: 5 m (16 ft)
Spread: 4 m (13 ft)
Hardiness: Zone 9

Diervilla
Caprifoliaceae

The three species of deciduous shrubs that make up this genus are all natives of North America. They are related to *Weigela* and are grown for their dense habit and autumn colour, as well as for their attractive yellow flowers. They will grow in any good soil and are suitable for either a sunny or a shady shrub border.

These shrubs can be cut back hard in spring before the new season's growth starts in order to improve vigour and maintain a compact habit.

Diervilla x splendens

This garden-raised deciduous hybrid between *D. lonicera* and *D. sessilifolia* develops into a thicket-forming shrub. It has glossy dark green,

Drimys
Winteraceae

This genus, composed of about 30 species of evergreen trees and shrubs, is native to Central and South America, Australasia and Southeast Asia. The following species are grown for their foliage and flower interest and require a moist, well-drained soil. They are best if planted in woodland conditions, and they require more shade and shelter in cooler, drier areas.

Drimys lanceolata

A conical, evergreen, aromatic shrub, sometimes tree-like, of upright habit and with red-purple shoots and deep green, leathery leaves, bronze when young. Clusters of small, greenish-white flowers open during late spring and early summer.

Drimys winteri

Common name: Mountain pepper
Native range: SE Australia, Tasmania
Height: 3 m (10 ft)
Spread: 2 m (6 ft)
Hardiness: Zone 8

Drimys winteri

An evergreen tree of upright, conical habit, often with several stems, with smooth, aromatic bark and glossy dark green, aromatic leaves. Large clusters of white, many-petalled, fragrant flowers open in spring and early summer.

Common name: Winter's bark
Native range: Mexico, South America
Height: 15 m (50 ft)
Spread: 8 m (26 ft)
Hardiness: Zone 8

Dryas
Rosaceae

A genus of three species of sun-loving evergreen shrubs with attractive foliage and flowers, widely distributed in arctic and high mountain regions of the northern hemisphere.

Dryas octopetala

This is a prostrate evergreen shrub with creeping stems that are densely clothed with glossy dark

Drimys lanceolata

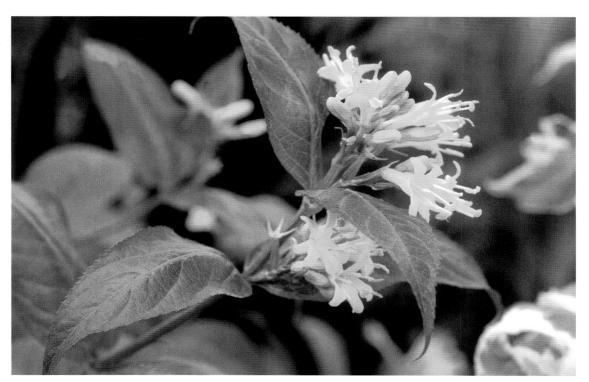

Diervilla x splendens

green leaves edged with rounded teeth. The creamy white flowers, each with a centre of yellow stamens, are borne on slender, upright stalks in spring and early summer, and these are followed by attractive silky seed heads.

Common name: Mountain avens
Native range: N Europe, N Asia, North America
Height: 10 cm (4 in)
Spread: 1.5 m (5 ft)
Hardiness: Zone 2

Elaeagnus pungens 'Maculata'

Elaeagnus x *ebbingei*

This garden-raised hybrid between *E. macrophylla* and *E. pungens* makes a vigorous and dense evergreen shrub with glossy dark green, leathery leaves, the undersides of which are covered in silvery scales. The small, creamy white and very fragrant flowers open during autumn.

Height: 3 m (10 ft)
Spread: 4 m (13 ft)
Hardiness: Zone 6
Variants: 'Gilt Edge' has leaves broadly margined with yellow. 'Limelight' has leaves blotched in the centre with deep yellow and pale green.

Elaeagnus pungens

This dense, evergreen shrub has spiny shoots and glossy dark green leaves, white beneath, with brownish scales. Clusters of white, fragrant flowers in autumn are followed by red, scaly fruits.

Native range: Japan
Height: 3 m (10 ft)
Spread: 4 m (13 ft)
Hardiness: Zone 6
Variants: 'Dicksonii' has leaves broadly margined with golden yellow. 'Frederici' is slow growing with creamy yellow leaves narrowly edged with green.

Elaeagnus
Elaeagnaceae

About 45 species of deciduous and evergreen shrubs, sometimes trees, natives of Asia, Europe and North America, make up this genus. Fast growing and tough, they are cultivated for their foliage and small but fragrant flowers. The variegated sorts sometimes produce reverting shoots, which should be promptly removed. They make excellent specimen shrubs or they can be used for hedging. *E. angustifolia* is best in full sun.

Elaeagnus angustifolia

A vigorous, deciduous, often spiny shrub or tree of conical-to-spreading habit, with slender, dark green leaves covered in silvery scales beneath. Small, pale yellow, fragrant flowers open in clusters in late spring to early summer, followed by edible yellow fruits covered in silvery scales.

Common names: Oleaster, Russian olive
Native range: W Asia
Height: 5 m (16 ft)
Spread: 5 m (16 ft)
Hardiness: Zone 2

Elaeagnus pungens 'Frederici'

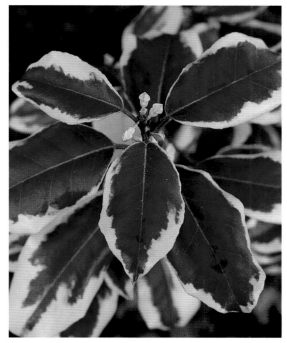

Elaeagnus x *ebbingei* 'Gilt Edge'

'Maculata' has leaves with a conspicuous deep yellow blotch in the centre.

Elaeagnus 'Quicksilver'

This garden-raised hybrid between *E. angustifolia* and *E. commutata* is a deciduous shrub with slender, very silvery leaves. Clusters of pale yellow, fragrant flowers open in late spring and early summer.

Height: 3 m (10 ft)
Spread: 5 m (16 ft)
Hardiness: Zone 2

Elaeagnus umbellata

This is a vigorous and large-growing deciduous shrub with a spreading habit. It has silvery, sometimes spiny shoots and often wavy edged, bright green leaves that are densely covered with silvery scales on their undersurfaces. The small, fragrant, white flowers open in late spring to early summer and these are followed by red, pea-sized fruits dotted with silvery scales.

Native range: China, Korea, Japan
Height: 5 m (16 ft)
Spread: 6 m (20 ft)
Hardiness: Zone 4

Elsholtzia
Labiatae

This genus contains about 35 species of annual and perennial herbs, shrubs and subshrubs, all of which are native to Asia. They have opposite, aromatic leaves and small, two-lipped flowers that are borne in dense spikes. They are suitable for growing in a border in any well-drained soil, but they do best if given a sunny position. They can be cut back hard to suitable buds just as the new growth starts in the spring.

Elsholtzia stauntonii

This deciduous subshrub, which spreads with age, has taper-pointed and sharply toothed, bright green, mint-scented leaves. The upright spikes of purple-pink flowers open during the late summer and autumn.

Native range: China
Height: 1.5 m (5 ft)
Spread: 1.5 m (5 ft)
Hardiness: Zone 5

Embothrium
Proteaceae

A genus of some eight species of evergreen or semi-evergreen trees and shrubs, natives mainly of the Andes of South America, reaching sea level in the south. Only the following species is in garden cultivation, primarily for its striking flowers. It requires a moist but well-drained, lime-free soil. It is suitable for a woodland setting, where surrounding trees can protect it from strong winds.

Elaeagnus umbellata

Embothrium coccineum

This is a vigorous evergreen or semi-evergreen tree with an upright habit and with narrow, glossy dark green to blue-green leaves. Dense clusters of striking, bright orange-red, tubular-shaped flowers open during late spring and early summer. The plant prefers a semi-shaded position.

Common name: Chilean fire bush
Native range: Chile, Argentina
Height: 9 m (30 ft)
Spread: 5 m (16 ft)
Hardiness: Zone 8

Enkianthus
Ericaceae

The ten species that make up this genus of deciduous and evergreen shrubs or small trees are all natives of the Himalayas and East Asia. The cultivated members are charming garden additions, grown both for their small drooping flowers, which vary in colour from white to red, as well as for their autumn colour, which can be a spectacular show of brilliant yellows and reds. They require a moist but well-drained, lime-free soil and do best in a bright but semi-shaded position. Pruning is not usually required, but dead, damaged or unwanted wood can be removed after flowering.

Enkianthus campanulatus

This is a deciduous shrub with a spreading habit that becomes more tree-like as it matures. Its dark green leaves, which are clustered at the ends of the shoots, turn orange, red and yellow in autumn. The small, pendulous, bell-shaped flowers are creamy yellow, veined variously with pink, and open in drooping clusters during the late spring to early summer.

Native range: Japan
Height: 5 m (16 ft)
Spread: 5 m (16 ft)
Hardiness: Zone 5
Variants: 'Albiflorus' has creamy.white flowers. 'Red Bells' is upright in habit and its flowers are conspicuously veined with deep pink.

Enkianthus cernuus f. rubens

This deciduous, bushy shrub has a rounded habit with bright green leaves that turn deep red-purple in autumn. Its slender, pendulous clusters of small, deep red flowers are fringed at the mouth, and open in the late spring and early summer.

Embothrium coccineum

Enkianthus campanulatus 'Albiflorus'

Native range: Japan
Height: 3 m (10 ft)
Spread: 3 m (10 ft)
Hardiness: Zone 5

Erica
Ericaceae

This is a large genus of more than 700 species of evergreen shrubs, sometimes small trees, that are natives mainly of South Africa, but are also found in Europe, North and East Africa and Turkey. They are invaluable in a heather garden, where they can be combined with forms of *Calluna vulgaris* and *Daboecia cantabrica* to create a patchwork of flower and foliage that is attractive throughout the year. *E. arborea* and *E. cinerea* require a lime-free soil, and all do best in full sun.

Erica arborea

A vigorous, upright shrub with short, slender, dark green leaves densely arranged on plume-like shoots. In early spring, clusters of small, white, fragrant flowers densely cover the shoots.

Common name: Tree heath
Native range: S Europe, N and E Africa, SW Asia
Height: 2.5 m (8 ft)
Spread: 3 m (10 ft)
Hardiness: Zone 7
Variants: 'Albert's Gold' has bright yellow young foliage; var. *alpina* is a particularly hardy form and flowers profusely.

Erica arborea

Erica carnea 'Ann Sparkes'

Erica carnea

This is a low, mound-forming evergreen shrub with a spreading habit and has slender, needle-like, bright green leaves. The upright spikes of tubular or bell-shaped flowers vary in colour from white to deep pink and they open during the winter and early spring.

Common name: Winter heath
Native range: Europe
Height: 25 cm (10 in)
Spread: 60 cm (24 in)
Hardiness: Zone 5
Variants: 'Ann Sparkes' has golden yellow foliage and purple-pink flowers. 'Foxhollow' has yellow foliage, tinged with red in winter, and pale pink flowers. 'Myretoun Ruby' has deep rose-pink flowers. 'Springwood White' bears a profusion of white flowers. 'Vivellii' has bronze-purple winter foliage and deep purple-pink flowers. 'Westwood Yellow' is compact with golden yellow foliage and deep pink flowers.

Erica cinerea

This is a mat-forming shrub that has slender, upright shoots densely clothed in narrow, dark green leaves. Urn-shaped flowers, varying in colour from white to pink or red-purple, open in clusters during summer and early autumn.

Common name: Bell heather
Native range: Europe
Height: 30 cm (12 in)
Spread: 75 cm (30 in)
Hardiness: Zone 6
Variants: 'C D Eason' has rich, deep pink flowers, while 'Pink Ice' is compact in form with bright green foliage and pale pink flowers.

Erica x darleyensis

This garden-raised hybrid between *E. carnea* and *E. erigena* makes a mound-forming shrub with a spreading habit and narrow, dark green leaves. The upright spikes of flowers, varying from white to deep pink, open in late winter and early spring.

Height: 60 cm (24 in)
Spread: 90 cm (35 in)
Hardiness: Zone 6
Variants: 'Arthur Johnson' has long sprays of magenta flowers. 'Darley Dale' bears a profusion of pale pink flowers over a long period. 'Ghost Hills' has bright green foliage tipped with cream in spring and pink flowers, deeper at the tips. 'Jack H

Erica tetralix 'Alba Mollis'

Brummage' has yellow foliage, red-tinged in winter, and deep pink flowers. 'Kramer's Rote' has bronze-green foliage and magenta-pink flowers. 'Silberschmelze' has profuse white flowers.

Erica erigena

This is a compact shrub with an essentially upright habit and with dark green, needle-like foliage.

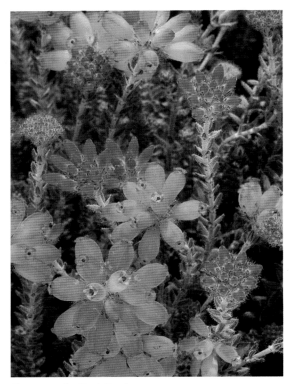

Erica tetralix 'Pink Star'

Fragrant deep pink flowers open over a long period during the spring months.

Synonym: *Erica mediterranea*
Common name: Irish heath
Native range: W Ireland, SW Europe, N Africa
Height: 60 cm (24 in)
Spread: 45 cm (18 in)
Hardiness: Zone 8
Variants: 'Brightness' has blue-green foliage that

Erica x darleyensis 'Silberschmelze'

turns bronze-green in winter and rose-pink flowers. 'Irish Dusk' is compact in habit with deep green foliage and rose-pink flowers. 'WT Rackliff' produces pure white flowers.

Erica tetralix

This dwarf shrub has a spreading habit with softly hairy, grey-green foliage. Nodding, urn-shaped flowers, varying in colour from white to pink, open in dense clusters at the ends of the shoots in the summer and autumn.

Common name: Cross-leaved heath
Native range: N and W Europe
Height: 25 cm (10 in)
Spread: 60 cm (24 in)
Hardiness: Zone 3
Variants: 'Alba Mollis' has grey foliage and white flowers. 'Con Underwood' has crimson flowers. 'Pink Star' has upright, lilac-pink flowers.

Erica vagans

This is a mound-forming shrub of dense habit and dark green foliage. White to pink or red flowers open in long, conical clusters from mid-summer to mid-autumn.

Common name: Cornish heath
Native range: W Europe
Height: 50 cm (20 in) or more
Spread: 90 cm (35 in)
Hardiness: Zone 5
Variants: 'Lyonesse' has white flowers. 'Mrs D F Maxwell' has deep cerise-pink flowers. 'Valerie Proudley' is low and compact, up to 15 cm (6in) high, with bright yellow foliage and white flowers.

Eriobotrya
Rosaceae

The 30 species or so of this genus of evergreen trees and shrubs are natives of the Himalayas and East Asia. The following is the most commonly grown species, due to its bold foliage and attractive flowers. It also produces edible fruits, but only in warm climates. It is suitable for any well-drained soil and prefers a sunny position sheltered from strong winds. It is at its best in warm climates; in cooler areas it can be grown against a sunny wall.

Eriobotrya japonica

This is a vigorous, stoutly branched, often multi-stemmed tree or large shrub of spreading habit

Erica x *darleyensis* 'Arthur Johnson'

Eriobotrya japonica

with large, leathery and prominently veined, glossy dark green leaves. Clusters of fragrant, white, five-petalled flowers open in late autumn or winter and these are followed by edible pear-shaped, yellow-coloured fruits. It is frost hardy but appreciates the protection of a sun-facing wall.

Common name: Loquat
Native range: China, Japan
Height: 6 m (20 ft)
Spread: 6 m (20 ft)
Hardiness: Zone 8

Escallonia rubra

Escallonia
Escalloniaceae

This genus is made up of some 40 species of evergreen shrubs and trees native to South America and popular for their bushy habit, foliage and flowers. They are easy to cultivate in any well-drained soil and are excellent for shelter and hedging in mild localities. They are also popular for coastal gardens. Prune lightly after flowering if necessary to retain a compact habit or to restrict growth; cut back hard to rejuvenate old plants.

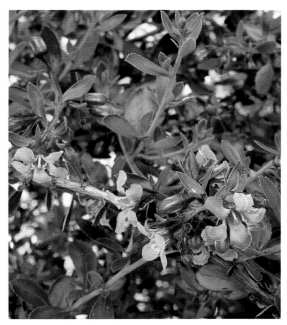

Escallonia 'Edinensis'

Escallonia 'C F Ball'

This is a vigorous, large evergreen shrub of dense habit with bold, aromatic, glossy dark green leaves. Clusters of showy, rich red flowers open over a long period during the summer months.

Height: 3 m (10 ft)
Spread: 4 m (13 ft)
Hardiness: Zone 8

Escallonia 'Edinensis'

A garden-raised hybrid making a compact evergreen shrub of bushy, spreading habit, with small, glossy dark green leaves. Pink flowers open from carmine-coloured buds during summer.

Height: 2.5 m (8 ft)
Spread: 3 m (10 ft)
Hardiness: Zone 8

Escallonia laevis

This vigorous and stoutly branched evergreen shrub has slightly sticky shoots and glossy dark green, aromatic leaves. Tubular, deep pink flowers open in the late summer and early autumn. It is mainly seen as the forms listed below.

Native range: Brazil
Height: 1.5 m (5 ft)

Spread: 1.5 m (5 ft)
Hardiness: Zone 8
Variants: 'Gold Brian' has golden-coloured young foliage that turns dark green as the seasons progress. 'Gold Ellen' has dark green leaves that are margined with yellow.

Escallonia 'Peach Blossom'

This garden-raised hybrid makes a bushy evergreen shrub with arching shoots and glossy dark green leaves. It bears clear peach-pink and white flowers that open in clusters during summer.

Height: 1.5 m (5 ft)
Spread: 1.5 m (5 ft)
Hardiness: Zone 8

Escallonia rubra

This is an evergreen shrub with a compact and vigorous habit and with aromatic, glossy dark green leaves. Clusters of tubular, deep pink to red flowers open during summer.

Native range: Chile, Argentina
Height: 4 m (13 ft)
Spread: 5 m (16 ft)
Hardiness: Zone 8
Variants: var. *macrantha* has larger leaves and larger, bright red flowers. 'Crimson Spire' is a very vigorous form of this, with deep red flowers, and is recommended for hedging.

Eucalyptus
Myrtaceae

This is a large genus with some 700 species of evergreen trees, sometimes shrubs, that are mainly natives of Australia. Young plants have opposite, usually rounded leaves, while on mature trees they are alternate, narrow and drooping. The following sorts have white flowers without petals but with numerous stamens.

Valued in gardens for their very rapid growth, their ornamental bark and their foliage, they are suitable for any well-drained, lime-free soil in a sunny position. Cut back hard to the base in spring if juvenile foliage is to be retained.

Eucalyptus coccifera

This is a vigorous, spreading tree that has smooth, grey and white peeling bark and aromatic foliage. Juvenile leaves are blue-grey and rounded, while adult leaves are blue-green with a hooked tip. The white flowers open in clusters of three to seven in the early summer.

Common name: Mount Wellington peppermint
Native range: Tasmania
Height: 15 m (50 ft)
Spread: 10 m (33 ft)
Hardiness: Zone 7

Eucalyptus dalrympleana

A large evergreen tree of vigorous, upright growth with grey-brown and cream peeling bark. Leaves are blue-green – juveniles rounded, adult leaves slender and pointed. White flowers are borne in clusters of three in late spring and summer.

Eucalyptus pauciflora subsp. *niphophila*

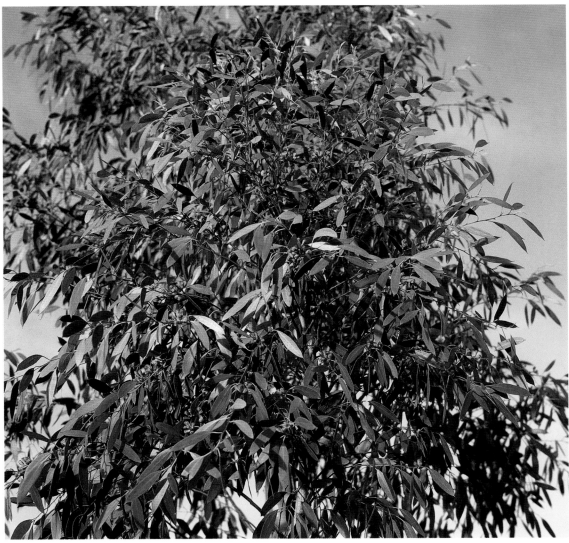

Eucalyptus coccifera

Common name: Mountain gum
Native range: SE Australia, Tasmania
Height: 25 m (80 ft)
Spread: 10 m (33 ft)
Hardiness: Zone 7

Eucalyptus gunnii

This is a fast-growing evergreen tree that has grey and green flaking bark and striking, silvery blue, rounded juvenile leaves. The adult leaves are narrow and pointed and grey-green in colour. White flowers open in clusters of three during the summer months.

Common name: Cider gum
Native range: Tasmania
Height: 20 m (65 ft)
Spread: 10 m (33 ft)
Hardiness: Zone 7

Eucalyptus pauciflora

This spreading evergreen tree, often with several stems, has grey and white peeling bark. Its juvenile leaves are leathery and oval to rounded, while on adult plants the leaves are glossy green, narrow and curved, opening from red shoots. Flowers are white and open in clusters of up to 12 blooms in summer.

Common name: Snow gum
Native range: SE Australia, Tasmania
Height: 15 m (50 ft)
Spread: 15 m (50 ft)
Hardiness: Zone 7
Variants: The subsp. *niphophila* (*E. niphophila*) is a particularly hardy form with bloomy shoots and fewer flowers in each cluster.

Eucalyptus perriniana

A fast-growing evergreen tree with grey and brown peeling bark. Juvenile leaves are joined around the stem, remaining attached and spinning around the stem with age. Adult leaves are deep blue-green, taper-pointed and drooping. White flowers are borne in small clusters during summer.

Common name: Spinning gum
Native range: SE Australia, Tasmania
Height: 8 m (26 ft)
Spread: 7 m (23 ft)
Hardiness: Zone 7

Eucryphia
Eucryphiaceae

This is a small genus of seven species of evergreen and deciduous trees, all with opposite leaves and showy white flowers. Natives of Australia and South America, they require a moist but well-drained, lime-free soil and should be planted where the base of the tree remains in cool shade.

Eucryphia glutinosa

This is a deciduous or semi-evergreen tree of upright habit. Its glossy dark green leaves, which turn orange-red in autumn, are divided into three to five leaflets. Large, white, four-petalled, fragrant flowers, with centres of numerous pink-tipped stamens, open in late summer.

Native range: Chile
Height: 10 m (33 ft)
Spread: 5 m (16 ft)
Hardiness: Zone 8

Eucryphia x intermedia 'Rostrevor'

A garden-raised hybrid between *E. glutinosa* and *E. lucida* making a bushy headed evergreen tree with undivided and divided leaves on the same tree. Leaves are glossy dark green above, grey-green beneath. Large, white flowers with pink-tipped stamens open in late summer and autumn.

Height: 10 m (33 ft)
Spread: 6 m (20 ft)
Hardiness: Zone 8

Eucryphia lucida

This is an evergreen tree of narrow, upright growth, with slender, glossy dark green leaves, blue-white beneath. Fragrant four-petalled flowers with pink-tipped stamens open during late summer.

Native range: Tasmania
Height: 7 m (23 ft)
Spread: 3 m (10 ft)
Hardiness: Zone 8

Eucryphia milliganii

A narrowly upright evergreen tree, sometimes shrubby with several branches from the base, and tiny, glossy dark green leaves, blue-white beneath. Small, white, cupped flowers with pink-tipped stamens open during late summer and autumn.

Eucryphia x *nymansensis* 'Nymansay'

Native range: Tasmania
Height: 6 m (20 ft)
Spread: 1.5 m (5 ft)
Hardiness: Zone 8

Eucryphia x nymansensis 'Nymansay'

A vigorous garden-raised hybrid between *E. cordifolia* and *E. glutinosa* making a columnar evergreen tree. Leaves are glossy and dark green above, paler beneath, either undivided or with up to three leaflets. The large, white, fragrant flowers have centres of numerous pink-tipped stamens and open during the late summer and autumn.

Height: 15 m (50 ft)
Spread: 6 m (20 ft)
Hardiness: Zone 8

Eucryphia x *intermedia* 'Rostrevor'

Euonymus
Celastraceae

This is a large genus of about 175 species of deciduous and evergreen trees, shrubs and climbers widely distributed throughout the world, but mainly in Asia. They have opposite leaves and small, usually greenish flowers. The lobed fruits split to release the often attractively coloured seeds. This genus provides a wide range of popular ornamentals suitable for the shrub border, specimen planting, hedging or for ground cover. Species can be grown in any well-drained soil.

Euonymus alatus

The shoots of this vigorous and densely branched deciduous shrub are edged with broad, corky wings. Dark green leaves reliably turn bright red early in autumn. Tiny, green flowers in late spring to early summer are followed by small, red fruits, which open to reveal orange-coated seeds.

Native range: China, Japan
Height: 2.5 m (8 ft)
Spread: 3 m (10 ft)
Hardiness: Zone 4
Variants: 'Compactus' is a more compact form.

Euonymus alatus 'Compactus'

Euonymus europaeus

This large deciduous shrub or small tree has a spreading habit with dark green leaves turning red in autumn. Clusters of small, greenish flowers in late spring to early summer are followed by pink, four-lobed fruits, which split to reveal bright orange-coated seeds. Some plants may be mostly male or female.

Common name: Spindle tree
Native range: Europe, W Asia
Height: 6 m (20 ft)
Spread: 6 m (20 ft)
Hardiness: Zone 4
Variants: 'Red Cascade' has arching branches, leaves that turn deep red in autumn and profusely borne fruits.

Euonymus fortunei

This is a variable evergreen shrub – prostrate in the juvenile form and climbing by aerial roots if given suitable support, such as that provided by a wall or tree. Juvenile plants that are allowed to climb will eventually reach the bushy adult stage and will then produce small, green flowers in summer. The flowers are followed by white or pinkish fruits, which open to reveal orange-coated seeds. The juvenile forms of *E. fortunei* make excellent ground cover.

Native range: China
Height: 30 cm (12 in) and more, but can climb to 10 m (33 ft) or more
Spread: 3 m (10 ft) or more
Hardiness: Zone 5
Variants: 'Coloratus' is a juvenile form with leaves that turn deep red-purple in winter. 'Emerald Gaiety' is a bushy adult form with leaves that are broadly margined with white. 'Emerald 'n' Gold' is a juvenile form, and its leaves have golden yellow margins. 'Kewensis' is a creeping juvenile form with tiny leaves. 'Silver Queen' is a bushy adult form of upright growth and with white-edged leaves. 'Sunspot' is a juvenile form and its leaves are blotched in their centres with yellow and are borne on yellow shoots.

Euonymus europaeus

Euonymus japonicus

This is a bushy and evergreen shrub with a dense, upright habit that often makes it look tree-like in appearance. It has glossy dark green leaves and bears clusters of greenish flowers in summer. The flowers are followed by pinkish-white fruits, which split to reveal orange-coated seeds. *E. japonicus* responds well to pruning and so it is useful as a hedging plant, even in shady places, and it is also suitable for coastal sites. Cut it back in spring to encourage a compact habit. Variegated plants sometimes produce shoots with all green or all yellow leaves – these should be removed as soon as they appear.

Common name: Japanese spindle
Native range: China, Japan
Height: 4 m (13 ft)
Spread: 3 m (10 ft)
Hardiness: Zone 7
Variants: 'Aureus' has leaves that are blotched with golden yellow but it often reverts. 'Latifolius Albomarginatus' ('Macrophyllus Albus') has broad, grey-green leaves that are edged with creamy white. 'Microphyllus Albovariegatus' is a dwarf form and is upright in habit with small leaves edged with white. 'Ovatus Aureus' has leaves broadly edged with golden yellow.

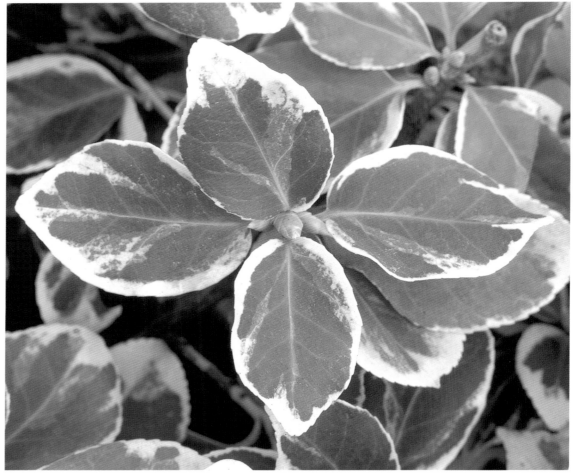

Euonymus fortunei 'Silver Queen'

Euonymus kiautschovicus

This semi-evergreen shrub grows vigorously and has a wide-spreading habit. Dark green leaves turn orange or red in the autumn and clusters of small, green flowers open in summer. The flowers are followed by pink fruits, which split to show orange-red seeds.

Native range: China
Height: 2.5 m (8 ft)
Spread: 4 m (13 ft)
Hardiness: Zone 5

Euonymus planipes

This vigorous deciduous shrub is among the most showy of the genus. *E. planipes* is particularly valued for its attractive fruit as well as for its dark green leaves, which turn a brilliant red colour in the autumn. Clusters of small, green flowers appear in summer and mature into large, slender-stalked, red fruits, which open to reveal bright orange-coated seeds. It has often been grown as *E. sachalinensis*.

Native range: China, Korea, Japan
Height: 3 m (10 ft)
Spread: 3 m (10 ft)
Hardiness: Zone 4

Euonymus planipes

Euryops
Compositae

This is a genus consisting of approximately 100 or so species of evergreen shrubs and perennial and annual herbs. They are popular for their attractive foliage and daisy-like flowers, and they are ideal for a border situation or a rock garden. These plants are natives mainly of South Africa, but their natural range also extends to northeast Africa and Arabia.

Species grow in any moist but well-drained soil, and they prefer a position in full sun. Once planted, however, they are best not moved, since they do not respond well to having their roots disturbed. Some species are fully hardy, but the following is frost-tender and so is suitable only for gardens in more mild locations.

Euryops pectinatus

This is a small evergreen shrub of upright growth with deeply cut, downy grey shoots and grey-green leaves. Large, rich yellow, daisy-like flowerheads are produced on long, slender stalks during late spring and early summer. Often there is a repeat flowering in winter.

Euryops pectinatus

Native range: South Africa
Height: 1 m (3 ft)
Spread: 1 m (3 ft)
Hardiness: Zone 8

Exochorda
Rosaceae

The four species in this small genus are all deciduous shrubs native to Central and East Asia. The following species is now the most commonly seen, and it is grown for its attractive habit and profuse flowers. Grow in any well-drained soil and in a sunny position for best flowering, but it may become chlorotic on shallow chalky soils.

Exochorda x macrantha 'The Bride'

A garden-raised hybrid between *E. korolkowii* and *E. racemosa* that makes a deciduous shrub of a dense, spreading habit. The clusters of large and showy white flowers densely wreathe the pendulous shoots in late spring and early summer.

Height: 2 m (6 ft)
Spread: 3 m (10 ft)
Hardiness: Zone 5

Exochorda x macrantha 'The Bride'

Fabiana
Solanaceae

This genus is made up of some 25 species of heath-like evergreen shrubs, natives mainly of the temperate regions of South America. Only the following is commonly grown, however. It requires a well-drained and not-too-rich soil in full sun and may become chlorotic if planted on very shallow, chalk soils. If necessary, it can be cut back lightly in spring before the new season's growth begins.

Fabiana imbricata

This loosely branched, upright evergreen shrub has plume-shoots that are densely covered in tiny, scale-like leaves. The branches are wreathed in white, tubular flowers during early summer.

Native range: Chile
Height: 2.5 m (8 ft)
Spread: 2 m (6 ft)
Hardiness: Zone 8
Variants: 'Prostrata' make a low, dense mound to 90 cm (35 in), while f. *violacea* has mauve flowers.

Fabiana imbricata f. *violacea*

Fagus sylvatica 'Pendula'

Fagus
Fagaceae

This is a genus of ten species of deciduous trees widely distributed in north temperate regions. The following is grown for its handsome stature and foliage as a specimen tree or for hedging. It is suitable for any well-drained soil.

Fagus sylvatica

A large, handsome tree with smooth grey bark and glossy dark green leaves that are pale and silkily hairy when young, turning yellow in autumn. Male and female flowers occur separately on the same tree – the male flowers in yellow-brown, tassel-like clusters in spring as the leaves emerge, and the females are followed by brown fruits covered in dense bristles.

Common name: Common beech
Native range: Europe
Height: 25 m (80 ft) or more
Spread: 20 m (65 ft)
Hardiness: Zone 4
Variants: 'Aspleniifolia' has narrow, slender-pointed and deeply lobed leaves. 'Atropurpurea' (purple beech) has bronze to purple leaves. 'Dawyck' is a conical form with upright branches, up to 8 m (26 ft)across. 'Dawyck Gold' is similar to 'Dawyck' except that it is columnar in habit with

Fagus sylvatica

Fagus sylvatica 'Dawyck Gold'

oliage that is yellow when young and later turns green. 'Dawyck Purple' is conical with deep red-purple foliage. 'Pendula' (weeping beech) has pendulous branches, often drooping to the ground. 'Purple Fountain' makes a slender tree with pendulous branches and deep red-purple foliage. 'Purpurea Pendula' is a weeping tree, to 4 m (13 ft) tall, with pendulous branches and red-purple foliage. 'Riversii' has deep red-purple foliage. 'Zlatia' has golden yellow young foliage later green.

Fargesia
Gramineae

This is a genus of four species of evergreen bamboos that are natives of the Himalayas and China. Grown for their elegant habit, they are suitable for any good, though not-too-dry, soil and ideally should be positioned away from strong winds. The following are not invasive and make excellent specimen plants.

Fargesia murieliae

This is a vigorous evergreen bamboo that forms dense clumps of arching, yellow-green culms, bloomy when young. It bears masses of slender,

Fagus sylvatica 'Dawyck Purple'

bright green, taper-pointed leaves. It has also been grown as *Thamnocalamus spathaceus*.

Synonym: *Arundinaria murieliae*
Native range: China
Height: 4 m (13 ft)
Spread: 5 m (16 ft)
Hardiness: Zone 7

Fargesia nitida

A dense, clump-forming evergreen bamboo of elegant habit with upright, later arching, purple-flushed culms. Very slender, deep green leaves tapering to a fine point weigh down the ends of the shoots. Excellent as a specimen or container plant.

Synonyms: *Arundinaria nitida, Sinarundinaria nitida*
Native range: China
Height: 4 m (13 ft)
Spread: 3 m (10 ft)
Hardiness: Zone 8

x Fatshedera lizei Araliaceae

An unusual garden-raised hybrid that makes a spreading evergreen shrub, somewhat scrambling if grown with support. The bold, glossy dark green

leaves are divided into five or seven lobes, and rounded heads of small white flowers open in large clusters during autumn. They make suitable plants for any good, well-drained soil.

Height: 2 m (6 ft)
Spread: 3 m (10 ft)
Hardiness: Zone 8
Variants: 'Annemieke' has leaves boldly blotched in the centre with bright yellow-green. 'Variegata' has the leaves edged with creamy white.

Fatsia
Araliaceae

A genus of three species of evergreen shrubs, natives of Japan and Taiwan. The following is grown for its bold leaves and white flowers. It is a shrub of architectural qualities and will grow in any good, not-too-dry soil. In cold areas it needs protection from strong winds. Flowering and fruiting is best if it is planted in full sun.

Fatsia japonica

This is a vigorous and stoutly branched evergreen shrub with large, deeply lobed, glossy dark green leaves. The long-stalked, rounded heads of small, white flowers open in large clusters in autumn, and these are followed by numerous green fruits, later turning black.

Common name: Japanese aralia
Native range: Japan
Height: 2.5 m (8 ft)
Spread: 3 m (10 ft)
Hardiness: Zone 8
Variants: 'Variegata' has leaf lobes that are prominently tipped with creamy white.

Fatsia japonica

Ficus
Moraceae

The figs make up a very large genus of more than 800 species of deciduous and evergreen trees, shrubs and climbers. They all bear inconspicuous flowers and the species are widely distributed – mainly in the tropical and subtropical regions of the world.

Ficus carica requires a warm and sunny position in the garden, and it grows well against a wall. *F. pumila* prefers a moist but well-drained soil and does best if grown in warm, humid areas. Given the appropriate conditions, it is an excellent plant for covering walls.

Ficus carica

This is a spreading deciduous tree that has stout branches and large, bold, glossy green leaves that turn yellow in autumn. The large, edible and fleshy green fruits, later turning brown or purple, ripen in the autumn.

Common name: Common fig
Native range: SW Asia
Height: 5 m (16 ft)
Spread: 5 m (16 ft)
Hardiness: Zone 7

Ficus pumila

This is a slender-stemmed, creeping evergreen shrub that produces small, dark green and rather puckered leaves. In warm climates it climbs vigorously, clinging firmly to it support by sending out aerial roots. Mature plants reach the adult stage, producing large leaves and, possibly, small, red fruits in autumn.

Common name: Creeping fig
Native range: E and SE Asia
Height: Prostrate to 10 m (33 ft) or more
Spread: 3 m (10 ft) or more
Hardiness: Zone 8

Fontanesia
Oleaceae

The single species in this genus is a deciduous shrub that is related to the privets (*Ligustrum*). Although it is little known in garden cultivation, the species is very hardy and can be used for screening as well as for hedges.

The shrub is suitable for any well-drained soil, and although it prefers a sunny position it will also

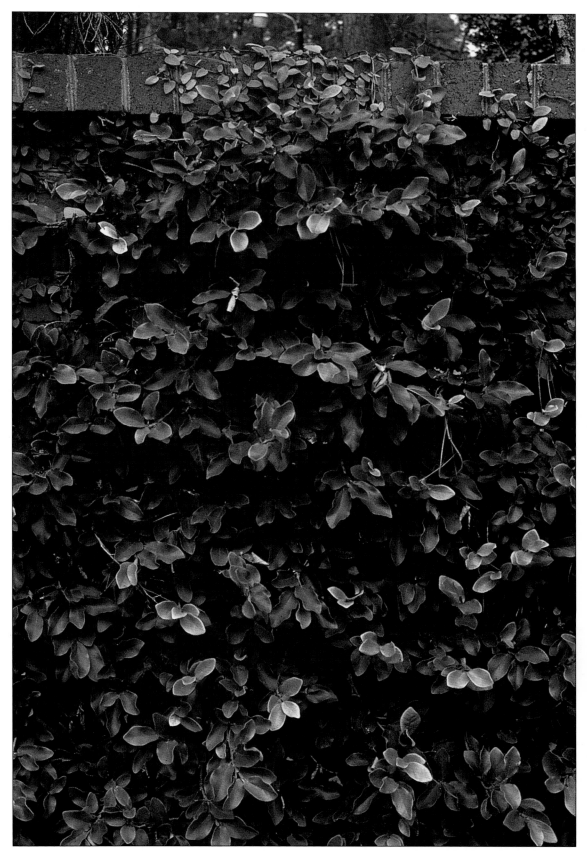

Ficus pumila

tolerate a position in light shade. A little light pruning in the spring will help to promote a good, compact habit.

Fontanesia phillyreoides

A vigorous deciduous or semi-evergreen shrub with upright branches and slender, drooping shoots bearing narrow, dark green, pointed leaves. Inconspicuous greenish-white flowers in early summer are followed by small, winged fruits.

Native range: SW Asia
Height: 5 m (16 ft)
Spread: 4 m (13 ft)
Hardiness: Zone 4
Variants: subsp. *fortunei* (*F. fortunei*) is also sometimes grown. It is similar in appearance and occurs in China.

Forsythia x *intermedia* 'Minigold'

toothed, dark green leaves are sometimes divided into three leaflets and can turn yellow, or occasionally purple, in autumn. Bright yellow flowers wreathe the shoots in early to mid-spring.

Height: 3 m (10 ft)
Spread: 3 m (10 ft)
Hardiness: Zone 6
Variants: 'Lynwood' has profuse, deep yellow flowers. 'Minigold' is compact and upright in habit with profuse, small, deep yellow flowers.

Forsythia ovata

This is a spreading, bushy deciduous shrub with a compact habit. It produces stiff shoots bearing dark green, sharply toothed leaves. The bright yellow, four-lobed flowers of *F. ovata* open very early in the spring, and it is among the earliest of all the forsythias.

Native range: Korea
Height: 1.5 m (5 ft)
Spread: 2.5 m (8 ft)
Hardiness: Zone 4

Forsythia
Oleaceae

This genus contains some seven species of deciduous shrubs, natives of southeast Europe and East Asia, with opposite leaves that are sometimes divided into three leaflets. These plants are popular for their four-lobed yellow flowers that open in early spring. They are suitable for any well-drained soil and flower best in a sunny position. To restrict growth or retain a compact habit they can be cut back – hard if necessary – after flowering.

Forsythia 'Arnold Dwarf'

A garden-raised hybrid making a low, wide-spreading deciduous shrub with bright green, sharply toothed leaves on creeping shoots. The yellow-green flowers in early spring are usually sparse, but the shrub makes good ground cover.

Height: 1 m (3 ft)
Spread: 2 m (6 ft)
Hardiness: Zone 5

Forsythia x *intermedia*

A group of garden-raised hybrids between *F. suspensa* and *F. viridissima* making vigorous, deciduous shrubs and containing some of the most popular plants in the entire genus. The sharply

Forsythia suspensa

Forsythia suspensa

A vigorous deciduous shrub that has slender, drooping shoots bearing dark green, sharply toothed leaves that are sometimes divided into three leaflets. Yellow, trumpet-shaped flowers open in clusters on the bare, arching shoots in early to mid-spring. This species can also be trained to grow against a wall.

Native range: China
Height: 3 m (10 ft)
Spread: 3 m (10 ft)
Hardiness: Zone 5

Forsythia viridissima

This is a deciduous or sometimes semi-evergreen shrub that has rigid, upright shoots bearing dark green, toothed or untoothed leaves growing from green shoots. Bright yellow flowers open singly or in small clusters on the shoots in early to mid-spring.

Native range: China
Height: 2.5 m (8 ft)
Spread: 2 m (6 ft)
Hardiness: Zone 5
Variants: 'Bronxensis' is a low, compact, densely growing form with a spreading habit and reaches a height of up to 30 cm (12 in) with a spread of about 75 cm (30 in). It has small, bright green leaves and primrose-yellow flowers.

Fothergilla
Hamamelidaceae

The witch alders make up a small genus of just two species of deciduous shrubs, both natives of the southeast of the United States of America. These plants are grown primarily for their autumn colour and their unusual, fragrant, spring flower clusters, the showy parts of which are the long stamens rather than the petals.

The witch alders require a good, lime-free soil rich in organic matter. The flowers are borne more profusely, and the autumn colour is more pronounced, if they are grown in a sunny position.

Fothergilla gardenii

This is a compact and densely growing deciduous shrub with a spreading, sometimes suckering, habit. The shrub produces dark green to blue-green leaves that turn colours of brilliant orange, yellow and red in autumn. The dense, cylindrical, bottlebrush-like spikes of fragrant,

Fothergilla gardenii

white flowers open in the late spring, before or as the young leaves begin to emerge.

Common name: Witch alder
Native range: SE United States of America
Height: 1 m (3 ft)
Spread: 1.5 m (5 ft)
Hardiness: Zone 5
Variants: 'Blue Mist' is a form that has attractive blue-green foliage but it produces less striking autumn colour.

Fothergilla major

This is a deciduous shrub of usually upright habit with dark green leaves, whitish beneath, turning yellow, orange and red in autumn. Its dense, bottlebrush-like spikes of fragrant, white flowers open in the late spring to early summer.

Common name: Witch alder
Native range: SE United States of America
Height: 2.5 m (8 ft)
Spread: 2 m (6 ft)
Hardiness: Zone 4

Fothergilla major

Fraxinus angustifolia 'Raywood'

Fraxinus
Oleaceae

This genus is made up of some 65 species of mainly deciduous trees and, sometimes, shrubs. Species of ash are usually fast growing and are widely distributed throughout the northern hemisphere. They have opposite leaves divided into several leaflets. The individual flowers are small and usually undistinguished and mostly without petals, although in some species white petals are present. They will grow on any well-drained soil, as long as it is not too dry, and they do particularly well on alkaline ones.

Ash will tolerate both wind and salt, making this genus suitable for coastal locations. Leaves do not change colour on all species before dropping in autumn, and the large root system associated with ash trees makes them difficult to accommodate in anything other than a very large area.

Fraxinus americana

A vigorous deciduous tree of broad, columnar habit, the leaves of which are composed of up to nine dark green leaflets, blue-green beneath and

Fraxinus pennsylvanica 'Summit'

turning yellow to red-purple in autumn. The tiny flowers lack petals and open in spring, males and females on separate plants. Female trees bear drooping clusters of small, slender, winged fruits, known as keys. Pruning is not usually necessary, though dead, damaged or crossing wood can be removed as necessary.

Common name: White ash
Native range: E North America
Height: 25 m (80 ft)
Spread: 15 m (50 ft)
Hardiness: Zone 4
Variants: 'Autumn Purple' is a selection with good red-purple autumn colour.

Fraxinus angustifolia

This elegant deciduous tree has a rounded to spreading habit, and its leaves are borne in whorls of three, with up to 13 narrow, slender-pointed leaflets. Bright and glossy green in summer, leaves turn yellow in autumn. It bears tiny flowers in spring, followed by slender, winged fruits.

Synonym: *Fraxinus oxycarpa*
Common name: Narrow-leaved ash
Native range: S Europe, North Africa
Height: 25 m (80 ft)
Spread: 15 m (50 ft)
Hardiness: Zone 5
Variants: 'Raywood' is broadly upright in habit with red-purple autumn colour.

Fraxinus excelsior

A vigorous deciduous tree that has a domed to rounded head and dark green leaves with up to 13 sharply toothed leaflets turning yellow in autumn. Tiny flowers open from black buds in spring, and these are followed by dense clusters of slender, winged fruits.

Common name: Common ash
Native range: Europe
Height: 30 m (100 ft)
Spread: 25 m (80 ft)
Hardiness: Zone 5
Variants: 'Jaspidea' has yellow young leaves, turning bright yellow in autumn, and yellow winter shoots contrasting with black buds. 'Pendula' (weeping ash) is a weeping tree with pendulous branches.

Fraxinus ornus

This is a deciduous tree that has a dense, rounded head and dark matt-green leaves divided up into nine leaflets, turning red-purple in autumn.

Fraxinus ornus

Flowers with white petals, fragrantly scented, open in dense, fluffy heads in the late spring to early summer, and these are followed by clusters of slender, winged fruits.

Common name: Flowering ash, manna ash
Native range: S Europe, SW Asia
Height: 20 m (65 ft)
Spread: 15 m (50 ft)
Hardiness: Zone 6

Fraxinus pennsylvanica

This vigorous deciduous tree has a broadly oval to spreading head. It bears dark green leaves, often velvety on their undersurfaces, divided up into as many as nine taper-pointed leaflets. Leaves turn yellow in the autumn. The tiny, insignificant flowers open in clusters during spring, male and female flowers on separate plants. Female trees bear clusters of slender, winged fruits in autumn.

Common name: Green ash, red ash
Native range: North America
Height: 20 m (65 ft)
Spread: 15 m (50 ft)
Hardiness: Zone 3
Variants: 'Summit' is conical with glossy foliage.

Fremontodendron
Sterculiaceae

The flannel bushes make up a genus of just two species of evergreen shrub, natives of California and northern Mexico, grown for their displays of showy flowers. Although in warm climates they will grow as free-standing plants, in cooler areas they are normally grown against a sunny wall. They need well-drained soil and a sunny position in order to thrive.

The hairs that cover these plants can be an irritant so care should be taken, especially when pruning. They can be cut back lightly after flowering if necessary. However, once planted they should not be moved, since they do not tolerate any disturbance to their roots.

Fremontodendron 'California Glory'

A garden-raised hybrid between *F. californicum* and *F. mexicanum* making a vigorous evergreen shrub with bold, glossy dark green, five-lobed leaves. The large, deep yellow flowers open over a long period during summer and autumn.

Height: 8 m (26 ft)
Spread: 6 m (20 ft)
Hardiness: Zone 8

Fremontodendron 'California Glory'

Fuchsia
Onagraceae

This genus is made up of some 100 species of deciduous and evergreen shrubs with opposite leaves, sometimes in whorls of three, native from Mexico to South America and New Zealand.

The prominent, showy flowers, which are nearly always pendulous, are produced over a long period during summer and autumn. The flowers have coloured petals in the centre and coloured, sometimes contrasting, sepals joined into a slender, coloured tube at the base. Upright forms can make dense shrubs, while trailing forms are suitable for hanging baskets. They will grow in any good, well-drained soil, and they can be cut back to the base in spring.

Fuchsia x bacillaris

A vigorous, naturally occurring hybrid between *F. microphylla* and *F. thymifolia* of spreading habit, with small, dark green leaves. Flowers are small but numerous, with red sepals and petals.

Native range: Mexico
Height: 1 m (3 ft)
Spread: 1.2 m (4 ft)
Hardiness: Zone 9

Fuchsia excorticata

This is a large deciduous shrub, sometimes tree-like, with pale brown, peeling bark. It is unusual in the genus as its dark green leaves, which are silvery white beneath, are alternate. The drooping flowers have pale green sepals becoming flushed red-purple with age, and deep purple petals.

Common name: Tree fuchsia
Native range: New Zealand
Height: 3 m (10 ft) or more
Spread: 3 m (10 ft) or more
Hardiness: Zone 9

Fuchsia magellanica

This spreading deciduous shrub has bright green to dark green leaves, usually arranged in threes, and pale brown, peeling bark on older shoots. The pendulous flowers have red sepals and violet-purple petals. *F. magellanica* can make an effective hedge in mild areas.

Native range: Chile, Argentina
Height: 2 m (6 ft) or more
Spread: 3 m (10 ft)
Hardiness: Zone 6

Fuchsia 'Corallina'

Fuchsia magellanica 'Sharpitor'

Variants: 'Aurea' has bright yellow foliage; var. *gracilis* produces slender flowers and its leaves usually grow in pairs; var. *molinae* produces white flowers that are tinged pale mauve. 'Sharpitor' is similar to var. *molinae* except that it has grey-green leaves edged with white. 'Variegata' has leaves that are edged with cream and pink. 'Versicolor' produces grey-green leaves edged with white, but they are pink-flushed when young.

Fuchsia procumbens

This low-growing, creeping plant, sometimes scrambling into small shrubs, has very slender shoots and small, rounded, bright green leaves. The small flowers are densely borne upright on the shoots, and they have green, sharply reflexed sepals that are deep purple at the tip and no petals. Flowers are often followed by large, deep red fruits.

Native range: New Zealand
Height: 10 cm (4 in)
Spread: 1 m (3 ft)
Hardiness: Zone 8

Garden hybrids

There are thousands of *Fuchsia* garden hybrids, many suitable only for frost-free conditions. The following can be grown outside except in the coldest areas. They are normally evergreen until they are cut back by frost.

Fuchsia 'Alice Hoffman'

This attractive garden-raised hybrid makes a small shrub of compact, bushy habit with densely

Fuchsia magellanica var. gracilis

Fuchsia magellanica var. molinae

clustered leaves tinged bronze-purple. Flowers are small and semi-double, with deep pink sepals and white petals veined with pink.

Height: 60 cm (24 in)
Spread: 60 cm (24 in)
Hardiness: Zone 8

Fuchsia 'Brutus'

This is a free-flowering shrub of upright growth. Flowers are single with cerise sepals and purple petals, shading to carmine at the base.

Height: 75 cm (30 in)
Spread: 75 cm (30 in)
Hardiness: Zone 8

Fuchsia 'Chillerton Beauty'

This spreading shrub has thick, sea-green, purple-stalked leaves. Flowers are single but are profusely borne, and have pale rose-pink sepals and violet-purple petals.

Height: 1 m (3 ft)
Spread: 1.2 m (4 ft)
Hardiness: Zone 8

Fuchsia 'Corallina'

This distinct and vigorous, spreading shrub has graceful, arching shoots and dark green leaves, flushed purple beneath, that are sometimes borne in threes or fours on the shoots. The flowers are single with scarlet sepals and purple-red petals.

Height: 60 cm (24 in)
Spread: 1 m (3 ft)
Hardiness: Zone 8

Fuchsia 'Display'

This vigorous, garden-raised hybrid has an upright habit and bears dark green leaves. The large, single flowers have carmine-coloured sepals and deep rose-pink petals.

Height: 75 cm (30 in)
Spread: 75 cm (30 in)
Hardiness: Zone 8

Fuchsia 'Dollar Princess'

This plant makes a strongly growing shrub with a bushy habit. The double flowers have cerise-coloured sepals and deep purple petals.

Fuchsia 'Prosperity'

Height: 50 cm (20 in)
Spread: 50 cm (20 in)
Hardiness: Zone 8

Fuchsia 'Garden News'

This is a vigorously growing shrub with an upright habit. The flowers are double and compactly formed, with pale pink sepals and tube, and deep magenta-pink petals.

Height: 90 cm (35 in)
Spread: 1 m (3 ft)
Hardiness: Zone 8

Fuchsia 'Genii'

This bushy, upright shrub has young foliage that is pale yellow, becoming yellow-green. Shoots are red. Flowers are single with cerise tubes and sepals, and deep violet petals.

Height: 75 cm (30 in)
Spread: 75 cm (30 in)
Hardiness: Zone 8

Fuchsia 'Lady Thumb'

This is a compact, bushy shrub of upright habit. Flowers are small but profusely borne, semi-double, with light carmine tubes and sepals and white petals veined with carmine.

Height: 45 cm (18 in)
Spread: 45 cm (18 in)
Hardiness: Zone 8

Fuchsia 'Lena'

This vigorously growing shrub has a spreading habit. Its flowers are large and semi-double with very pale pink tubes and sepals, and deep rose-purple petals.

Height: 60 cm (24 in)
Spread: 75 cm (30 in)
Hardiness: Zone 8

Fuchsia 'Margaret'

This is a vigorous and bushy shrub with an upright habit. Its flowers are double and profusely borne, and they have deep rose-pink sepals and violet-purple petals.

Height: 1 m (3 ft)
Spread: 1 m (3 ft)
Hardiness: Zone 8

Fuchsia 'Margaret Brown'

This shrub grows vigorously and has profusely borne single flowers. The flower sepals and the slender tubes are coloured pink, and the petals are a deep rose-pink.

Fuchsia 'Genii'

Height: 1 m (3 ft)
Spread: 1 m (3 ft)
Hardiness: Zone 8

Fuchsia 'Mrs Popple'

This is a vigorous and spreading bushy shrub with dark green foliage. Its flowers are single and have scarlet-coloured tubes and sepals, and deep violet-purple petals.

Height: 1 m (3 ft)
Spread: 1.2 m (4 ft)
Hardiness: Zone 8

Fuchsia 'Phyllis'

This very strongly growing shrub has an upright habit. Its flowers are semi-double and small, but profusely borne, with rose-red sepals and tubes, and deep rose-coloured petals.

Height: 1.2 m (4 ft)
Spread: 1 m (3 ft)
Hardiness: Zone 8

Fuchsia 'Prosperity'

This is a vigorous shrub of strong, upright growth. Its flowers are very large and double, its sepals are deep rose-pink, and its petals white flushed with pink. An extremely attractive and hardy hybrid.

Height: 1.2 m (4 ft)
Spread: 90 cm (35 in)
Hardiness: Zone 8

Fuchsia 'Riccartonii'

This vigorous and upright shrub has arching branches and dark green, bronze-tinged leaves, sometimes borne in threes, on red shoots. Its flowers are small and single, with scarlet tubes and sepals, and broad, violet petals.

Height: 1.5 m (5 ft)
Spread: 1.5 m (5 ft)
Hardiness: Zone 6

Fuchsia 'Tom Thumb'

This is a compact, dwarf shrub of bushy, upright habit. The flowers are small but profusely borne, with carmine-pink tubes and sepals, and violet-purple petals.

Height: 60 cm (24 in)
Spread: 60 cm (24 in)
Hardiness: Zone 8

Garrya
Garryaceae

A genus of about 13 species of evergreen shrubs with opposite leaves, natives of the western United States of America, Mexico and the West Indies. The following is the most commonly grown, for its winter catkins. The individual flowers are small; males and females on separate plants.

It is suitable for any good, well-drained soil, and can be grown in the border or as a specimen shrub.

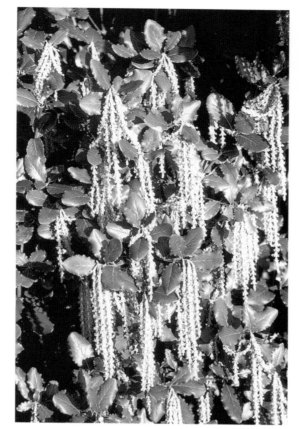
Garrya elliptica

In cold areas it should be given protection from strong winds, such as that provided by a sun-facing wall. It can be lightly pruned if necessary after flowering has finished.

Garrya elliptica

This vigorous evergreen shrub has glossy dark green, wavy edged, leathery leaves. The male is the most commonly grown form. It has long, slender, grey catkins from which yellow anthers protrude. Catkins open in winter and early spring.

Common name: Silk-tassel bush
Native range: W United States of America
Height: 4 m (13 ft)
Spread: 3 m (10 ft)
Hardiness: Zone 8
Variants: 'James Roof' is a male form with very long catkins.

Gaultheria
Ericaceae

This genus contains about 170 species of evergreen shrubs, often spreading by suckers, and is widely distributed in the New World, as well as from the Himalayas to East Asia and Australasia. Grown for their small, usually white flowers and often ornamental fruits, they require a moist, peaty, lime-free soil and do best in shade or semi-shade.

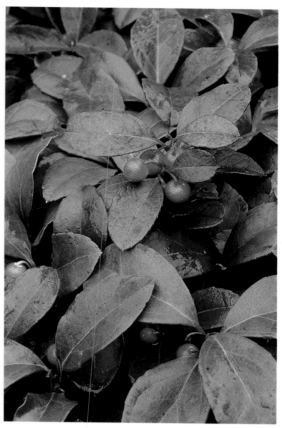
Gaultheria procumbens

Gaultheria cuneata

This low, spreading shrub has a compact habit and small, pointed, glossy leaves. Small clusters of nodding, urn-shaped, white flowers open in late spring to early summer, and these are followed by ivory-white fruits.

Native range: China
Height: 30 cm (12 in)
Spread: 90 cm (35 in)
Hardiness: Zone 6

Gaultheria mucronata

This is a vigorously growing, thicket-forming and stiffly branched shrub with glossy dark green, sharply pointed and leathery leaves. Small, nodding, white flowers open in the late spring to early summer, and these are followed by showy marble-like fruits. The fruits range in colour from white to pink and red.

Synonym: *Pernettya mucronata*
Native range: Chile, Argentina
Height: 1 m (3 ft)
Spread: 1.5 m (5 ft)
Hardiness: Zone 6
Variants: 'Bell's Seedling' has large, deep red fruits. 'Crimsonia' has very large, crimson fruits. 'Parelmoer' ('Mother of Pearl') has pale pink fruits. 'Signaal' has very large, persistent, cherry-red fruits. 'Sneeuwwitje' ('Snow White') produces white fruits spotted with pink.

Gaultheria shallon

Gaultheria procumbens

This low, creeping shrub, bearing glossy dark green, aromatic leaves, forms dense mats and is an excellent candidate for ground cover. Small, nodding, urn-shaped, white or pale pink flowers appear in summer, and these are followed by long-persistent, aromatic, red fruits.

Common names: Checkerberry, wintergreen
Native range: E North America
Height: 10 cm (4 in)
Spread: 1 m (3 ft) or more
Hardiness: Zone 4

Gaultheria shallon

This is an extremely vigorous and thicket-forming shrub. It spreads strongly by suckers and its leaves are leathery, appearing from red shoots. Slender, arching clusters of small, pink-tinged, white flowers open at the ends of the shoots in mid- to late spring, and the flowers are followed by deep purple-coloured fruits.

Common name: Salal
Native range: W North America
Height: 1.2 m (4 ft)
Spread: 3 m (10 ft) or more
Hardiness: Zone 5

Gaultheria x wisleyensis

This vigorous, garden-raised hybrid between *G. mucronata* and *G. shallon* develops into a

dense, thicket-like shrub. It spreads by sending out suckers and has dark green leaves. It produces clusters of small, white, urn-shaped flowers opening during the late spring and early summer. It is usually grown as named forms.

Synonym: x *Gaulnettya wisleyensis*
Height: 1.2 m (4 ft)
Spread: 2 m (6 ft) or more
Hardiness: Zone 5
Variants: 'Pink Pixie' has pink-tinged flowers and purple-red fruits. 'Wisley Pearl' has deep ox-blood red fruits.

Genista
Leguminosae

This widely distributed genus is made up of about 80 species of deciduous and evergreen, often sparsely leafy, shrubs and trees, natives of Europe, North Africa and West Asia. Grown for their yellow, pea-like flowers, several species are popular plants for the shrub border and rock garden, while *G. aetnensis* is probably best as a specimen tree.

These plants do best if they are grown in a not-too-rich, well-drained soil in full sun. If necessary, they can be pruned after flowering but take care not to cut into the old wood.

Genista aetnensis

This deciduous, rounded tree, sometimes shrubby on more than one trunk, has slender, bright green shoots and small, sparse leaves, which fall early. The fragrant, golden yellow, pea-like flowers are profusely borne in mid- to late summer.

Genista lydia

Common name: Mount Etna broom
Native range: Sardinia, Sicily
Height: 10 m (33 ft)
Spread: 8 m (26 ft)
Hardiness: Zone 8

Genista hispanica

This is a deciduous shrub that makes a dense mound with deep green, very spiny shoots. The small, slender leaves are borne only on the flowering shoots, each of which ends in a dense

Genista pilosa

Spread: 1.5 m (5 ft)
Hardiness: Zone 5
Variants: Several good selections include 'Goldilocks', which grows to 60 cm (24 in) tall, and 'Vancouver Gold,' which has very profuse, golden yellow flowers and reaches up to 30 cm (12 in).

Genista tinctoria

A deciduous shrub that varies from low and spreading to upright, with green shoots and small, slender, dark green leaves. Upright clusters of bright yellow flowers open during summer.

Common name: Dyer's greenweed
Native range: Europe, Turkey
Height: 60 cm (24 in)
Spread: 90 cm (35 in)
Hardiness: Zone 4
Variants: 'Flore Pleno' is dwarf and spreading, up to 30 cm (12 in) tall, with double flowers, and does best in a rock garden. 'Royal Gold' is vigorous and upright, up to 1 m (3 ft), with large flower clusters.

cluster of bright golden yellow, pea-like flowers. *G. hispanica* makes an excellent shrub for a large rock garden.

Common name: Spanish gorse
Native range: SW Europe
Height: 60 cm (24 in)
Spread: 1 m (3 ft)
Hardiness: Zone 7

Genista lydia

A deciduous shrub of compact habit with slender, green, arching shoots and sparsely borne, small, blue-green leaves. Small clusters of bright yellow, pea-like flowers open during late spring and early summer. Good in a dry border or rock garden.

Native range: SE Europe, SW Asia
Height: 60 cm (24 in)
Spread: 1 m (3 ft)
Hardiness: Zone 6

Genista pilosa

This is a dwarf, deciduous shrub of dense, spreading habit that forms a low mat. It has slender shoots and small, narrow leaves. The small, bright yellow, pea-like flowers are densely borne along the shoots during late spring and early summer. It makes excellent ground cover for a dry, sunny site and in a large rock garden.

Native range: Europe
Height: 45 cm (18 in)

Genista aetnensis

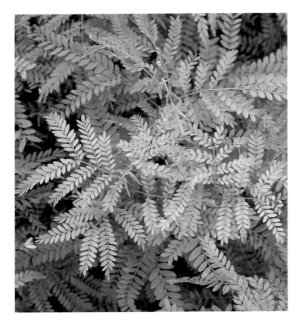

Gleditsia triacanthos

Gleditsia
Leguminosae

This is a small genus made up of only about 12 species of deciduous, often very spiny, graceful trees. The leaves, which appear late in the season, are distinct in that they are divided up into numerous leaflets.

The species in this genus are grown principally for their habit and foliage – the flowers are inconspicuous but they are followed by often large, striking pods. They are suitable for any good, fertile, well-drained soil and they do best if they are provided with a sunny position. When mature, trees are fully hardy, but young specimens may succumb to frost damage in cold areas.

Pruning is not usually required, but dead, damaged or crossing wood can be removed in spring. Wind damage is not unusual as branches tend to be brittle.

Gleditsia triacanthos

This is a large-growing deciduous tree of columnar to spreading habit, with a trunk and shoots that are often very spiny. Its glossy bright green, fern-like leaves are divided into numerous leaflets, turning yellow in autumn. Spikes of small, yellow-green flowers open in early summer, and these are followed by long, often twisted pods.

Common name: Honey locust
Native range: North America
Height: 30 m (100 ft)
Spread: 15 m (50 ft)
Hardiness: Zone 4
Variants: 'Rubylace' has deep red-purple young leaves that turn dark green as it matures, but it is viciously spiny. 'Sunburst' is a smaller, spineless

Gleditsia triacanthos 'Sunburst'

Grevillea rosmarinifolia

ree, growing up to 12 m (40 ft) tall, its bright yellow young foliage contrasting attractively with the dark green of its older leaves.

Grevillea
Proteaceae

This is a large genus made up of approximately 250 species of evergreen shrubs and trees, natives mainly of Australia. They are grown for their striking and unusual flowers, which have long, projecting styles, and they need a well-drained, lime-free soil in a sunny position. Suitable for the shrub border or dry garden, theses trees and shrubs should be provided with a sheltered position or be planted against a wall in cool areas.

Grevillea juniperina f. sulphurea

A stoutly branched evergreen shrub of spreading habit with arching shoots and slender, pointed, bright green leaves. The dense clusters of pale yellow flowers open at the ends of the shoots in late spring and early summer.

Native range: New South Wales (Australia)
Height: 2 m (6 ft)
Spread: 2 m (6 ft)
Hardiness: Zone 8

Grevillea rosmarinifolia

This is a spreading evergreen shrub of vigorous growth with rosemary-like foliage. Its shoots are covered with slender, grey-green leaves that are silvery beneath. Clusters of deep red flowers open over a long period from winter to summer.

Native range: Australia (New South Wales)
Height: 1.5 m (5 ft)
Spread: 2.5 m (8 ft)
Hardiness: Zone 8

Griselinia
Griseliniaceae

The six species of evergreen shrubs and trees that make up this small genus are natives of New Zealand and South America. A handsome foliage plant, the following will grow in any well-drained soil, in sun or shade. In mild areas it is suitable for shelter and hedging and does particularly well in coastal areas. To restrict growth, cut back in spring.

Gymnocladus dioica 'Variegata'

Griselinia littoralis

This vigorous, dense evergreen shrub has bright apple-green, leathery foliage. Small clusters of pale green flowers open in late spring, males and females on separate plants. In very mild areas it can reach a height of 10 m (33 ft) or more.

Native range: New Zealand
Height: 5 m (16 ft) or more
Spread: 3 m (10 ft) or more
Hardiness: Zone 8
Variants: 'Variegata' is slower growing and smaller in size, with leaves edged with creamy white.

Gymnocladus
Leguminosae

This is a small genus consisting of about five species of deciduous tree that are natives of East Asia and North America. Only the following is commonly seen in gardens, however, where it is grown for its bold foliage.

In order to do well, it requires a good, moist but well-drained soil. It is fully hardy, but is at its best if planted in a sunny position. The flowers and fruits will probably be produced only in areas that have reliably hot summers.

Gymnocladus dioica

This is a slow-growing deciduous tree with stout shoots and very large leaves divided into four to seven pairs of dark green leaflets. Leaves are bronze when they are young, often turning yellow in autumn. Conical clusters of fragrant, greenish-white, star-shaped flowers open in late spring to early summer, the males and females usually on separate plants, and these are followed by leathery, persistent, red-brown pods.

Common name: Kentucky coffee tree
Native range: C and E United States of America
Height: 20 m (65 ft)
Spread: 15 m (50 ft)
Hardiness: Zone 4
Variants: 'Variegata' has leaves that are blotched with creamy white.

Halesia monticola

Halesia monticola var. vestita

Halesia
Styracaceae

This is a small genus of plants that encompasses some five species of attractive, spring-flowering deciduous trees or shrubs that are natives of the southeast region of the United States of America and of East China.

They are grown for their beautiful white or pinkish, snowdrop-like flowers, which are followed by winged fruits. They need a good, moist but well-drained, lime-free soil that is rich in organic matter, and they are ideal for planting among other trees or in woodland situations.

Halesia carolina

This is a broadly conical to spreading deciduous tree with bright green, taper-pointed leaves that turn yellow in the autumn. Prolific clusters of white or pink-flushed, bell-shaped flowers open in mid- to late spring on bare branches before the young leaves emerge, and these are followed by four-winged, green-coloured fruits that turn pale brown in autumn.

Synonym: *Halesia tetraptera*
Common name: Snowdrop tree
Native range: SE United States of America
Height: 10 m (33 ft)
Spread: 8 m (26 ft)
Hardiness: Zone 4

Halesia monticola

This is a fast-growing, deciduous tree that is very similar to *H. carolina*, except that it produces larger and showier flowers and reaches a greater height and spread.

Common name: Mountain snowdrop tree
Native range: SE United States of America
Height: 15 m (50 ft)
Spread: 10 m (33 ft)
Hardiness: Zone 5
Variants: var. *vestita* produces large, white flowers that are flushed with pink.

x Halimiocistus
Cistaceae

These garden-raised hybrids between *Cistus* and *Halimium* are evergreen shrubs with opposite leaves grown for their showy flowers. They require essentially similar treatment to *Cistus*, and so are best in a well-drained soil, not too rich, in a warm, sunny position and with shelter from cold winds.

x Halimiocistus wintonensis

A low-growing evergreen shrub of spreading habit with grey-green leaves that are covered in white hairs when young. The white flowers in late spring and early summer are heavily marked with a ring of deep red blotches. They also have a contrasting yellow centre and yellow marks at the base.

Height: 45 cm (18 in)
Spread: 75 cm (30 in)
Hardiness: Zone 8
Variants: 'Merristwood Cream' has creamy yellow flowers with red blotches.

Hamamelis x intermedia 'Diane'

Halimium
Cistaceae

This is a small genus made up of about ten species of evergreen shrubs with opposite leaves. They are natives of the Mediterranean region as well as Southwest Asia, and are grown for their attractive, conspicuous flowers.

Related to *Cistus* and *Helianthemum*, these species are suitable for coastal gardens and require well-drained soil that is not too rich. They do best in a sunny position, while in cold regions they need protection from winds.

Halimium lasianthum

This is a low evergreen shrub of spreading habit and with arching shoots covered in grey-hairy leaves. The bright yellow, saucer-shaped flowers, each marked with red blotches near the bases of the petals, open during the late spring and early summer.

Native range: S Spain, S Portugal
Height: 60 cm (24 in)
Spread: 1 m (3 ft)
Hardiness: Zone 8

Halimium 'Susan'

A garden-raised hybrid that makes an evergreen shrub of upright growth, later spreading, with small, grey-green leaves. Profusely borne, deep yellow flowers, blotched with maroon in the centre, open in early summer.

Height: 45 cm (18 in)
Spread: 60 cm (24 in)
Hardiness: Zone 8

Hamamelis
Hamamelidaceae

The witch hazels are a small genus of five species, providing gardens with some of the best known winter-flowering deciduous shrubs. In addition, they give good autumn colour.

Natives of China, Japan and North America, they require a good, deep, lime-free soil. No pruning is usually needed but it may be necessary to remove suckers from the base as plants are sometimes produced on grafted root stock.

Hamamelis x intermedia

This group of garden-raised hybrids between *H. japonica* and *H. mollis* make deciduous shrubs of usually vase-shaped habit with bold, dark green, hazel-like leaves turning from yellow to orange, red and purple in autumn. The four-petalled, spidery, fragrant flowers open on the bare shoots during mid- and late winter. It is normally grown only as selected forms. Autumn colour is yellow unless otherwise stated.

Height: 5 m (16 ft)
Spread: 5 m (16 ft)
Hardiness: Zone 5
Variants: There are now numerous named forms, including 'Arnold Promise', which has large, yellow flowers in late winter and early spring. 'Diane' has

deep red flowers and purple-red autumn colour. 'Jelena' is upright in habit, with deep orange flowers opening early, and orange-red autumn colour. 'Pallida' (*H. mollis* 'Pallida') has very profuse, large yellow flowers.

Hamamelis mollis

A large deciduous shrub of upright to spreading habit with bold, hazel-like leaves, felted beneath, and turning yellow in autumn. The four-petalled, deep yellow, spidery flowers, each petal stained with red at the base, are very fragrant and open on the bare shoots in mid- to late winter.

Common name: Chinese witch hazel
Native range: China
Height: 5 m (16 ft)
Spread: 4 m (13 ft)
Hardiness: Zone 5

Hamamelis vernalis

This is a deciduous shrub of upright habit that becomes rounded to spreading with age. It has dark green leaves, often bronze when young and usually turning yellow in autumn. The small, yellow to orange or sometimes reddish, fragrant flowers open in late winter to early spring.

Hamamelis mollis

Common name: Ozark witch hazel
Native range: SC United States of America
Height: 4 m (13 ft)
Spread: 5 m (16 ft)
Hardiness: Zone 4
Variants: 'Sandra' is an upright and open shrub, with deep bronze-purple young foliage, which later turns to shades of orange, yellow, red and purple in autumn. The flowers are fragrant, small and deep yellow in colour.

Hebe albicans

Hebe
Scrophulariaceae

This is a large genus containing more than 100 species of plants. Found mainly in New Zealand but also naturally occurring in Australia and the south of South America, the shrubby veronicas, as they are sometimes known, are evergreen shrubs, occasionally trees, with opposite leaves.

Grown principally for their flowers, which, although individually small, are usually borne in dense, showy, often spike-like clusters, or racemes, as well as their foliage, larger species make ideal specimens for the border while the smaller types are suitable for a rock garden. In addition, some of the denser-growing species can be used for hedging, particularly in mild areas.

Hebes can be grown successfully in any well-drained soil, as long as it is not too rich. In general, they prefer a position in full sun but they will also tolerate partial shade. Pruning is not usually necessary, although the more vigorous, larger-growing sorts can be cut back lightly in spring, before the new season's growth starts. Leggy plants will also benefit from light pruning in the spring, and any frost-damaged branches should be removed at the same time.

Hebe albicans

Hebe albicans

This is a compact, bushy shrub that forms a wide mound with densely arranged, blue-grey leaves. Small, white flowers with purple anthers open in very dense clusters in early to mid-summer.

Native range: New Zealand
Height: 60 cm (24 in)
Spread: 1 m (3 ft)
Hardiness: Zone 8

Hebe 'Autumn Glory'

This is a popularly grown garden-raised hybrid. It makes an evergreen, upright shrub that becomes more spreading with age. It bears rounded, dark green leaves, attractively edged with red-purple, that open from purple buds. Dense clusters of deep violet flowers with white tubes open over a long period from mid-summer to autumn.

Height: 75 cm (30 in)
Spread: 1 m (3 ft)
Hardiness: Zone 8

Hebe 'Baby Marie'

This attractive hybrid shrub has been grown incorrectly under the name *H. buxifolia* 'Nana'. It develops into a compact, dwarf mound of bright green foliage composed of small, thick leaves. Suitable for a rock garden, during mid- to late spring the whole plant is covered in clusters of pale lilac flowers.

Height: 30 cm (12 in)
Spread: 45 cm (18 in)
Hardiness: Zone 8

Hebe cupressoides

This unusual-looking shrub is one of a group known as the whipcord hebes, plants that have shoots that are densely covered in tiny, scale-like leaves. *H. cupressoides* is an upright shrub, developing a more rounded, conifer-like appearance as it develops. It has blue-green foliage and, on mature plants, tiny, pale lilac flowers that open during the period from early to mid-summer.

Native range: New Zealand
Height: 1.5 m (5 ft)
Spread: 1.5 m (5 ft)
Hardiness: Zone 6
Variants: 'Boughton Dome' makes a compact, rounded bush growing to a height of about 75 cm (30 in), with bright green foliage. This is strictly a foliage plant, however, since it does not bear flowers.

Hebe 'Emerald Green'

Found as a naturally occurring hybrid in New Zealand, this dwarf-growing shrub makes a low, spreading mound. The densely arranged, upright shoots are covered in small, glossy green, scale-like leaves. It is grown principally for its foliage, since it rarely flowers.

Hebe 'Midsummer Beauty'

Hebe cupressoides 'Boughton Dome'

Height: 30 cm (12 in)
Spread: 45 cm (18 in)
Hardiness: Zone 7

Hebe x *franciscana*

This popular garden-raised hybrid is commonly found in mild areas, and since it will tolerate salt-laden air it is particularly suitable for coastal gardens, where it is often seen planted up as bedding and hedging. It makes a compact bush with a spreading habit and it has densely arranged, rather thick, dark green leaves. It bears dense, showy spikes of lilac-coloured flowers over a long period during the summer and autumn seasons.

Height: 1 m (3 ft)
Spread: 1.5 m (ft)
Hardiness: Zone 8
Variants: 'Blue Gem' has densely growing, mid-green leaves and bears spikes of individually small, pale mauve flowers between mid-summer and early winter. 'Variegata' has leaves edged with creamy white.

Hebe hulkeana

This is a very distinct and attractive species that makes a spreading evergreen bush with an open habit. The shrub produces oval-shaped, bright glossy green, toothed leaves narrowly edged with red. The tiny, white or lilac-coloured flowers are borne in prolific, large, open clusters in late spring and early summer.

Common name: New Zealand lilac
Native range: New Zealand
Height: 45 cm (18 in)

Spread: 75 cm (30 in)
Hardiness: Zone 8
Variants: 'Lilac Hint' is a much larger growing shrub, up to about 1.5 m (5 ft) in height and with a similar spread. It has glossy pale green leaves, and bears a profusion of pale lilac flowers in spring and early summer.

Hebe 'Midsummer Beauty'

This is a vigorous and popularly grown garden-raised hybrid that makes a rounded bush with purple-tinged shoots and long, slender, bright green leaves, which are flushed with purple on their undersurfaces. Small violet-purple flowers, which fade to white as they age, are borne in long, slender clusters during the summer and autumn seasons.

Height: 1.5 m (5 ft)
Spread: 1.5 m (5 ft)
Hardiness: Zone 8

Hebe 'Mrs Winder'

This is a garden-raised hybrid that makes a dense, rounded bush with upright, purple shoots bearing narrow, densely arranged, dark green

Hebe x *franciscana* 'Variegata'

leaves that are purple when young. Dense clusters of small, violet-blue flowers open in the late summer and autumn.

Height: 1 m (3 ft)
Spread: 1.5 m (5 ft)
Hardiness: Zone 8

Hebe ochracea

This distinct and popular, slow-growing, whipcord hebe has an upright habit with slender, arching shoots that are densely covered in small, ochre-coloured leaves. Tiny white flowers are borne along the shoots in late spring and early summer. It is sometimes grown in gardens under the name *H. armstrongii*.

Native range: New Zealand
Height: 1.2 m (4 ft)
Spread: 1.5 m (5 ft)
Hardiness: Zone 6
Variants: 'James Stirling' is a dwarf form with a compact and flat-topped habit that reaches a height of about 40 cm (16 in).

Hebe rakaiensis

Hebe ochracea 'James Stirling'

Hebe 'Pewter Dome'

This garden-raised hybrid makes a compact, spreading mound with densely arranged, grey-green leaves. Short, dense spikes of small, white flowers open during the summer.

Height: 90 cm (35 in)
Spread: 1.5 m (5 ft)
Hardiness: Zone 8

Hebe pimeleoides

This very variable species is grown in several forms, differing in habit and leaf size. Leaves are usually grey-green to blue-green in colour, often with red margins, rather thick, and they emerge from purple shoots. The flowers range from pale lilac to blue-purple and are borne in small clusters during the summer season.

Native range: New Zealand
Height: 40 cm (16 in)
Spread: 60 cm (24 in)
Hardiness: Zone 7
Variants: 'Quicksilver' is a wide-spreading shrub with very deep purple shoots and tiny silvery leaves. Its flowers are violet-blue and are borne in small clusters.

Hebe pinguifolia

This is a variable and low-growing shrub that has a spreading, rounded or upright habit. It has small, thick, blue-green leaves appearing on often purple-tinged shoots. Small, dense clusters of white flowers open during the late spring and early summer seasons.

Native range: New Zealand
Height: 45 cm (18 in)
Spread: 60 cm (24 in)
Hardiness: Zone 6
Variants: 'Pagei' is the most commonly seen garden form. It is low and spreading, reaching a height of only about 20 cm (8 in) but with a spread of about 1 m (3 ft). It has blue-grey, slightly cup-shaped leaves and makes excellent ground cover. Spikes of small, white flowers appear in spring or early summer. 'Sutherlandii' has a compact and rounded habit, growing to a height of about 45 cm (18 in), and bears attractive, grey-green foliage.

Hebe rakaiensis

This popular evergreen species develops into a dense mound of purple-tinged shoots and bright glossy green leaves. Its dense spikes of small, white flowers open during early to mid-summer.

This versatile shrub works well in a border or it can also be used as ground cover.

Native range: New Zealand
Height: 75 cm (30 in)
Spread: 1.5 m (5 ft)
Hardiness: Zone 6

Hebe 'Red Edge'

This garden-raised hybrid grows into a low, sprawling mound. Its grey-green leaves have a distinct red margin and those at the ends of the shoots are red in winter. Clusters of pale violet-blue flowers open in mid- to late summer.

Height: 60 cm (24 in)
Spread: 1 m (3 ft)
Hardiness: Zone 8

Hebe topiaria

This is a compact, dome-shaped bush with a neat habit and densely arranged, small and thick, grey-green leaves. Dense clusters of small, white flowers open during the summer season.

Native range: New Zealand
Height: 80 cm (32 in)
Spread: 1.5 m (5 ft)
Hardiness: Zone 8

Hebe vernicosa

This is a low-growing, spreading shrub with a compact habit. Its green shoots are purple at the leaf bases. The leaves themselves are small, oval-shaped and leathery, and are bright glossy green. Dense and prolific spikes of small, white flowers open from mid-spring to early summer.

Native range: New Zealand
Height: 50 cm (20 in)
Spread: 1 m (3 ft)
Hardiness: Zone 7

Hebe 'Youngii'

This attractive and popular garden-raised hybrid has a low, spreading habit with dark, nearly black, shoots and glossy green, red-edged leaves. Short spikes of violet-blue flowers open during mid- to late summer, fading to white as they age.

Synonym: *Hebe* 'Carl Teschner'
Height: 20 cm (8 in)
Spread: 60 cm (24 in)
Hardiness: Zone 8

Helianthemum
Cistaceae

The rock roses are a genus of more than 100 species of usually dwarf evergreen shrubs. They are mainly found in the Mediterranean region, but they are also widely distributed throughout Europe, western Asia, North Africa and both North and South America.

These plants are grown for their flowers, which occur in a wide range of colours, and they make excellent flowering shrubs for the rock garden, provided they are given well-drained soil and a position in full sun. Individual flowers are short-lived but are borne in profusion. They can be cut back lightly after flowering to retain a compact habit and to promote further flowering. Removing spent blooms also helps to promote flower growth.

Helianthemum nummularium

This dwarf, spreading shrub forms mats of bright green foliage, grey-green beneath. The bright yellow, occasionally white or pink, flowers open during late spring and early summer.

Native range: Europe, SW Asia
Height: 10 cm (4 in) or more
Spread: 45 cm (18 in)
Hardiness: Zone 5

Variants: The most common rock roses in garden cultivation are forms or hybrids of this and other species. Recommended types are: 'Amy Baring', which is deep yellow with orange in the centre; 'Ben Afflick' has bronze-orange with copper centres; 'Ben Fhada' is golden yellow with orange centres and grey-green foliage; 'Ben Ledi' is bright pink; 'Ben More' is rich orange, deeper coloured in the centre; 'Boughton Double Primrose', a double, primrose yellow with deeper centres; 'Cerise Queen', which is double and coloured scarlet; 'Chocolate Blotch' is pale buff, blotched chocolate-brown in the centre; 'Fire Dragon' has bright orange-red flowers and grey-green foliage; 'Georgeham', is large and pink with paler pink centres; 'Jubilee' has double, nodding, primrose yellow flowers with deeper centres; 'Mrs C W Earle' is double, scarlet, with yellow centres; 'Raspberry Ripple' is white with deep pink centres and grey-green foliage; 'Rhodanthe Carneum' is pale pink with yellow centres and silver-grey foliage; 'The Bride' is creamy white with yellow centres and silver-grey foliage; 'Wisley Primrose' has primrose yellow flowers with deep yellow centres and grey-green foliage.

Helianthemum 'The Bride'

Helianthemum 'Mrs C W Earle'

128 TREES, SHRUBS AND BAMBOOS

Helichrysum
Compositae

This is a large genus made up of some 500 species of annual and perennial herbs and evergreen shrubs and subshrubs. These summer- and autumn-flowering plants are widely distributed, particularly in Australia and South Africa.

As well as their showy flowers, many species of *Helichrysum* make valuable garden additions because of their attractive grey- or silver-coloured foliage. Flower arrangers also sometimes use these plants in their arrangements, since once the blooms have been dried they are then very long-lasting.

Helichrysum need to be grown in very well-drained soil in order to grow and thrive, and they also require full sun. The following sorts are suitable for a garden border or a rock garden. Pruning is not usually essential, but in order to retain a compact habit they can be cut back lightly after flowering, and dead or damaged wood should be removed as necessary.

Helichrysum italicum

This is a compact and bushy evergreen subshrub with upright, grey-hairy shoots bearing slender, silver-grey, aromatic leaves. Sometimes grown under the name *H. angustifolium*, it produces clusters of small, golden yellow flowerheads, which open over a long period during the summer and autumn seasons.

Native range: S Europe
Height: 60 cm (24 in)
Spread: 60 cm (24 in)
Hardiness: Zone 8
Variants: The subsp. *serotinum* (curry plant) makes a more compact plant, growing to a height of only about 40 cm (16 in). Its foliage is intensely aromatic and distinctly curry-scented.

Helichrysum splendidum

This compact and evergreen shrub grows with a dense, bushy, upright habit. Its shoots are covered in white,woolly hairs and they produce small, silver-grey leaves. *H. splendidum* eventually forms a spreading mound of a size suitable for a large border. Dense clusters of small, deep yellow flowerheads open over a long period during the summer and autumn seasons, sometimes extending into winter.

Native range: South Africa
Height: 1 m (3 ft)
Spread: 1.2 m (4 ft)
Hardiness: Zone 7

Hibiscus syriacus 'Woodbridge'

Hibiscus syriacus 'Hamabo'

Hibiscus
Malvaceae

This genus is made up of about 200 species of deciduous and evergreen shrubs, trees and herbaceous plants widely distributed in mainly tropical regions. They are grown for their very showy flowers that have centres of long clusters of prominent stamens. The following example is the most commonly seen hardy species in garden cultivation. It is suitable for a shrub border as long as it receives full sun and is provided with good, well-drained soil. *H. rosa-sinensis* is an evergreen species commonly grown in warm regions and, in colder parts of the world, under glass.

Pruning is not usually required. However, dead, damaged, crossing or straggly growth can be cut back in spring.

Hibiscus syriacus

This deciduous shrub has an upright habit with dark green, variously three-lobed leaves. A succession of large, widely funnel-shaped flowers opens over a long period from late summer through to the autumn. It is normally grown as selected forms, with flowers that vary in colour from white to pink, mauve or blue, with deeper blotches at the bases of the petals. Pruning is not usually necessary.

Native range: E Asia
Height: 4 m (13 ft)
Spread: 3 m (10 ft)
Hardiness: Zone 5

Variants: 'Diana' has large, pure white flowers. 'Hamabo' has very pale pink flowers with deep crimson central blotches. 'Oiseau Bleu' ('Blue Bird') has deep violet-blue flowers that are blotched red in their centres. 'Pink Giant' has very large, rich pink flowers that are deep red in their centres. 'Woodbridge' has large, deep pink flowers with red centres.

Hippophae
Elaeagnaceae

This small genus is made up of three species of deciduous shrubs and trees widely distributed across Europe and Asia. The following is the most commonly grown and is cultivated for its foliage and persistent fruits.

Suitable for a wide range of soils, except those that are very dry, it can be grown in the border or to provide shelter, and it is excellent for exposed coastal positions. Male and female flowers are borne on separate plants so both need to be present in order to produce fruit.

Hippophae rhamnoides

This is a thicket-forming, spiny deciduous shrub, sometimes a tree, with slender grey-green leaves that are white beneath. Inconspicuous flowers appear in spring followed, on female plants, by striking, bright orange, long-persistent fruits.

Common name: Sea buckthorn
Native range: Europe, Asia
Height: 5 m (16 ft) or more
Spread: 4 m (13 ft) or more
Hardiness: Zone 4

Hoheria
Malvaceae

The members of this small genus of five species of deciduous and evergreen trees and shrubs are natives of New Zealand. Grown for their white flowers, they are suitable for any well-drained soil and can be planted in the shrub border or in woodland conditions. Evergreen species should be given protection from cold winds, and in cooler areas they can be grown against a wall.

Hoheria angustifolia

This compact and relatively hardy evergreen tree of columnar habit has small, glossy dark green

Hippophae rhamnoides

Hoheria glabrata

leaves. In mid-summer the plant is covered in masses of small, white flowers. It makes an excellent small specimen tree.

Native range: New Zealand
Height: 8m (26 ft)
Spread: 3 m (10 ft)
Hardiness: Zone 8

Hoheria glabrata

A broadly conical to spreading deciduous tree, sometimes shrubby, with dark green, taper-pointed, sharply toothed leaves that turn yellow in autumn. Clusters of white flowers open during summer.

Common name: Mountain ribbonwood
Native range: New Zealand
Height: 10 m (33 ft)
Spread: 8 m (26 ft)
Hardiness: Zone 8

Hoheria 'Glory of Amlych'

This garden-raised hybrid between *H. glabrata* and *H. sexstylosa* makes a small, semi-evergreen tree with slender-pointed, toothed, glossy green leaves. Profuse white flowers open in clusters in summer.

Height: 8 m (26 ft)
Spread: 7 m (23 ft)
Hardiness: Zone 8

Hoheria lyallii

This is a broadly conical to spreading deciduous tree with taper-pointed and sharply toothed, grey-green, downy leaves. Clusters of white flowers open during the summer season.

Common name: Mountain ribbonwood
Native range: New Zealand
Height: 6 m (20 ft)
Spread: 6 m (20 ft)
Hardiness: Zone 8

Hoheria sexstylosa

A vigorous evergreen tree of broad, columnar habit with upright branches bearing glossy dark green, sharply toothed and taper-pointed leaves. Clusters of small, white flowers open during summer.

Common name: Lacebark
Native range: New Zealand
Height: 8 m (26 ft)
Spread: 5 m (16 ft)
Hardiness: Zone 8

Hydrangea arborescens 'Annabelle'

Hoheria sexstylosa

Variants: 'Stardust' is a selection of compact, upright habit with profusely borne flowers.

Hydrangea
Hydrangeaceae

This genus is made up of some 23 species of deciduous and evergreen shrubs and climbers with opposite leaves that are natives of East Asia and North and South America. They are grown principally for their flowers, which, although they are individually small, are borne in showy, prominent clusters. A feature of many species of the genus is the presence of sterile flowers, which consist of large, sometimes coloured, sepals.

They require a good, humus-rich, moist but well-drained soil and they are an excellent choice for the shrub border or a woodland setting. The flower colour of *H. macrophylla* forms is influenced by soil pH values: pink on alkaline soils; blue on acidic soils. Proprietary bluing agents are available to change the flower colour.

Hydrangea arborescens

This clump-forming, rounded deciduous shrub has slender shoots and broad, heart-shaped, dark green leaves. Domed heads of white flowers containing scattered, sterile flowers open during summer. To rejuvenate, cut back hard in spring. Cutting back after flowering may promote further flowers in late summer or autumn.

Native range: E United States of America
Height: 1.5 m (5 ft)
Spread: 2 m (6 ft)
Hardiness: Zone 4
Variants: 'Annabelle' has very large heads of mainly sterile, white flowers. 'Grandiflora' has dense heads of large, white, sterile flowers.

Hydrangea aspera subsp. *sargentiana*

Hydrangea aspera

This sparsely branched deciduous shrub has an upright habit and bears bold, dark green leaves. It is also notable for its peeling bark. The broad, flattened flowerheads that appear in late summer and autumn contain small, pink to blue-purple, fertile flowers that are surrounded by a ring of conspicuous, white to pink or purple-coloured, sterile flowers.

Native range: Himalayas to China and Taiwan
Height: 4 m (13 ft)
Spread: 3 m (10 ft)
Hardiness: Zone 7
Variants: The subsp. *sargentiana* (*H. sargentiana*) has densely bristly shoots. Villosa Group (*H. villosa*) has narrower leaves and, usually, smaller flowerheads.

Hydrangea involucrata

This is a low-growing deciduous shrub with a spreading, open habit and has bristly, dark green, heart-shaped leaves. The open flower heads of blue, fertile flowers, which are produced in late summer, are surrounded by blue to pink sterile flowers.

Hydrangea macrophylla

This is a vigorous, dome-shaped bush with bold, glossy dark green leaves on shoots that are often distinctly spotted. Two types are cultivated: the hortensias, which bear dense, hemispherical heads of mainly sterile flowers; and the more delicate-looking lacecaps, which have flattened heads of pink or blue fertile flowers edged with a ring of large, sterile flowers. They are susceptible to late frosts in cold areas and can be cut back hard in early spring if necessary.

Native range: Japan
Height: 2 m (6 ft) or more
Spread: 3 m (10 ft) or more
Hardiness: Zone 6
Variants: 'Alpenglühen', hortensia type with large, crimson-coloured flowerheads. 'Ami Pasquier' is a compact hortensia with deep crimson to purple-blue flowerheads. 'Europa', hortensia type with large, deep pink to blue-purple flowerheads. 'Générale Vicomtesse de Vibraye', hortensia type with large heads of pale pink or blue flowers. 'Hamburg', hortensia with large heads of deep pink or blue flowers with large sterile flowers. 'King George', hortensia with large heads of pink or blue flowers. 'Lanarth White', lacecap with white, sterile flowers. 'Mariesii Perfecta' ('Blue Wave'), lacecap with large, sterile flowers – either pink or blue. 'Nigra', hortensia type with pink or blue flowerheads and dark, nearly black stems. 'Pia',

Hydrangea involucrata 'Hortensis'

Native range: Japan, Taiwan
Height: 90 cm (35 in)
Spread: 1.5 m (5 ft)
Hardiness: Zone 7
Variants: 'Hortensis' is the most commonly seen form in garden cultivation, with profuse, pink and white, sterile, double flowers.

compact hortensia, up to 60 cm (24 in) high, with purple-red flowerheads. 'Quadricolor', lacecap with leaves variegated with dark and pale green and cream and yellow, and pale pink sterile flowers. 'Veitchii', lacecap with white, sterile flowers turning pink. 'White Wave', lacecap with large, white, sterile flowers.

Hydrangea paniculata

This is a large, vigorous and very hardy deciduous shrub with an upright habit. The branches are often arching, bearing bold, dark green leaves. Large, conical clusters of white flowers open in the late summer and autumn, the blooms containing varying amounts of cream-coloured sterile flowers, which often turn pink as they age. Pruning of this species is unusual in that it can be cut back hard in spring to encourage the production of large flowerheads. Pruning may also be needed in order to restrict growth.

Native range: E Asia
Height: 5 m (16 ft)
Spread: 3 m (10 ft)
Hardiness: Zone 3
Variants: 'Grandiflora' has large, dense heads of mainly sterile flowers that turn from white to pink as they age. 'Kyushu' is a vigorous and upright shrub, with bright glossy green foliage and heads of mixed fertile and sterile flowers. 'Tardiva' produces large flowerheads with both sterile and fertile flowers, opening in autumn. 'Unique' has huge flowerheads of mainly sterile flowers produced over a long period, turning from white to deep pink with age.

Hydrangea 'Preziosa'

This is a garden-raised hybrid between *H. macrophylla* and *H. serrata*. It makes a small deciduous shrub of upright growth with attractive, purple-red stems and glossy green leaves that are bronze when young. The domed heads of sterile flowers open white and turn to pink, red, mauve or blue.

Height: 1.5 m (5 ft)
Spread: 1 m (3 ft)
Hardiness: Zone 6

Hydrangea quercifolia

This is a very distinct, late-deciduous shrub that makes a spreading mound. Its branches usually arch to the ground and the bark tends to peel on the older shoots. The bold, deeply lobed, oak-like leaves are dark green, turning to orange, red and purple in late autumn and winter. White flowers open in the summer and early autumn. These are borne in large, usually arching or drooping, conical clusters, with the sterile flowers turning pink.

Common name: Oakleaf hydrangea
Native range: SE United States of America
Height: 2 m (6 ft)
Spread: 3 m (10 ft)
Hardiness: Zone 5

Hydrangea paniculata 'Tardiva'

Hydrangea macrophylla 'Quadricolor'

Hydrangea serrata 'Grayswood'

Variants: Several selections are grown, including 'Snow Flake', with double sterile flowers, and 'Snow Queen', with large, upright flower clusters.

Hydrangea serrata

This small deciduous shrub has an upright habit, similar to *H. macrophylla* but differing in its smaller size, leaves and flowerheads.

Native range: Korea, Japan
Height: 1.5 m (5 ft)
Spread: 1.2 m (4 ft)
Hardiness: Zone 6
Variants: 'Bluebird', lacecap, produces pale blue to pink, sterile flowers. 'Grayswood', lacecap, has white, sterile flowers that turn to a deep red colour as they age. 'Rosalba', lacecap, has white, sterile flowers that become blotched with red as the season progresses.

Hypericum
Guttiferae

This is a genus made up of approximately 400 species of annual and perennial herbs as well as deciduous and evergreen subshrubs and shrubs, occasionally trees, with opposite leaves. Species of this genus are widely distributed throughout the world.

The cultivated species are grown principally for their prominent yellow flowers, which are usually borne over a long part of the year. The flowers are made even more conspicuous by their centres of long, yellow stamens. Although many species are suitable for growing in a shrub border, others can be planted in a rock garden or used for ground cover. These are generally easy plants to grow and will do well in any well-drained soil. Where they find conditions to their liking, *H. androsaemum* and the very tough *H. calycinum* will grow well in shade, while *H. olympicum* prefers a position in full sun.

Low-growing types can be cut back hard in spring, almost to soil level, to encourage dense new stems, while the taller-growing varieties should have their branches reduced in length only by about a third, again in the spring.

Hypericum androsaemum

This clump-forming deciduous or semi-evergreen shrub has sparsely branched, upright shoots bearing dark green leaves that turn orange and red in autumn. Clusters of small, yellow flowers open in summer and these are followed by fleshy, black fruits that are initially red.

Common name: Tutsan
Native range: Europe, W Asia, North Africa
Height: 1 m (3 ft)
Spread: 1 m (3 ft)
Hardiness: Zone 6
Variants: 'Albury Purple' has attractive, purple-flushed leaves.

Hypericum calycinum

This is a low, compact evergreen shrub that spreads by sending out underground stems. It bears dark green leaves and its large, bright yellow flowers are produced over a long period between summer and autumn. It makes good, dense ground cover and is suitable for either sun or shade.

Common names: Aaron's beard, rose of Sharon
Native range: Bulgaria, Turkey
Height: 45 cm (18 in)
Spread: 2 m (6 ft) or more
Hardiness: Zone 5

Hypericum androsaemum

Hypericum x moserianum

Hypericum frondosum

This is a stoutly branched and low-growing deciduous shrub. It has an essentially rounded habit with pale brown, peeling bark and blue-green, oblong-shaped leaves. It bears bright yellow flowers, opening in summer, and each bloom has a central mass of conspicuous, long, yellow stamens.

Common name: Golden St John's wort
Native range: SE United States of America
Height: 1 m (3 ft)
Spread: 1 m (3 ft)
Hardiness: Zone 5

Hypericum 'Hidcote'

This is a very commonly grown garden-raised hybrid. It makes a vigorous evergreen or semi-evergreen shrub of dense, rounded habit and it bears dark green leaves. The large, golden yellow flowers are borne over a long period from the summer to the early autumn. Flowers are very open in shape and the shrub makes an ideal specimen for a large border.

Height: 1.5 m (5 ft)
Spread: 2 m (6 ft)
Hardiness: Zone 6

Hypericum 'Hidcote'

Hypericum olympicum

Hypericum x *moserianum*

This garden-raised hybrid between *H. calycinum* and *H. patulum* makes a dwarf, clump-forming evergreen shrub with arching, red shoots and dark green leaves. Suitable for a rock garden, this shrub produces small, golden yellow flowers with prominent clusters of stamens that are tipped with conspicuous, reddish-coloured anthers. The bowl-shaped flowers are borne over a long period from mid-summer to autumn.

Height: 45 cm (18 in)
Spread: 90 cm (35 in)

Hardiness: Zone 7
Variants: With its attractive three-coloured foliage, 'Tricolor' is by far the most commonly found form of *H.* x *moserianum* in cultivation. Its name derives from its foliage – its green leaves being conspicuously edged with cream and pink. It is less vigorous and a little less hardy than most other hypericums and so it may benefit from being grown in a more sheltered position in the garden.

Hypericum olympicum

This is a dwarf, mound-forming deciduous shrub with slender, upright shoots that are densely clothed with small, oval-shaped, grey-green leaves. The shrub's relatively large, deep yellow flowers open in clusters at the ends of the shoots throughout the summer season. *H. olympicum* makes an excellent shrub for the rock garden.

Native range: SE Europe, Turkey
Height: 30 cm (12 in)
Spread: 45 cm (18 in)
Hardiness: Zone 6

Ilex
Aquifoliaceae

This is a large, widely distributed genus of about 400 species of deciduous and evergreen trees, shrubs and, more rarely, climbers. The leaves of holly are very variable, and on evergreen species they are sometimes spiny. The distinct male and female flowers are usually white and are borne on separate plants. Both types need to be present for the females to produce fruit, which takes the form of red, or sometimes black, berries.

Hollies are suitable for any good, well-drained soil, either in sun or shade, and they can be planted in the shrub border or used as specimens. *I. aquifolium* is suitable for use as hedging. Prune, or cut, hedges in the early spring, before the new season's growth starts. Specimen shrubs should be trimmed in the summer. Cut out any single-colour reversions on variegated plants as soon as they appear. If necessary, hollies can be cut back hard without causing them any lasting damage.

Ilex x *altaclerensis*

This is a garden-raised hybrid between *I. aquifolium* and *I. perado*. It makes a vigorous evergreen tree of conical, later columnar, habit with broad, dark green and often spiny leaves. Small, white flowers, often flushed on the outside with purple, are borne in clusters in spring and these are followed, on female plants, by bright red berries. This tree is suitable for planting in exposed sites and also for growing in coastal regions. It is normally grown only as selected forms.

Common name: Highclere holly
Height: 20 m (66 ft)
Spread: 15 m (50 ft)
Hardiness: Zone 7
Variants: The following are all female selections and bear red berries. 'Belgica Aurea' has nearly spineless leaves that are edged with yellow when young but later turn cream. 'Camelliifolia' produces nearly spineless leaves that are purple when young. 'Golden King' has leaves that are boldly margined with yellow. 'Hendersonii' has matt-green, spineless or sparsely spined leaves and goes on to produce deep red berries. 'Lawsoniana' has leaves that are boldly blotched with yellow and pale green.

Ilex aquifolium

This is an evergreen tree that is conical when young, later becoming columnar. The glossy dark green leaves are spiny on young plants. As the plants develop, however, adult foliage begins to

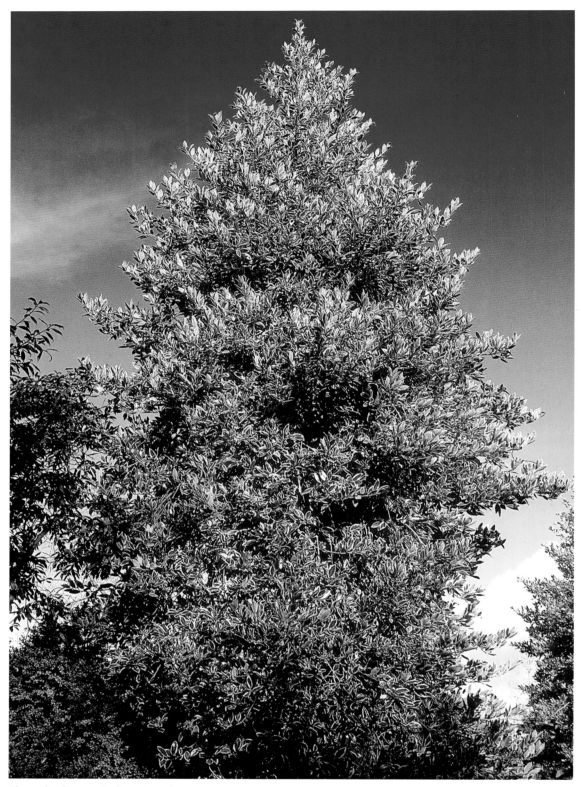

Ilex x *altaclerensis* 'Belgica Aurea'

appear, and on mature trees leaves are spineless. White flowers, often tinged purple, open in the spring, and these are are followed, on female plants, by red berries.

Common name: Common holly
Native range: Europe, W Asia, N Africa
Height: 20 m (66 ft)
Spread: 10 m (33 ft)
Hardiness: Zone 6
Variants: 'Amber' is a female form with orange berries. 'Argentea Marginata' is female with leaves edged with creamy white. 'Argentea Marginata Pendula' (Perry's silver weeping holly)

is female with weeping shoots and grows to about 3 m (10 ft) tall. 'Bacciflava' is a female form and bears yellow berries. 'Ferox Argentea' is male and slow growing, eventually reaching about 8 m (26 ft) in height. Its leaves are edged with creamy white and they are very spiny, both on the surface as well as around the margin. 'Golden van Tol' is female with leaves that are broadly margined with yellow. 'Handsworth New Silver' is female with purple shoots and white-margined leaves. 'Madame Briot' is female with leaves that are edged with golden yellow. 'Pyramidalis Fructu Luteo' is a conical female form with nearly spineless leaves and bears a profusion of yellow berries.

Ilex x altaclerensis 'Hendersonii'

Ilex cornuta

This ia a dense, rounded evergreen shrub that is sometimes tree-like, with glossy dark green, rigidly spiny leaves. Clusters of small, white flowers open in the spring and these are followed by large, persistent, red berries on the female plants.

Common name: Horned holly
Native range: China, Korea
Height: 5 m (16 ft)
Spread: 4 m (13 ft)
Hardiness: Zone 7
Variants: 'Burfordii' is a female form with usually spineless leaves and profuse, very long-persistent berries. 'Rotunda' is female and makes a low, compact mound, about 1 m (3 ft) or more tall, with very spiny leaves. It bears few fruits.

Ilex crenata

This is a variable, bushy evergreen shrub, sometimes tree-like, with small, glossy dark green leaves. Clusters of small, greenish-white flowers open in late spring to early summer, and these are followed, on female plants, by glossy black berries. It can be used for hedging and is very tolerant of heavy pruning.

Ilex aquifolium 'Amber'

Common name: Japanese holly
Native range: Japan, Sakhalin, Korea
Height: 5 m (16 ft) or more
Spread: 4 m (13 ft)
Hardiness: Zone 5
Variants: 'Convexa' is a female form that makes a dense, rounded bush, growing up to about 2 m (6 ft) or more in height, and with convex leaves. 'Fastigiata' is narrowly upright in habit. 'Golden Gem' is slow growing, eventually reaching up to about 1 m (3 ft) in height, with young foliage that is golden yellow in colour. It does best in full sun and although it is a female form it bears few fruits. 'Helleri' has a compact and spreading habit,

Ilex aquifolium 'Pyramidalis Fructu Luteo'

reaching up to about 1 m (3 ft) in height. It is an excellent choice where ground cover is required. Although it is female it rarely fruits. 'Mariesii' is female, slow growing and has stout, upright shoots and small, rounded leaves.

Ilex x meserveae

This group of garden-raised hybrids between *I. aquifolium* and *I. rugosa* makes large, evergreen, upright to rounded shrubs, spreading by suckers when mature, with purple shoots and glossy dark blue-green, spine-toothed leaves. Clusters of

Ilex aquifolium 'Madame Briot'

Ilex crenata 'Golden Gem'

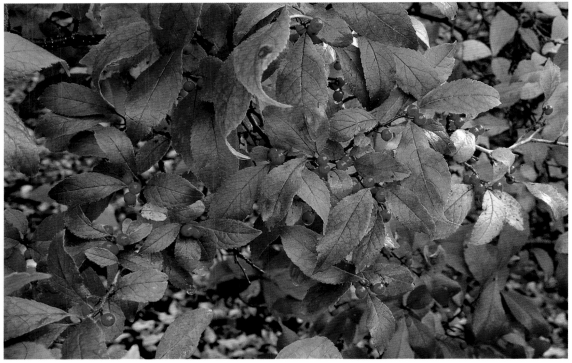

Ilex 'Sparkleberry'

white flowers open in spring and these are followed, on female plants, by bright red berries. It is normally grown only as selected forms.

Common name: Blue holly
Height: 3 m (10 ft) or more
Spread: 3 m (10 ft)
Hardiness: Zone 5
Variants: 'Blue Angel' is a compact, female form that bears large, glossy red berries. 'Blue Prince' is a compact, conical male form that has very glossy foliage and is a good pollinator. 'Blue Princess' is a female form that produces a profusion of deep red fruits.

Ilex opaca

This compact evergreen tree has a conical habit with deep matt-green to yellow-green, spine-edged leaves. Clusters of small, white flowers open in late spring, and these are followed, on female plants, by red berries. There are numerous selected forms, varying in the glossiness of their foliage, vigour, habit and fruit colour – some bearing orange or yellow berries.

Common name: American holly
Native range: E United States of America
Height: 10 m (33 ft)

Spread: 6 m (20 ft)
Hardiness: Zone 5

Ilex 'Sparkleberry'

A splendid garden-raised hybrid between *I. serrata* and *I. verticillata* making a vigorous, large deciduous shrub, sometimes tree-like, with dark green leaves attractively flushed with deep bronze-purple when young. Clusters of white flowers in spring are followed by small, glossy bright red, very profuse and long-persistent berries. It needs a suitable male to pollinate it, such as the similar 'Apollo' or a male *I. verticillata*.

Height: 5 m (16 ft)
Spread: 4 m (13 ft)
Hardiness: Zone 4

Ilex verticillata

A spreading deciduous shrub with dark green leaves, sometimes turning yellow in autumn. Clusters of small, white flowers in spring are followed, on females, by persistent, bright red berries. A suitable pollinator is required, such as a male *I. verticillata*.

Common name: Winterberry
Native range: E North America
Height: 3 m (10 ft)
Spread: 4 m (13 ft)
Hardiness: Zone 3
Variants: There are several selections, some dwarf, some with either orange or yellow fruits. 'Winter Red' has very profuse, bright red fruits that persist throughout winter.

Indigofera heterantha

Itea virginica

Indigofera
Leguminosae

This is a large and widely distributed, mainly tropical, genus made up of some 700 species of herbaceous perennials and deciduous and evergreen trees and shrubs. The cultivated species have leaves divided into several small leaflets and bear spikes of small, pea-like flowers.

They can be grown in any good, well-drained soil, and are suitable for a shrub border. In cold regions they can be trained against a wall for protection. They can be pruned as necessary in spring before the new season's growth starts and they respond well to being cut back to the base.

Indigofera amblyantha

This is a deciduous shrub of upright habit with arching shoots bearing deep green leaves divided into seven to eleven small leaflets. Slender, upright spikes of small, pink, pea-like flowers open over a long period during the summer and early autumn.

Native range: China
Height: 2 m (6 ft)
Spread: 2 m (6 ft)
Hardiness: Zone 6

Indigofera heterantha

A vigorous deciduous shrub of spreading habit with arching branches bearing deep grey-green leaves divided into numerous small leaflets. The dense spikes of deep purple-pink flowers open over a long period from summer to early autumn.

Native range: NW Himalayas
Height: 2 m (6 ft)
Spread: 3 m (10 ft)
Hardiness: Zone 7

Itea
Escalloniaceae

This genus is made up of ten species of deciduous and evergreen shrubs, natives of the Himalayas and East and Southeast Asia, with just one species native in the east of the United States of America. Cultivated for their foliage and flowers, the two most commonly grown species are very different in general appearance. *I. ilicifolia* requires a well-drained soil and is suitable for a shrub border or woodland, or for growing against a wall. *I. virginica* requires a moist, lime-free soil and is best planted in full sun. It can be pruned after flowering if necessary.

Itea ilicifolia

A spreading, evergreen shrub with glossy dark green, holly-like leaves edged with small teeth. The long, pendulous and slender, catkin-like clusters of small, greenish-white flowers remain attractive over a long period during summer.

Native range: China
Height: 4 m (13 ft)
Spread: 5 m (16 ft)
Hardiness: Zone 8

Itea virginica

This deciduous, thicket-forming shrub spreads by suckers. It has upright, later arching, shoots bearing dark green, long-persistent leaves, which sometimes turn yellow, red or purple in autumn. Dense, upright spikes of slightly fragrant, white flowers open during the summer.

Common name: Sweetspire
Native range: E United States of America
Height: 1.5 m (5 ft) or more
Spread: 2 m (6 ft) or more
Hardiness: Zone 5
Variants: 'Henry's Garnet' has rich red-purple autumn colour.

Jasminum
Oleaceae

The jasmines make up a very widely distributed genus of 200 or more species of deciduous and evergreen shrubs and woody stemmed climbers with opposite or alternate leaves. These plants are natives of Africa and Asia to the Pacific Islands and Australia, as well as being found throughout Europe. The shrubby species all have yellow flowers. However, unlike many of the climbing species of jasmine, the shrubs are not strongly fragrant.

The following species all require good, well-drained soil in order to thrive, and all do best if they are planted in full sun. They can be pruned by cutting back to suitable buds after flowering. On mature plants, some of the older shoots can be cut to the base in order to encourage new growth. (*See also chapter on Climbers.*)

Jasminum humile

This is a vigorous, semi-evergreen, bushy shrub with graceful, green shoots and alternate leaves. The leaves are usually divided up into seven dark green leaflets. Clusters of bright yellow, slightly fragrant flowers open from summer through to autumn, and these are followed by glossy black berries.

Common names: Italian jasmine, yellow jasmine
Native range: Himalayas to China
Height: 2.5 m (8 ft)
Spread: 3 m (10 ft)
Hardiness: Zone 8
Variants: This is an extremely variable species with several forms. Particularly popular in garden cultivation is 'Revolutum', an evergreen that has large leaves and large, more fragrant, tubular-shaped flowers.

Jasminum mesnyi

This very vigorous evergreen or semi-evergreen shrub has upright, later arching, green shoots bearing opposite leaves that are divided into three dark green leaflets. The attractive, bright yellow, double flowers open during the late spring and summer, but the blooms fade to white as they age. The woody stems of this species allow it to be effectively trained as a climber against a suitable wall.

Common name: Primrose jasmine
Native range: China
Height: 4 m (13 ft)
Spread: 3 m (10 ft)
Hardiness: Zone 8

Jasmimum nudiflorum

Jasmimum mesnyi

Jasminum nudiflorum

This is a deciduous shrub that produces long, arching, green shoots bearing opposite, glossy dark green leaves that are divided up into three oval-shaped leaflets. Its bright yellow flowers open on the bare shoots during late winter and early spring, making it a valuable addition in the garden when colour is often at a premium. Although it is not strictly a climber, this species is nearly always grown trained against a wall. Such plants are best cut back after flowering. This is an easy to grow plant that does well in any well-drained soil.

Common name: Winter jasmine
Native range: China
Height: 4 m (13 ft)
Spread: 4 m (13 ft)
Hardiness: Zone 6

Jovellana
Scrophulariaceae

This is a small genus made up of just six species of southern hemisphere herbaceous perennials and subshrubs, all of which are native to Chile and New Zealand.

Grown for its showy flowers, the following species is suitable for any good, well-drained soil, and it prefers a position in full sun. In mild areas it can be grown in the shrub border, but in cooler regions it often requires the protection of being grown against a wall. Light pruning in spring helps to maintain a compact habit.

Jovellana violacea

This evergreen or semi-evergreen subshrub has upright shoots and dark green leaves edged with large teeth. The clusters of unusual, pale violet flowers that open during summer are blotched yellow inside and have purple spots.

Native range: Chile
Height: 1 m (3 ft)
Spread: 1 m (3 ft)
Hardiness: Zone 9

Juglans
Juglandaceae

The walnuts comprise a genus of some 15 species of deciduous trees that are natives of southeast Europe, Asia and North and South America. All have bold leaves divided into several leaflets. Male and female flowers are borne separately on the same tree – the males in pendulous catkins. Several species produce edible nuts.

Walnuts require a good, deep, well-drained soil and a sunny position. They should be planted when small rather than as well-grown specimens.

Juglans nigra

This fast-growing deciduous tree of spreading habit has large, dark green, aromatic leaves with up to 23 taper-pointed leaflets. The pendulous, green male catkins open in late spring to early summer, while the small female flowers develop into rounded, edible nuts enclosed in a green husk.

Common name: Black walnut
Native range: E United States of America
Height: 25 m (80 ft) or more
Spread: 15 m (50 ft)
Hardiness: Zone 4

Juglans regia

A large deciduous tree with distinctive pale grey bark and large, aromatic leaves, bronze when young, with five to nine glossy green leaflets. Green male flowers open in pendulous catkins in late spring to early summer, and the female flowers ripen to edible nuts confined in a green husk. Selected forms are often grown for their nuts.

Common name: Common walnut
Native range: SE Europe to China
Height: 30 m (100 ft)
Spread: 20 m (65 ft)
Hardiness: Zone 6

Juglans regia

Jovellana violacea

Kalmia angustifolia f. *rubra*

Kalmia
Ericaceae

The seven species in this genus are natives of North America, with one occurring in Cuba. Mainly evergreen shrubs with alternate or opposite leaves, they are grown in gardens for their attractive clusters of ornamental flowers, which are pink or, sometimes, white. They require a moist, acid soil that is rich in organic matter, and they do best if given a sunny position – as long as the soil is not too dry.

Kalmia angustifolia

This is an extremely hardy evergreen shrub of compact habit that makes a low, spreading mound with deep blue-green, opposite or whorled leaves. Clusters of small, pink to purple-pink flowers open during early to mid-summer.

Common name: Sheep laurel
Native range: E North America
Height: 60 cm (24 in)
Spread: 1.5 m (5 ft)
Hardiness: Zone 1
Variants: The flowers are variable in colour – white in f. *candida* and deep red-purple in f. *rubra*.

Kalmia latifolia

This is a compact evergreen shrub of rounded habit with alternate, glossy dark green leaves. The pale to deep pink, sometimes white, flowers, which are often spotted or banded on the inside,

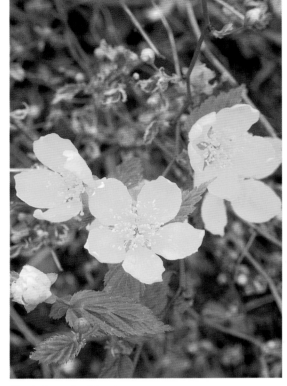

Kerria japonica 'Picta'

open from distinctively crimped buds in the late spring and early summer. Both the size and colouring of the flowers are extremely variable.

Common names: Calico bush, mountain laurel
Native range: E North America
Height: 2 m (6 ft) or more
Spread: 3 m (10 ft) or more
Hardiness: Zone 4
Variants: 'Carousel' has white flowers that are heavily marked with deep red inside. 'Freckles' has pink buds opening to creamy white, spotted with purple. 'Little Linda' is a compact dwarf form up to

Kalmia latifolia

1 m (3 ft) tall, with deep pink flowers opening from red buds. 'Minuet' is compact and dwarf, up to 1 m (3 ft) tall, with small leaves and white flowers that are banded with deep red. 'Olympic Fire' has large, red buds opening to pink flowers. 'Ostbo Red' has bright red buds opening to pale pink flowers.

Kerria
Rosaceae

The single species in this genus is an invaluable garden plant that is grown in several forms for its bright, early-opening flowers. Easy to grow in any well-drained soil, it is particularly suitable for the shrub border. The double form, 'Plena', is extremely vigorous and should be used with care in small gardens. Pruning can be carried out in spring if necessary. On mature plants, some of the older shoots can be cut back right to the base.

Kerria japonica

A vigorous deciduous shrub spreading by suckers, with arching, green shoots bearing alternate, bright green, sharply toothed and taper-pointed leaves, sometimes turning yellow in autumn. The buttercup-like, golden yellow flowers open early in the year, in mid- to late spring or sometimes earlier.

Native range: China
Height: 2 m (6 ft)
Spread: 3 m (10 ft)
Hardiness: Zone 5
Variants: 'Golden Guinea' has very large flowers. 'Picta' ('Variegata') is smaller, up to 1.2 m (4 ft) tall, with leaves that are edged with white. 'Pleniflora' ('Plena') is extremely vigorous and upright, forming dense thickets with large, fully double flowers.

Koelreuteria
Sapindaceae

A genus of three species of deciduous trees native to East Asia, with leaves divided into numerous leaflets. The following is a useful small tree, grown not only for its elegant foliage but also its flowers and fruits. Suitable for any good, well-drained soil, it flowers and fruits best if grown in full sun.

Koelreuteria paniculata

This spreading deciduous tree has fern-like, bright green leaves, bronze coloured when young, that

Kolkwitzia amabilis 'Pink Cloud'

turn yellow in autumn. Each leaf is divided up into about 15 leaflets, which themselves are further divided, lobed, or toothed. The large clusters of small, bright yellow flowers, marked with red in the centre, open in mid- to late summer, followed by green, bladder-like fruits ripening to pale brown, or pink in some forms.

Common names: Golden rain tree, pride of India
Native range: China, Korea
Height: 10 m (33 ft)
Spread: 10 m (33 ft)
Hardiness: Zone 5

Kolkwitzia
Caprifoliaceae

The single species that makes up this small genus develops into a splendid, large shrub that is valued in gardens for its display of profusely borne flowers. Suitable for planting in a shrub border or for growing as a specimen plant, it will grow in any good, well-drained soil. It does best if positioned in full sun, since it may become leggy if it is given too much shade.

Ideally, it should be left uncut in order to attain full size, but can be pruned if necessary by trimming it back lightly after flowering. Damaged wood should also be removed at this time. On mature plants, some of the older shoots can be cut back right to the base.

Kolkwitzia amabilis

This is a vigorous deciduous shrub with opposite, dark green, taper-pointed leaves borne on arching shoots. On older wood, the bark develops a tendency to peel. The beautiful, bell-shaped, usually pale pink flowers, coloured yellow in the throat, are profusely borne in arching clusters during the late spring and early summer. The small fruits are densely covered in long bristles.

Common name: Beauty bush
Native range: China
Height: 4 m (13 ft)
Spread: 5 m (16 ft)
Hardiness: Zone 5
Variants: 'Pink Cloud' is a deciduous shrub bearing masses of bright pink flowers in mid-spring.

Koelreuteria paniculata

Kerria japonica 'Pleniflora'

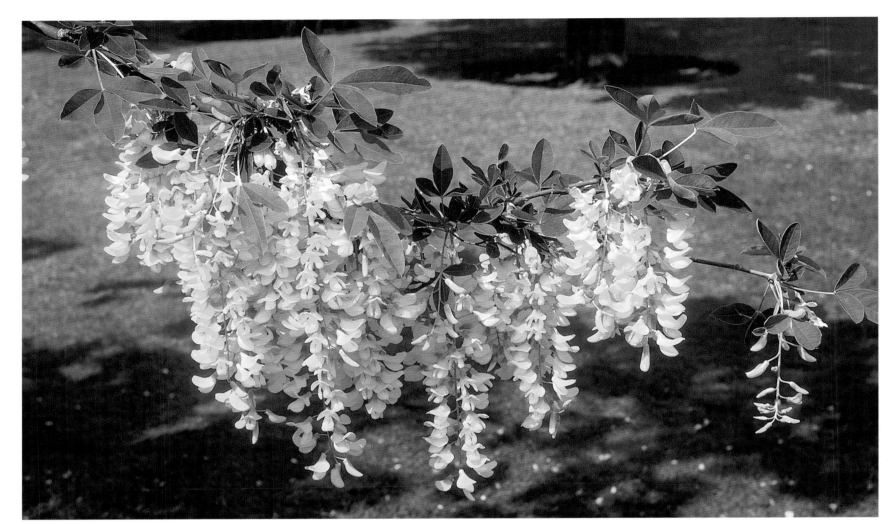

Laburnum x watereri 'Vossii'

+ *Laburnocytisus*
Leguminosae

The plant listed here is known as a 'graft hybrid'. It is not a true hybrid but originated when a purple broom was grafted on to a *Laburnum*. The tissues of the two plants combined to produce a completely new third plant.

The plant will grow on any well-drained soil and prefers a sunny position.

+ *Laburnocytisus* 'Adamii'

This is a graft hybrid between *Laburnum anagyroides* and *Chamaecytisus purpureus*. It makes a small deciduous tree with spreading branches bearing dark green leaves that are divided into three leaflets. The short, pendulous clusters of pink, pea-shaped flowers flushed with yellow open from late spring to early summer. The tree usually also carries long, pendulous clusters of yellow laburnum flowers as well as the purple-pink flowers of purple broom.

Height: 6 m (20 ft)
Spread: 6 m (20 ft)
Hardiness: Zone 5

Laburnum
Leguminosae

This is a small genus of just two species of deciduous trees that are popular for their flowers. Their size makes them suitable for small gardens and they are also easy to grow in any reasonably good, well-drained soil. Take note that all parts of the trees are poisonous.

Laburnun alpinum

This deciduous, spreading tree, which is sometimes shrubby and with several branches coming from the base, has dark green leaves composed of three leaflets. The long, slender chains of small, bright yellow, pea-like flowers open in the early summer. This species is less frequently seen than the other laburnums described here, and it is most commonly grown in the weeping form listed below.

Common name: Scotch laburnum
Native range: C and S Europe
Height: 8 m (26 ft)
Spread: 6 m (20 ft)
Hardiness: Zone 4

Variants: 'Pendulum' is shorter, with pendulous shoots weeping right to the ground.

Laburnum anagyroides

This is a spreading deciduous tree with dark green leaves divided up into three leaflets, grey with hairs on their undersurfaces. The dense, pendulous chains of yellow flowers open in the late spring. The flowers are larger than those of *L. alpinum*, although its flowering period is shorter. This was once the most commonly found laburnum in cultivation, but it has now been largely superseded by the hybrid *L.* x *watereri*.

Common name: Common laburnum
Native range: C and S Europe
Height: 8 m (26 ft)
Spread: 6 m (20 ft)
Hardiness: Zone 5

Laburnum x *watereri*

This is a popularly grown, vigorous hybrid between *L. alpinum* and *L. anagyroides* and it makes a spreading deciduous tree with dark green leaves. It combines the best characters of its parents – the long chains of *L. alpinum* and the larger flowers of

L. anagyroides, which open in late spring to early summer. It has been raised in gardens and it also occurs naturally.

Native range: Austria, Switzerland
Height: 8 m (26 ft)
Spread: 6 m (20 ft)
Hardiness: Zone 5
Variants: 'Vossii' is the form commonly grown and it has very long flower clusters.

Laurus
Lauraceae

The two species that make up this small genus are evergreen trees or shrubs, natives of the Mediterranean region. Only the following is commonly grown in gardens, however, where it is valued for its very aromatic foliage. It is an excellent specimen shrub or tree, but it is also suitable for growing in containers and for hedging.

Plant in any good, well-drained soil, and in colder areas it will benefit from the protection afforded by a wall. Prune trees if necessary in spring, while hedges should be cut and pot-grown specimens trimmed in the summer. Both male and female trees are needed to obtain fruit.

Laurus nobilis

This dense, conical evergreen tree, which is often suckering at the base, has glossy dark green, very aromatic leaves that are often wavy-edged. Small clusters of yellow-green flowers open in the spring – males and females on separate plants – and these are followed by fleshy berries that ripen from green to black.

Common name: Bay laurel
Native range: Mediterranean region
Height: 15 m (50 ft)
Spread: 10 m (33 ft)
Hardiness: Zone 8
Variants: 'Angustifolia' is a form with very narrow leaves. 'Aurea' has golden yellow foliage.

Lavandula
Labiatae

The lavenders make up a genus comprising some 25 species of evergreen shrubs, all with opposite leaves, that are distributed from the Mediterranean region through to India.

Lavenders are popular in gardens for their grey or grey-green, aromatic foliage and for their dense

Laburnum anagyroides

Laurus nobilis

clusters of fragrant flowers. They require a not-too-rich, very well-drained soil and a position in full sun in order to thrive. They can be used effectively to create low hedges or garden divisions. They are best pruned lightly but regularly in spring to encourage a compact growth habit.

Lavandula angustifolia

This is a bushy, rounded shrub with a compact habit and slender, aromatic, grey-green leaves. The dense, long-stalked clusters of small pale to deep purple flowers open during mid- to late summer.

Common name: Lavender
Native range: Mediterranean region
Height: 1 m (3 ft)
Spread: 1.5 m (5 ft)
Hardiness: Zone 5
Variants: 'Alba' has white flowers. 'Folgate' is compact with lavender blue flowers. 'Hidcote' is very compact, up to 60 cm (24 in) tall, with silvery foliage and deep purple flowers. 'Hidcote Pink' resembles 'Hidcote' but has pale pink flowers. 'Loddon Pink' has soft pink flowers. 'Nana Alba' is a dense, dwarf form, growing only up to 30 cm (12 in) high, and bearing white flowers.

Lavandula x intermedia

These garden-raised hybrids between *L. angustifolia* and *L. latifolia* make vigorous and robust, rounded evergreen shrubs with aromatic, grey-green foliage. In summer, they bear long-stalked clusters of blue to purple flowers.

Height: 1 m (3 ft)
Spread: 1.5 m (5 ft)
Hardiness: Zone 5
Variants: The flower colour of 'Grappenhall' is blue-purple.

Lavandula stoechas

This compact evergreen shrub has upright shoots and slender, grey-green, aromatic leaves. The short-stalked clusters of small, purple flowers, which open in late spring and summer, are topped with conspicuous purple bracts.

Common name: French lavender
Native range: Mediterranean region
Height: 60 cm (24 in)
Spread: 60 cm (24 in)
Hardiness: Zone 8
Variants: f. *leucantha* has white flowers and bracts, while subsp. *pedunculata* has flower clusters growing on long stalks.

Lavandula angustifolia 'Hidcote'

Lavandula stoechas subsp. *pedunculata*

Lavatera 'Rosea'

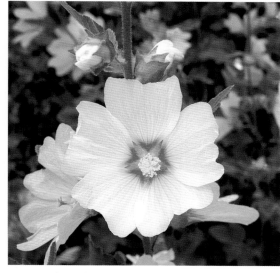

Lavatera 'Barnsley'

Lavatera
Malvaceae

The 25 species in this genus are all herbaceous annuals and perennials, natives of Europe and Asia, with some species found in Australia and California. The cultivated woody members are mainly garden-raised hybrids between *L. olbia* and *L. thuringiaca*, making vigorous semi-evergreen shrubs with lobed, grey-green leaves. The large and showy mallow-like flowers are borne over a long period in summer. They will grow in any well-drained soil and prefer a position in full sun. They are best cut back hard to a woody base in spring before the new season's growth starts.

Height: 2 m (6 ft)
Spread: 2 m (6 ft)
Hardiness: Zone 8
Variants: 'Barnsley' has white flowers with red centres and they turn to pale pink with age. It occasionally reverts to 'Rosea', of which it is a sport. 'Blushing Bride' is very similar to 'Barnsley' but is more compact in habit and does not revert. 'Bredon Springs' has deep dusky pink flowers. 'Burgundy Wine' has deep purple-pink flowers. 'Candy Floss' has very pale pink flowers. 'Kew Rose' has purple shoots and large, bright pink flowers. 'Rosea' has deep pink flowers.

Leptospermum
Myrtaceae

The 80 or so species in this genus of evergreen shrubs and trees are largely natives of Australia, with a few occurring in New Zealand and Southeast Asia. The cultivated species are grown for their attractive foliage and small, starry flowers. They prefer a not-too-rich soil in a sunny position.

The less hardy species can be grown with wall protection. Pruning is rarely required.

Leptospermum lanigerum

This vigorous, tree-like evergreen shrub has upright growth with silver-grey, aromatic foliage. Profusely borne, small, white flowers open during the late spring and early summer.

Common name: Woolly tea tree
Native range: SE Australia, Tasmania
Height: 5 m (16 ft)
Spread: 2.5 m (8 ft)
Hardiness: Zone 8

Leptospermum rupestre

This is a compact, spreading evergreen shrub making a low mound with arching branches densely covered in small, glossy dark green leaves. The leaves turn bronze-purple in winter. The whole plant is studded with numerous small, white flowers in late spring and early summer.

Synonym: *Leptospermum humifusum*
Native range: Tasmania
Height: 1 m (3 ft)
Spread: 5 m (16 ft)
Hardiness: Zone 8

Leptospermum scoparium

A graceful evergreen shrub with arching shoots and aromatic, dark green, sharply pointed leaves. Flowers, usually white but pink in some forms, are profusely borne in late spring and early summer.

Common name: Tea tree
Native range: New Zealand
Height: 2.5 m (8 ft) or more
Spread: 3 m (10 ft)
Hardiness: Zone 8
Variants: 'Chapmanii' is compact and upright with bronze foliage and bright pink flowers. 'Kiwi' is a compact, dwarf form, to 1 m (3 ft) tall, with bronze foliage and deep pink flowers. 'Nicholsii' has bronze foliage and carmine-red flowers. 'Red Damask' has deep red, double flowers.

Leptospermum lanigerum

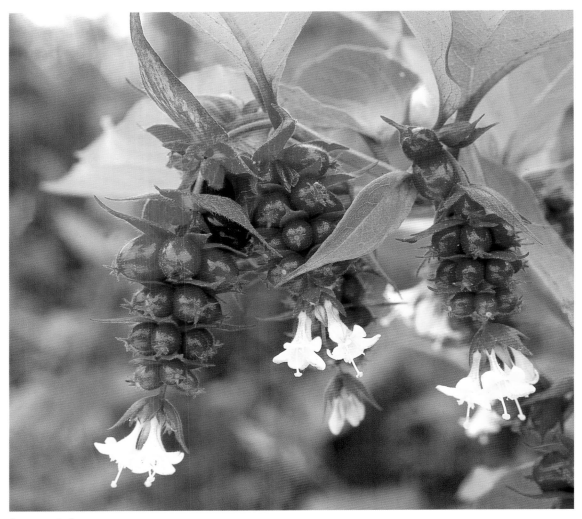

Leycesteria formosa

Lespedeza
Leguminosae

This is a genus of about 40 species of herbaceous annuals and perennials and deciduous shrubs, with leaves divided into three leaflets and small pea-like flowers. They are natives of North America, Asia and Australia.

The following is the most commonly grown and makes an excellent border shrub for its late and showy flowers. In cold areas it often behaves like a herbaceous plant, and the old shoots should be cut to the ground in spring.

Lespedeza thunbergii

This vigorous deciduous shrub or subshrub has long, arching shoots bearing blue-green leaves divided into three leaflets. The plant has large clusters of deep rose-purple, pea-like flowers that open at the ends of the shoots in late summer and early autumn.

Native range: China, Japan
Height: 1.5 m (5 ft)
Spread: 3 m (10 ft)
Hardiness: Zone 5

Leucothoe
Ericaceae

This is a genus made up of approximately 45 species of deciduous, evergreen and semi-evergreen shrubs that are natives of North and South America, East Asia and Madagascar.

The following species is grown for its attractive foliage and for its small white flowers, and is also

Leucothoe fontanesiana 'Rainbow'

useful for growing in shady places. In order to thrive it requires a moist, but well-drained, lime-free soil that is rich in organic matter, and it prefers a shaded or partially shaded site.

Little pruning is usually required. However, with established plants some of the old shoots can be cut back right to the base in spring in order to encourage new growth.

Leucothoe fontanesiana

This vigorous evergreen shrub has long, arching shoots, which are red when young, and deep glossy green, leathery, taper-pointed leaves that are sometimes bronze when young. The leaves also turn bronze in autumn. The small, slightly fragrant, white, urn-shaped flowers hang in attractive clusters along the shoots in late spring.

Native range: SE United States of America
Height: 1.5 m (5 ft)
Spread: 2.5 m (8 ft)
Hardiness: Zone 5
Variants: 'Rainbow' has leaves that are mottled with cream and pink. 'Scarletta' has deep red-purple young foliage that turns bronze-red in autumn and winter.

Leycesteria
Caprifoliaceae

The six species that make up this genus are deciduous shrubs, with opposite leaves, and all are natives of the Himalayas and China.

The following species is popular in gardens due to its vigorous habit and long period of interest in flowers and fruit. It is suitable for any good, well-drained soil, and it does best if given a sunny position, although it will tolerate semi-shade. Some of the old stems should be cut back right to the ground each year.

Leycesteria formosa

This is a vigorous deciduous shrub that forms dense clumps and spreads by sending out suckers. It produces upright, blue-green, hollow shoots that bear taper-pointed, dark green leaves. In summer and autumn, drooping clusters of white flowers mixed with deep red-purple bracts, ripen to glossy red-purple berries.

Common name: Himalayan honeysuckle
Native range: Himalayas, W China
Height: 2 m (6 ft)
Spread: 2 m (6 ft)
Hardiness: Zone 7

Ligustrum
Oleaceae

The privets are a widely distributed genus that is composed of some 40 species of deciduous and evergreen shrubs and trees with opposite leaves. They are natives of Europe, North Africa, and West Asia and from the Himalayas to East Asia and Australia.

The privets are grown principally for their foliage: *L. ovalifolium* is used most often for hedging, while *L. lucidum* can be planted as a specimen tree. They can be grown in any well-drained soil and will often do well in either full sun or in shade.

Hedges can be cut as necessary to keep them in shape during late spring and summer. Specimen trees and shrubs do not usually require any pruning. However, any damaged, straggly or unwanted branches can be removed in spring.

Ligustrum japonicum

This vigorous evergreen shrub, which is sometimes tree-like, has an upright habit with arching shoots and glossy dark green, leathery leaves. Dense, conical clusters of small, white, rather unpleasantly scented flowers open at the ends of the shoots in summer, and these are followed by black fruits covered in a white bloom. It thrives best in areas with hot summers.

Common name: Japanese privet
Native range: China, Korea, Japan
Height: 3 m (10 ft)
Spread: 2 m (6 ft)
Hardiness: Zone 7
Variants: 'Rotundifolium' is a very compact and slow-growing shrub, to 1.5 m (5 ft), with a congested habit and thick, rounded, black-green leaves. 'Silver Star' has leaves edged with white.

Ligustrum lucidum 'Excelsum Superbum'

Liquidambar styraciflua

Ligustrum lucidum

This is a vigorous evergreen tree – upright when young, later spreading – with bold, dark green leaves. The large, conical clusters of white flowers are attractive over a long period during late summer and autumn, and these are followed by blue-black fruits, which are most profusely borne in areas that experience hot summers.

Common name: Chinese privet
Native range: China
Height: 10 m (33 ft)
Spread: 10 m (33 ft)
Hardiness: Zone 8
Variants: 'Excelsum Superbum' has leaves with a yellow edge, turning to creamy white. 'Tricolor' has young leaves that are flushed with pink, later becoming edged with white.

Ligustrum ovalifolium

This vigorous semi-evergreen or deciduous shrub has upright growth, with glossy green leaves that are sometimes purple-flushed in late autumn or winter. Dense clusters of rather unpleasantly scented, small, white flowers open during summer at the ends of the shoots, and these are followed by small, glossy black fruits. It is most frequently used as a hedging plant.

Common name: Privet
Native range: Japan
Height: 5 m (16 ft)
Spread: 3 m (10 ft)
Hardiness: Zone 5
Variants: 'Argenteum' has leaves that are edged with white. 'Aureum' (golden privet) has leaves broadly edged with yellow. Any shoots producing all-yellow leaves should be cut out.

Liquidambar
Hamamelidaceae

This small genus of four species of deciduous trees, natives of North America, Turkey and East Asia, provides gardens with valuable autumn colour. The following is the most commonly grown species, and it does best in a good, deep, moist but well-drained, lime-free soil, colouring best in full sun.

Liquidambar styraciflua

This is a deciduous tree of conical habit whose shoots often have conspicuous corky wings and bear bold, glossy green, deeply lobed, maple-like leaves, each normally with five pointed lobes. The leaves turn to brilliant shades of orange, yellow, red and purple over a long period in autumn. The inconspicuous, yellow-green flowers open in late spring and these are followed by spherical, pendulous fruit clusters. It only flowers and fruits freely in regions that experience hot summers.

Common name: Sweet gum
Native range: E United States of America, Mexico
Height: 25 m (80 ft)
Spread: 15 m (50 ft)
Hardiness: Zone 5
Variants: Numerous forms have been selected, mainly for their autumn colour. 'Golden Treasure' is slow growing and has leaves that are broadly edged with deep yellow, the centre turning deep purple in autumn. 'Lane Roberts' has deep red-purple autumn colouring, starting early in the season. 'Silver King' has leaves that are edged with creamy yellow, later turning white. 'Variegata' has leaves that are blotched with yellow and pale green. 'Worplesdon' has deeply lobed leaves that turn purple and then orange and yellow in autumn.

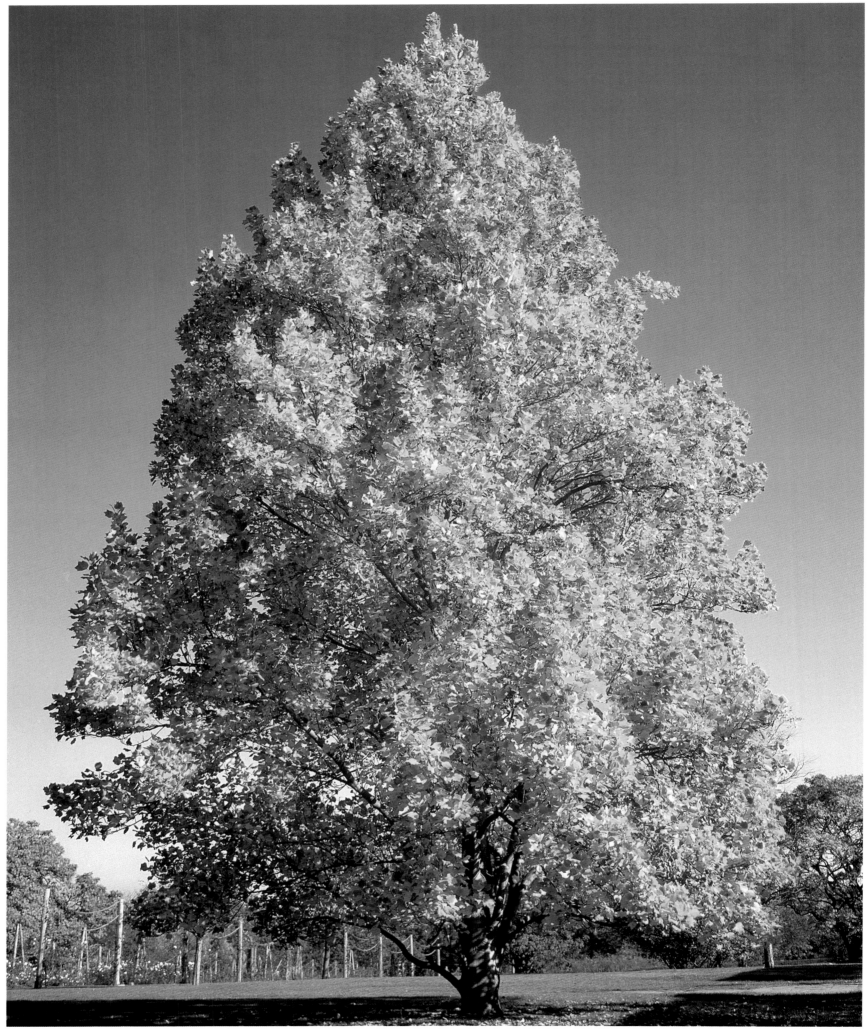

Liriodendron tulipifera 'Fastigiatum'

Liriodendron
Magnoliaceae

The two similar species of deciduous tree that make up this small genus are found in North America and China

With leaves of a unique shape, the North American species is the more commonly grown – usually as a specimen tree in large gardens and parks – for its flowers, foliage and autumn colour. It does best in a good, moist but well-drained, slightly acidic soil. Apart from the removal of any dead, damaged or crossing wood, no pruning is required.

Liriodendron tulipifera

This is a vigorous, large-growing deciduous tree of broadly columnar habit, with bold, dark green leaves that turn yellow in autumn. The unusually shaped leaves have two lobes at the truncated tip, and two more at the base. Cup-shaped, tulip-like flowers, which are orange at the base and banded with green towards the tip, open in early to mid-summer. Trees may take as long as ten years, or even longer, to flower from seed.

Common name: Tulip tree
Native range: E North America
Height: 30 m (100 ft)
Spread: 20 m (65 ft)
Hardiness: Zone 4
Variants: 'Aureomarginatum' has leaves broadly margined with golden yellow, eventually turning to green. 'Fastigiatum' ('Arnold') is a form with a narrow, conical habit and upright branches.

Lithodora
Boraginaceae

This is a genus made up of seven species of evergreen shrub that are natives of southern Europe and North Africa. The most popular species is a delightful rock garden plant, which is grown for its blue flowers, and requires a well-drained, acidic soil and a sunny position. Pruning is not usually necessary, but it can be trimmed lightly after flowering.

Lithodora diffusa

This sprawling, evergreen shrub, which forms dense ground cover, has slender, bristly shoots and narrow, dark green leaves. The five-lobed flowers have a tubular base and are bright blue. They open in profusion during the late spring and early summer seasons.

Liriodendron tulipifera

Lithodora diffusa 'Heavenly Blue'

Synonym: Lithospermum diffusum
Native range: SW Europe
Height: 30 cm (12 in)
Spread: 1.5 m (5 ft)

Hardiness: Zone 7
Variants: 'Alba' produces white flowers. 'Cambridge Blue' has pale blue flowers. 'Heavenly Blue' has azure-blue flowers.

Lonicera
Caprifoliaceae

This is a genus made up of some 200 species of deciduous and evergreen shrubs and climbers, with opposite leaves, and widely distributed in mainly temperate regions of the northern hemisphere. The shrubby species are grown for their sometimes fragrant flowers or their foliage. Most are suitable for the shrub border, while *L. nitida* and its forms are useful for hedging and *L. pileata* makes an excellent groundcover plant.

It can be grown in any well-drained soil, and the winter-flowering sorts do best in full sun. Prune hedges of *L. nitida* as necessary in summer. Winter-flowering sorts can be cut back after flowering if required. (See also chapter on *Climbers*.)

Lonicera fragrantissima

This is a spreading late-deciduous or semi-evergreen shrub with arching shoots bearing dark green leaves. Very fragrant white flowers open in pairs during winter and early spring and these are sometimes followed by red berries in summer. It flowers best in areas with hot summers, or when grown against a warm wall.

Native range: China
Height: 2 m (6 ft)
Spread: 2.5 m (8 ft)
Hardiness: Zone 4

Lonicera nitida

This vigorous and densely bushy evergreen shrub has small, dark green leaves. Its small, creamy white flowers open in spring, sometimes followed by violet-purple berries. Its vigorous growth, dense habit and ability to withstand clipping make *L. nitida* very useful as a hedging plant.

Native range: China
Height: 3 m (10 ft)
Spread: 4 m (13 ft)
Hardiness: Zone 7
Variants: 'Baggesen's Gold' has bright yellow foliage. 'Lemon Beauty' has leaves broadly edged with creamy white. 'Maigrün' is low and spreading, making dense ground cover. 'Red Tips' has deep red-purple young leaves. 'Silver Beauty' has leaves edged with silvery white.

Lonicera pileata

This is a low-growing shrub with a dense, spreading habit and small, dark green, leathery leaves. Pairs of small, creamy white flowers open

Lonicera fragrantissima

Lonicera nitida 'Baggesen's Gold'

Lonicera x purpusii

Lonicera x purpusii

Luma
Myrtaceae

The two South American species of evergreen trees or shrubs that make up this small genus are sometimes found listed under the name *Myrtus*, a genus to which they are closely related. They are natives of Chile and Argentina and have opposite-growing, aromatic leaves. They bear white flowers with conspicuous stamens.

The following is the most commonly seen species in cultivation, and it is best grown as a specimen tree or shrub in an open position. However, if it is grown in cold regions it will benefit from the protection afforded by a wall.

Luma apiculata

This is a fast-growing evergreen shrub or tree, often with several stems from the base. Mature stems bear cinnamon-brown bark, which peels to reveal striking, creamy white patches. The glossy dark green leaves are aromatic when crushed and white flowers with numerous protruding white stamens open over a long period during summer and autumn. These are followed by red and then purple-black, fleshy, edible fruits.

Synonym: *Myrtus luma*
Native range: Argentina, Chile
Height: 10 m (33 ft)
Spread: 10 m (33 ft)
Hardiness: Zone 8
Variants: 'Glanleam Gold' is slower growing and shrubby, with pink-tinged young leaves that become dark green edged with creamy yellow.

---

in late spring, and these are followed by violet-coloured berries. It is a useful plant for ground cover in either sun or shade.

Native range: China
Height: 75 cm (30 in)
Spread: 2 m (6 ft)
Hardiness: Zone 6
Variants: 'Silver Lining' has leaves that are narrowly edged with white.

Lonicera x *purpusii*

This garden-raised hybrid between *L. fragrantissima* and *L. standishii* has dark green leaves remaining late into the season. Creamy white and very fragrant flowers, with yellow anthers, open during winter, and these are sometimes followed by small, red berries in summer.

Height: 2 m (6 ft)
Spread: 3 m (10 ft)
Hardiness: Zone 5
Variants: 'Winter Beauty' flowers very profusely over a long period, from early winter to mid-spring.

Lonicera syringantha

This bushy, spreading deciduous shrub has a graceful habit, with slender, arching shoots bearing blue-green leaves often arranged in whorls of three. The soft pink, bell-shaped, fragrant flowers open in drooping pairs during late spring and early summer, most profusely in a sunny position.

Native range: China
Height: 1.5 m (5 ft)
Spread: 3 m (10 ft)
Hardiness: Zone 4

Magnolia campbellii

Magnolia
Magnoliaceae

The 120 or so species of deciduous and evergreen trees and shrubs that make up this genus are widely distributed in North, Central and South America, as well as from the Himalayas to Southeast Asia. Because of their strikingly attractive, often highly fragrant flowers, some of the trees and shrubs in this genus should ideally be grown as specimens.

In order to do best, magnolias require a good, humus-rich, moist but well-drained soil that is acidic or neutral. They also benefit from the application of mulch around the base. They are usually best grown in a sheltered position, among other trees and shrubs. However, *M. grandiflora* flowers best in full sun. All species may bear fruit clusters in autumn from which glossy, red-coated seeds emerge. The flowers of early-flowering sorts can be damaged by late frosts.

Magnolia campbellii

This is a vigorous deciduous tree of broadly conical habit that produces large, dark green leaves that are bronze when young. The very large, fragrant, pink-coloured flowers, with a characteristic 'cup-and-saucer' shape, open in late winter and early

Magnolia denudata

spring before the leaves emerge. Young trees of this species may take many years to produce flowers.

Native range: Himalayas, China
Height: 20 m (66 ft) or more
Spread: 15 m (50 ft)
Hardiness: Zone 8
Variants: There are several selected grafted forms that produce flowers at an earlier age than seedlings.

'Alba' has white flowers; 'Charles Raffill' purple-pink flowers; and 'Lanarth' deep lilac-purple flowers.

Magnolia denudata

This deciduous shrub or small tree is conical when young, but as it matures takes on more of a spreading or rounded habit. The large, fragrant, pure white, cup-shaped flowers open in spring on the bare shoots, before the new season's leaves start to emerge.

Common names: Lily tree, yulan
Native range: China
Height: 8 m (26 ft)
Spread: 10 m (33 ft)
Hardiness: Zone 5

Magnolia grandiflora

This is an evergreen tree with a conical habit. It produces bold, glossy dark green leaves that are pale to bronzy green beneath or with a dense layer of rust-coloured hairs. The very large and extremely fragrant creamy white, cup-shaped flowers open during the summer and autumn seasons. *M. grandiflora* flowers best and grows to a greater size in regions that experience hot summers, while in cool areas it can be grown or trained against a sunny wall. It is an adaptable species that is also suitable for alkaline soils.

Common name: Bull bay
Native range: SE United States of America
Height: 10 to 20 m (33 to 66 ft) or more
Spread: 10 m (33 ft)

Magnolia liliiflora 'Nigra'

Hardiness: Zone 7
Variants: Numerous selections have been made. These include 'Bracken's Brown Beauty', which is a compact and very hardy conical form with extremely glossy dark green, wavy-edged leaves that are covered with rust-coloured hairs on their undersurfaces. 'Exmouth' is a very hardy form with leaves that are pale green beneath. 'Goliath' produces very large flowers and has rather wavy-edged leaves. 'Little Gem' is compact and upright in habit, up to 5 m (16 ft) in height, with smaller, very dark green leaves, covered in brown hairs beneath, and smaller flowers. 'Victoria' is an extremely hardy form with leaves that are covered in rust-coloured hairs beneath.

Magnolia 'Heaven Scent'

This is a very vigorous, garden-raised hybrid between *M. liliiflora* 'Nigra' and *M. x veitchii*. It makes a small, spreading, attractive deciduous tree with dark green, taper-pointed leaves. The upright, vase-shaped and fragrant flowers are pale pink in colour, shading to deep pink at the flower base. The blooms open during the spring and early summer, either before or just as the young leaves start to emerge.

Height: 10 m (33 ft)
Spread: 10 m (33 ft)
Hardiness: Zone 7

Magnolia 'Heaven Scent'

Magnolia x *loebneri* 'Merrill'

Magnolia kobus

This is a strong-growing deciduous tree with a broadly conical habit that bears dark green leaves on aromatic shoots. The slightly fragrant, creamy white flowers, measuring about 10 cm (4 in) across, are often tinged pink at the base and are held horizontally. The flowers open in early to mid-spring before the leaves emerge. This species is also suitable for alkaline soils.

Native range: Japan, South Korea
Height: 10 m (33 ft)
Spread: 8 m (26 ft)
Hardiness: Zone 4

Magnolia liliiflora

A deciduous shrub of compact, bushy habit with dark green leaves. The slightly fragrant, upright, vase-shaped flowers are red-purple outside and white inside. They start to open in spring with the young leaves and continue well into summer.

Native range: China
Height: 3 m (10 ft)
Spread: 3 m (10 ft)
Hardiness: Zone 5
Variants: 'Nigra' has very deep red-purple flowers opening over a long period into late summer.

Magnolia x loebneri

This is a group of garden-raised hybrids between *M. kobus* and *M. stellata* and it combines some of the best features of both parents. The group is

Magnolia salicifolia

This is a deciduous tree of conical habit with slender, aromatic shoots and dark green leaves, bronzy when young. The leaves are blue-green beneath. The fragrant, pure white flowers are held horizontally, and are about 10 cm (4 in) across. Flowers open in spring before the leaves appear.

Common name: Willow-leaved magnolia
Native range: Japan
Height: 12 m (40 ft)
Spread: 7 m (23 ft)
Hardiness: Zone 4
Variants: 'Wada's Memory' is a very floriferous selection, with red-purple young leaves and large, profusely borne flowers.

Magnolia x soulangeana

This group of garden-raised hybrids between *M. denudata* and *M. liliiflora* contains some of the

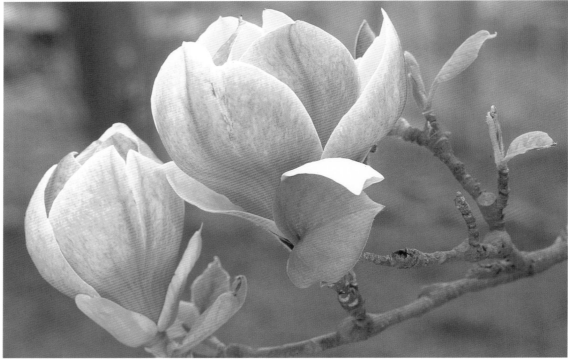

Magnolia x *soulangeana* 'Rustica Rubra'

made up of deciduous shrubs or small trees of upright to spreading habits, with dark green leaves that are bronze-coloured when young. The fragrant flowers open in early to mid-spring and vary in colour from white to pink.

Height: 8 m (26 ft)
Spread: 6 m (20 ft)
Hardiness: Zone 5
Variants: 'Leonard Messel' is spreading and graceful, with lilac-pink flowers with drooping petals that are deeper in bud. 'Merrill' is vigorous and upright, with profusely borne white flowers that are pale pink in bud.

most popular of all the cultivated magnolias. They generally make rounded to spreading deciduous trees that are often multi-stemmed and shrubby in habit, and have broad, dark green leaves. The prominent, upright, goblet-shaped flowers are white, streaked with purple-pink towards their bases. The flowers, which are large and fragrant, begin to open before the young leaves appear and continue as the leaves break in late spring to early summer.

Height: 8 m (26 ft)
Spread: 8 m (26 ft)
Hardiness: Zone 4

Magnolia salicifolia 'Wada's Memory'

Magnolia stellata

Magnolia virginiana

This is a deciduous to semi-evergreen or evergreen tree of conical habit, sometimes shrubby and multi-stemmed, with glossy green leaves that are silvery white beneath. The lemon-scented, creamy white flowers open during summer. This species flowers and grows best in regions with hot summer, where it will grow in wet soils.

Common name: Sweet bay
Native range: E United States of America
Height: 8 m (26 ft)
Spread: 6 m (20 ft)
Hardiness: Zone 5

Magnolia wilsonii

This is a spreading deciduous shrub, often tree-like, with dark green leaves that are velvety beneath. The white, pendulous, cup-shaped

Magnolia stellata

Variants: Popular forms of *M.* x *soulangeana* include 'Alba', which has pure white flowers, 'Lennei', which produces large, purple-pink flowers, and 'Rustica Rubra', which has large, deep red-purple flowers.

Magnolia stellata

This is a very popular garden selection due to its relatively small size and profusely borne flowers. *M. stellata* makes a dense, bushy, rounded, deciduous shrub with dark green, narrow leaves. The fragrant, white, star-like flowers have numerous slender petals and open on the bare branches from distinctly furry buds in early to mid-spring before the new season's leaves emerge.

Common name: Star magnolia
Native range: Japan

Height: 2.5 m (8 ft)
Spread: 3 m (10 ft)
Hardiness: Zone 4
Variants: There are several selections, including 'Rosea', which has pale pink flowers that are deeper coloured in bud, and 'Royal Star', which produces large, white flowers from pink-coloured buds.

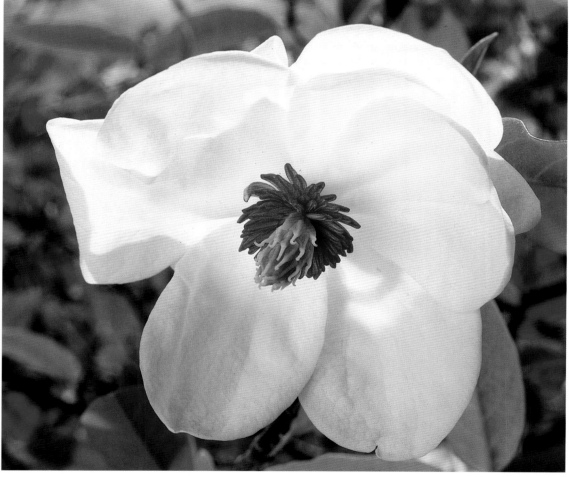

Magnolia wilsonii

flowers, up to 10 cm (4 in) across, have conspicuous centres of red-purple stamens and open with the young leaves in late spring and early summer.

Native range: China
Height: 7 m (23 ft)
Spread: 7 m (23 ft)
Hardiness: Zone 6

Mahonia japonica

leaves are divided up into a maximum of 19 very spiny leaflets. Slender spikes of fragrant, rather pale yellow flowers open in clusters at the ends of the shoots in late autumn and winter, and these are followed by deep blue-purple berries.

Native range: China
Height: 2 m (6 ft)
Spread: 2.5 m (8 ft)
Hardiness: Zone 6

Mahonia x media

These vigorous evergreen shrubs of upright habit are garden-raised hybrids between *M. japonica* and *M. lomariifolia*. Their stout shoots have deeply ridged bark when mature and they bear large, glossy green leaves with up to 21 sharply toothed leaflets. In late autumn and winter the long, clustered spikes of yellow flowers open at the ends of the shoots.

Mahonia
Berberidaceae

The 70 or so species in this genus are evergreen shrubs found in western North America, Central America and in the Himalayas and East Asia. They are grown for their foliage and flowers and often have bold leaves divided into several to numerous leaflets, and small, but usually densely clustered, sometimes fragrant, flowers, usually yellow in colour. Suitable for a border, the larger sorts make impressive specimen shrubs while the lower-growing ones make good ground cover. They will grow in any well-drained soil that is not too dry.

To prune, cut back lightly after flowering if necessary. Leggy plants of *M. aquifolium* can have their older shoots cut back right to ground level.

Mahonia aquifolium

This is a variable evergreen shrub that is thicket-forming and spreads by underground stems. The glossy bright green leaves have up to nine leaflets edged with spiny teeth, and often turn bronzy in winter. Dense, upright clusters of bright yellow flowers open at the ends of the shoots in spring, and these are followed by blue-black berries.

Common name: Oregon grape
Native range: W North America
Height: 1 m (3 ft)
Spread: 2 m (6 ft)
Hardiness: Zone 5
Variants: 'Apollo' is low and spreading, with large clusters of bright yellow flowers. 'Atropurpurea' has leaves that turn to deep red-purple in winter.

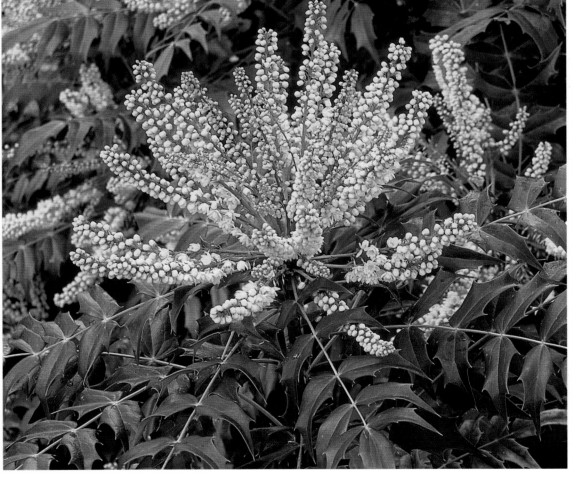
Mahonia x media

'Smaragd' is compact and upright with handsome, glossy foliage and dense flower clusters.

Mahonia japonica

This is a sparsely branched evergreen shrub with stout shoots bearing bold, dark green leaves. The

Height: 4 m (13 ft)
Spread: 5 m (16 ft)
Hardiness: Zone 7
Variants: This hybrid is grown normally only as selected forms, which include 'Buckland', with long, spreading flower spikes; 'Charity', with dense clusters of upright then spreading flower spikes; and 'Winter Sun' with dense, upright spikes.

Malus floribunda

Height: 10 m (33 ft)
Spread: 8 m (26 ft)
Hardiness: Zone 4

Malus hupehensis

This strong-growing tree develops a dense, spreading habit. It has flaking, purple-brown bark and dark green, taper-pointed and finely toothed leaves. Clusters of white, fragrant flowers open in mid-spring from pink buds, and these are followed in autumn by pea-sized, deep red fruits.

Native range: China
Height: 12 m (40 ft)
Spread: 12 m (40 ft)
Hardiness: Zone 4

Malus 'John Downie'

The upright branches of this garden-raised hybrid give it a characteristically narrow crown with bright green foliage, making it useful in confined spaces. Clusters of white flowers open from soft pink buds in late spring, and these are followed by egg-shaped, orange-yellow fruits flushed with red.

Height: 9 m (30 ft)
Spread: 5 m (16 ft)
Hardiness: Zone 4

Malus
Rosaceae

The crab apples are a genus of about 35 species of deciduous trees and shrubs found in temperate regions of the northern hemisphere.

Grown for their flowers, fruit, and sometimes their ornamental foliage, they provide some very tough and easy-to-grow trees that are particularly useful for small gardens. They are suitable for any good, well-drained soil and do best in full sun.

Malus floribunda

This popular crab apple is a hybrid of Japanese origin. It makes a bushy headed small tree of dense, spreading habit with dark green, taper-pointed leaves opening from arching shoots. Masses of small, white flowers, pale pink at first, open from deep red buds in mid-spring, and these are followed by small, yellow fruits.

Common name: Japanese crab apple
Height: 6 m (20 ft)
Spread: 8 m (26 ft)
Hardiness: Zone 4

Malus 'Golden Hornet'

Malus 'Golden Hornet'

This vigorous, garden-raised hybrid makes a rounded tree, upright when young, with bright green, sharply toothed leaves. The white flowers in late spring are 4 cm (1½ in) across and open from deep pink buds. They are followed by profuse, spherical, deep yellow fruits 2.5 cm (1 in) across.

Malus 'Royalty'

This is one of the best of all the purple-leaved crab apples. It is a garden-raised hybrid that makes a small, spreading tree with arching shoots bearing glossy red-purple leaves that are sometimes lobed. The leaves retain their colour right through summer until they turn red in the autumn. Deep red-purple flowers open from prominent red buds in mid- to late spring, and these are followed by deep purple-coloured fruits.

Height: 6 m (20 ft)
Spread: 8 m (26 ft)
Hardiness: Zone 4

Malus tschonoskii

Popular for its narrow habit and good autumn colour, this crab apple is frequently seen as a street-planted tree, but it can also make a useful addition to a small garden. It develops a broadly conical habit with upright branches bearing glossy green leaves, grey and hairy when young and turning to bright red, yellow and purple in autumn. Clusters of white flowers, flushed with pink, open in late spring, and these are followed by yellow-green fruits flushed with red.

Native range: Japan
Height: 15 m (50 ft)
Spread: 8 m (26 ft)
Hardiness: Zone 4

Mespilus
Rosaceae

The single species in this genus is a small tree or shrub grown for its picturesque habit, its flowers and its unusual, edible fruits. It is suitable for any reasonably good, well-drained soil, and it prefers a sunny position. It is usually grown as forms selected for the quality and size of their fruits, which are edible only after the first frosts.

Mespilus germanica

This is a deciduous tree with a spreading habit, sometimes having spiny shoots, and, on mature plants, flaking bark. The bold leaves are dark green in colour, turning yellow-brown in autumn. Large, white flowers, 5 cm (2 in) across, open singly at the ends of the shoots in late spring and early summer, and sometimes there is a repeat flowering in late summer. The russet-brown fruits, with sunken tips and conspicuous, projecting sepals, ripen in the late autumn and early winter.

Common name: Medlar
Native range: SW Asia, SE Europe
Height: 6 m (20 ft)
Spread: 8 m (26 ft)
Hardiness: Zone 5
Variants: Selections recommended for their fruit include 'Dutch' and 'Nottingham'.

Malus hupehensis

Mespilus germanica 'Nottingham'

Mitraria
Gesneriaceae

This small genus is made up of just a single species – an evergreen shrub with opposite leaves that is grown for its attractive and showy flowers.

It requires a cool, moist but well-drained, lime-free soil, and it does best if provided with a bright position. In drier regions, however, it may require a more shaded spot in which to grow. In areas that experience mild winters and cool, moist summers, it can sometimes climb vigorously.

Apart from the removal of any dead, damaged or unwanted wood, little in the way of pruning is usually necessary, but it can be trimmed back lightly before the new season's growth starts in spring if required.

Mitraria coccinea

This is an evergreen shrub with trailing shoots that will often climb over low shrubs if it finds the conditions favourable. It bears toothed, glossy dark green leaves. The long-stalked, bright red, tubular-shaped flowers have protruding yellow anthers and open in late spring and early summer and, intermittently, until autumn.

Native range: Chile, Argentina
Height: 1.5 m (5 ft) or more
Spread: 2 m (6 ft)
Hardiness: Zone 8

Morus nigra

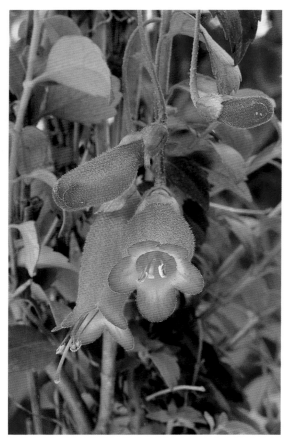
Mitraria coccinea

Morus
Moraceae

The mulberries are a small, widely distributed genus made up of some ten species of deciduous trees and shrubs, natives of North and South America, Africa, southern Europe and Asia. The individual flowers are small but are borne in profuse clusters, the males and females on the same or separate plants, and these are followed by dense clusters of edible fruits.

They are grown for their attractive foliage as well as their fruits, and are suitable for any reasonably good, well-drained soil. They do best if provided with a position in full sun.

Morus alba

This is a spreading deciduous tree with smooth, glossy bright green, toothed and taper-pointed leaves that turn yellow in autumn. The small, dense, drooping clusters of tiny, greenish flowers open in early summer, and these are followed by cylindrical, white to pink or red, edible fruits.

Common name: White mulberry
Native range: China
Height: 10 m (33 ft)
Spread: 12 m (40 ft)
Hardiness: Zone 5
Variants: 'Pendula' is a smaller-growing selection, weeping in habit and reaching up to about 3 m (10 ft) in height, with shoots hanging right down to the ground.

Morus nigra

This is a spreading deciduous tree that bears broad, heart-shaped, dark green leaves that are roughly hairy on both sides and edged with numerous teeth. Small, pendulous clusters of greenish-coloured flowers open in the early summer, and these are followed by dense, edible, blackish-red fruits. This is the best species to grow for edible fruits.

Common name: Black mulberry
Native range: Uncertain, but probably SW Asia
Height: 10 m (33 ft)
Spread: 12 m (40 ft)
Hardiness: Zone 5

Morus nigra

Myrtus
Myrtaceae

This is a small genus made up of two species of evergreen, aromatic shrubs, with opposite leaves, natives of the Mediterranean region and Southwest Asia. Only the following is commonly cultivated. It has handsome foliage and flowers and is suitable for any well-drained soil in a sunny position. It can be used as a specimen or grown in a border. In areas where it is not fully hardy, it does best when grown against a sunny wall. Prune in spring before growth starts.

Myrtus communis

This is a vigorous and bushy evergreen shrub with glossy dark green, pointed leaves that are very aromatic when crushed. The fragrant, white flowers, with their dense central clusters of white stamens, are borne on slender stalks in summer, followed by fleshy, purple-black berries.

Common name: Common myrtle
Native range: Mediterranean region
Height: 3 m (10 ft)
Spread: 4 m (13 ft)
Hardiness: Zone 8
Variants: The subsp. *tarentina* (Tarentum myrtle) is compact and has small leaves, pink-flushed flowers and white fruits. 'Variegata' has leaves edged with creamy white.

Myrtus communis

Myrtus communis subsp. *tarentina*

Nandina
Berberidaceae

The single species in this genus is an evergreen shrub grown for its attractive foliage as well as its flowers and fruits. It is suitable for any well-drained soil, and shows the best foliage colour, as well as flowering and fruiting better, in sun rather than shade. It is ideal for a sunny border or for growing against a wall. The low-growing, compact forms make good ground cover. Cutting back lightly in spring will encourage a compact habit.

Nandina domestica

This is an evergreen shrub with upright shoots bearing bold leaves divided into numerous slender, blue-green leaflets. Leaves are bronzy when young and they often turn red-purple in winter. Conical panicles of small, white flowers in summer are followed by bright red berries that persist through winter. It flowers and fruits best in areas that experience hot summers.

Common name: Sacred bamboo
Native range: China, Japan
Height: 2 m (6 ft)
Spread: 1.5 m (5 ft)
Hardiness: Zone 6
Variants: 'Fire Power' is one of several dwarf selections, reaching 60 cm (24 in) tall with bright red winter foliage.

Nandina domestica 'Fire Power'

Neillia
Rosaceae

The ten species in this genus are thicket-forming, deciduous shrubs with lobed leaves. They are natives of the Himalayas and East Asia and are grown for their clusters of small, pink flowers. Easy to grow in any reasonably good, well-drained soil they are suitable for the shrub border. Cut back some of the older shoots to the base after flowering.

Neillia thibetica

This vigorous deciduous shrub forms dense clumps of arching shoots with peeling bark and has dark green, sharply toothed and lobed leaves. Large clusters of small, bell-shaped, pink flowers open in late spring and early summer.

Native range: China
Height: 2 m (6 ft)
Spread: 2 m (6 ft)
Hardiness: Zone 5

Nothofagus
Fagaceae

The 34 species in this genus include both deciduous and evergreen trees. They have a wide distribution in the southern hemisphere, stretching from South America to Australia, New Zealand, New Caledonia and New Guinea. They provide gardens with some splendid foliage trees, with the deciduous species giving good autumn colour as well. Grow plants in a good, moist but well-drained, lime-free soil, in a site sheltered from strong winds – perhaps among other trees.

Nothofagus alpina

This is a vigorous deciduous tree with a broadly conical habit. It bears deep green leaves, up to 10 cm (4 in) long, with conspicuous veins in numerous parallel pairs. Bronze when young, the leaves turn to orange and yellow in autumn. Separate, inconspicuous male and female flowers open on the same tree in late spring.

Synonyms: *Nothofagus nervosa, Nothofagus procera*
Common name: Rauli
Native range: Chile, Argentina
Height: 25 m (80 ft)
Spread: 12 m (40 ft)
Hardiness: Zone 7

Nothofagus antarctica

This is a deciduous tree with a conical habit, often shrubby and branching low down. It has glossy dark green leaves that turn yellow in autumn. The attractive leaves are shallowly lobed, wavy edged and have fine teeth at their margins. Small flower clusters – the males and females being borne separately on the same tree – open in the late spring.

Common name: Antarctic beech
Native range: S Chile, S Argentina
Height: 15 m (50 ft)
Spread: 8 m (26 ft)
Hardiness: Zone 7

Nothofagus antarctica

Nothofagus dombeyi

This is a large and fast-growing, broadly conical tree with dark grey bark that cracks with age. The small, glossy dark green leaves have tiny spots on their undersurfaces and they are edged with fine, sharp teeth. Small flower clusters, males and females borne separately on the same tree, open in the late spring.

Native range: Chile, Argentina
Height: 20 m (65 ft)
Spread: 15 m (50 ft)
Hardiness: Zone 8

Nothofagus obliqua

This is a vigorously growing, large deciduous tree with pale grey bark that flakes on mature trees. The dark green leaves, which are blue-green on their undersurfaces, each have eight to ten parallel veins. Leaves turn clear yellow in autumn. Small flower clusters, the males and females borne separately on the same tree, open in late spring. The tree can come into growth early in the season, when it will be susceptible to damage by late spring frosts.

Common name: Roble beech
Native range: Argentina, Chile
Height: 20 m (65 ft)
Spread: 15 m (50 ft)
Hardiness: Zone 8

Nothofagus obliqua

Nyssa sylvatica

Nyssa
Cornaceae

This is a small genus made up of five species of deciduous tree from the east of North America and China. The following species are grown for their striking autumn colour. The tiny, green flowers are borne in long-stalked clusters, males and females separate but on the same tree, and these are followed by small, bluish fruits.

These trees require a moist, lime-free soil and colour best in a sunny position. Nyssas should always be planted when small. Remove dead or damaged wood in autumn.

Nyssa sinensis

This medium-sized deciduous tree has a broad to spreading habit, often with several stems and branching from low down. The narrow, taper-pointed, deep green leaves are up to 20 cm (8 in) long. These attractive leaves are bronze when young and then turn to brilliant shades of orange, red and yellow in autumn.

Common name: Chinese tupelo
Native range: China
Height: 10 m (33 ft)
Spread: 12 m (40 ft)
Hardiness: Zone 6

Nyssa sylvatica

This is a slow-growing deciduous tree of conical to columnar habit, the lower branches often drooping. The variable leaves are up to 15 cm (6 in) long and end in a short point. Glossy dark green above, blue-green beneath, leaves turn to orange, red and yellow in autumn. Inconspicuous flowers are followed by blue-black berries,

Common names: Black gum, sour gum, tupelo
Native range: E North America
Height: 15 m (50 ft) or more
Spread: 12 m (40 ft) or more
Hardiness: Zone 4

Olearia
Compositae

The 130 or so species in this genus are evergreen shrubs, occasionally trees, or herbaceous perennials, from New Zealand and Australia. Grown for their foliage and their daisy-like, usually white flowerheads, they are ideal for the shrub border, or the larger ones for specimen planting.

They require a well-drained soil in a sunny position, while in colder regions they need shelter from strong winds. In mild, coastal areas O. x *haastii* and O. *macrodonta* can be used for hedging. To restrict their growth, prune in spring as the new growth starts to emerge.

Olearia avicenniifolia

This vigorous evergreen shrub has white-hairy shoots and deep grey-green leaves, to 10 cm (4 in) long, densely covered with white hairs beneath. The small, fragrant, white, daisy-like flowerheads are borne in broad clusters during summer.

Native range: New Zealand
Height: 4 m (13 ft)
Spread: 3 m (10 ft)
Hardiness: Zone 8

Olearia x haastii

A naturally occurring hybrid between O. *avicenniifolia* and O. *moschata* that makes a dense, bushy evergreen shrub. Its white shoots are densely covered with small, leathery, glossy green leaves, which are also white beneath. Clusters of white, daisy-like flowerheads, yellow in the centre, open in mid- to late summer.

Native range: New Zealand
Height: 2 m (6 ft)
Spread: 2.5 m (8 ft)
Hardiness: Zone 8

Olearia macrodonta

This vigorous evergreen shrub, sometimes tree-like, has flaking bark and leathery, dark grey-green, aromatic, holly-like leaves – white beneath and edged with pointed teeth. Broad clusters of fragrant, white, daisy-like flowerheads with small, reddish centres open in early summer.

Common name: New Zealand holly
Native range: New Zealand
Height: 5 m (16 ft)
Spread: 4 m (13 ft)
Hardiness: Zone 8

Olearia x haastii

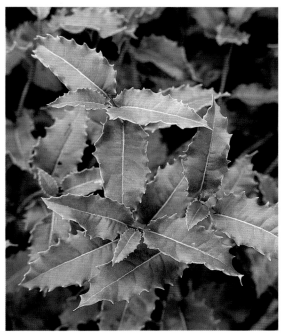

Olearia macrodonta

Olearia nummulariifolia

This is a densely branched, evergreen shrub with a rounded habit. The plant has stout, upright shoots bearing small, leathery, dark green leaves. The white undersides of the leaves are partly hidden by the recurved leaf edges. The small, daisy-like, white flowerheads, which have yellowish centres, are attractively fragrant and open in mid-summer.

Native range: New Zealand
Height: 2 m (6 ft)
Spread: 2.5 m (8 ft)
Hardiness: Zone 8

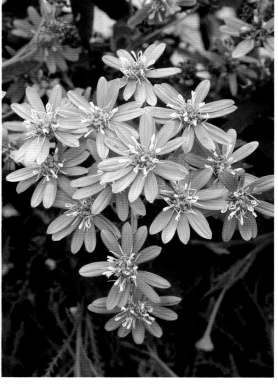

Olearia phlogopappa Splendens Group

Olearia phlogopappa

This evergreen shrub has upright, white-felted shoots and grey-green, wavy edged leaves. The undersurfaces of the oblong-shaped leaves are covered in white hairs. Large and showy clusters of usually white, daisy-like flowerheads, yellow in the centre, open in profusion in mid- to late spring.

Native range: SE Australia, Tasmania
Height: 2.5 m (8 ft)
Spread: 2 m (6 ft)
Hardiness: Zone 8
Variants: Forms of O. *phlogopappa* that have coloured flowerheads are known as Splendens Group. These include 'Comber's Blue', which produces heads of blue flowers, and 'Comber's Pink', which bears pink flowerheads.

Olearia x scilloniensis

This is a garden-raised hybrid between O. *lirata* and O. *phlogopappa*. It makes a vigorous evergreen shrub, upright at first, later becoming more rounded in habit, with slender, grey-green, wavy edged leaves that have white undersurfaces. The extremely profuse and showy, daisy-like, white-coloured flowerheads, yellow in the centre, open in large clusters in the late spring. This shrub does best if it is cut back lightly after flowering has finished.

Height: 2.5 m (8 ft)
Spread: 2 m (6 ft)
Hardiness: Zone 8

Osmanthus
Oleaceae

This is a genus made up of about 30 species of evergreen shrubs and trees with opposite leaves, natives of the southeast of the United States of America, East Asia and the Pacific Islands. Often of holly-like appearance, these shrubs and trees are grown principally for their foliage and fragrant flowers. They make suitable subjects for the shrub border or they can be grown as specimens among other trees and plants. They can be grown in any reasonably good, well-drained soil, but they will require some shelter from strong wind in cold regions. *O.* x *burkwoodii* and *O. heterophyllus* can be used for hedging.

Pruning is not usually required, apart from the removal of dead, damaged or diseased wood. If necessary, prune spring-flowering species after flowering, *O. heterophyllus* in spring. Cut hedges as necessary during the summer.

Osmanthus x burkwoodii

This is an attractive, garden-raised hybrid between *O. delavayi* and *O. decorus*. It makes a dense and bushy shrub with a rounded habit and bears leathery, dark green, tooth-edged leaves. Clusters of white, tubular, very fragrant flowers open in mid- to late spring.

Height: 3 m (10 ft)
Spread: 4 m (13 ft)
Hardiness: Zone 6

Osmanthus delavayi

This is a rather slow-growing, rigidly branched evergreen shrub with a spreading habit, and bears small, glossy dark green, leathery leaves edged with small teeth. Clusters of pure white and very fragrant, tubular-shaped flowers open in mid- to late spring, and these are sometimes followed by small, blue-black, egg-shaped fruits. This species is suitable for growing against a wall.

Native range: China
Height: 2 m (6 ft) or more
Spread: 3 m (10 ft)
Hardiness: Zone 7

Osmanthus x fortunei

This is a vigorous, garden-raised hybrid between *O. fragrans* and *O. heterophyllus* making a large evergreen shrub, sometimes tree-like. The bold, glossy dark green, holly-like leaves are sharply toothed on young plants, but they become

Osmanthus x *burkwoodii*

Osmanthus heterophyllus 'Variegatus'

Osmanthus delavayi

untoothed towards the tops of mature plants. Clusters of small, white, very fragrant flowers open in the autumn.

Height: 5 m (16 ft)
Spread: 4 m (13 ft)
Hardiness: Zone 7

Osmanthus heterophyllus

This is an evergreen holly-like shrub with a dense, upright to rounded habit, sometimes tree-like in stature. *O. heterophyllus* has glossy dark green leaves edged with spiny teeth, but becoming spineless towards the tops of mature plants. Small, white, fragrant flowers open during the autumn.

Native range: Japan
Height: 5 m (16 ft) or more
Spread: 4 m (13 ft)
Hardiness: Zone 6
Variants: 'Aureomarginatus' has attractively yellow-edged leaves. 'Goshiki' ('Tricolor') has leaves that are mottled with yellow, bronze when young. 'Purpureus' has glossy, deep purple young foliage. 'Variegatus' has leaves that are edged with creamy white.

Osmanthus heterophyllus 'Goshiki'

Oxydendrum
Ericaceae

The single species in this genus is grown for its late flowers and its autumn colour. It requires a moist but well-drained, acidic and humus-rich soil. Although shade-tolerant, it flowers and produces its best autumn colour in a sunny position.

Oxydendrum arboreum

This is a deciduous tree of conical habit, sometimes shrubby, with deeply furrowed bark when mature. Its bold, dark green, finely toothed leaves, up to 20 cm (8 in) long, turn to shades of orange, red and purple in autumn. Small, urn-shaped, fragrant, white flowers open in large clusters at the ends of the shoots in autumn, or in summer in hot regions.

Common name: Sorrel tree
Native range: E North America
Height: 10 m (33 ft)
Spread: 6 m (20 ft)
Hardiness: Zone 5

Ozothamnus
Compositae

A genus of some 50 species of evergreen shrubs related to *Helichrysum* and grown for their attractive, sometimes aromatic foliage and their small, but usually clustered flowerheads. The following species require well-drained soil and a sunny position sheltered from strong winds. They can be pruned in spring if necessary.

Ozothamnus ledifolius

This strongly aromatic, small, rounded shrub has a dense habit, with yellowish shoots and small, dark green leaves, yellow beneath. Dense clusters of small, white flowerheads open in early summer.

Common name: Kerosene bush
Native range: Tasmania
Height: 1.2 m (4 ft)
Spread: 1.5 m (5 ft)
Hardiness: Zone 8

Ozothamnus rosmarinifolius

This is a vigorous evergreen shrub with upright shoots covered in white hairs, and densely arranged, narrow, dark green, rosemary-like leaves

Pachysandra terminalis

that are white beneath. Dense clusters of small, fragrant, white flowerheads open from striking red buds in the early summer.

Native range: SE Australia, Tasmania
Height: 3 m (10 ft)
Spread: 2 m (6 ft)
Hardiness: Zone 8

Pachysandra
Buxaceae

The four or five species that make up this small genus are evergreen or semi-evergreen subshrubs and herbaceous perennials from China, Japan and the southeast of the United States of America. The following is a useful groundcover plant in shady places, where it is grown for its foliage and flowers. It should be planted in a shaded or partially shaded site in a moist but well-drained soil rich in organic matter.

Pachysandra terminalis

This evergreen subshrub spreads vigorously by underground stems. It has glossy dark green, leathery leaves concentrated towards the ends of short, upright shoots. Clusters of small, white flowers open at the ends of the shoots during the spring and early summer.

Native range: China, Japan
Height: 25 cm (10 in)
Spread: 3 m (10 ft) or more
Hardiness: Zone 4
Variants: 'Green Carpet' is a very compact form, good for ground cover. 'Variegata' is less vigorous and its leaves are edged with white.

Paeonia
Paeoniaceae

The peonies are a genus of some 30 species of mainly herbaceous perennials, natives of East Asia and the west of North America. The shrubby species, often referred to as tree peonies, are deciduous, sparsely branched plants that spread by suckers, and are grown for their showy flowers and bold, deeply cut leaves. Suitable for any good, well-drained soil they are excellent border plants. Little pruning is necessary but wayward branches on vigorous plants can be cut back in early spring before growth starts. Foliage, particularly of forms of *P. suffruticosa*, can emerge very early in the year and is then subject to damage by late frosts.

Paeonia delavayi

This is an upright, deciduous shrub with large, dark green leaves, blue-green on their undersides, deeply cut into slender, pointed segments. The nodding, cup-shaped flowers, which open in early summer, are coloured deep red and have conspicuous centres composed of golden anthers.

Native range: China
Height: 2 m (6 ft)
Spread: 2 m (6 ft)
Hardiness: Zone 6

Paeonia lutea var. *ludlowii*

This vigorous deciduous shrub has stout shoots and deep green leaves that are deeply cut into slender-pointed lobes. Large, yellow, cup-shaped flowers, 12 cm (5 in) across, open in late spring.

Common name: Tibetan peony
Native range: Tibet
Height: 2.5 m (8 ft)
Spread: 4 m (13 ft)
Hardiness: Zone 6

Paeonia suffruticosa

This is a sparsely branched deciduous shrub with stout, upright shoots bearing large, deep green leaves. The leaves are bronze when they are young and are cut into pointed lobes. The very large flowers, sometimes growing up to 30 cm (12 in) across, can be single to semi-double or double. Flowers vary in colour, ranging from white to pink and red.

Common name: Moutan peony
Native range: China
Height: 2 m (6 ft)
Spread: 2 m (6 ft)
Hardiness: Zone 7

Parahebe
Scrophulariaceae

This southern hemisphere genus is made up of about 30 species of evergreen subshrubs and herbaceous perennials. All plants are natives of Australasia and have opposite leaves. They are closely related to *Hebe* and *Veronica*.

Grown for their small flowers, they are suitable for any well-drained soil in a sunny position. They make excellent rock garden plants.

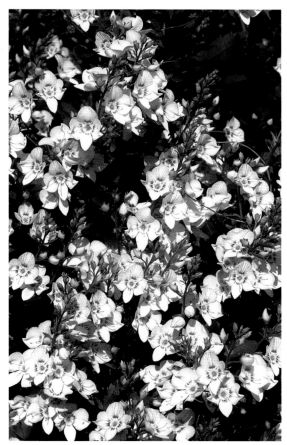

Parahebe cattaractae

Parahebe cattaractae

This is an evergreen or semi-evergreen subshrub with a sprawling habit, and with slender, upright, purple shoots and glossy green, oval-shaped and toothed leaves. The small, funnel-shaped flowers, which bloom in upright, open clusters during the summer, vary in colour from white to pink or blue. The flowers are often prominently veined with pink or purple.

Native range: New Zealand
Height: 30 cm (12 in)
Spread: 60 cm (24 in)
Hardiness: Zone 8
Variants: The form 'Delight' bears blue-coloured, summer-opening flowers.

Parahebe perfoliata

This is an evergreen, clump-forming subshrub, which is sometimes known as *Veronica perfoliata*. It produces attractively arching and usually unbranched shoots bearing rounded, blue-green leaves with overlapping bases. The slender, branched spikes of deep blue flowers open in the late summer.

Common name: Digger's speedwell
Native range: SE Australia
Height: 60 cm (24 in)
Spread: 1 m (3 ft)
Hardiness: Zone 8

Paeonia delavayi

Parrotia
Hamamelidaceae

The single species in this genus is a deciduous tree grown for its handsome foliage, which colours well in autumn, as well as for its bark and unusual winter flowers. Suitable for growing as a specimen tree in woodland conditions, the species requires a moist but well-drained, preferably lime-free soil.

Parrotia persica

This is a deciduous tree with a spreading habit, often branching low down, with grey-brown bark flaking on mature plants to leave creamy white patches. Its glossy green leaves, which are often edged with red when young, turn to brilliant shades of orange, yellow, red and purple in autumn. Small, red flower clusters open on the bare shoots during winter and early spring.

Common name: Persian ironwood
Native range: Caucasus, N Iran
Height: 10 m (33 ft)
Spread: 12 m (40 ft)
Hardiness: Zone 5

Paulownia
Scrophulariaceae

The six species that make up this small genus are all deciduous trees. They have stout shoots and bold, opposite leaves, and are grown principally for their flowers.

The following species is excellent as a specimen tree and does best in a good, deep, well-drained soil in a sunny position, preferably sheltered from strong winds among other trees. By cutting back annually in early spring it can be grown as a foliage plant, producing enormous leaves.

Paulownia tomentosa

This vigorous deciduous tree bears bold, angled, dark green leaves up to 30 cm (12 in) long. The large, foxglove-like, pale purple flowers, marked with yellow on the insides, are borne in large, upright clusters before the leaves emerge. Many plants grown as *P. fargesii* are, in fact, *P. tomentosa*.

Common names: Empress tree, foxglove tree, princess tree
Native range: China
Height: 15 m (50 ft)
Spread: 10 m (33 ft)
Hardiness: Zone 6

Parrotia persica

Perovskia
Labiatae

The seven species in this genus are all deciduous subshrubs with opposite, aromatic leaves, and are native from Southwest Asia to the Himalayas.

The following is grown for its attractive foliage and small, profusely borne flowers. It is ideal for planting in groups in a dry border or against a sunny wall. It is suitable for any not-too-rich, well-drained soil in full sun. Cut back to just above the base in spring, as the new foliage starts to emerge.

Perovskia atriplicifolia

This deciduous subshrub has upright shoots densely covered in white hairs, and bearing toothed, grey-green, aromatic leaves. Large, open clusters of deep violet-blue flowers open in the late summer and early autumn.

Native range: W Himalayas
Height: 1.5 m (5 ft)
Spread: 1 m (3 ft)
Hardiness: Zone 5
Variants: 'Blue Spire' has deeply cut leaves and very large flower clusters.

Perovskia atriplicifolia 'Blue Spire'

Philadelphus
Hydrangeaceae

The mock oranges include about 65 species of deciduous shrubs with opposite leaves, from eastern Europe, Asia and North and Central America. Grown for their often very fragrant, white or pink-blotched flowers, double in some forms, they make ideal border or specimen plants.

They are suitable for any good, well-drained soil. They mainly benefit from regular pruning – cut back some of the older shoots to ground level in spring before growth starts, leaving the younger shoots to flower. To renovate old plants, cut all the shoots to the base, but the plant will then not flower until the following year.

Philadelphus 'Beauclerk'

This vigorous, garden-raised hybrid is a deciduous shrub with arching shoots bearing dark green leaves. Large, single, white flowers, up to 7.5 cm (2 in) across, flushed pink at the base of the petals, open in clusters during early to mid-summer.

Height: 2 m (6 ft)
Spread: 2.5 m (8 ft)
Hardiness: Zone 5

Philadelphus coronarius 'Aureus'

Philadelphus 'Belle Etoile'

A compact deciduous shrub with arching shoots bearing dark green, toothed or untoothed leaves. The very fragrant, white flowers in late spring and early summer are cupped at first, later opening more widely, and are conspicuously blotched with red-purple in their centres.

Height: 1.5 m (5 ft)
Spread: 2 m (6 ft)
Hardiness: Zone 5

Philadelphus coronarius

This is a large-growing deciduous shrub with upright shoots, dark green, toothed leaves, and peeling bark on the older branches. Creamy white and very fragrant flowers, about 2.5 cm (1 in) across, open in clusters at the ends of the shoots in the early summer. In its typical form, this species has largely been replaced by hybrids and it is now most commonly seen in the forms listed below.

Native range: SE Europe, SW Asia
Height: 3.5 m (11 ft)
Spread: 2.5 m (8 ft)
Hardiness: Zone 4

Philadelphus 'Manteau d'Hermine'

Philadelphus 'Virginal'

Variants: 'Aureus' has golden yellow foliage but may scorch in full sun. 'Variegatus' is slower growing and has creamy white-edged leaves.

Philadelphus 'Innocence'

A garden-raised hybrid making a deciduous shrub with upright, later arching, shoots and bright green leaves blotched and mottled with yellow. Clusters of very fragrant, cup-shaped, white flowers, 4 cm (1½ in) across, open in early to mid-summer.

Height: 2.5 m (8 ft)
Spread: 2.5 m (8 ft)
Hardiness: Zone 5

Philadelphus 'Manteau d'Hermine'

This garden-raised hybrid is a dwarf deciduous shrub with small, dark green leaves. The double, fragrant, creamy white flowers are produced in small clusters during early to mid-summer.

Height: 1 m (3 ft)
Spread: 1.2 m (4 ft)
Hardiness: Zone 5

Philadelphus microphyllus

This is a very distinct species that makes a dense bush with slender, upright shoots bearing small, untoothed, bright green leaves. The leaves are grey with hairs beneath. The small, very fragrant flowers, only about 2.5 cm (1 in) across, are borne singly on the shoots, but only in profusion if the shrub is grown in a hot, sunny position.

Native range: SW United States of America
Height: 1 m (3 ft)
Spread: 1.5 m (5 ft)
Hardiness: Zone 6

Philadelphus 'Sybille'

A popular garden-raised hybrid that makes a graceful deciduous shrub with arching, pink shoots and dark green, nearly untoothed leaves. The showy, white and very fragrant, saucer-shaped flowers, about 5 cm (2 in) across, are marked with deep purple-pink at the base of the petals and are profusely borne during early to mid-summer.

Height: 1.2 m (4 ft)
Spread: 1.5 m (5 ft)
Hardiness: Zone 5

Philadelphus 'Virginal'

This is a very vigorous deciduous shrub of upright habit, with sharply toothed to nearly untoothed leaves. The large, white, double or semi-double, fragrant flowers, 5 cm (2 in) across, open in clusters in mid-summer.

Height: 3 m (10 ft) or more
Spread: 2.5 m (8 ft)
Hardiness: Zone 5

Phlomis
Labiatae

This is a genus of some 100 species of shrubs and herbaceous perennials with opposite leaves, natives of Europe, Asia and North Africa. The following species are not only attractive foliage plants, but they are also grown for their whorled, two-lipped flowers.

Suitable for a border or for growing against a wall, they require well-drained soil in full sun.

Little pruning is usually required but stray branches may occasionally need removing. To rejuvenate old plants, cut back hard in spring.

Phlomis fruticosa

This compact, mound-forming evergreen shrub has stout, upright shoots densely covered in grey hairs and sage-like, grey-green, deeply veined leaves. Large, deep yellow flowers open in dense whorls along the shoots in summer.

Common name: Jerusalem sage
Native range: E Mediterranean region
Height: 1.2 m (4 ft)
Spread: 1.5 m (5 ft)
Hardiness: Zone 7

Phlomis italica

This is an evergreen shrub with upright shoots covered in white, woolly hairs and slender, grey-white, woolly leaves. Whorls of pale lilac-pink flowers open along the shoots in summer.

Native range: Balearic Islands
Height: 60 cm (24 in)
Spread: 45 cm (18 in)
Hardiness: Zone 8

Photinia
Rosaceae

The 40 species in this genus are deciduous and evergreen trees and shrubs, native from the Himalayas to East and Southeast Asia.

The evergreen species are mainly grown for their often attractively coloured young foliage, with forms of *P.* x *fraseri* being useful for hedging. *P. villosa* is grown for its fruits and autumn colour. Grow in any well-drained soil, although *P. villosa* needs lime-free soil. Cut hedges as necessary.

Photinia davidiana

This is a vigorous evergreen tree or tree-like shrub, with dark green, leathery leaves that usually turn red before they fall. Broad clusters of small, white flowers in summer are followed by small, long-persistent, crimson-coloured fruits.

Synonym: *Stranvaesia davidiana*
Native range: China
Height: 6 m (20 ft)
Spread: 5 m (16 ft)
Hardiness: Zone 6

Photinia x fraseri 'Red Robin'

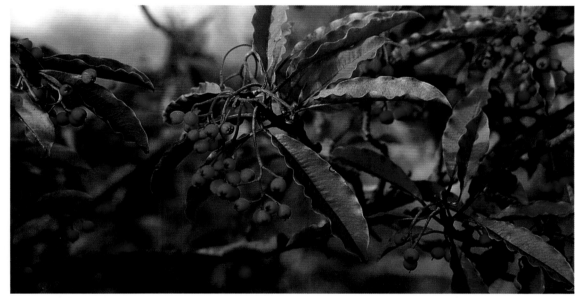

Photinia davidiana

Variants: 'Palette' is smaller in size and slower growing, up to about 3 m (10 ft), with leaves that are variously blotched with creamy white.

Photinia x fraseri

This garden-raised hybrid between *P. glabra* and *P. serratifolia* makes a small evergreen tree or large shrub, with bright red young foliage maturing to dark green. Small, white flowers open in flattened heads during the spring, sometimes followed by small, red fruits. On mature plants, the young foliage is bronze rather than bright red.

Height: 6 m (20 ft)
Spread: 5 m (16 ft)

Hardiness: Zone 7
Variants: 'Birmingham', 'Red Robin' and 'Robusta' are recommended forms.

Photinia villosa

A spreading deciduous tree with finely toothed, taper-pointed, dark green leaves, often bronze or bronze-edged when young, turning to bright orange and red in autumn. Small, white flowers in late spring are followed by egg-shaped red berries.

Native range: China, Japan, Korea
Height: 5 m (16 ft)
Spread: 6 m (20 ft)
Hardiness: Zone 4

Phygelius x *rectus* 'Salmon Leap'

Phygelius
Scrophulariaceae

The two species that make up this genus are both evergreen shrubs with opposite leaves, and are natives of South Africa.

Grown for their showy, tubular flowers, they require a well-drained but moist, light soil and they do best if given a sunny position. In good conditions they can spread extensively by suckers. In cold areas they may be deciduous or herbaceous, dying down to ground level during winter. Shrubs usually grow taller if they are planted against a sunny wall. Unpruned plants can become tall and leggy and grow best if they are cut back hard in spring as the young growth emerges. Removing spent flowerheads will often prolong the flowering period.

Phygelius aequalis

This is a suckering shrub with upright, angled shoots and dark green leaves. One-sided spikes of tubular flowers, up to 6 cm (2½ in) long, red to pink outside, yellow in the throat, open during summer and early autumn.

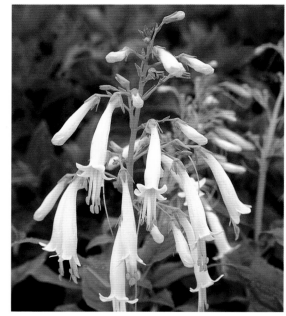

Phygelius x *rectus* 'Moonraker'

Native range: South Africa
Height: 1 m (3 ft)
Spread: 1 m (3 ft)
Hardiness: Zone 8
Variants: 'Sensation' ('Sani Pass') bears deep magenta-purple flowers. 'Trewidden Pink' has dusky pink flowers. 'Yellow Trumpet' produces pale yellow flowers.

Phygelius capensis

This vigorous shrub has angled, upright shoots and glossy dark green leaves. The long, upright spikes of orange-red, tubular flowers, yellow in the throat, open on all sides of the spike over a long period during the summer and early autumn.

Common name: Cape figwort
Native range: South Africa
Height: 1.2 m (4 ft)
Spread: 1 m (3 ft)
Hardiness: Zone 8

Phygelius x rectus

These garden-raised hybrids between *P. aequalis* and *P. capensis* make suckering shrubs with upright shoots bearing dark green leaves and spikes of tubular-shaped flowers. It is mainly grown as the selected forms listed below, with flowers varying in colour from yellow to orange, pink or red.

Height: 1–1.2 m (3–4 ft)
Spread: 1 m (3 ft)
Hardiness: Zone 8
Variants: 'African Queen' produces pale red flowers. 'Devil's Tears' has deep pinkish-red flowers. 'Moonraker' has pale yellow flowers. 'Salmon Leap' has orange flowers. 'Sunshine' has yellow-flushed foliage and dusky reddish-pink flowers. 'Winchester Fanfare' has dusky reddish-pink flowers.

Phyllostachys
Gramineae

This is a genus of some 80 species of clump-forming or spreading evergreen bamboos, native from the Himalayas to East Asia. Characterized by their canes, which are distinctly grooved on one side, they do best in a good, moist but well-drained soil, and should be sheltered from strong winds, particularly in colder areas.

Phyllostachys aurea

This vigorous evergreen bamboo has stout, erect, yellow-green canes, the joints crowded together at the base. It is a lush and strongly spreading species bearing masses of dark green, taper-pointed leaves, up to 15 cm (6 in) long, blue-green beneath.

Common name: Fishpole bamboo
Native range: China
Height: 8 m (26 ft) or more

Phyllostachys aurea

Spread: 6 m (20 ft)
Hardiness: Zone 7
Variants: It is a variable species with selected forms, including 'Boryana' with green to yellow-green canes that are blotched with purple.

Physocarpus
Rosaceae

The ten species in this genus are deciduous shrubs, natives of North America and East Asia. Grown for their lobed leaves, coloured in some forms, and their densely clustered flowers, they are suitable for any well-drained soil – except shallow chalk. To prune, cut them back lightly or remove some of the older shoots after they have flowered.

Physocarpus opulifolius

This is a vigorous deciduous shrub, the bark of older stems peeling, with sharply toothed, usually three-lobed leaves. Dense, hemispherical heads of small, white flowers tinged with pink in early summer are followed by clusters of small, inflated pods that turn red-purple when they are ripe.

Common name: Ninebark
Native range: E North America

Physocarpus opulifolius 'Dart's Gold'

Phyllostachys nigra

Spread: 5 m (16 ft) or more
Hardiness: Zone 6

Phyllostachys nigra

This is an elegant and vigorous evergreen bamboo that forms a dense clump of slender, arching canes, green at first but eventually becoming shiny black. The rather glossy dark green leaves, blue-green beneath and up to 12 cm (5 in) long, end in tapered points.

Common name: Black bamboo
Native range: China
Height: 6 m (20 ft)

Height: 2.5 m (8 ft)
Spread: 3 m (10 ft)
Hardiness: Zone 2
Variants: 'Dart's Gold' is a compact form with conspicuous, bright yellow foliage. 'Diabolo' produces striking, deep red-purple foliage. 'Luteus' has leaves that are yellow when young, turning green in summer.

Pieris
Ericaceae

The seven species of evergreen shrub within this genus are natives of North America, the Himalayas and East Asia. They provide a range of valuable garden evergreens that are grown for their small, profusely borne flowers, which are usually white and are often ornamental in bud before they open, and attractive foliage, which is often strikingly coloured when the leaves are young.

They can be grown in moist but well-drained, lime-free soil that is rich in organic matter. They may come into growth early and as a result young foliage can be damaged by late frosts. Little pruning is usually needed apart from the removal of damaged or unwanted branches, but they do benefit from being dead-headed after flowering.

Pieris 'Flaming Silver'

This is a sport of 'Forest Flame' that makes an evergreen shrub with slender-pointed leaves. The leaves are bright red when they first emerge and later turn to dark green with a silvery white margin. Drooping clusters of small, white flowers open in spring.

Height: 1.5 m (5 ft)
Spread: 1.2 m (4 ft)
Hardiness: Zone 5

Pieris 'Forest Flame'

This is a vigorous, garden-raised hybrid between *P. formosa* and *P. japonica* with slender-pointed, glossy dark green leaves that emerge bright red in spring, before turning to pink, creamy white and eventually green. Large, drooping clusters of small, white flowers open in spring.

Height: 5 m (16 ft)
Spread: 2.5 m (8 ft)
Hardiness: Zone 5

Pieris formosa

This vigorous evergreen shrub, often spreading by suckers, has bold, glossy dark green, leathery leaves that are bronze to red when young. The large, conical clusters of nodding, white flowers open at the ends of the shoots in spring. It is mainly cultivated as the forms listed below.

Native range: Himalayas, China
Height: 5 m (16 ft)
Spread: 5 m (16 ft)
Hardiness: Zone 8

Pieris formosa 'Wakehurst'

Variants: 'Jermyns' has deep red-purple young foliage and white flowers emerging from red buds; buds are conspicuous during winter. 'Wakehurst' has brilliant red young foliage.

Pieris japonica

This is a compact and bushy evergreen shrub with an essentially rounded habit. It has glossy dark green leaves that vary in colour from pale green to bronze when young. Large clusters of white flowers open at the ends of the shoots in early to mid-spring. There are now numerous selections commonly available, varying in habit, foliage and flower colour.

Native range: Japan, China, Taiwan
Height: 3 m (10 ft) or more
Spread: 4 m (13 ft) or more
Hardiness: Zone 5
Variants: 'Blush' produces white flowers flushed with pink that emerge from deep pink buds. 'Little Heath' is a dwarf and compact form, up to 60 cm (24 in) in height, with leaves edged in creamy white. 'Little Heath Green' is similar to 'Little Heath' but with green leaves, bronze when young. 'Purity' is a compact and rounded form, growing up

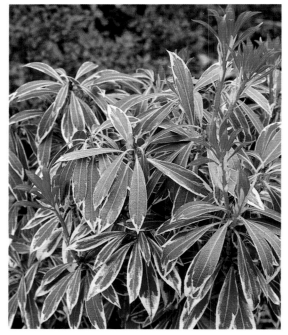

Pieris 'Flaming Silver'

to 1 m (3 ft) tall, with pale green young foliage. 'Valley Rose' has deep pink buds that open as rose-pink and then fade to white. 'Valley Valentine' produces large clusters of deep dusky red flowers. 'Variegata' is a compact form, up to 1.5 m (5 ft) tall, with leaves edged with creamy white.

Piptanthus
Leguminosae

The two species in this genus are deciduous or semi-evergreen shrubs, natives of the Himalayas and China. Only the following is commonly grown in the garden, however, where it is valued for its fine foliage and showy flowers.

Suitable for any well-drained soil, the species can be grown in the border or trained against a wall. In cold areas it should be given protection from the effects of the wind. Little pruning is usually necessary, but some of the older shoots can be cut back right to the base in spring.

Piptanthus nepalensis

This is a vigorous deciduous or semi-evergreen shrub with upright shoots and leaves composed of three blue-green leaflets that are whitish beneath. Dense, upright clusters of large, bright yellow, pea-like flowers open at the ends of the shoots in late spring, and these are followed by pendulous, flattened pods up to 12 cm (5 in) in length.

Synonym: *Piptanthus laburnifolius*
Common name: Evergreen laburnum
Native range: Himalayas, China
Height: 3 m (10 ft)
Spread: 3 m (10 ft)
Hardiness: Zone 8

Piptanthus nepalensis

Pittosporum
Pittosporaceae

This is a large genus of some 200 species of evergreen shrubs and trees, natives of Australia and New Zealand, with some species in South Africa, the Pacific Islands and East Asia. The cultivated species provide gardens with valuable ornamentals, grown for their foliage and their often fragrant flowers. They are suitable for use in the shrub border, as specimen plants, or – as with *P. tenuifolium* – for hedging, and they can be grown in any well-drained soil.

Provide protection from winds in cold areas by growing them against a wall or among other trees and shrubs. Pruning is not essential but trim them in spring as growth starts for a compact habit, and cut hedges again in summer if necessary.

Pittosporum 'Garnettii'

This is a garden-raised hybrid between *P. ralphii* and *P. tenuifolium* and makes an evergreen tree or large shrub or columnar habit. The grey-green

Pittosporum tenuifolium 'Tom Thumb'

leaves are edged with an irregular border of creamy white, which turns more pink-tinged in cold weather. Small, deep red-purple, fragrant flowers open in late spring and early summer.

Height: 6 m (20 ft)
Spread: 3 m (10 ft)
Hardiness: Zone 8

Pittosporum tenuifolium

This vigorous, evergreen tree of columnar habit, sometimes shrubby, has deep purple-black shoots and glossy bright green, wavy edged leaves. The small, red-purple flowers open in late spring and early summer and are strongly scented of honey, especially in the evening.

Common name: Kohuhu
Native range: New Zealand
Height: 10 m (33 ft)
Spread: 5 m (16 ft)
Hardiness: Zone 8
Variants: 'Abbotsbury Gold' has young leaves blotched in the centre with yellow-green. 'Irene Paterson' is slower growing, to 3 m (10 ft), with nearly white young leaves becoming mottled with dark green. 'Purpureum' has glossy red-purple foliage, pale green when young. 'Silver Queen' has grey-green leaves edged with white. 'Tom Thumb' is a compact, rounded, dwarf bush with red-purple foliage, pale green when young. 'Warnham Gold' has pale green foliage turning yellow in winter.

Pittosporum tobira

This bushy evergreen shrub has a dense, spreading habit and leathery, glossy dark green leaves. The extremely fragrant white flowers that open during spring in dense clusters at the ends of the shoots turn yellow with age. It does best in areas with hot summers, where it will thrive in sun or shade.

Native range: China, Japan, Taiwan
Height: 5 m (16 ft)
Spread: 5 m (16 ft)
Hardiness: Zone 8
Variants: 'Variegatum' is a slower-growing form and is less hardy. It has grey-green leaves that are edged with creamy white.

Platanus
Platanaceae

The planes are a small genus of six species of large, deciduous trees found in North America and Mexico, the southeast of Europe and Southeast

Pittosporum tenuifolium 'Irene Paterson'

Platanus x hispanica

Asia. The following are grown for their bold, maple-like leaves, their stately habit and their attractive peeling bark. The tiny, inconspicuous flowers that are borne in clusters in the spring are followed by rounded fruit clusters, which can persist on the trees throughout the entire winter season.

These trees are suitable for planting in any well-drained soil and they prefer a sunny position. However, due to their mature size, they are ideal only in parks or large gardens. They should never be planted close to buildings.

Platanus x hispanica

This vigorous, garden-raised hybrid between *P. occidentalis* and *P. orientalis* makes a large deciduous tree. The trunk is grey and brown and features cream-coloured, flaking bark. The large, bright glossy green leaves can be up to 25 cm (10 in) across and are divided into three to five toothed lobes.

Synonym: *Platanus x acerifolia*
Common name: London plane
Height: 30 m (100 ft)
Spread: 25 m (80 ft)
Hardiness: Zone 5
Variants: 'Suttneri' has leaves mottled with white.

Platanus occidentalis

This is a large, vigorous deciduous tree, usually taller than it is broad, with mottled, flaking bark and large, dark green, usually three-lobed leaves up to 20 cm (8 in) or more across. This tree needs hot summers to thrive and succeeds only in continental climates, such as those in mainland Europe or in North America.

Common name: American sycamore
Native range: E North America
Height: 30 m (100 ft) or more
Spread: 25 m (80 ft)
Hardiness: Zone 4

Platanus orientalis

A large deciduous tree, broadly columnar in habit, or often low and wide-spreading, with a flaking patchwork of grey and cream bark. The broad, glossy green leaves, up to 25 cm (10 in) across, are deeply cut into five, sometimes seven, lobes.

Common name: Oriental plane
Native range: SE Europe
Height: 30 m (100 ft)
Spread: 25 m (80 ft)
Hardiness: Zone 7

Pleioblastus auricomus

Pleioblastus
Gramineae

This is a genus with a narrow distribution made up of about 20 species of clump-forming or spreading evergreen bamboos. They have slender, upright, usually hollow, canes and are natives of China and Japan.

Grown for their graceful canes and foliage, which is sometimes variegated, they are suitable for any moist but well-drained soil that is rich in organic matter. The following species can be grown in open positions among other shrubs or in containers.

Pleioblastus auricomus

This is an evergreen bamboo that forms small clumps and spreads slowly by sending out underground shoots. The upright, slender, purple-green canes bear slender, pointed leaves, up to 20 cm (8 in) long, that are striped with bright yellow and green.

Synonyms: *Arundinaria auricoma, Arundinaria viridistriata*
Native range: Japan
Height: 1.5 m (5 ft)
Spread: 2 m (6 ft)
Hardiness: Zone 7

Pleioblastus pygmaeus

This dwarf evergreen bamboo forms dense clumps of slender, upright canes and spreads by sending out underground stems. The dark green, densely arranged leaves are up to 10 cm (4 in) long. It is useful for ground cover, and it does best in a sunny position. It is taller growing in shady conditions.

Synonym: *Arundinaria pygmaea*
Native range: Japan
Height: 20 cm (8 in)
Spread: 1.5 m (5 ft)
Hardiness: Zone 6
Variants: var. *distichus* (*Arundinaria disticha*) is taller, more vigorous and has larger leaves.

Pleioblastus variegatus

This is a vigorous evergreen bamboo that forms dense clumps of slender, upright, pale green canes. The narrow leaves, up to 20 cm (8 in) long, are dark green and conspicuously striped with creamy white. It is an excellent specimen plant for the garden or container.

Synonyms: *Arundinaria fortunei, Arundinaria variegata*
Native range: Japan
Height: 1.5 m (5 ft)
Spread: 1.5 m (5 ft)
Hardiness: Zone 7

Polygala
Polygalaceae

This very large genus of some 500 species of annual and perennial herbaceous plants and evergreen shrubs is widely distributed throughout the world. The following is grown for its unusual flowers and it requires a moist but well-drained, lime-free soil. It prefers a sunny position, ideally in a peat or rock garden.

Polygala chamaebuxus

This dwarf evergreen shrub has a low, spreading habit, slender, creeping stems and narrow, dark green leaves. The small, rather pea-like flowers, which open in late spring to early summer, are creamy white and tipped with bright yellow.

Native range: Europe
Height: 10 cm (4 in)
Spread: 30 cm (12 in)
Hardiness: Zone 6
Variants: var. *grandiflora* (var. *rhodoptera*) has purple-pink flowers that are tipped with yellow.

Populus
Salicaceae

The 35 species that make up this genus are mainly deciduous trees and are widely distributed in Europe, Asia, North Africa and North America.

Most species are grown only in plantations for timber, while others can be useful as fast-growing screens. Even the few species grown in gardens are vigorous trees with invasive roots systems and should not be planted anywhere close to buildings. Flowers are borne in catkins – males and females on separate plants.

Populus alba

This is a deciduous tree with a broadly upright to spreading habit. The young shoots are densely covered with white wool. The leaves, which are covered in white hairs, becoming dark green above, are five-lobed and maple-like on vigorous shoots, while on other shoots they are oval and only shallowly lobed.

Common names: Abele, white poplar
Native range: Europe, C and W Asia, North Africa
Height: 25 m (80 ft)
Spread: 15 m (50 ft)
Hardiness: Zone 3

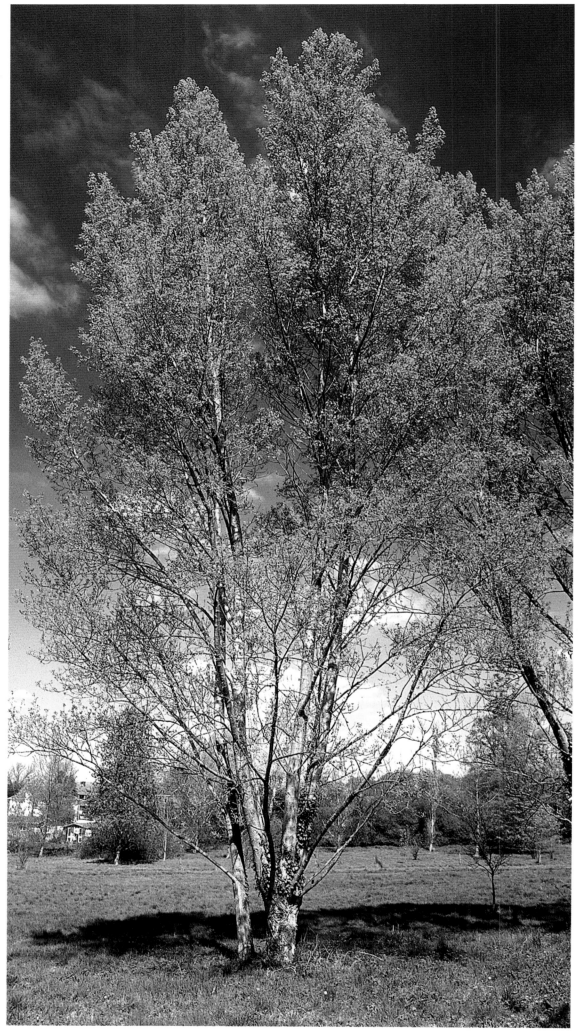

Populus nigra

Variants: 'Racket' is a fast-growing form with a conical habit. 'Richardii' produces golden yellow foliage.

Populus x jackii

This naturally occurring hybrid between *P. balsamifera* and *P. deltoides* makes a vigorous, broadly columnar deciduous tree with dark green, heart-shaped leaves that are whitish beneath. The female form is most commonly grown, bearing green, pendulous catkins in early spring. It is most commonly seen as the form listed below.

Synonym: *Populus x candicans*
Common name: Balm of Gilead
Native range: E North America
Height: 15 m (50 ft)
Spread: 8 m (26 ft)
Hardiness: Zone 2
Variants: 'Aurora' has leaves that are conspicuously mottled with creamy yellow, and are flushed with pink when young.

Populus nigra

This is a vigorous deciduous tree with a spreading habit when mature, and with nearly triangular, glossy dark green leaves ending in a fine, tapered point. The leaves are bronze when they are young and turn yellow in the autumn. In garden cultivation, *P. nigra* is most frequently seen as the form listed below.

Common name: Black poplar
Native range: Europe, W Asia
Height: 30 m (100 ft)
Spread: 25 m (80 ft)
Hardiness: Zone 3
Variants: 'Italica' (Lombardy poplar) is a male form of narrow habit and with upright branches.

Populus tremula

This spreading deciduous tree has long-stalked, grey-green leaves edged with small, rounded teeth. Foliage is bronze when young and turns yellow in the autumn. The flattened leaf stalks cause the leaves to flutter in the wind. Male plants have pendulous, red catkins in early spring before the leaves emerge.

Common name: Aspen
Native range: Europe, North Africa, Asia
Height: 20 m (65 ft)
Spread: 15 m (50 ft)
Hardiness: Zone 2
Variants: 'Erecta' is a slender tree with upright branches. 'Pendula' is a weeping form.

Potentilla fruticosa 'Elizabeth'

Potentilla

Rosaceae

This large genus of some 500 species of mainly herbaceous perennials and shrubs provides gardens with numerous ornamental plants. The following is the most commonly grown shrubby species.

Variable and of wide distribution, it has given rise to many different garden forms. It is suitable for any well-drained soil in a sunny position, and it can be used for ground cover; the more vigorous forms are ideal for hedging. They benefit from regular pruning and should be cut back lightly after flowering to maintain a compact habit.

Potentilla fruticosa

This is a bushy deciduous shrub of a spreading to rounded or upright habit. Its small, dark green to blue-green leaves are usually divided into five or seven leaflets. The saucer-shaped flowers vary in colour from yellow to orange, red, pink and white, and open over a long period from late spring to autumn. Those with orange, red or pink flowers tend to fade in hot sun.

Common name: Shrubby cinquefoil
Native range: Europe, N Asia, North America
Height: up to 1.5 m (5 ft)
Spread: up to 1 m (3 ft)
Hardiness: Zone 2
Variants: 'Abbotswood', up to 75 cm (30 in), with white flowers. 'Abbotswood Silver' is similar but with leaflets edged with white, often reverting. 'Beesii' is compact, to 60 cm (24 in), with silvery foliage and yellow flowers. 'Elizabeth' is spreading,

up to 1 m (3 ft), with golden yellow flowers. 'Goldfinger' is compact, to 90 cm (35 in), with large, rich yellow flowers. 'Katherine Dykes' is spreading, to 1.5 m (5 ft), with grey-green foliage and primrose yellow flowers. Marion Red Robin ('Marrob', Red Robin) is low and spreading with red flowers. 'Princess' ('Blink'), to 60 cm (24 in), has pale pink flowers. 'Red Ace', spreading to 75 cm (30 in), has vermilion flowers. 'Sunset' has orange flowers. 'Tangerine' is spreading, to 1 m (3 ft), with coppery yellow flowers. 'Tilford Cream' is compact and spreading, to 60 cm (24 in), with creamy white flowers. 'Vilmoriniana' is vigorous and upright, to 1.2 m (4 ft), with silvery foliage and creamy flowers.

Prostanthera

Labiatae

The mint bushes are a genus of about 50 species of aromatic evergreen shrubs with opposite leaves, natives of Australia and Tasmania. Grown in gardens for their neat habit, attractive foliage and their small, two-lipped flowers, they are suitable for a sheltered border or for growing against a sunny wall in well-drained soil. Prune lightly after flowering if necessary.

Prostanthera cuneata

This compact and rounded, bushy evergreen shrub has very densely arranged, small, thick, glossy dark green and very aromatic leaves, only about 5 mm (⅛ in) long. Clusters of tubular, two-lipped flowers, blotched inside with yellow and purple, open during the summer.

Common name: Alpine mint bush
Native range: SE Australia, Tasmania
Height: 60 cm (24 in)
Spread: 90 cm (35 in)
Hardiness: Zone 9

Prostanthera rotundifolia

This is an evergreen shrub with a bushy, spreading habit and slender, grey-hairy shoots. Its small, aromatic, dark green, rounded leaves have only a few shallow teeth. Dense clusters of purple, bell-shaped flowers open at the ends of the shoots in the spring.

Common name: Round-leaved mint bush
Native range: SE Australia, Tasmania
Height: 2 m (6 ft)
Spread: 3 m (10 ft)
Hardiness: Zone 9
Variants: 'Rosea' has pink flowers.

Prunus 'Accolade'

Prunus avium 'Plena'

Prunus
Rosaceae

This is a large and varied genus of some 200 species of deciduous and evergreen trees and shrubs, widely distributed mainly in the temperate regions of the northern hemisphere and extending to South America.

It provides a wide range of ornamental flowering shrubs and trees, many of which are of a size suitable for smaller gardens, including the Japanese cherries. Several, such as *P.* x *cistena*, *P. spinosa*, *P. laurocerasus* and *P. lusitanica*, can be used for hedging. Prune deciduous hedges after flowering; evergreens in spring.

Prunus 'Accolade'

This garden-raise hybrid between *P. sargentii* and *P.* x *subhirtella* makes a spreading tree with dark green, taper-pointed and sharply toothed leaves. In early spring, deep pink buds open to pale pink, semi-double flowers about 4 cm (1½ in) across, with yellow anthers in their centres.

Height: 8 m (26 ft)
Spread: 8 m (26 ft)
Hardiness: Zone 4

Prunus 'Amanogawa'

This popular Japanese cherry makes a small deciduous tree of narrow habit with upright branches and dark green, sharply toothed leaves. Foliage is bronze when young, turning red and orange in autumn. Upright clusters of semi-double, fragrant, pale pink flowers open in late spring.

Height: 8 m (26 ft)
Spread: 3 m (10 ft)
Hardiness: Zone 5

Prunus avium

A vigorous deciduous tree with red-brown bark peeling in horizontal bands. Taper-pointed and sharply toothed leaves are bronze when young, turning to deep green, then red and yellow in autumn. Clusters of white flowers open in mid-spring before or as the leaves emerge, followed by small, edible, red fruits.

Common name: Gean
Native range: Europe, W Asia
Height: 20 m (65 ft)
Spread: 15 m (50 ft)
Hardiness: Zone 3
Variants: The form 'Plena' has double flowers.

Prunus cerasifera

This is a small, vigorous, spreading tree or thicket-forming shrub of garden origin with glossy dark green leaves. Small, white flowers are profusely borne on the bare shoots before the leaves emerge in early spring, and these are followed by red, edible, plum-like fruits.

Common names: Cherry plum, myrobalan
Height: 8 m (26 ft)
Spread: 8 m (26 ft)
Hardiness: Zone 5
Variants: 'Nigra' has deep red-purple foliage and pink flowers. 'Pissardii' has deep red-purple foliage and white flowers.

Prunus x cistena

This is a garden-raised hybrid between
P. cerasifera 'Pissardii' and *P. pumila* that makes a deciduous shrub with slender, upright shoots bearing glossy red-purple leaves. Small, fragrant, pink flowers open singly on the shoots in late spring after the leaves have emerged, and these are sometimes followed by deep red-purple, cherry-like fruits.

Common name: Purple-leaved sand cherry
Height: 3 m (10 ft)
Spread: 2 m (6 ft)
Hardiness: Zone 4

Prunus dulcis

This spreading deciduous tree has slender, glossy green, taper-pointed and finely toothed leaves. Large white or pink flowers, 5 cm (2 in) across, open singly or in small clusters on the bare shoots before the leaves emerge in early spring. The velvety green fruits, about 6 cm (2⅛ in)long with a dry flesh, contain the familiar edible nuts.

Common name: Almond
Native range: North Africa, SW and C Asia
Height: 8 m (26 ft)
Spread: 8 m (26 ft)
Hardiness: Zone 7
Variants: 'Roseoplena' has double pink flowers.

Prunus glandulosa

This is a spreading deciduous shrub with slender, arching shoots and taper-pointed, finely toothed

Prunus glandulosa 'Alba Plena'

leaves. Small, white or pink flowers are borne in mid-spring, sometimes followed by small, bright red fruits. It is nearly always grown as one of the double-flowered forms listed below.

Native range: N China, Korea, Japan
Height: 1.5 m (5 ft)
Spread: 2 m (6 ft)
Hardiness: Zone 4
Variants: 'Alba Plena' has double, white flowers. 'Sinensis' ('Rosea Plena') has double, pink flowers.

Prunus incisa

This is a small, bushy, spreading tree, often shrubby, with small, dark green, sharply toothed leaves. Foliage is bronze when young and turns red and yellow in autumn. White or pale pink flowers, 2 cm (¾ in) across, are borne in small clusters of two or three in mid-spring before the leaves emerge, and these are sometimes followed by small, purple-black cherries.

Common name: Fuji cherry
Native range: Japan
Height: 8 m (26 ft)
Spread: 10 m (33 ft)
Hardiness: Zone 5
Variants: 'February Pink' has pale pink flowers throughout winter. 'Kojo-no-mai' has zigzag shoots and pale pink flowers. 'Praecox' has white flowers opening from pink buds in early winter.

Prunus cerasifera 'Nigra'

Prunus 'Kanzan'

Prunus 'Kanzan'

This is one of the most popular of the Japanese cherries. This vigorous deciduous tree is vase shaped when young with upright branches that later spread more widely. The sharply toothed leaves end in a fine, tapered point and are deep bronze when young. Clusters of large, purple-pink, double flowers, 5cm (2 in) across, open in spring as the young leaves emerge.

Height: 10 m (33 ft)
Spread: 10 m (33 ft)
Hardiness: Zone 5

Prunus 'Kiku-shidare-zakura'

This Japanese cherry has a very distinct habit and is normally grafted on the top of a stem to make a small, weeping tree. The hanging branches often reach right to the ground. The taper-pointed leaves are bronze when young, and fully double, rich pink flowers open as the young leaves emerge in mid- to late spring.

Synonym: *Prunus* 'Cheal's Weeping'
Height: 2.5 m (8 ft)
Spread: 3 m (10 ft)
Hardiness: Zone 5

Prunus laurocerasus

This large, vigorous evergreen shrub, sometimes tree-like, bears bold, leathery, glossy dark green leaves, to 20 cm (8 in) long, on short, stout stalks. Upright spikes of small, white flowers start to emerge early in the year. The flowers open in mid-spring, and these are followed by green, then red and finally glossy black fruits. It is very variable in size and is normally grown as garden selections.

Common name: Cherry laurel
Native range: E Europe, SW Asia
Height: 6 m (20 ft) or more

Spread: 8 m (26 ft)
Hardiness: Zone 6
Variants: 'Castlewellan' ('Marbled White') has heavily white-mottled foliage. 'Otto Luyken' makes a dense mound of narrow, very dark green leaves, up to 1 m (3 ft) tall. 'Rotundifolia' is compact and upright, the best form for hedges. 'Zabeliana' is wide spreading, to 1.5 m (5 ft), with slender leaves.

Prunus lusitanica

This vigorous evergreen shrub or tree has very dark, glossy green leaves on slender, red stalks. Slender, spreading spikes, up to 25 cm (10 in) long, of small white flowers open in mid-summer, followed by small, glossy black fruits.

Common name: Portugal laurel
Native range: SW Europe
Height: 10 m (33 ft) or more
Spread: 10 m (33 ft)
Hardiness: Zone 7

Prunus laurocerasus 'Otto Luyken'

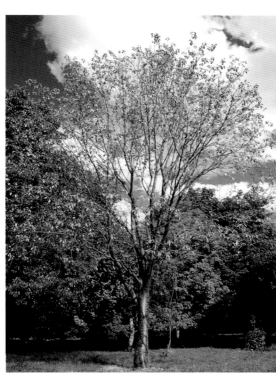

Prunus maackii

Prunus maackii

A broadly conical deciduous tree notable for its striking, glossy yellow-brown, peeling bark. Finely toothed and taper-pointed dark green leaves turn yellow in autumn. Small, fragrant, white flowers open in dense, short clusters as the leaves emerge in mid-spring, followed by small, glossy black fruits.

Common name: Manchurian cherry
Native range: NE Asia
Height: 12 m (40 ft)
Spread: 8 m (26 ft)
Hardiness: Zone 3

Prunus padus 'Colorata'

Prunus 'Okame'

This is a garden-raised hybrid between *P. campanulata* and *P. incisa* that makes a small deciduous tree. The tree is upright when young, becoming rounded in habit as it matures, with sharply toothed, dark green leaves that turn orange-red in autumn. Small clusters of bright pink flowers, up to about 2.5 cm (1 in) across, open in the early spring.

Height: 8 m (26 ft)
Spread: 6 m (20 ft)
Hardiness: Zone 6

Prunus padus

This fast-growing deciduous tree has a spreading habit and dark matt-green, taper-pointed and finely toothed leaves. Small, fragrant, white flowers open in slender, upright, spreading or drooping spikes in mid- to late spring, and these are followed by glossy black fruits.

Common name: Bird cherry
Native range: Europe, N Asia
Height: 15 m (50 ft)
Spread: 12 m (40 ft)
Hardiness: Zone 3
Variants: 'Colorata' has deep red-purple leaves, becoming dark green, and pink flowers. 'Watereri' produces very long flower spikes.

Prunus 'Pink Perfection'

This spreading deciduous tree has taper-pointed, dark green leaves that are bronze as they emerge. Drooping clusters of large, pink, double flowers open in late spring.

Height: 8 m (26 ft)
Spread: 8 m (26 ft)
Hardiness: Zone 5

Prunus sargentii

This is one of the most striking of all the cherries. It is a spreading deciduous tree with glossy green leaves ending in long, tapered points. Deep bronze-red when young, the leaves turn to brilliant shades of orange, red and yellow in autumn. Pale

Prunus sargentii

Prunus 'Shirofugen'

Among the best of the Japanese cherries, this spreading tree has dark green leaves that emerge bronze and turn to orange and red in the autumn. The large, double flowers are pink in bud, turning white as they open in the late spring, before turning pink again before they fall.

Height: 10 m (33 ft)
Spread: 10 m (33 ft)
Hardiness: Zone 5

Prunus 'Shirotae'

This is a small deciduous tree with spreading and slightly drooping branches bearing dark green leaves. The leaves – which end in long, tapered points – are pale green when young and turn orange and red in autumn. Pendulous clusters of large, semi-double, white flowers, up to 5 cm (2 in) across, open in mid-spring.

Synonym: *Prunus* 'Mount Fuji'
Height: 6 m (20 ft)
Spread: 8 m (26 ft)
Hardiness: Zone 5

Prunus spinosa

This is a dense, spiny deciduous shrub, sometimes a tree, often spreading by suckers, with dark green, sharply toothed leaves. Profuse, small, white flowers open on the bare shoots before the leaves emerge in the early spring, and these are followed by edible but bitter, blue-black fruits. It is a useful plant for hedging.

Common names: Blackthorn, sloe
Native range: Europe, W Asia
Height: 5 m (16 ft)
Spread: 4 m (13 ft)
Hardiness: Zone 4
Variants: 'Plena' produces double, rosette-like, white flowers. 'Purpurea' has purple leaves and pink flowers.

Prunus 'Shirotae'

pink flowers, up to 4 cm (1½ in) across, open in clusters in mid-spring.

Native range: Japan
Height: 15 m (50 ft)
Spread: 15 m (50 ft)
Hardiness: Zone 4

Prunus serrula

Grown primarily for its smooth, strikingly coloured, glossy red-brown bark, which peels in long horizontal strips, this medium-sized *Prunus* species makes a spreading deciduous tree with slender, taper-pointed, dark green leaves, which turn yellow in autumn. Nodding, five-petalled, white flowers open singly or in small clusters as the young leaves first emerge in spring, and these are followed by small red fruits.

Native range: China
Height: 10 m (33 ft)
Spread: 10 m (33 ft)
Hardiness: Zone 5

Prunus x subhirtella

This is a naturally occurring hybrid between *P. incisa* and *P. pendula*. It makes a small deciduous tree of spreading habit with taper-pointed and sharply toothed, deep green leaves. The leaves are bronze when young and turn yellow in autumn. Small clusters of pink or white flowers, up to about 2 cm (¾ in) across, open in the early spring before or as the young leaves emerge.
P. x *subhirtella* is most commonly grown as the two forms listed below.

Prunus serrula

Prunus 'Pink Perfection'

flowers, up to 4 cm (1½ in) across, are pale yellow-green. The flowers are flushed with pink at first, but later turn to white.

Height: 8 m (26 ft)
Spread: 10 m (33 ft)
Hardiness: Zone 5

Prunus x yedoensis

A naturally occurring hybrid between *P. pendula* and *P. speciosa* making a spreading deciduous tree with widely arching branches bearing glossy green, sharply toothed leaves. Masses of pale pink flowers, fading to white, open in clusters along the bare shoots in early spring, and these are followed by small, red fruits that ripen to black.

Common name: Yoshino cherry
Native range: Japan
Height: 10 m (33 ft)
Spread: 12 m (40 ft)
Hardiness: Zone 5

Common name: Spring cherry
Native range: Japan
Height: 8 m (26 ft)
Spread: 6 m (20 ft)
Hardiness: Zone 5
Variants: 'Autumnalis' produces semi-double, white flowers that open from pink buds over a long period from late autumn through to early spring. 'Autumnalis Rosea' is similar, except that it bears pink flowers.

Prunus tenella

This small deciduous shrub spreads by suckers and has slender, upright shoots bearing glossy dark green, sharply toothed leaves. Pink flowers, 2–3 cm (about 1 in) across, open along the shoots in mid-spring. It prefers a warm, sunny position and old plants can be rejuvenated by cutting them back hard after they have flowered.

Common name: Russian almond
Native range: C and E Europe, W Asia
Height: 1.5 m (5 ft)
Spread: 1.5 m (5 ft)
Hardiness: Zone 2
Variants: 'Fire Hill' produces deep pink flowers.

Prunus 'Ukon'

This is a very distinct Japanese cherry that makes a vigorous deciduous tree. The branches, which are upright at first, later spreading, bear dark green, taper-pointed and finely toothed leaves that are bronze when young. The unusual double

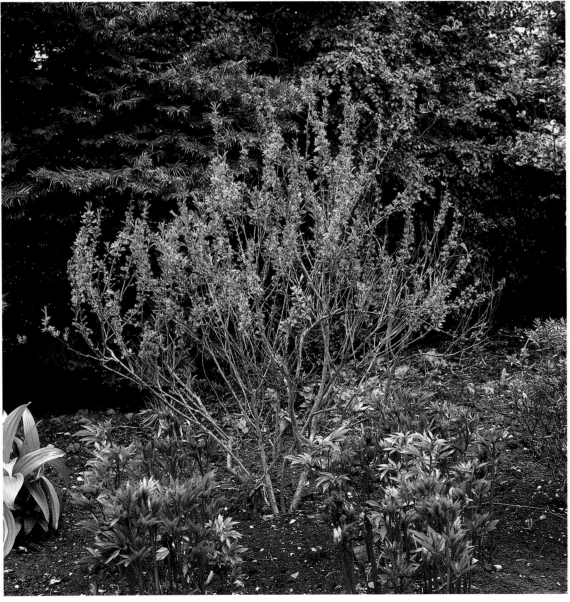

Prunus tenella 'Fire Hill'

Pseudosasa
Gramineae

This is a small genus made up of six species of evergreen bamboos that spread by sending out underground stems, and are natives of Japan, Taiwan and Korea.

The following species is best grown as a specimen plant or it can also be used to form an effective screen. It is suitable for any good, moist but well-drained soil. The size of clumps can be controlled by cutting out unwanted canes.

Pseudosasa japonica

This is a vigorous and evergreen bamboo with upright, green canes that later turn yellow-brown. It makes dense clumps and spreads by underground stems. The large, dark green, taper-pointed leaves, which are blue-green beneath, can grow up to about 35 cm (14 in) long. Flowers are rarely produced.

Synonym: *Arundinaria japonica*
Common name: Arrow bamboo
Native range: Japan
Height: 5 m (16 ft)
Spread: 8 m (26 ft) or more
Hardiness: Zone 6

Ptelea
Rutaceae

This is a small genus comprising about ten species of deciduous shrubs and small trees, all natives of North America. Grown for their aromatic foliage, they have leaves that are divided up into three leaflets. Small flowers are followed by winged fruits.

The following is the most commonly seen species in garden cultivation. It is suitable for any well-drained soil, but requires a sunny position in order to thrive.

Ptelea trifoliata

This is a vigorous, though small-growing, deciduous tree with a spreading habit. The leaves, which are very aromatic when crushed, are composed of three glossy dark green leaflets turning yellow in the autumn. Rounded clusters of small, yellow-green flowers at the ends of the shoots appear in summer, and these are followed by pale green fruits, which later turn pale brown. The fruits are surrounded by a broad, circular wing.

Pseudosasa japonica

Common name: Hop tree
Native range: E North America
Height: 6 m (20 ft)
Spread: 6 m (20 ft)
Hardiness: Zone 3
Variants: 'Aurea' produces foliage that is bright yellow when young.

Pterocarya
Juglandaceae

This small genus, made up of ten species of vigorous deciduous trees, is related to the walnuts. The trees produce large leaves that are divided into numerous leaflets, and the flowers are borne in catkins – males and females separate but on the same tree. Male catkins are pendulous, while females develop into long, hanging clusters of small, winged fruits.

Grown for their foliage and fruits, they are suitable for any good, moist but well-drained soil. They do best if given a position in full sun.

Pterocarya fraxinifolia

This vigorous, large-growing and spreading deciduous tree, often branching low down, bears bold, glossy dark green leaves that turn yellow in the autumn. The leaves grow up to about 40 cm (16 in) in length, and are divided up into as many as 23 or more individual leaflets. The tree bears pendulous, male catkins, up to about 12 cm (5 in) long, in the spring and slender drooping clusters, up to about 15 cm (6 in) long, of winged fruits in the autumn.

Common name: Caucasian wingnut
Native range: Caucasus, N Iran
Height: 25 m (80 ft) or more
Spread: 20 m (65 ft)
Hardiness: Zone 6

Pterostyrax
Styracaceae

The four species that make up this small genus of hardy deciduous shrubs and trees are all natives of East Asia.

The following is the most commonly seen species in garden cultivation and it is grown for its bold foliage as well as its fragrant flowers. It can be grown as a specimen tree or planted in a woodland situation. It requires a good depth of well-drained soil and a sunny position in order to thrive.

Ptelea trifoliata 'Aurea'

Pterostyrax hispida

Pterostyrax hispida

This deciduous tree is upright when young but later adopts a spreading habit. It has bold, bright green leaves, up to 20 cm (8 in) long, that are grey-green beneath. The pendulous clusters of small, fragrant, white flowers reach a length of up to 20 cm (8 in) and open in early to mid-summer. The flowers are followed by small, persistent, bristly fruits.

Common name: Epaulette tree
Native range: China, Japan
Height: 10 m (33 ft)
Spread: 10 m (33 ft)
Hardiness: Zone 5

Punica
Punicaceae

The two species of shrubs or trees in this genus are natives of West Asia. Only the following is commonly grown for its showy flowers and its edible fruits. In warm regions it makes a handsome specimen shrub, where it is also useful for screening. In regions where winters are cooler, it can be grown in a sheltered border or against a wall. It is suitable for any well-drained soil in full sun and it can be cut back in spring if necessary to restrict growth.

Punica granatum

This vigorous deciduous or semi-evergreen shrub, sometimes a tree (evergreen in warm climates) has glossy dark green leaves that are bronze when young. Striking, bright orange-red flowers open over a long period during the summer and early autumn, followed in warm climates by edible fruits.

Common name: Pomegranate
Native range: W Asia
Height: 5 m (16 ft)
Spread: 4 m (13 ft)
Hardiness: Zone 8
Variants: var. *nana* is a dwarf form of compact habit, up to 1 m (3 ft) high, with smaller leaves, flowers and fruits. 'Plena' has double flowers.

Pyracantha
Rosaceae

The firethorns are a genus of seven species of spiny evergreen shrubs that are natives of southeast Europe, West Asia, the Himalayas and

Pyracantha 'Dart's Red'

East Asia. Grown for their dense habit, their flowers and their showy fruits, they are ideal for the shrub border, for hedging and screening, or for training against a wall.

Suitable for any well-drained soil, they flower and fruit best when positioned in full sun. Although pruning is not essential, they can be cut back in spring to restrict growth. Cut hedges in spring and, as necessary, during the summer.

Pyracantha angustifolia

This dense and bushy evergreen shrub has spiny shoots covered in grey hairs when young. The narrow-shaped leaves are dark green above with a thick, grey felt beneath. Clusters of small, white flowers open in mid-summer, and these are followed by long-persistent, orange-yellow berries.

Native range: China
Height: 3 m (10 ft)
Spread: 3 m (10 ft)
Hardiness: Zone 7

Pyracantha coccinea

This vigorous evergreen shrub has a dense, rounded habit with spiny shoots and glossy dark green leaves. Clusters of small, white flowers open in early summer followed by orange-red berries.

Pyracantha 'Soleil d'Or'

Native range: SE Europe, W Asia
Height: 3 m (10 ft)
Spread: 4 m (13 ft)
Hardiness: Zone 5
Variants: 'Lalandei' is a very vigorous shrub and fruits profusely. 'Red Column' is upright in habit and has bright red fruits.

Pyracantha rogersiana

This is a vigorous and compact evergreen shrub with arching, spiny shoots, red when young, and slender, glossy dark green leaves. Dense clusters of white flowers appear in late spring, and these are followed by orange-red berries.

Native range: China
Height: 3 m (10 ft)
Spread: 4 m (13 ft)
Hardiness: Zone 7
Variants: 'Flava' produces yellow berries.

Pyracantha hybrids

Numerous hybrids between the various species have been raised in gardens, varying in habit and fruit colour. These include 'Dart's Red' – vigorous with red berries. 'Golden Charmer' – vigorous, to 3 m (10 ft), with arching shoots and bright orange berries. 'Mohave' – vigorous and upright, to 4 m (13 ft), with broad, glossy green leaves and profuse, bright red berries. 'Orange Glow' – upright with arching branches and profuse, long-persistent, bright orange-red berries, good for growing against a wall. 'Soleil d'Or' – large clusters of golden yellow berries. 'Teton' – compact and upright, with small, glossy green leaves and orange-yellow berries.

Pyrus
Rosaceae

The pears comprise a genus of about 20 species of deciduous trees and shrubs from Europe, North Africa and Asia. Well known for providing the edible pear, the ornamental species are grown for their habit, foliage and flowers. Although they do best on good, well-drained soils, they are very tough trees and also perform well in moist and dry conditions. They prefer a sunny position.

Pyrus calleryana

This vigorous, usually broadly conical, deciduous tree produces glossy green leaves that remain late into autumn or early winter, when they turn red-purple in colour. Clusters of small, white flowers with pink anthers open in the spring followed by

Pyrus salicifolia 'Pendula'

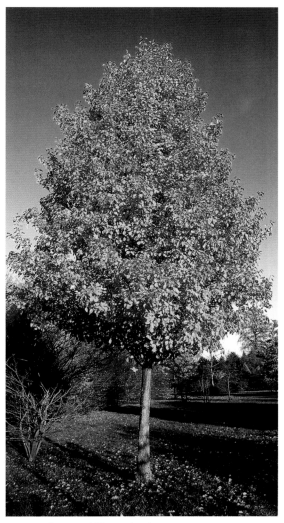

Pyrus calleryana 'Chanticleer'

rounded to pear-shaped, russet-coloured fruits. It is mainly grown as selected forms below.

Native range: China
Height: 15 m (50 ft)
Spread: 10 m (33 ft)
Hardiness: Zone 5
Variants: There are many forms selected mainly for their habit and autumn colour, the most common of which are: 'Bradford' (United States of America), which is broadly conical but spreading, and often splitting with age; and 'Chanticleer' (Britain), narrowly conical even in old trees.

Pyrus salicifolia

Only commonly seen as the following form, this small deciduous tree has slender, grey-green leaves that are silvery grey when young. Small, creamy white flowers with pink anthers open in dense clusters as the young foliage emerges, and the flowers are followed by small, green fruits.

Common name: Willow-leaved pear
Native range: Caucasus, NE Turkey
Height: 10 m (33 ft)
Spread: 8 m (26 ft)
Hardiness: Zone 4
Variants: 'Pendula' is the form seen in gardens. It makes a dense, strongly weeping, small-sized tree, reaching up to about 6 m (20 ft) in height.

Quercus
Fagaceae

The oaks are a large genus of about 500 species of deciduous and evergreen trees and shrubs widely distributed throughout the temperate and tropical regions of the northern hemisphere. Flowers are borne in catkins in spring: males pendulous and usually yellow-green; the small, female flowers ripening to form the acorns. The cultivated species are grown for their habit and their foliage.

Preferring a good, deep, well-drained soil, the following species can make large trees and are suitable only for sizable gardens. Some require a lime-free soil.

Quercus alba

This is a spreading tree of rounded habit with bold, shallowly to deeply lobed leaves. The leaves are pink-tinged as they open, turning blue-green, then bright green, and finally red-purple in the autumn. This species prefers areas that experience hot summers and is most commonly grown in North America. It requires a lime-free soil.

Common name: White oak
Native range: E North America
Height: 25 m (80 ft) or more
Spread: 30 m (100 ft)
Hardiness: Zone 4

Quercus cerris

This is a large, fast-growing deciduous tree with deeply ridged bark. The glossy dark green leaves, up to 12 cm (5 in) long, are edged with up to six, usually rounded, lobes on each side, turning yellow

Quercus cerris 'Argenteovariegata'

to yellow-brown in autumn. Large acorns, to 2.5 cm (1 in) long, ripen in 18 months and are borne in a cup densely covered with slender scales. This tree is the alternate host to the knopper gall wasp, which causes deformed acorns on English oak (*Q. robur*). In North America, the name turkey oak is applied to a different species (*Q. laevis*).

Common name: Turkey oak
Native range: Europe, SW Asia

Height: 30 m (100 ft)
Spread: 25 m (80 ft)
Hardiness: Zone 5
Variants: 'Argenteovariegata', also known as 'Variegata', has leaves with a creamy yellow margin when young, turning creamy white with age. It is a smaller tree – about 10 m (33 ft) tall and across.

Quercus coccinea

This vigorous deciduous tree is spreading to broadly columnar in habit. The glossy dark green leaves, up to 15 cm (6 in) long, are deeply cut into lobes ending in bristle-tipped teeth, and they turn bright red in autumn. It needs a lime-free soil.

Common name: Scarlet oak
Native range: E North America
Height: 25 m (80 ft)
Spread: 20m (65 ft)
Hardiness: Zone 4
Variants: 'Splendens' is a form selected for its excellent deep red, autumn colour.

Quercus frainetto

This is a vigorous deciduous tree with a broadly upright to spreading habit. Among the finest species for general planting, the bold, dark green

Quercus cerris 'Argenteovariegata'

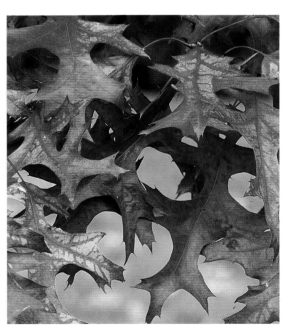

Quercus coccinea

leaves, up to 20 cm (8 in) long, are deeply and conspicuously cut into numerous, often notched, lobes. The leaves turn yellow in autumn.

Common name: Hungarian oak
Native range: SE Europe
Height: 30 m (100 ft)
Spread: 25 m (80 ft)
Hardiness: Zone 5
Variants: 'Hungarian Crown' is a selection with a compact, broadly upright habit.

Quercus ilex

This is an evergreen tree, typically with a dense, rounded habit. The leathery, taper-pointed leaves are untoothed, or nearly so, on mature plants, but on younger leaves and shoots from the base of old trees can be spiny edged. Emerging grey and hairy, they become glossy dark green on their upper surfaces. The yellow, male catkins are conspicuous as the leaves emerge in early summer.

Common name: Holm oak
Native region: Mediterranean region
Height: 20 m (65 ft)
Spread: 20 m (65 ft)
Hardiness: Zone 7

Quercus imbricaria

This deciduous tree is upright when young, wide-spreading with age, and with lower branches that often droop. The untoothed leaves, up to 15 cm (6 in) long, end in small, bristle-tipped points. Pale green to bronze when young, leaves turn glossy dark green and then yellow-green or red-brown in the autumn. It requires a lime-free soil.

Common name: Shingle oak
Native range: C and E United States of America
Height: 20 m (65 ft) or more
Spread: 20 m (65 ft)
Hardiness: Zone 4

Quercus palustris

A vigorous deciduous tree with a characteristic broadly conical habit, with the lower branches wide-spreading and drooping. The glossy dark green leaves are cut into deep lobes, ending in bristle-tipped teeth, and turn red in autumn. This species requires a lime-free soil.

Common name: Pin oak
Native range: E North America
Height: 20 m (65 ft)
Spread: 15 m (50 ft)
Hardiness: Zone 4

Quercus robur

Quercus robur

Quercus rubra

Quercus phellos

This is a vigorous, deciduous tree that is conical when young, but becoming dense and rounded as it matures. The distinct willow-like leaves are slender and without teeth, ending in small, bristle-like points. Pale green to bronze when young, the leaves mature to a dark green colour and usually turn yellow to yellow-brown in the autumn.

Common name: Willow oak
Native range: E United States of America
Height: 20 m (65 ft) or more
Spread: 15 m (50 ft) or more
Hardiness: Zone 5

Quercus robur

A wide-spreading deciduous tree of rounded habit. The dark green leaves are blue-green beneath and have three to six rounded lobes on each side. Borne on very short stalks, the leaves usually turn yellow-brown in autumn. There are many selected forms varying in habit and leaf shape.

Common names: English oak, pedunculate oak
Native range: Europe
Height: 25 m (80 ft) or more
Spread: 20 m (65 ft) or more
Hardiness: Zone 4
Variants: 'Concordia' has bright yellow young foliage. 'Fastigiata' (Cypress oak) is a narrow tree.

Quercus rubra

This very fast-growing deciduous tree has a rounded, spreading habit. The bold leaves are shallowly cut into several lobes, each ending in a bristle-tipped tooth. Dark matt-green above and usually rather blue-green beneath, they turn yellow-brown in autumn, or red on young trees.

Common name: Red oak
Native range: E North America
Height: 25 m (80 ft)
Spread: 20 m (65 ft)
Hardiness: Zone 4
Variants: 'Aurea' has bright yellow young foliage and does best in a partially shaded position.

Rhamnus
Rhamnaceae

This is a large genus comprising some 150 species of deciduous and evergreen trees and shrubs, with alternate or opposite leaves. Species are widely distributed, mainly in the northern hemisphere but also extending to South Africa and South America.

The buckthorns have inconspicuous flowers and are grown principally for their attractive foliage and fruits. The following species are suitable for any well-drained soil, while *R. frangula* will tolerate wet soil. Apart from the removal of dead, damaged or unwanted wood, no pruning is usually necessary.

Rhamnus alaternus

This is a variable evergreen shrub or small tree with alternate, leathery, glossy dark green leaves. Tiny, yellow-green flowers open in clusters in late spring and early summer, and these are followed by small, red fruits, which ripen to black. It is most commonly grown as the form listed below.

Common name: Italian buckthorn
Native range: Mediterranean region
Height: 5 m (16 ft)
Spread: 5 m (16 ft)
Hardiness: Zone 8
Variants: 'Argenteovariegata' produces leaves that are edged with white.

Rhamnus frangula

This vigorous and bushy, often spiny, deciduous shrub or small tree has glossy dark green, alternate leaves that turn red in autumn. Clusters of tiny, yellow-green, pink-tinged flowers open during summer, and these are followed by red, later black, fruits. This species can be used for hedging.

Synonym: *Frangula alnus*
Common name: Alder buckthorn
Native range: Europe, W Asia, North Africa
Height: 5 m (16 ft)
Spread: 5 m (16 ft)
Hardiness: Zone 3

Rhaphiolepis
Rosaceae

This is a small, narrowly distributed genus comprising about 15 species of evergreen shrubs, sometimes trees. All are natives of East Asia.

Rhaphiolepis umbellata

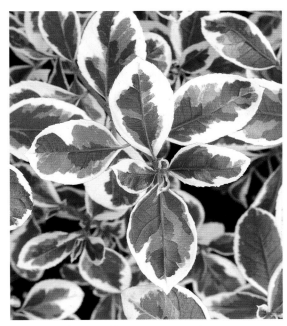

Rhamnus alaternus 'Argenteovariegata'

The following species are cultivated for their foliage, flowers and fruits. In warm areas they can be used as specimen shrubs, for ground cover, or for hedging. In cooler regions, however, they generally require more of a sheltered site. They do best in well-drained soil and when given a position in full sun.

Rhaphiolepis x delacourii

This garden-raised hybrid between *R. indica* and *R. umbellata* makes a rounded evergreen shrub with glossy dark green leaves that are often bronze when young. Clusters of pink flowers open over a long period during the spring and summer.

Height: 1 m (3 ft)
Spread: 1.5 m (5 ft)
Hardiness: Zone 8
Variants: 'Coates' Crimson' has deep pink flowers. 'Enchantress' is a compact form with large clusters of rose-pink flowers.

Rhaphiolepis umbellata

A stiffly branched evergreen shrub with very thick and leathery glossy dark green leaves, usually clustered at the ends of the shoots. Dense clusters of white flowers open in late spring to early summer, followed by long-persistent, blue-black fruits.

Native range: Japan, Korea
Height: 1.5 m (5 ft)
Spread: 1.5 m (5 ft)
Hardiness: Zone 8

Rhododendron augustinii

Rhododendron 'Blue Tit'

Rhododendron
Ericaceae

The 700 or more evergreen, semi-evergreen and deciduous species that make up this large genus range from dwarf shrubs of no more than 1m (3 ft) in height to sizable tree-like shrubs. Species are widely distributed, mainly in the northern hemisphere but also extending to Australasia.

The great variation in the genus gives them many uses in the garden. While the larger species are suitable for woodland situations, the dwarf species are ideal for the peat garden, or the rock garden where summers are not too dry. Those known as hardy hybrids can withstand exposure and make good hedges.

Rhododendrons need a moist but well-drained, lime-free soil, and any yellowing of the leaves is usually an indication of poor drainage or incorrect soil chemistry. Plants benefit from dead-heading and leggy stems can be cut back hard in spring.

Rhododendron augustinii

This vigorous evergreen shrub of bushy, upright habit has scaly young shoots and dark green, taper-pointed leaves, scaly beneath, to 10 cm (4 in) long. Widely funnel-shaped flowers, in various shades of blue, sometimes pink or white, 6 cm (2½ in) across, open in small clusters in mid- to late spring.

Native range: China
Height: 4 m (13 ft)
Spread: 3 m (10 ft)
Hardiness: Zone 6

Rhododendron 'Blue Diamond'

A garden-raised hybrid between R. augustinii and R. 'Intrifast' making a compact, upright evergreen shrub with small leaves. The funnel-shaped flowers, up to 5 cm (2 in) long, are deep violet-blue and open in small clusters in mid- to late spring.

Height: 2 m (6 ft)
Spread: 1.5 m (5 ft)
Hardiness: Zone 6

Rhododendron 'Blue Tit'

A garden-raised hybrid between R. augustinii and R. impeditum making a dense, dwarf evergreen shrub with small, light green leaves up to 2.5 cm (1 in) long. Small clusters of funnel-shaped, pale lavender blue flowers open in early to mid-spring.

Height: 1.2 m (4 ft)
Spread: 2 m (6 ft)
Hardiness: Zone 6

Rhododendron 'Bow Bells'

This charming garden-raised hybrid between R. 'Corona' and R. williamsianum makes a dome-shaped evergreen shrub of compact habit with nearly rounded, purple-stalked leaves, which are bronze when young. Profuse clusters of pale pink, widely bell-shaped flowers, 6 cm (2½ in) across, open from deep pink buds in late spring.

Height: 2 m (6 ft)
Spread: 2 m (6 ft)
Hardiness: Zone 7

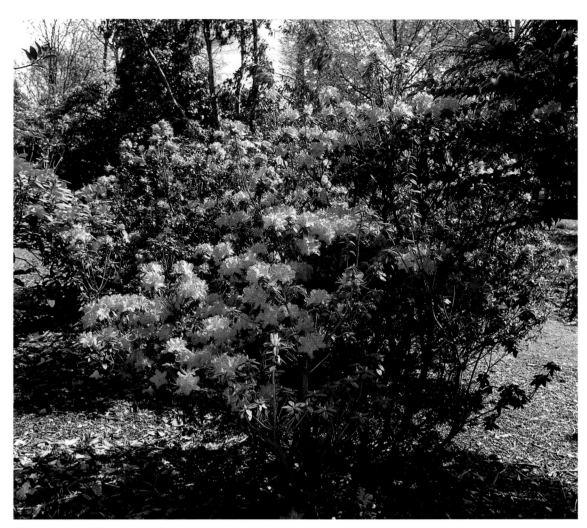

Rhododendron 'Blue Diamond'

Rhododendron 'Britannia'

This popular, hardy hybrid makes a compact, spreading evergreen shrub with light green leaves. Large clusters of broadly bell-shaped, scarlet flowers, up to about 7 cm (3 in) long, open in the late spring.

Height: 1.5 m (5 ft)
Spread: 2 m (6 ft)
Hardiness: Zone 6

Rhododendron calostrotum

This low-growing and compact evergreen shrub has scaly young shoots and small, rather rounded, blue-green leaves, up to about 3 cm (1 in) long, covered with brown scales beneath. Purple-pink flowers, often with deeper spots, open in the late spring.

Native range: N Burma (Myanmar), NE India, SE Tibet, SW China
Height: 1 m (3 ft)
Spread: 1.2 m (4 ft)
Hardiness: Zone 6
Variants: 'Gigha' has red flowers. The subsp. *keleticum* is dwarf and spreading, to 30 cm (12 in) tall, with red-purple flowers.

Height: 60 cm (24 in)
Spread: 1 m (3 ft)
Hardiness: Zone 5

Rhododendron 'Chikor'

This compact, dwarf evergreen shrub is a garden-raised hybrid of *R. rupicola* var. *chryseum* and *R. ludlowii*. It has small, dark green leaves, up to 5 cm (2 in) long, that turn bronze in cold weather. Clusters of pale yellow flowers, up to 4 cm (1½ in) across, open in mid- to late spring.

Height: 60 cm (24 in)
Spread: 90 cm (35 in)
Hardiness: Zone 6

Rhododendron 'Cunningham's White'

This compact, hardy hybrid has dark green leaves up to 10 cm (4 in) long. The white, funnel-shaped flowers, 5 cm (2 in) across, are pale mauve as they open, and have yellow-brown spots in the throat. Reasonably lime-tolerant if the soil is not too dry.

Height: 2.5 m (8 ft)
Spread: 3 m (10 ft)
Hardiness: Zone 5

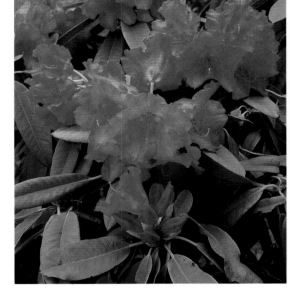

Rhododendron 'Britannia'

Rhododendron 'Carmen'

This garden-raised hybrid between *R. forrestii* and *R. sanguineum* subsp. *didymum* makes a dwarf, spreading evergreen shrub producing dark green leaves up to 5 cm (2 in) long. Clusters of conspicuous, bell-shaped, blood-red flowers, growing up to 4 cm (1½ in) across, open in mid- to late spring.

Rhododendron 'Cynthia'

Rhododendron 'Cynthia'

This is a large-growing and vigorous, hardy hybrid making a dome-shaped evergreen shrub with dark green leaves reaching up to 15 cm (6 in) in length. Large, funnel-shaped, deep pink flowers, up to about 7 cm (3 in) across, and with darker spots inside, are borne in dense, conical clusters in the late spring.

Height: 5 m (16 ft) or more
Spread: 5 m (16 ft)
Hardiness: Zone 5

Rhododendron 'Dopey'

This is a garden-raised hybrid involving
R. yakushimanum and makes a compact
evergreen shrub with an upright habit. Dense,
rounded clusters of bell-shaped, bright orange-
red flowers with wavy edged lobes open in the
late spring.

Height: 2 m (6 ft)
Spread: 2 m (6 ft)
Hardiness: Zone 6

Rhododendron 'Egret'

This is a compact, garden-raised hybrid between
R. racemosum 'White Lace' and *R. campylogynum*.
It makes a free-flowering, dwarf shrub of neat
habit with dark glossy green leaves growing up to
about 2.5cm (1 in) long. Broadly funnel-shaped,
white flowers, up to about 2 cm (¾ in) across,
tinged with green, open in clusters 7cm (3 in)
across in the late spring.

Height: 60 cm (24 in)
Spread: 1 m (3 ft)
Hardiness: Zone 6

Rhododendron 'Elizabeth'

This popular garden-raised hybrid between
R. forrestii and *R. griersonianum* makes a dense,
spreading evergreen shrub bearing small, red-
stalked leaves up to about 8 cm (3 in) long.
Clusters of bright red, funnel-shaped flowers
open in mid-spring.

Height: 1 m (3 ft)
Spread: 2 m (6 ft)
Hardiness: Zone 6

Rhododendron
'Fastuosum Flore Pleno'

This is a compact, hardy hybrid that makes a large
evergreen shrub with dark matt-green leaves up to
12 cm (5 in) long. Mauve-blue, funnel-shaped,
double flowers, up to about 7 cm (3 in) across,
flushed with yellow-brown inside, open in dense
clusters in late spring to early summer.

Height: 4 m (13 ft)
Spread: 5 m (16 ft)
Hardiness: Zone 5

Rhododendron 'Ginny Gee'

Rhododendron 'Fastuosum Flore Pleno'

Rhododendron 'Fragrantissimum'

A garden-raised hybrid between *R. edgeworthii* and *R. formosum* making an open-branched evergreen shrub with veined leaves. Large and extremely fragrant, funnel-shaped, white flowers, up to 10 cm (4 in) across, with a conspicuous yellow flare inside, open in mid-spring. Suitable for a conservatory where it cannot be grown outdoors.

Height: 2 m (6 ft)
Spread: 2 m (6 ft)
Hardiness: Zone 8

Rhododendron 'Ginny Gee'

A dwarf, garden-raised hybrid between *R. keiskei* 'Yaku Fairy' and *R. racemosum* making a spreading evergreen shrub with small, dark green leaves. The widely funnel-shaped, pale pink flowers, 2.5 cm (1 in) long, are deeper in bud, opening in mid-spring and fading to nearly white, edged with pink.

Height: 60 cm (24 in)
Spread: 90 cm (35 in)
Hardiness: Zone 5

Rhododendron 'Gomer Waterer'

A vigorous, tough, hardy hybrid making a compact evergreen shrub with dark green leaves up to 12 cm (5 in) long. Funnel-shaped, white flowers, 8 cm (3 in) across, edged with mauve-pink and flushed yellow-brown in the centre, open from mauve buds in dense, rounded clusters in early summer.

Height: 2 m (6 ft)
Spread: 2.5 m (8 ft)
Hardiness: Zone 5

Rhododendron 'Grumpy'

A garden-raised hybrid of *R. yakushimanum* making a spreading evergreen shrub with dark green leaves up to 8 cm (3 in) long. The funnel-shaped flowers, 5 cm (2 in) across, cream flushed with pale pink at the edges and spotted orange-yellow, open in rounded clusters in mid-spring.

Height: 1 m (3 ft)
Spread: 1.5 m (5 ft)
Hardiness: Zone 6

Rhododendron impeditum

A dwarf evergreen shrub of compact, upright habit with very small, blue-green leaves up to about

Rhododendron impeditum

1 cm (⅓ in) long. The widely funnel-shaped, blue-purple flowers, up to 2.5 cm (1 in) across, open in small clusters in mid- to late spring.

Native range: China
Height: 60 cm (24 in)
Spread: 60 cm (24 in)
Hardiness: Zone 4

Rhododendron 'Loderi King George'

This magnificent garden-raised hybrid between *R. fortunei* and *R. griffithianum* makes a large evergreen shrub of open habit with bold leaves up to 30 cm (12 in) long. The white, funnel-shaped, fragrant flowers, up to 15 cm (6 in) across, open from pink buds in late spring and early summer.

Height: 4 m (13 ft)
Spread: 5 m (16 ft)
Hardiness: Zone 7

Rhododendron lutescens

This is a vigorous evergreen shrub with upright shoots and slender-pointed, dark green leaves, bronze when young, scaly beneath. Broadly

funnel-shaped, pale yellow flowers, up to 2.5 cm (1 in) across, open in early to mid-spring.

Native range: China
Height: 3 m (10 ft)
Spread: 4 m (13 ft)
Hardiness: Zone 7

Rhododendron macabeanum

This large evergreen, stoutly branched shrub, sometimes tree-like, has bold, glossy dark green leaves, up to 30 cm (12 in) long, densely covered with pale brown hairs beneath. Clusters of bell-shaped, pale to deep yellow flowers, about 7 cm (3 in) long, and blotched red-purple inside at the base, open in early to mid-spring.

Native range: NE India
Height: 6 m (20 ft) or more
Spread: 6 m (20 ft)
Hardiness: Zone 8

Rhododendron 'Morning Cloud'

This is a garden-raised hybrid of *R. yakushimanum* that makes a compact evergreen shrub bearing narrow, dark green leaves densely covered in

Rhododendron 'Pink Pearl'

brown hairs beneath. Dense clusters of white flowers, flushed with pink, open from the late spring to early summer.

Height: 1.5 m (5 ft)
Spread: 2 m (6 ft)
Hardiness: Zone 6

Rhododendron 'Mrs GW Leak'

This is a large-growing, compact and vigorous, hardy hybrid with dark matt-green leaves reaching up to 15 cm (6 in) in length. The widely funnel-shaped flowers are up to about 8 cm (3 in) across. Flowers are pale pink, flushed with deeper pink, and with a conspicuous flare of deep red-brown markings inside. They open in dense, conical clusters in late spring.

Height: 3 m (10 ft)
Spread: 4 m (13 ft)
Hardiness: Zone 7

Rhododendron 'Patty Bee'

This is a compact, garden-raised hybrid between *R. fletcherianum* and *R. keiskei* 'Yaku Fairy' that makes a vigorous, dwarf shrub with dark green leaves growing up to about 4.5 cm (2 in) long. The leaves turn bronze in winter. Pale yellow, funnel-shaped flowers, up to about 4.5 cm (2 in) across, with wavy margins, open in dense clusters in the early spring.

Height: 75 cm (30 in)
Spread: 1 m (3 ft)
Hardiness: Zone 6

Rhododendron 'Percy Wiseman'

This is a compact, garden-raised hybrid of *R. yakushimanum* that makes a small-growing evergreen shrub bearing glossy dark green leaves up to about 7.5 cm (3 in) in length. The funnel-shaped flowers, up to about 5 cm (2 in) across, are cream, flushed with pink, and fade to creamy white. The flowers are borne in rounded clusters in mid- to late spring.

Height: 1.5 m (5 ft)
Spread: 2 m (6 ft)
Hardiness: Zone 6

Rhododendron 'Pink Pearl'

This is an old and very popular, hardy hybrid that makes a strongly growing evergreen shrub producing large, dark green leaves. The profusely borne, broadly funnel-shaped, pink flowers, reaching up to about 10 cm (4 in) across, have wavy edges and open in large clusters in mid- to late spring. The flowers fade nearly to white after they open.

Height: 3 m (10 ft)
Spread: 4 m (13 ft)
Hardiness: Zone 6

Rhododendron 'PJM'

This is a popular, garden-raised hybrid between *R. minus* and *R. dauricum* valued in the garden for its great hardiness. It is a medium-sized, compact evergreen shrub bearing dark green leaves that turn a bronze-purple colour in winter. Clusters of bright, lavenderpink, saucer-shaped flowers, up to about 4 cm (1½ in) across, open in the early spring.

Height: 2 m (6 ft)
Spread: 1.5 m (5 ft)
Hardiness: Zone 4

Rhododendron ponticum

This species is largely represented in gardens by hybrids that make vigorous, large shrubs with dark green leaves up to about 20 cm (8 in) long. The large clusters of funnel-shaped, blue-purple flowers, marked with yellow-green spots, open in late spring and early summer.

Native range: S Spain, S Portugal, SW Asia
Height: 5 m (16 ft)
Spread: 5 m (16 ft)
Hardiness: Zone 5
Variants: 'Variegatum' is smaller, up to 3 m (10 ft) high, and has leaves edged with creamy white.

Rhododendron ponticum 'Variegatum'

Rhododendron williamsianum

Rhododendron 'Scarlet Wonder'

Rhododendron 'Praecox'

Valuable for its very early flowers, this semi-evergreen shrub is a garden-raised hybrid between *R. ciliatum* and *R. dauricum*. A compact and rather upright bush, it has glossy, dark green, aromatic leaves that are scaly beneath. Open, funnel-shaped, rose-purple flowers, up to about 5 cm (2 in) across, open in late winter and early spring.

Height: 1.5 m (5 ft)
Spread: 1.5 m (5 ft)
Hardiness: Zone 6

Rhododendron 'Princess Anne'

An evergreen, garden-raised hybrid between *R. hanceanum* and *R. keiskei* making a dense, spreading mound with rather light green leaves, 6 cm (2½ in) long, bronze when young. Funnel-shaped flowers, 3 cm (1 in) across, are green in bud but open pale yellow, and are faintly spotted green.

Height: 60 cm (24 in)
Spread: 1 m (3 ft)
Hardiness: Zone 6

Rhododendron 'Ptarmigan'

This is a garden-raised hybrid between *R. leucaspis* and *R. orthocladum* var. *microleucum* forming a low-spreading, compact shrub with dark green, scaly leaves, 1–2 cm (¾ in) long. Pure white, saucer-shaped flowers, 3 cm (1 in) across, are profusely borne in small clusters in early to mid-spring.

Height: 60 cm (24 in)
Spread: 1 m (3 ft)
Hardiness: Zone 7

Rhododendron 'Purple Splendour'

This is an old and popular, vigorous, hardy hybrid making a compact shrub with dark green leaves to 15 cm (6 in) long. The widely funnel-shaped, wavy edged flowers, about 8 cm (3 in) across, are deep purple with conspicuous, nearly black, markings within, and open in late spring and early summer.

Height: 3 m (10 ft)
Spread: 4 m (13 ft)
Hardiness: Zone 6

Rhododendron 'Ramapo'

This is a very hardy, garden-raised hybrid between *R. fastigiatum* and *R. minus* that makes a dwarf,

Rhododendron yakushimanum

Height: 1 m (3 ft)
Spread: 1.5 m (5 ft)
Hardiness: Zone 6

Rhododendron 'Titian Beauty'

This is a garden-raised hybrid involving *R. yakushimanum* that makes a small evergreen shrub with a compact, rather upright habit. The dark green leaves have a thin layer of brown hairs on their undersurfaces. Clusters of waxy red, bell-shaped flowers open in the late spring and early summer.

Height: 2 m (6 ft)
Spread: 2 m (6 ft)
Hardiness: Zone 6

Rhododendron williamsianum

This dome-shaped evergreen shrub has a dense habit with nearly rounded, dark green leaves, growing up to about 5 cm (2 in) in length. The leaves are blue-green beneath and bronze-coloured when young. Open clusters of widely bell-shaped, pink or sometimes white flowers, up to 5 cm (2 in) across, open in mid-spring.

compact evergreen shrub with attractive, blue-grey young foliage. Small, violet-blue flowers are profusely borne in small clusters in early to mid-spring.

Height: 60 cm (24 in)
Spread: 60 cm (24 in)
Hardiness: Zone 4

Rhododendron 'Sappho'

This is a vigorous, hardy hybrid that makes a large, dome-shaped evergreen shrub with glossy dark green leaves up to 18 cm (7 in) long. The widely funnel-shaped flowers, 8 cm (3 in) across, are mauve in bud, opening in mid-spring to pure white with a blotch of rich purple-black.

Height: 3 m (10 ft)
Spread: 3 m (10 ft)
Hardiness: Zone 6

Rhododendron 'Scarlet Wonder'

A hardy, garden-raised hybrid between R. 'Essex Scarlet' and *R. forrestii* forming a compact mound of dense foliage, with glossy green leaves up to 8 cm (3 in) long. Funnel-shaped, ruby-red flowers, 5 cm (2 in) long, with frilly edged lobes are borne in loose trusses at the ends of the shoots.

Rhododendron 'Daviesii' (deciduous azalea)

Native range: China
Height: 1.2 m (4 ft)
Spread: 1.5 m (5 ft)
Hardiness: Zone 7

Rhododendron yakushimanum

This dense evergreen shrub forms a spreading dome with thick, dark green leaves, white-felted when young, and covered beneath with a thick layer of pale brown hairs. Dense clusters of white, funnel-shaped flowers, up to 5 cm (2 in) across, open from deep pink buds in mid-spring.

Native range: Japan
Height: 1.2 m (4 ft)
Spread: 1.5 m (5 ft)
Hardiness: Zone 5

Deciduous azaleas

The deciduous azaleas that make such striking shrubs generally reach about 2 m (6 ft) in height, with showy, usually fragrant flowers in spring and leaves often colouring in autumn. They flower best in a bright position and can be grown in full sun. They are generally hardy to Zone 5.

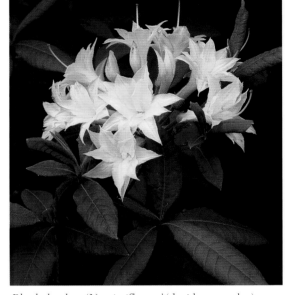

Rhododendron 'Narcissiflorum' (deciduous azalea)

R. **'Berryrose'** Bright salmon-pink flowers with a red tube, and young foliage that is bronze coloured.
R. **'Daviesii'** Large, very fragrant, white flowers, cream flushed with pink when they first open.
R. **'Gibraltar'** Large clusters of rich, orange-red, frilly edged flowers.
R. **'Homebush'** Dense, rounded clusters of bright pink, double flowers.

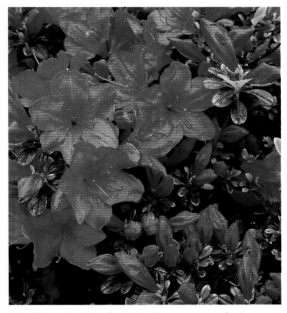

Rhododendron 'Mother's Day' (evergreen azalea)

R. **'Klondyke'** Golden yellow flowers with a red flush, opening from yellow buds flushed red.
R. *luteum* Very fragrant, bright yellow flowers.
R. **'Narcissiflorum'** Pale yellow, very fragrant double flowers in dense clusters.
R. **'Silver Slipper'** Creamy white flowers flushed with yellow, pink-tinged in bud.
R. **'Strawberry Ice'** Pale pink flowers, flushed deep pink, with a yellow flare.

Evergreen azaleas

Generally of compact habit and growing to about 1 m (3 ft) tall, these are excellent for mass planting and prefer light shade, except where summers are cool. The foliage often turns bronze in winter.

R. **'Addy Wery'** Deep vermilion-red flowers.
R. **'Amoenum'** Bright rose-purple, double flowers.
R. **'Blaauw's Pink'** Salmon-pink flowers.
R. **'Blue Danube'** Large violet-purple flowers.
R. **'Hatsugiri'** Compact, with profusely borne, magenta-purple flowers.
R. **'Hino-crimson'** Profuse, bright red flowers.
R. **'Hinode-giri'** Clusters of bright crimson flowers.
R. **'Hinomayo'** Compact, with profusely borne, clear pink flowers.
R. **'Kirin'** Rich pink, double flowers, silvery pink on the outside.
R. **'Madame van Hecke'** Small, rose-pink flowers.
R. **'Mother's Day'** Deep crimson, often semi-double flowers.
R. *nakaharae* Dwarf and spreading, to 30 cm (12 in) tall, with orange-red to pink flowers. (Zone 7)
R. **'Orange Beauty'** Bushy, spreading habit with orange-red, frilly edged flowers.
R. **'Squirrel'** Dwarf and compact, with deep reddish-orange flowers.
R. **'Vuyk's Rosyred'** Large, deep rose pink flowers with a deeper flush in the centre.
R. **'Vuyk's Scarlet'** Large, bright crimson flowers, and a low, spreading habit.

Rhododendron 'Blaauw's Pink' (evergreen azalea)

Rhodotypos
Rosaceae

The single species in this small genus is a deciduous shrub with opposite leaves, and is grown for its showy white flowers, which can open very early in the year given a warm spring.

This species is suitable for the shrub border and will grow in any good, well-drained soil, and does best in a sunny position. Little pruning is generally needed but some of the shoots that have flowered can be cut back after flowering.

Rhodotypos scandens

This deciduous shrub is upright at first and later develops arching shoots. The dark green and sharply toothed leaves are taper-pointed and have conspicuous, parallel veins. White, four-petalled flowers with yellow stamens in their centres, open at the ends of the shoots in late spring and early summer, sometimes earlier, followed by clusters of small, glossy black, persistent fruits.

Native range: China, Japan
Height: 2 m (6 ft)
Spread: 2.5 m (8 ft)
Hardiness: Zone 4

Rhus glabra

Rhus typhina 'Dissecta'

Rhus
Anacardiaceae

The sumachs are a large and widely distributed genus made up of deciduous and evergreen shrubs and trees, and occasionally climbers as well.

The following species are grown for their foliage, which colours up richly in autumn, and for their often conspicuous fruit clusters. They are suitable for any well-drained soil in full sun, but they are generally too invasive for the border – however, *R. glabra* and *R. typhina* are suitable as specimen plants. Planting them in a lawn that is cut regularly will prevent them spreading. Remove suckers as necessary, and cut back hard in spring to rejuvenate them or to encourage the production of large, showy leaves.

Rhus aromatica

This is a spreading deciduous shrub with dark green to blue-green, aromatic foliage. The leaves are divided into three sharply toothed leaflets and turn orange-red in autumn. Upright spikes of small, yellow flowers open in spring, and these are followed by clusters of small red fruits. It does best in regions with hot summers.

Common name: Fragrant sumach
Native range: E North America
Height: 1.5 m (5 ft)
Spread: 2.5 m (8 ft)
Hardiness: Zone 3

Rhus glabra

This is a vigorous, sturdily branched and upright shrub with stout, bloomy shoots that spreads by suckers. It has dark green leaves with numerous, up to 31, sharply toothed leaflets that turn brilliant orange- to purple-red in autumn. Small, yellow-green flowers open in large, conical clusters at the ends of the shoots during summer and these are followed by red-ripening fruits.

Common name: Smooth sumach
Native range: North America
Height: 3 m (10 ft)
Spread: 3 m (10 ft)
Hardiness: Zone 3

Rhus typhina

This is a vigorous, thicket-forming deciduous shrub, sometimes a tree, with stout, velvety shoots. The bold, dark green leaves are divided up into as many as 27 leaflets, and leaves turn to brilliant shades of orange and red in autumn. Dense heads of small, yellow-green flowers in summer ripen to conical, long-persistent, matted clusters of red fruits.

Common name: Stag's-horn sumach
Native range: E North America
Height: 6 m (20 ft)
Spread: 5 m (16 ft)
Hardiness: Zone 4
Variants: 'Dissecta' is lower growing with deeply lobed leaflets. It is sometimes known as 'Laciniata'.

Ribes sanguineum 'Pulborough Scarlet'

Ribes alpinum

Ribes

Grossulariaceae

The currants are a genus of some 150 species of deciduous and evergreen, sometimes spiny shrubs. They are widely distributed mainly in temperate regions of the northern hemisphere, with some species found in South America.

While the ornamental species are grown principally for their flowers, others, such as the gooseberry, redcurrant and blackcurrant, have edible fruits. Suitable for any reasonably good, well-drained soil, in general they do best if given a position in full sun.

Ribes alpinum

This compact deciduous shrub has bright green, three- to five-lobed leaves. Tiny, yellow-green flowers are borne in dense clusters in spring, males and females usually on separate plants. Females bear small, glossy red berries. This species will grow well in sun or shade.

Common name: Moutain currant
Native range: Europe
Height: 1.2 m (4 ft) or more
Spread: 1.5 m (5 ft)
Hardiness: Zone 2
Variants: 'Aureum' produces foliage that is bright yellow when young.

Ribes laurifolium

This is a low-growing and spreading evergreen shrub bearing dark green, leathery leaves that grow up to 12 cm (5 in) long. Large, drooping clusters of pale greenish-white flowers open in late winter and early spring. The male and female flowers are borne on separate plants; the males distinguished by being more showy. It is an excellent groundcover plant, especially for shady places.

Native range: China
Height: 1 m (3 ft)
Spread: 3 m (10 ft)
Hardiness: Zone 8

Ribes odoratum

This is a clump-forming deciduous shrub with upright shoots that become arching with age. The bright green, deeply lobed leaves turn to yellow, red and purple in autumn. Drooping clusters of clove-scented, bright yellow flowers open in mid- to late spring.

Common name: Buffalo currant
Native range: C United States of America
Height: 2 m (6 ft)
Spread: 2.5 m (8 ft)
Hardiness: Zone 4

Ribes sanguineum

This is a vigorous deciduous shrub of a dense, upright habit with aromatic, three- to five-lobed leaves, useful as a specimen shrub, in a border or as hedging. Drooping clusters of pink flowers open in spring, and these are followed by blue-black, bloomy berries. To prune, cut some of the older shoots to the base after flowering.

Common name: Flowering currant
Native range: W North America
Height: 2.5 m (8 ft)
Spread: 2 m (6 ft)
Hardiness: Zone 5
Variants: 'Brocklebankii' produces yellow foliage and pale pink flowers. 'King Edward VII' is spreading and has deep red flowers. 'Pulborough Scarlet' is vigorous and upright, with deep red flowers. 'White Icicle' produces white flowers.

Ribes speciosum

This vigorous, upright deciduous shrub has red, bristly shoots and small, glossy green, three- to five-lobed leaves. Slender, pendulous, bright red, fuchsia-like flowers open in small clusters in mid- to late spring. It can be trained effectively against a sunny wall.

Common name: Fuchsia-flowered currant
Native range: California, USA
Height: 2.5 m (8 ft) or more
Spread: 2 m (6 ft)
Hardiness: Zone 7

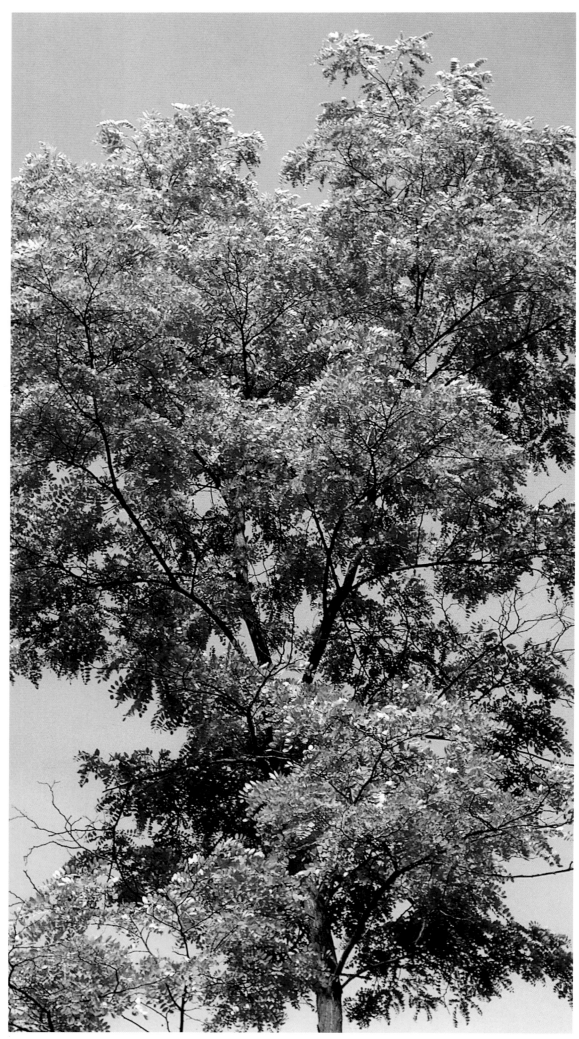

Robinia pseudoacacia 'Frisia'

R[obinia]

Leg[uminosae]

This is a small genus of only about ten species of deciduous trees and shrubs, all natives of North America. They have leaves divided into numerous leaflets and pendulous clusters of pea-like flowers.

Species are suitable for any well-drained soil and they are particularly useful on dry soils. They all thrive in a sunny position. *R. pseudoacacia* can produce invasive suckers.

Robinia hispida

This is a deciduous shrub with an open habit that spreads by sending out suckers. The blue-green, bristly stalked leaves are divided up into as many as 13 leaflets, and leaves are borne on densely bristly shoots. Drooping clusters of large, pea-like, deep pink flowers open in late spring and early summer. However, fruit is rarely produced.

Common name: Bristly locust
Native range: SE United States of America
Height: 3 m (10 ft)
Spread: 4 m (13 ft)
Hardiness: Zone 5

Robinia pseudoacacia

This vigorous deciduous tree of broadly columnar habit often has spiny branches and bears blue-green leaves divided up into as many as 21 leaflets. Drooping clusters of fragrant, white, pea-like flowers, blotched yellow-green, hang from the shoots in early to mid-summer, and these are followed by dark brown pods.

Common name: Black locust
Native range: SE United States of America
Height: 25 m (80 ft)
Spread: 15 m (50 ft)
Hardiness: Zone 4
Variants: 'Frisia' is a smaller tree with pale yellow foliage. 'Tortuosa' is a small, slow-growing tree with conspicuously twisted shoots.

Robinia x slavinii 'Hillieri'

This garden-raised hybrid of *R. pseudoacacia* makes a vigorous, rounded tree with spreading, slightly bristly shoots and dark green leaves bearing up to 19 leaflets. Drooping clusters of fragrant, lilac-pink flowers hang from the shoots in late spring.

Height: 10 m (33 ft)
Spread: 10 m (33 ft)
Hardiness: Zone 5

Robinia hispida

Romneya
Papaveraceae

The single species in this genus is a subshrub grown for its strikingly large flowers. Suitable for a border, it may need restricting as it can spread vigorously by underground stems. In cold areas it can be grown against a sunny wall.

Grow in any good, well-drained soil in full sun. The old shoots can be cut to the ground in spring.

Romneya coulteri

A vigorous, suckering subshrub with upright, bloomy shoots bearing deeply cut, blue-grey leaves. Large, white, poppy-like flowers, 12 cm (5 in) across, have petals with crinkled edges and a conspicuous central boss of golden yellow stamens. They open singly at the ends of the young shoots over a long period during summer.

Romneya coulteri 'White Cloud'

Common name: Tree poppy
Native range: California, USA, N Mexico
Height: 2 m (6 ft)
Spread: 5 m (16 ft) or more
Hardiness: Zone 7
Variants: 'White Cloud' produces very large flowers and spreads vigorously.

Rosa
Rosaceae

The roses are some of the most widely grown of all woody plants. The 150 or so species are deciduous or sometimes evergreen shrubs, widely distributed in temperate regions of the northern hemisphere. With often spiny or bristly stems and leaves divided into several leaflets, the wild species have flowers with normally five petals, and these are often followed by ornamental fruits (hips). Most roses prefer a good, moist but well-drained soil rich in organic matter and a position in full sun.

The vast number of garden hybrids have given a diverse array of plants suitable for many purposes in the garden, from specimen shrubs, hedging, bedding, growing up a wall, over a pergola or into trees. Others are suitable for ground cover or for growing in containers.

The species roses and their immediate hybrids are often left unpruned, but they can be cut back as necessary in late summer after flowering, or in late winter if they continue flowering into the autumn. Most other roses benefit from regular pruning. The various methods are discussed below under the different groups to which roses are assigned.

All roses that are planted when they are dormant, with the exception of climbers, should be pruned hard immediately to ensure that the subsequent growth breaks from the base.

Some roses are offered under selling names or trademarks. These are shown without quotation marks. If the plant also has a cultivar name, then this is given afterwards in parentheses.

Alba

These old hybrids are vigorous and hardy, usually sparsely spiny shrubs with grey-green foliage and white to pink, usually fully double, fragrant flowers. Useful as specimens or for hedging. Prune in late summer after flowering by cutting old shoots back by about one-third. Any long shoots can also be cut back in autumn. To renovate, after flowering or in spring, cut all the old shoots to the base, and cut back vigorous young shoots by one-third.

Bourbon

A group of old hybrids making vigorous, sometimes climbing, shrubs. The usually double flowers are borne in summer through to autumn, and so they should be pruned in the dormant season. Prune as for Alba roses, but in late winter, when any thin and overcrowded shoots should also be removed.

Centifolia

These are old hybrids involving the Alba roses that make open shrubs with thorny stems and large, usually double, fragrant flowers. Prune immediately after flowering, as for Alba roses.

Climbers

These are vigorous shrubs with long, thorny shoots useful for training against a wall or on to a pergola. Do not cut back on planting. Provide a support of wires and tie in lateral shoots to these as they develop. When established, prune as necessary to restrict growth. Cut some older stems back to young, developing shoots. When mature, the oldest stems can be cut back to the ground.

Cluster-flowered (Floribunda)

Vigorous, upright shrubs with single to double, clustered flowers borne over a long period from summer to autumn. Useful for bedding and for a border. Cut out any dead or diseased wood during the growing season and dead-head regularly. Prune in late winter by cutting out any weak or dead shoots and reducing other shoots to about 30 cm (12 in). Some have climbing forms.

Damask

This group of old hybrids makes open shrubs with thorny stems and semi-double or double, white to pink flowers. Prune as for Alba roses.

Gallica

This is an old group of hybrids deriving from *R. gallica*, with single to fully double, white to pink flowers. Prune as for Alba roses.

Ground cover

These are low-growing shrubs all with a spreading to trailing habit, and with long, prickly shoots and profuse, single to double flowers. They are shrubs ideal for trailing over low walls and banks. Prune as necessary in late winter to restrict growth.

Hybrid musk

This is a group of vigorous hybrids with clustered, usually fragrant flowers produced from summer through to autumn. They are useful for hedging. Prune in late winter by removing any dead or weak shoots and by cutting some of the oldest shoots back to the base. Reduce the remaining shoots by about one-third.

Large-flowered (Hybrid Tea)

These are vigorous, upright shrubs with large, usually double and fragrant flowers. The flowers are borne singly or in small clusters in summer and autumn. They are mainly used for bedding. Prune in late winter as for cluster-flowered roses, cutting stems back to 20 cm (8 in). Some have climbing forms.

Pimpinellifolia hybrid

Also known as Burnet or Scotch roses, these hybrids make vigorous, suckering shrubs deriving from *R. pimpinellifolia*, with small leaves that often colour well in autumn. Flowers are single to semi-double, white to pink or red-purple in colour, sometimes yellow. To prune, cut the stems back lightly after flowering. They are suitable for bedding or for planting in a shrub border.

Polyantha

These are compact, free-flowering shrubs suitable for bedding or growing in containers, producing clustered, single to double flowers. Prune shrubs in late winter, as for large-flowered roses.

Rambler

These vigorous shrubs have long, thorny shoots bearing profuse clusters of small, usually unscented flowers. Useful for growing on walls, fences, or into trees and as weeping standards. Given space they can be left to grow freely. Prune on planting by cutting back to about 40 cm (16 in). Cut back after flowering to restrict growth, and remove some of the old shoots by cutting back to ground level to encourage new growth from the base.

Rosa 'Albéric Barbier'

Rugosa hybrid

These vigorous hybrids of *R. rugosa* have distinctive and prominently veined leaves that often colour up well in autumn. The usually large, single to semi-double flowers are often followed by conspicuous fruits. After flowering cut some of the older shoots right back to the base and reduce the length of the remaining shoots slightly by cutting out the tips.

Shrub

These are vigorous, modern hybrids with single to semi-double flowers. The flowers open in summer and again usually in autumn. They are useful shrubs for the border but they can also do service as bedding plants. Prune them after they have finished flowering by lightly cutting back shoots. Remove some of the older stems, cutting them right back to the base, of any plants that have become congested.

Rosa 'Abraham Darby'

This is a vigorous and bushy shrub rose with large, double, fragrant, apricot-pink flowers up to about 11cm (4–5 in) across. The flowers open in summer through to autumn.

Height: 1.5 m (5 ft)
Spread: 1.5 m (5 ft)
Hardiness: Zone 5

Rosa 'Albéric Barbier'

This is a strong-growing and popular rambler, a hybrid of *R. wichurana*, with handsome, glossy foliage. Double, fragrant, creamy white flowers, 8 cm (3 in) across, open in summer.

Height: 5 m (16 ft)
Spread: 3 m (10 ft)
Hardiness: Zone 5

Rosa 'Albertine'

This is an extremely vigorous rambler – a hybrid of *R. wichurana* – with strongly growing, thorny shoots and glossy green foliage that is bronze when young. The profuse and very fragrant, double, pale pink flowers, up to 8 cm (3 in) across, are flushed with orange when they first open.

Height: 5 m (16 ft)
Spread: 3 m (10 ft)
Hardiness: Zone 5

Rosa 'American Pillar'

This is a vigorous rambler deriving from *R. wichurana* with long, stout, very thorny shoots and large, glossy green leaves. In summer, the shrub bears large clusters of single, red flowers, up to 5 cm (2 in) across, white in the centre and fading to deep pink.

Height: 5 m (16 ft)
Spread: 3 m (10 ft)
Hardiness: Zone 5

Rosa 'Arthur Bell'

This cluster-flowered rose produces glossy green foliage. The semi-double yellow or creamy flowers, up to 8 cm (3 in) across, are fragrant and have a centre of golden-coloured stamens. Flowers open from summer to autumn.

Rosa 'Blanc Double de Coubert'

Height: 1 m (3 ft)
Spread: 75 cm (30 in)
Hardiness: Zone 5

Rosa 'Ballerina'

This is a bushy Polyantha type rose with a good, compact habit. The shrub bears large sprays of small, single, pink-coloured flowers, about 3 cm (1 in) across, each with a white centre. It is a useful plant, equally suitable for growing in containers or planted out for bedding.

Height: 1.2 m (4 ft)
Spread: 1 m (3 ft)
Hardiness: Zone 5

Rosa banksiae

This is a vigorous evergreen climber with long, slender shoots and light green leaves that are composed of up to seven leaflets. A useful plant where children may play as its shoots are thornless. Flowers, which may be white or yellow, single or double, open in late spring. It prefers a Mediterranean climate and in colder regions it benefits from being grown up a sun-facing wall.

Native range: China
Height: 10 m (33 ft)
Spread: 6 m (20 ft)
Hardiness: Zone 7
Variants: 'Lutea' produces attractive, double, yellow flowers.

Rosa 'Blanc Double de Coubert'

This is a vigorous rugosa hybrid with densely prickly shoots and dark green, deeply veined leaves. The large, loosely semi-double, pure white, strongly fragrant flowers, up to 8cm (3 in) across, have conspicuous yellow stamens and open from summer through to autumn. The flowers are sometimes followed by large, orange-red fruits.

Height: 1.5 m (5 ft)
Spread: 1.2 m (4 ft)
Hardiness: Zone 2

Rosa Blessings

This vigorous, large-flowered rose has dark green foliage, and fragrant, double, salmon-pink flowers that open during the summer and autumn.

Height: 1 m (3 ft)
Spread: 75 cm (30 in)
Hardiness: Zone 5

Rosa Blue Moon ('Tannacht')

This is a large-flowered rose with dark green foliage. It bears fragrant, double, lilac-coloured flowers, up to 10 cm (4 in) across, from summer through to the autumn.

Height: 1 m (3 ft)
Spread: 75 cm (30 in)
Hardiness: Zone 5

Rosa 'Bobbie James'

This is a vigorous rambler with lush, bright green foliage, red when young. The white flowers, in large clusters of semi-double, very fragrant, blooms, up to 5 cm (2 in) across, have centres of white stamens and open in summer from cream buds.

Height: 10 m (33 ft)
Spread: 8 m (26 ft)
Hardiness: Zone 5

Rosa 'Boule de Neige'

This vigorous, upright and sparsely thorny Bourbon rose has dark green, leathery leaves. The fully double and strongly fragrant flowers are globular in shape, opening white in summer and autumn from red-flushed buds.

Height: 1.2 m (4 ft)
Spread: 90 cm (35 in)
Hardiness: Zone 4

Rosa 'Buff Beauty'

This is an extremely beautiful Hybrid Musk rose with a spreading habit and arching shoots bearing dark green leaves that are bronze when young. Clusters of large, fully double, buff-yellow to apricot, fragrant flowers, up to about 9 cm (3½ in) across, open from summer to autumn.

Height: 1.5 m (5 ft)
Spread: 1.5 m (5 ft)
Hardiness: Zone 5

Rosa 'Cardinal de Richelieu'

This compact Gallica rose has slender, almost thornless shoots and dark green, occasionally purple-edged, foliage. The sweetly fragrant, fully double, rounded blooms have rich purple-red, velvety petals and flowers open in clusters during the summer.

Height: 1.2 m (4 ft)
Spread: 90 cm (35 in)
Hardiness: Zone 4

Rosa 'Cécile Brünner'

This slender-stemmed, upright Polyantha rose produces small, dark green, rather sparse leaves. Pale pink, double and delicately scented flowers, up to about 4 cm (1½ in) across, open in clusters, on long stalks, during summer and autumn. Another form, 'Climbing Cécile Brünner', is similar but is a vigorous climber.

Height: 1.2 m (4 ft)
Spread: 60 cm (24 in)
Hardiness: Zone 5

Rosa 'Céleste'

This dense and vigorous Alba rose has an upright habit with grey-green foliage and sparsely prickly shoots. Soft pink, loosely double, sweetly fragrant flowers, up to 8 cm (3 in) across, open in summer.

Height: 2 m (6 ft)
Spread: 1.2 m (4 ft)
Hardiness: Zone 5

Rosa x centifolia

The Centifolia roses are old, complex hybrids. The typical form makes a vigorous shrub with arching, spiny shoots and matt-green foliage. Fully double, fragrant, pink flowers, up to 9 cm (3½ in) across, and with incurved petals, open in summer.

Rosa x centifolia 'Muscosa'

Common names: Holland rose, Provence rose
Height: 1.5 m (5 ft)
Spread: 1.5 m (5 ft)
Hardiness: Zone 5
Variants: 'Cristata' (crested moss rose) produces conspicuous, green, moss-like crests on its sepals. 'Muscosa' (moss rose) has shoots and sepals covered in moss-like bristles.

Rosa Chinatown

This is a vigorous, cluster-flowered rose of an upright habit that produces dark green leaves. The large, double, very fragrant flowers, growing up to about 10 cm (4 in) across, are yellow, sometimes flushed with pink or red, and open in the summer and autumn.

Height: 1.5 m (5 ft)
Spread: 1 m (3 ft)
Hardiness: Zone 5

Rosa 'Climbing Iceberg'

This climbing, cluster-flowered rose has glossy light green foliage and almost thornless shoots. Pure white, double flowers, up to about 8 cm (3 in) across, open in large clusters over an extended period from summer to autumn.

Height: 6 m (20 ft)
Spread: 3 m (10 ft)
Hardiness: Zone 5

Rosa Compassion

This is a climbing, large-flowered rose that produces glossy dark green foliage. The large, double, fragrant flowers are salmon-pink flushed apricot and yellow, and they open from summer through to the autumn.

Height: 3 m (10 ft)
Spread: 2 m (6 ft)
Hardiness: Zone 5

Rosa 'Complicata'

This is a vigorous Gallica rose that has arching shoots and matt-grey-green foliage. The large, single, bright pink flowers, up to about 11 cm (4–5 in) across, have paler centres and a dense cluster of yellow stamens. Flowers are borne in clusters in mid-summer. It can be grown as a specimen or trained on a pillar or as a climber.

Height: 3 m (10 ft)
Spread: 2 m (6 ft)
Hardiness: Zone 5

Rosa Compassion

Rosa Constance Spry ('Austance')

This is an extremely beautiful shrub rose with large, grey-green leaves produced on arching, thorny shoots. The large, slightly nodding, fragrant, double flowers, which grow up to about 12 cm (5 in) across, are a soft pink colour and open in mid-summer. It can be trained as a climber if required.

Height: 2 m (6 ft) or more
Spread: 1.5 m (5 ft)
Hardiness: Zone 5

Rosa 'Cornelia'

This is a vigorous Hybrid Musk rose with glossy, dark green leaves that are bronze when young. Its small, double and sweetly fragrant flowers, growing up to about 5 cm (2 in) across, are an apricot-pink colour and they are attractively flushed with shades of a deeper pink. The flowers are borne in small clusters during the summer and larger clusters of flowers are produced in the autumn.

Height: 1.5 m (5 ft)
Spread: 1.5 m (5 ft)
Hardiness: Zone 5

Rosa Constance Spry

Rosa 'Crimson Shower'

This is a vigorous, rambling rose with glossy bright green foliage. The small, scented, semi-double flowers, up to about 3 cm (1 in) across, are a deep crimson colour that does not fade. The flowers open in large, pendulous clusters over a long period during the summer and autumn.

Height: 4 m (13 ft)
Spread: 3 m (10 ft)
Hardiness: Zone 5

Rosa Danse du Feu

This is a climbing rose with lush, dark green foliage. Double, bright scarlet flowers, up to 8 cm (3 in) across are profusely borne, opening from summer through to autumn.

Height: 4 m (13 ft)
Spread: 3 m (10 ft)
Hardiness: Zone 5

Rosa 'Deep Secret'

This is a vigorous, large-flowered rose with glossy dark green foliage. The large, fully double and fragrant flowers, up to 10 cm (4 in) across, are deep crimson in colour and open from summer through to autumn.

Height: 1 m (3 ft)
Spread: 75 cm (30 in)
Hardiness: Zone 5

Rosa 'Dorothy Perkins'

This is a popular and well-known, vigorous rambler – a hybrid of *R. wichurana* – with glossy dark green foliage. Small, double, clear pink and slightly fragrant flowers, about 2 cm (¾ in) across, are profusely borne in large drooping clusters in late summer.

Height: 3 m (10 ft)
Spread: 2.5 m (8 ft)
Hardiness: Zone 5

Rosa 'Fantin-Latour'

This vigorous Centifolia hybrid produces dark green foliage. The large, soft pink, double flowers, growing up to about 10 cm (4 in) across, have strongly folded petals and a small, green centre. The flowers, which open in summer, have the extra benefit of being richly scented.

Height: 1.5m (5 ft)
Spread: 1.2 m (4 ft)
Hardiness: Zone 4

Rosa 'Felicia'

This vigorous Hybrid Musk rose is among the very best of its type, making a rounded bush with rich green foliage. The loosely double, sweetly fragrant flowers, up to about 8 cm (3 in) across, open a deep pink colour, but this pales as the blooms age. Flowers open in large clusters in summer and autumn. It can be used for hedging.

Rosa filipes 'Kiftsgate'

Height: 1.5 m (5 ft)
Spread: 2 m (6 ft)
Hardiness: Zone 5

Rosa 'Félicité Perpetué'

This rambler, a hybrid of *R. sempervirens*, has nearly evergreen dark green leaves on sparsely thorny shoots. Double, creamy white flowers, flushed pink, 4 cm (1½ in) across, open in summer.

Height: 5 m (16 ft)
Spread: 3 m (10 ft)
Hardiness: Zone 6

Rosa filipes

This vigorous species is a strong-growing climber with glossy, rather pale green leaves on arching, thorny shoots. Fragrant, white flowers, 2.5 cm (1 in) across, open in clusters from cream buds in late summer, followed by orange, later scarlet, fruits.

Native range: China
Height: 10 m (33 ft)
Spread: 6 m (20 ft)
Hardiness: Zone 5
Variants: 'Kiftsgate' is the most popular form. It is extremely vigorous with large flower clusters.

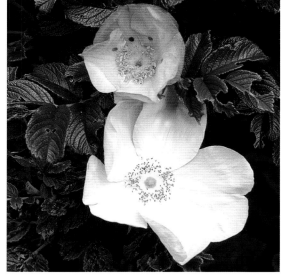

Rosa 'Fru Dagmar Hastrup'

Rosa Fragrant Cloud ('Tanduft')

This large-flowered rose produces dark green foliage. It flowers are double, growing up to 8 cm (3 in) across, deep scarlet in colour and very fragrant. The flowers open from summer through to the autumn.

Height: 1 m (3 ft)
Spread: 75 cm (30 in)
Hardiness: Zone 5

Rosa 'Fru Dagmar Hastrup'

This dense and bushy Rugosa hybrid has densely prickly shoots and deeply veined leaves that turn yellow in autumn. The large and sweetly fragrant, clear silvery pink flowers, up to about 9 cm (3½ in) across, have a centre of yellow stamens and open in clusters during summer. The flowers are followed by conspicuous, bright red fruits.

Height: 1.2 m (4 ft)
Spread: 1.5 m (5 ft)
Hardiness: Zone 2

Rosa 'Frühlingsgold'

This vigorous Pimpinellifolia hybrid has arching, spiny shoots and small, dark green leaves. The semi-double flowers, up to 10 cm (4 in) across, are very fragrant and open a rich golden yellow in early summer, fading to creamy white with age.

Height: 2 m (6 ft)
Spread: 2.5 m (8 ft)
Hardiness: Zone 4

Rosa 'Frühlingsmorgen'

A Pimpinellifolia hybrid of open, upright habit and with dark grey-green leaves. The single, strongly fragrant flowers, 10 cm (4 in) across, are rich pink with a yellow centre and maroon stamens. They open in early summer, often with a second flush in autumn, and are followed by red-purple fruits.

Height: 2 m (6 ft)
Spread: 1.5 m (5 ft)
Hardiness: Zone 4

Rosa gallica

This species makes a suckering shrub with slender, upright stems and leaves with up to seven leaflets. The single, deep pink to red, fragrant flowers, growing to about 8 cm (3 in) across, open singly or in small clusters in summer, and these are followed by red fruits. It is mainly represented in gardens by the forms listed below.

Common name: Red rose
Native range: Europe, W Asia
Height: 1.2 m (4 ft)
Spread: 1 m (3 ft)
Hardiness: Zone 5
Variants: 'Officinalis' (apothecaries' rose) is bushy and upright, with grey-green foliage and very fragrant, semi-double, deep pinkish-red flowers. 'Versicolor' ('Rosa Mundi') has pale pink, semi-double flowers streaked with red.

Rosa glauca

Rosa 'Golden Wings'

This is a popular and compact shrub rose of bushy, upright habit with light green foliage on prickly shoots. The large, single, sweetly fragrant, pale yellow flowers are deeper coloured in the centre and have golden stamens. They start to open in early summer and continue until autumn.

Height: 1.5 m (5 ft)
Spread: 1.5 m (5 ft)
Hardiness: Zone 5

Rosa 'Graham Thomas'

This vigorous shrub rose has arching shoots bearing bright green foliage. Its fully double, fragrant, rich yellow flowers are up to about 11 cm (4–5 in) across and open from summer through to the autumn.

Height: 1.2 m (4 ft)
Spread: 1.2 m (4 ft)
Hardiness: Zone 5

Rosa 'Grandpa Dickson'

This is a large-flowered rose with glossy green foliage. The very large, clear yellow, double flowers, up to 18 cm (7 in) across, are well-shaped with a high centre and are highly fragrant. Flushed with pink on the outer petals, the flowers open freely in summer and autumn.

Height: 90 cm (35 in)
Spread: 60 cm (24 in)
Hardiness: Zone 5

Rosa Heritage ('Ausblush')

This is a bushy and vigorous shrub rose with glossy dark green foliage. The double, pale pink flowers, up to about 11 cm (4–5 in) across, are deeper coloured in their centres and have a strong scent reminiscent of lemons. They are freely borne during summer and into autumn.

Height: 1.2 m (4 ft)
Spread: 1.2 m (4 ft)
Hardiness: Zone 5

Rosa glauca

This is a vigorous and upright shrub with arching, bloomy shoots and purple-grey leaves. The shrub produces single, deep pink flowers, reaching up to 4 cm (1½ in) across, that have paler centres each with a cluster of yellow stamens. The flowers open in small clusters in summer, and these are followed by rounded, red fruits.

Synonym: *Rosa rubrifolia*
Native range: Europe
Height: 2.5 m (8 ft)
Spread: 2 m (6 m)
Hardiness: Zone 2

Rosa 'Gloire de Dijon'

This is an old and popular climbing rose of vigorous growth. It produces purple shoots bearing glossy dark green leaves that are bronze when young. The large and very fragrant double flowers, reaching up to 10 cm (4 in) across, are pale apricot in colour and open in summer. There is a repeat flowering in autumn.

Height: 4 m (13 ft)
Spread: 3 m (10 ft)
Hardiness: Zone 5

Rosa 'Geranium'

Rosa 'Geranium'

This hybrid of *R. moyesii* develops into a compact, bushy shrub with arching branches bearing bright green leaves. The single, bright red flowers, up to 6 cm (2½ in) across, have centres of golden stamens and open during summer. They are followed by bright orange-red, bottle-shaped fruits.

Height: 2.5 m (8 ft)
Spread: 2.5 m (8 ft)
Hardiness: Zone 5

Rosa 'Louise Odier'

This vigorous Bourbon rose has slender, arching shoots and grey-green foliage. The double, bright pink, camellia-like flowers, about 9 cm (3½ in) across, are richly fragrant and are heavily borne in summer and autumn.

Rosa 'New Dawn'

Height: 1.5 m (5 ft)
Spread: 1.2 m (4 ft)
Hardiness: Zone 4

Rosa 'Madame Alfred Carrière'

A climber with light green foliage on sparsely thorny shoots. The white, fully double flowers, flushed pale pink, are 6 cm (2½ in) across, and open over a long period from summer to autumn.

Height: 4 m (13 ft)
Spread: 3 m (10 ft)
Hardiness: Zone 5

Rosa 'Madame Grégoire Staechelin'

A vigorous climber with arching shoots and dark green foliage. The double, clear pink flowers, 12 cm (5 in) across, are flushed deeper pink. Flowers open early summer, followed by orange-red fruits.

Height: 5 m (16 ft)
Spread: 3 m (10 ft)
Hardiness: Zone 5

Rosa 'Madame Hardy'

An old but popular Damask rose making a vigorous bush with bright green foliage. The pure white, fragrant, fully double flowers, 10 cm (4 in) across, have a green eye and open during summer.

Height: 1.5 m (5 ft)
Spread: 1.5 m (5 ft)
Hardiness: Zone 4

Rosa 'Madame Isaac Pereire'

This is a vigorous Bourbon rose with arching, sometimes climbing, shoots and dark green foliage. The very large and fully double, rich purple-pink flowers, reaching about 15 cm (6 in) across, are strongly fragrant and open from summer through to autumn.

Height: 2.5 m (8 ft)
Spread: 2 m (6 ft)
Hardiness: Zone 4

Rosa 'Maiden's Blush'

This vigorous Alba rose has arching shoots bearing blue-grey foliage. The fully double, pale pink flowers, up to about 7 cm (3 in) across, are extremely fragrant and open in large clusters from creamy buds in mid-summer.

Height: 1.5 m (5 ft)
Spread: 1.5 m (5 ft)
Hardiness: Zone 4

Rosa Margaret Merril ('Harkuly')

This is a cluster-flowered rose with a bushy, upright habit bearing dark green foliage. The pale pink to almost white, double flowers, reaching up to about 10 cm (4 in) across, are fragrant and open from silvery pink buds in clusters from summer through to the autumn.

Height: 1.2 m (4 ft)
Spread: 90 cm (35 in)
Hardiness: Zone 5

Rosa Mary Rose ('Ausmary')

This is a vigorous and bushy shrub rose with dense foliage. The deep pink, double, highly fragrant flowers, up to 9 cm (3½ in) across, open from summer through to autumn.

Height: 1.2 m (4 ft)
Spread: 1.2 m (4 ft)
Hardiness: Zone 5

Rosa 'Mermaid'

This beautiful, nearly evergreen climber, is a hybrid of *R. bracteata* and has strongly spiny, red-brown shoots and glossy dark green foliage. The large, single, fragrant yellow flowers, up to 10 cm (4 in) across, have centres of deep yellow stamens and open from summer to autumn. It is best grown against a sunny wall.

Height: 8 m (26 ft)
Spread: 6 m (20 ft)
Hardiness: Zone 7

Rosa moyesii

This vigorous species has arching, spiny shoots and dark green leaves that are blue-green beneath. Deep crimson flowers, up to 6 cm (2½ in) across, with centres of golden stamens, open during the summer, and these are followed by profusely borne, bright orange-red, bottle-shaped fruits.

Native range: China
Height: 3 m (10 ft)
Spread: 3 m (10 ft)
Hardiness: Zone 5

Rosa 'Nevada'

A very attractive shrub rose with a dense habit and arching, purple-brown, sparsely thorny shoots bearing light green foliage. The large, semi-double, fragrant, creamy white flowers, 10 cm (4 in) across, have contrasting centres of golden stamens and are profusely borne, mainly during summer.

Height: 2 m (6 ft)
Spread: 2.5 m (8 ft)
Hardiness: Zone 5

Rosa 'New Dawn'

A vigorous climber with arching shoots and glossy green foliage. The semi-double, pale blush pink, fragrant flowers, 8 cm (3 in) across, are freely borne over a long period from summer to autumn.

Rosa pimpinellifolia 'Canary'

Rosa pimpinellifolia 'Bicolor'

Height: 3 m (10 ft)
Spread: 2.5 m (8 ft)
Hardiness: Zone 5

Rosa 'Nozomi'

This miniature groundcover rose of compact habit has low, arching shoots and dark green foliage. Small, single, very pale pink flowers, 2.5 cm (1 in) across, open in clusters along the shoots in summer. It can be grown as a weeping standard.

Height: 60 cm (24 in)
Spread: 2 m (6 ft)
Hardiness: Zone 5

Rosa x *odorata* 'Mutabilis'

This is a slender-stemmed, open shrub with purple, sparsely thorny shoots and glossy dark green leaves that are purple when young. Single, fragrant flowers, up to 6 cm (2½ in) across, open buff yellow and then turn coppery pink followed by deep pink as they age. It is in almost continuous flower from spring to late autumn, and it can be trained as a climber against a wall.

Height: 2.5 m (8 ft)
Spread: 2.5 m (8 ft)
Hardiness: Zone 7

Rosa Pascali ('Lenip')

This is a large-flowered rose with dark green foliage. Double, white flowers, up to about 9 cm (3½ in) across, open from summer to autumn.

Height: 75 cm (30 in)
Spread: 50 cm (20 in)
Hardiness: Zone 5

Rosa 'Paul's Himalayan Musk'

This very vigorous climber has glossy dark green foliage, bronze when young, and shoots bearing large, hooked thorns. Small, double, pale pink flowers, 4 cm (1½ in) across, are profusely borne in large, drooping clusters.

Height: 8 m (26 ft)
Spread: 6 m (20 ft)
Hardiness: Zone 5

Rosa 'Paul's Lemon Pillar'

This is a vigorously climbing, large-flowered rose with stout shoots and large, dark green leaves. The very large, fully double and fragrant flowers, about 12 cm (5 in) across, are creamy white flushed with lemon yellow, and open in summer.

Height: 5 m (16 ft)
Spread: 3 m (10 ft)
Hardiness: Zone 5

Rosa 'Paul's Scarlet Climber'

This is a vigorous climber with dark green foliage borne on sparsely thorny, arching shoots. The double, bright scarlet flowers, up to about 8 cm (3 in) across, open in clusters during summer.

Height: 3 m (10 ft)
Spread: 2.5 m (8 ft)
Hardiness: Zone 5

Rosa Peace ('Madame A Meilland')

One of the best known of all the roses, this classic large-flowered plant is vigorous and upright with glossy deep green foliage. The double, fragrant and beautifully shaped flowers are 15 cm (6 in) across with a high centre. Opening in summer to autumn, the flowers are creamy to golden yellow, the petals attractively edged with pink or red.

Height: 1.5 m (5 ft)
Spread: 1 m (3 ft)
Hardiness: Zone 5

Rosa 'Penelope'

This Hybrid Musk rose has a dense, bushy habit and dark green foliage flushed red. The large, semi-double, fragrant flowers, about 7 cm (3 in) across, are creamy pink with frilly edged petals and open in clusters from summer to autumn.

Height: 1.2 m (4 ft)
Spread: 1.5 m (5 ft)
Hardiness: Zone 5

Rosa pimpinellifolia

This is a low-growing, thicket-forming shrub that spreads by suckers. It has upright, spiny shoots and small, dark green leaves. Single, creamy white, sometimes pink, flowers, about 4 cm (1½ in) across, with centres of yellow stamens, open in late spring, and these are followed by glossy black fruits.

Synonym: *Rosa spinosissima*
Common names: Burnet rose, Scotch rose
Height: 1 m (3 ft)

Spread: 1.5 m (5 ft)
Hardiness: Zone 4
Variants: It is grown in several forms, with single or double, white or pink flowers. 'Dunwich Rose' is low growing and spreading.

Rosa 'Pink Perpétué'

A climber with very dark green foliage flushed purple. The double, fragrant, deep pink flowers, 8 cm (3 in) across, open from summer to autumn.

Height: 4 m (13 ft)
Spread: 3 m (10 ft)
Hardiness: Zone 5

Rosa 'Prosperity'

This Hybrid Musk rose has arching shoots and dark green foliage. Fully double, creamy white, fragrant flowers, 5 cm (2 in) across, open from creamy pink buds in clusters that weigh down the shoots in summer and autumn.

Height: 2 m (6 ft)
Spread: 1.5 m (5 ft)
Hardiness: Zone 5

Rosa 'Rambling Rector'

This old, vigorous rambler has long, arching shoots and grey-green foliage. Fragrant, creamy white, semi-double flowers, 4 cm (1½ in) across, with centres of golden stamens, open in clusters during summer, followed by profuse, rounded, red fruits.

Height: 6 m (20 ft)
Spread: 5 m (16 ft)
Hardiness: Zone 5

Rosa rugosa 'Scabrosa'

Rosa 'Roseraie de l'Haÿ'

Rosa 'Reine Victoria'

This is a slender, upright Bourbon rose with elegant, light green foliage. The globular, silky, double flowers, about 8 cm (3 in) across, are fragrant and rich pink.

Height: 2 m (6 ft)
Spread: 1.2 m (4 ft)
Hardiness: Zone 4

Rosa 'Roseraie de l'Haÿ'

This is a vigorous Rugosa hybrid with a dense, bushy habit and very prickly shoots. The glossy dark green, deeply veined leaves turn yellow in autumn. Large, semi-double, strongly scented, deep red-purple flowers, up to about 11cm (4–5 in) across, open from summer to autumn.

Height: 2 m (6 ft)
Spread: 2 m (6 ft)
Hardiness: Zone 2

Rosa rubiginosa

This vigorous shrub rose has arching, prickly shoots and dark green leaves. Single, pale pink flowers, 2.5 cm (1 in) across, open in summer, followed by bright red, egg-shaped fruits.

Synonym: *Rosa eglanteria*
Common names: Eglantine, sweet briar
Native range: Europe, N Africa, W Asia
Height: 2.5 m (8 ft)
Spread: 2.5 m (8 ft)
Hardiness: Zone 4

Rosa rugosa

This vigorous, thicket-forming shrub has upright, densely prickly shoots and dark green, deeply veined leaves that turn yellow or red in autumn. The fragrant, usually purple-pink flowers, up to about 9 cm (3½ in) across, open from summer to autumn, followed by tomato-like, bright red fruits.

Native range: NE Asia
Height: 2 m (6 ft)
Spread: 3 m (10 ft)
Hardiness: Zone 2
Variants: 'Alba' bears white flowers. 'Rubra' has deep crimson-purple flowers. 'Scabrosa' has large, violet-crimson flowers and large orange-red fruits.

Rosa 'Sarah van Fleet'

A vigorous Rugosa hybrid of bushy, upright habit with dark green, deeply veined leaves, bronze when young. Semi-double, fragrant, silvery pink flowers, 8 cm (3 in) across, open from summer to autumn.

Height: 2.5m (8 ft)
Spread: 1.5 m (5 ft)
Hardiness: Zone 2

Rosa 'Schneezwerg'

This is a Rugosa hybrid with an upright habit and dark green, wrinkled leaves. Fragrant, semi-double, white flowers, up to 5 cm (2 in) across, with centres of yellow stamens, open in summer and autumn, followed by orange-red fruits.

Height: 1.5 m (5 ft)
Spread: 1.2 m (4 m)
Hardiness: Zone 2

Rosa 'Seagull'

This is a vigorous rambler with arching shoots and grey-green leaves. White, semi-double, very fragrant flowers, about 2.5 cm (1 in) across, with centres of yellow stamens, open in large clusters during summer.

Height: 6 m (20 ft)
Spread: 5 m (16 ft)
Hardiness: Zone 5

Rosa 'The Queen Elizabeth'

A vigorous and upright, cluster-flowered rose with large, dark green leaves. Semi-double, silvery pink, long-stalked flowers, 10 cm (4 in) across, open from pointed buds in summer and autumn.

Height: 2 m (6 ft)
Spread: 1 m (3 ft)
Hardiness: Zone 5

Rosa 'Veilchenblau'

This vigorous rambler has nearly thornless shoots and glossy bright green leaves. Semi-double, sweetly scented flowers, about 3 cm (1 in) across, open violet-purple marked with white from crimson-purple buds, and fade to lilac-grey.

Height: 5 m (16 ft)
Spread: 4 m (13 ft)
Hardiness: Zone 5

Rosa Whisky Mac ('Tanky')

This is a large-flowered rose with very thorny shoots and dark green, bronze-tinged leaves. The double, fragrant, amber-yellow flowers, 10 cm (4 in) across, open from summer to autumn.

Rosa rugosa

Height: 90 cm (35 in)
Spread: 60 cm (24 in)
Hardiness: Zone 7

Rosa 'William Lobb'

A vigorous and upright Moss rose with small, dark green leaves and flower stems densely covered with pale green 'moss'. Large, semi-double flowers, 8 cm (3 in) across, open during summer, deep crimson-purple at first, fading to lavender-grey.

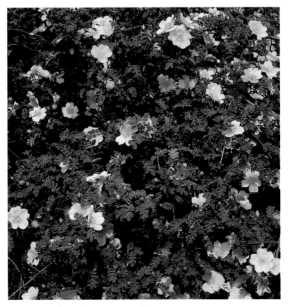

Rosa xanthina 'Canary Bird'

Height: 2.5 m (8 ft)
Spread: 1.5 m (5 ft)
Hardiness: Zone 3

Rosa xanthina 'Canary Bird'

This is a strong-growing shrub with a dense habit and arching, sparsely spiny shoots bearing dark green, fern-like leaves. The single, fragrant, rich yellow flowers, up to about 5 cm (2 in) across, are profusely borne in spring and sometimes again later in the year.

Height: 3 m (10 ft)
Spread: 4 m (13 ft)
Hardiness: Zone 5

Rosa 'Zéphirine Drouhin'

This is a very popular Bourbon rose with foliage that is bronze when young, later turning grey green, borne on thornless shoots. The fragrant, semi-double, deep cerise-pink flowers, up to about 8 cm (3 in) across, open over a long period from summer through to autumn. It can also be trained as a climber.

Height: 3 m (10 ft)
Spread: 2 m (6 ft)
Hardiness: Zone 4

Rosmarinus
Labiatae

This is a small genus of three species of evergreen shrubs, all with opposite leaves and natives of the Mediterranean. Only one species, however, is commonly found in garden cultivation, where it is valued for its flowers and aromatic foliage.

Suitable for any soil that is not too rich, this species needs a position in full sun, and it can be grown successfully in a border, dry garden or against a wall. It can also be grown to form an effective hedge.

Cut plants back after flowering in order to restrict their growth, or to renovate old plants, cut them back hard. Hedges can be cut after flowering and again as necessary during the summer.

Rosmarinus officinalis

This is a vigorous, evergreen shrub with a dense, bushy habit and intensely aromatic, slender, dark green leaves that are white beneath. Clusters of small, violet-blue, two-lipped flowers open among the foliage at the ends of the shoots during spring, and sometimes again in autumn.

Common name: Rosemary
Native range: Mediterranean region
Height: 2 m (6 ft)
Spread: 2 m (6 ft)
Hardiness: Zone 7
Variants: var. *albiflorus* produces white flowers. 'Benenden Blue' has rich blue flowers. 'Majorca Pink' is upright with lilac-pink flowers. 'Miss Jessopp's Upright' is a vigorous, upright form that is good for hedging. 'Prostratus' is low and spreading, but less hardy, and does well on a wall or in a rock garden. 'Roseus' has lilac-pink flowers. 'Severn Sea' is spreading and has arching shoots. 'Tuscan Blue' has deep blue flowers, often borne in winter.

Rubus
Rosaceae

This widely distributed genus contains more than 250 species of often thorny deciduous and evergreen shrubs, sometimes climbing, as well as herbaceous perennials. The ornamental species are grown for their flowers and foliage, and also sometimes for their attractive winter shoots.

These plants will grow in any well-drained soil. Those grown for their winter shoots do best in full sun and any shoots that have flowered should be cut back right to the ground after flowering is over. Other members of the genus are grown for their edible fruits.

Rosmarinus officinalis 'Roseus'

Rubus 'Benenden'

Rubus 'Benenden'

This is a garden-raised hybrid between *R. deliciosus* and *R. trilobus* that makes a vigorous, thornless deciduous shrub. The arching branches are covered with pale brown, peeling bark and bear three- to five-lobed leaves. Its large, showy white flowers, up to about 7 cm (3 in) across, have conspicuous centres of yellow stamens.

Height: 3 m (10 ft)
Spread: 4 m (13 ft)
Hardiness: Zone 5

Rubus cockburnianus

This vigorous deciduous shrub spreads by suckers and forms a dense thicket of spiny, white, bloomy shoots that look particularly striking in winter. The dark green leaves are white beneath and have prickly stalks and up to nine leaflets. Small, purple, relatively inconspicuous flowers open in summer, and these are followed by small, black fruits.

Common name: Ghost bramble
Native range: China
Height: 2.5 m (8 ft)
Spread: 5 m (16 ft) or more
Hardiness: Zone 6
Variants: 'Goldenvale' is less vigorous and lower growing, to 1 m (3 ft), with equally white shoots.

Rubus spectabilis

This deciduous shrub has upright, sparsely prickly shoots and bold, glossy green leaves divided into three sharply toothed leaflets. Small, fragrant, purple-pink flowers open in clusters at the ends of the shoots in mid-spring and these are followed by orange-yellow fruits.

Common name: Salmonberry
Native range: W North America
Height: 2 m (6 ft)
Spread: 2.5 m (8 ft)

Rubus thibetanus

Rubus cockburnianus 'Goldenvale'

Hardiness: Zone 5
Variants: 'Olympic Double' has large, very showy, double flowers.

Rubus thibetanus

This deciduous shrub has upright, arching, prickly shoots covered in a conspicuous white bloom. The dark green leaves have up to 13 sharply toothed leaflets, white beneath. Clusters of small, purple flowers at the ends of the shoots in summer are sometimes followed by small, black fruits.

Native range: China
Height: 2 m (6 ft)
Spread: 2 m (6 ft)
Hardiness: Zone 6

Rubus tricolor

A vigorous, sprawling evergreen shrub with long shoots densely covered in red bristles. The glossy dark green leaves are sharply toothed and sometimes shallowly lobed, white and bristly beneath. Clusters of white flowers at the ends of the shoots in summer are followed by red, raspberry-like, edible fruits. An excellent quick-growing, groundcover plant.

Native range: China
Height: 60 cm (24 in)
Spread: 5 m (16 ft) or more
Hardiness: Zone 7

Ruscus
Ruscaceae

This is a small, widely distributed genus of some six species of evergreen subshrubs, natives of Europe, North Africa and West Asia. The apparent leaves are actually modified flattened shoots on which the plant's rather inconspicuous flowers are borne.

Grown for their foliage and fruits, they are suitable for any well-drained soil, and can be planted in either sun or shade. Most plants are male or female only and both are needed to produce fruit. Some forms of *R. aculeatus* have flowers that are both male and female. Cut any dead shoots back to the base in spring.

Ruscus aculeatus

This is a small evergreen shrub that makes a dense clump of upright, green shoots and spreads by sending out underground stems. Glossy dark green 'leaves', which end in a sharp point, have small, greenish flowers on their surfaces in winter and spring, and these are followed – on female plants – by conspicuous and persistent, bright red berries.

Common name: Butcher's broom
Native range: Europe, North Africa, W Asia
Height: 90 cm (35 in)
Spread: 75 cm (30 in)
Hardiness: Zone 7

Ruta
Rutaceae

The eight species that make up this small genus are aromatic herbs and shrubs, natives of the Mediterranean region, North Africa and Southwest Asia.

The following species is grown for its foliage, which is used as a flavouring, as well as its flowers. Suitable for a dry border or rock garden, it requires a well-drained soil in full sun in order to thrive. Prune by reducing shoots by one-half in spring.

Ruta graveolens

This is an evergreen shrub with upright shoots bearing blue-green, very aromatic leaves divided into numerous lobes. Clusters of small, four-petalled, mustard yellow flowers open at the ends of the shoots in summer, making an effective contrast with the foliage. All parts of the plant can be an irritant.

Common name: Rue
Native range: SE Europe
Height: 90 cm (35 in)
Spread: 75 cm (30 in)
Hardiness: Zone 5
Variants: 'Jackman's Blue' is a compact form with vivid, blue-grey foliage.

Salix
Salicaceae

The 300 or more species of willows vary from dwarf shrubs to large trees and are widely distributed, mainly in the northern hemisphere. The flowers are borne in catkins, males and females on separate plants.

Grown in gardens for their habit, foliage, flowers and sometimes their coloured winter shoots, they prefer a moist but well-drained soil and a sunny position. The very dwarf willows do not need pruning, while shrubby species can have some of the older shoots removed after flowering or be cut back hard if renovation is required. Forms of S. *alba* grown for their winter shoots should be cut back every two years. The large tree-willows should never be planted close to buildings.

Salix alba

This is a vigorous deciduous tree, usually broadly columnar, with sharply toothed leaves ending in long, tapering points. Young leaves are silvery hairy – becoming green above, blue-green beneath. Small catkins open as the leaves emerge in spring.

Common name: White willow
Native range: Europe, W Asia
Height: 25 m (80 ft)
Spread: 15 m (50 ft)
Hardiness: Zone 2
Variants: The young shoots of 'Britzensis' are bright orange-red in winter.

Salix babylonica

This deciduous tree was once the commonly grown weeping willow, but it has largely been replaced by S. x *sepulcralis* 'Chrysocoma'. It is a spreading tree with pendulous branches and bears dark green, taper-pointed leaves that are blue-green beneath. Small catkins open in spring as the young leaves emerge.

Common name: Chinese weeping willow
Native range: Of cultivated origin in China
Height: 12 m (40 ft)
Spread: 15 m (50 ft)
Hardiness: Zone 6
Variants: 'Tortuosa' (dragon's claw willow) is upright in habit with twisted shoots and leaves.

Salix 'Boydii'

This hybrid between S. *lapponum* and S. *reticulata* was originally found in the Scottish mountains. It makes a slow-growing, dwarf shrub of congested,

Salix alba 'Britzensis'

upright habit, and with rather twisted shoots and small, red buds. The grey-green, rounded and deeply veined leaves are only about 2 cm (¾ in) long. Small, female catkins are occasionally produced. It does best in a rock garden or trough.

Height: 45 cm (18 in)
Spread: 25 cm (10 in)
Hardiness: Zone 3

Salix caprea 'Kilmarnock'

This is a small deciduous tree with a dense, spreading head of shoots that weep to the ground. Its broad, dark green leaves are grey-green on their undersurfaces. It is particularly attractive when its silky, grey, male catkins open in early spring before the leaves. Flowers become covered with yellow

stamens. It tends to become congested and top-heavy and then some of the older shoots should be cut out. Prune in spring before growth restarts.

Common name: Kilmarnock willow
Height: 1.5–2 m (5–6 ft)
Spread: 2.5 m (8 ft)
Hardiness: Zone 4

Salix daphnoides

A fast-growing, small deciduous tree of broadly conical habit, with bloomy young shoots and slender, dark green, taper-pointed leaves that are blue-green beneath. Small catkins open in spring, as or before the leaves emerge. This species can be cut back every two years to induce the production of vigorous and attractive winter shoots.

Common name: Violet willow
Native range: Europe
Height: 10 m (33 ft)
Spread: 10m (33 ft)
Hardiness: Zone 5
Variants: 'Aglaia' produces red shoots in winter and profuse silvery, then yellow, male catkins.

Salix elaeagnos

A deciduous shrub with slender, upright shoots densely covered in grey hairs when young. Narrow, dark green, rosemary-like leaves, grey at first and blue-white beneath, turn yellow in autumn. Slender catkins open as the young leaves emerge in spring.

Common name: Hoary willow
Native range: S and C Europe, SW Asia
Height: 3 m (10 ft)
Spread: 2 m (6 ft)
Hardiness: Zone 4

Salix 'Erythroflexuosa'

A garden-raised hybrid between the weeping willow, S. x sepulcralis 'Chrysocoma', and S. babylonica 'Tortuosa', making a small, spreading tree with pendulous, twisted shoots, bright orange-yellow in winter. The glossy green leaves are also twisted, and yellow catkins appear with the leaves in spring.

Height: 5 m (16 ft)
Spread: 5 m (16 ft)
Hardiness: Zone 6

Salix gracilistyla

This is a bushy deciduous shrub with grey, hairy shoots and grey-green leaves, which are silky with

Salix hastata 'Wehrhahnii'

Salix daphnoides 'Aglaia'

hairs when young, blue-green beneath. The catkins open in early to mid-spring, before the leaves emerge; the males are particularly attractive, with red-tinged, later yellow, anthers.

Native range: Japan, Korea, NE China
Height: 2.5 m (8 ft)
Spread: 4 m (13 ft)
Hardiness: Zone 5
Variants: 'Melanostachys' is a male form with blackish catkins, showing brick red later, and yellow anthers.

Salix hastata

This is a small-growing, spreading deciduous shrub with stout, purple-brown shoots and dark green leaves. The leaves are covered in hairs when young, but become smooth as they mature. The catkins open initially grey and silky before or as the young leaves emerge. The females later turn green and the males yellow.

Native range: Europe, W Asia
Height: 1 m (3 ft)
Spread: 1 m (3 ft)
Hardiness: Zone 5
Variants: 'Wehrhahnii' is a male form that flowers profusely.

Salix integra 'Hakuro-nishiki'

Normally grafted on top of a stem, this makes a miniature deciduous tree with a spreading head of arching shoots. The opposite leaves open nearly white, tinged with pink, later becoming blotched with green. The green-leaved form is native to Japan and makes a graceful shrub with pendulous shoots, but is rarely seen in gardens.

Height: 1.5 m (5 ft)
Spread: 1.2 m (4 ft)
Hardiness: Zone 5

Salix x sepulcralis 'Chrysocoma'

This popular tree is thought to be a hybrid between S. babylonica and S. alba. It makes a very vigorous, wide-spreading tree with slender, pendulous, gold yellow shoots, often reaching to the ground. The slender, taper-pointed, glossy green leaves are blue-green beneath and open early in spring. It is not suitable for small gardens.

Common name: Golden weeping willow
Height: 15 m (50 ft) or more
Spread: 20 m (65 ft)
Hardiness: Zone 6

Salvia
Labiatae

This is a very large genus comprising some 900 or more species of annual and perennial herbaceous plants, shrubs and subshrubs, all with opposite leaves and widely distributed – mainly in the warm regions.

The following is the hardiest of the shrubby species, and is grown for its aromatic foliage and its flowers. Sage is suitable for any well-drained soil, as long as it is not too rich, and it needs a position in full sun in order to thrive.

Sage can be trimmed lightly in spring to retain its compact habit, and again after flowering. If plants have become leggy, cut them back hard in spring to renovate them.

Salvia officinalis 'Purpurascens'

Salvia officinalis

This is a bushy, mound-forming evergreen shrub producing grey-green, aromatic and deeply veined leaves. Spikes of two-lipped, whorled, blue-purple flowers open at the ends of the shoots during the summer.

Common name: Common sage
Native range: Mediterranean region, North Africa
Height: 60 cm (24 in)
Spread: 1 m (3 ft)
Hardiness: Zone 5
Variants: 'Icterina' produces leaves with yellow margins. 'Purpurascens' has young foliage that is red-purple in colour. 'Tricolor' has striking foliage, with leaves edged with creamy white and pink.

Sambucus
Caprifoliaceae

The elders are a widely distributed genus made up of about 25 species of deciduous shrubs, trees and herbaceous perennials. All have opposite leaves that are divided up into several leaflets.

Grown for their attractive, sometimes coloured foliage as well as for their small flowers and fruits, the elders are suitable for any well-drained soil, as long as it is not too dry, and they usually prefer a sunny position. Once established, they do best if cut back hard in spring to ensure there is a good crop of new foliage.

Sambucus nigra

This vigorous and upright deciduous shrub, sometimes tree-like, has bold, dark green leaves divided into five or seven leaflets. Flattened heads

Sambucus racemosa 'Sutherland Gold'

of small, fragrant, white flowers open in early summer, followed by black, glossy fruits. It is mainly grown as the selected forms listed below.

Common name: Common elder
Native range: Europe, North Africa, SW Asia
Height: 5 m (16 ft)
Spread: 4 m (13 ft)
Hardiness: Zone 5
Variants: 'Aurea' produces yellow leaves. 'Black Beauty' has blackish-purple foliage and pink flowers. 'Guincho Purple' has purple foliage and pink-budded flowers. 'Laciniata' (fern-leaved elder) has leaves with finely cut leaflets. 'Madonna'

Sambucus nigra 'Guincho Purple'

produces leaves edged with bright yellow. 'Marginata' has leaves edged with creamy white.

Sambucus racemosa

This vigorous deciduous shrub has arching shoots bearing dark green leaves divided into usually five sharply toothed leaflets. The conical heads of small, pale creamy yellow flowers open in mid-spring, followed by glossy red fruits in summer.

Common name: Red-berried elder
Native range: Europe, W Asia
Height: 3 m (10 ft)
Spread: 3 m (10 ft)
Hardiness: Zone 4
Variants: 'Plumosa Aurea' has finely cut, yellow foliage but can scorch if it is positioned in full sun. 'Sutherland Gold' is similar to 'Plumosa Aurea', except with foliage of a less intense yellow and is not as likely to scorch. 'Tenuifolia' is low and spreading with finely cut leaflets.

Santolina
Compositae

The lavender cottons are a small genus of some five species of evergreen shrubs, natives of the Mediterranean. They have small, aromatic leaves and tiny flowers on long-stalked heads.

Suitable for any well-drained soil in full sun, they can be used in the border or for creating a low hedge. To retain a compact habit, trim them lightly in autumn after flowering, and cut them back hard every two or three years in the spring.

Santolina chamaecyparissus

This is a compact and rounded evergreen shrub, becoming open with age. Small, aromatic, white-felted leaves, edged with tiny teeth, are densely arranged on white-hairy shoots. The dense, button-like, bright yellow flowerheads open on long stalks during mid- to late summer.

Common name: Lavender cotton
Native range: Mediterranean region
Height: 60 cm (24 in)
Spread: 75 cm (30 in)
Hardiness: Zone 6
Variants: 'Lemon Queen' produces lemon-yellow heads of flowers.

Santolina rosmarinifolia

This evergreen shrub has a compact, rounded habit, and aromatic foliage composed of small, bright green leaves that are deeply cut into toothed lobes. Tiny flowers are borne in dense, button-like, bright yellow flowerheads carried on long, slender, upright stalks in mid-summer.

Common name: Holy flax
Native range: SW Europe
Height: 60 cm (24 in)
Spread: 1 m (3 ft)
Hardiness: Zone 7
Variants: 'Primrose Gem' produces pale yellow heads of flowers.

Sarcococca
Buxaceae

The Christmas boxes comprise a genus of about 14 species of clump-forming or suckering evergreen shrubs, natives of the Himalayas and East Asia. They are grown for their attractive foliage and their fragrant winter flowers, as well as for their fruits. Male and female flowers are borne

Santolina chamaecyparissus

separately on the same plant, both without petals. The male flowers are more conspicuous, with protruding stamens; the female are followed by fleshy, black or red berries.

They are suitable for any good, moist but well-drained soil, and they prefer a shady position where they make effective ground cover. Little pruning is usually required, but any wayward or weak shoots can be cut to the base in spring.

Sarcococca confusa

This is a dense, clump-forming evergreen shrub of rounded habit with glossy dark green, slightly wavy edged leaves. Clusters of small, white, fragrant flowers open in winter as the glossy black berries from the previous year's flowers ripen.

Native range: Probably China
Height: 1.5 m (5 ft)
Spread: 2 m (6 ft)
Hardiness: Zone 7

Sarcococca hookeriana

This is a vigorous evergreen shrub producing upright shoots that form a dense thicket. It spreads by underground stems and bears dark matt-green leaves. Clusters of white or pink-flushed, fragrant flowers open in winter, and these are accompanied by black berries.

Native range: Himalayas, Tibet
Height: 1.5 m (5 ft)
Spread: 2 m (6 ft)
Hardiness: Zone 6
Variants: var. *digyna* has slender-pointed leaves and conspicuously pink-tinged flowers. var. *humilis* is low-growing, up to 60 cm (24 in) high.

Santolina rosmarinifolia 'Primrose Gem'

Sarcococca hookeriana var. *humilis*

Sarcococca ruscifolia

This clump-forming evergreen shrub has arching shoots bearing glossy dark green, taper-pointed leaves. Clusters of white, fragrant flowers in winter are accompanied by red berries. It is commonly confused in gardens with *S. confusa*.

Native range: China
Height: 1.2 m (4 ft)
Spread: 1.5 m (5 ft)
Hardiness: Zone 7
Variants: var. *chinensis* is the most commonly grown form and has narrow, pointed leaves.

Sassafras albidum

Sasa veitchii

Sasa
Gramineae

The 40 or so species that make up this genus are evergreen bamboos that spread by sending out underground stems. Relatively low-growing and with broad leaves, they are grown for their foliage and are useful for ground cover.

They are suitable for moist, well-drained soil that is rich in organic matter. The following species will grow in sun or shade.

Sasa veitchii

This low, thicket-forming bamboo has slender, upright, green, later purple, canes that spread vigorously by underground stems. The broad, dark green leaves, blue-green beneath, are up to 20 cm (8 in) or more long. In autumn the leaves develop a broad, white margin that lasts through winter, thus creating a variegated effect.

Native range: Japan
Height: 1 m (3 ft)
Spread: 5 m (16 ft) or more
Hardiness: Zone 8

Sassafras
Lauraceae

The three species of deciduous trees in this genus are natives of North America and East Asia. The following is commonly grown for its foliage, which colours well in autumn. It needs a good, moist but well-drained, acidic soil, preferably rich in organic matter, and does best in a sunny position.

Sassafras albidum

This deciduous tree of a usually broadly columnar habit produces numerous suckers from the base, often some distance from the trunk. The distinctive, bright green, aromatic leaves are either unlobed or have three prominent lobes, and turn yellow to orange and red in autumn. Clusters of small, yellow flowers, males and females on separate trees, open as the leaves emerge in spring.

Common name: Sassafras
Native range: E North America
Height: 15 m (50 ft) or more
Spread: 10 m (33 ft)
Hardiness: Zone 4

Senecio
Compositae

This very large and widely distributed genus contains more than 1,000 species of annual and perennial herbs, shrubs, climbers and trees. The following is grown for its attractive foliage and requires a well-drained and not-too-rich soil and full sun. For the shrubby New Zealand species sometimes listed here, see *Brachyglottis*.

Senecio viravira

This spreading evergreen subshrub has young shoots densely covered in white hairs. The silvery leaves are deeply cut into slender lobes. Clusters of small, pale yellow flowerheads open over a long period from summer to autumn.

Native range: Argentina
Height: 60 cm (24 in)
Spread: 1 m (3 ft)
Hardiness: Zone 8

Skimmia
Rutaceae

The four species in this genus are evergreen shrubs and trees, native from the Himalayas to East Asia. The following are grown for their foliage, flowers (often attractive in bud), and their fruits. They need a moist but well-drained soil rich in organic matter. Forms of *S. japonica* should be grown in shade or semi-shade and usually both male and female plants need to be grown to produce fruit. *S.* x *confusa* 'Kew Green' will tolerate full sun. Little pruning is usually necessary, but any wayward shoots can be cut out

Skimmia japonica 'Rubella'

Skimmia japonica

in spring. Their compact habit makes them useful in the garden for ground cover in shady places.

Skimmia x *confusa* 'Kew Green'

This vigorous, male shrub is a garden-raised hybrid between S. *anquetilia* and S. *japonica*. It makes a dense, spreading, dome-shaped bush with aromatic foliage. The large, conical clusters of fragrant, creamy white flowers in spring make it perhaps the most attractive of the genus in flower.

Height: 1.2 m (4 ft)
Spread: 2 m (6 ft)
Hardiness: Zone 7

Skimmia japonica

This is an evergreen shrub of very variable habit, ranging from low and spreading to upright, with aromatic, dark green, leathery leaves. In spring, dense clusters of small, fragrant, white flowers open at the ends of the shoots, often from red buds, and these are followed on female plants by bright red, persistent berries that are conspicuous in winter.

Native range: China, Japan
Height: 1–2 m (3–6 ft)
Spread: 1–2 m (3–6 ft)
Hardiness: Zone 7
Variants: 'Fragrans' is a compact male form that flowers profusely. 'Kew White' is a female form that produces large, white berries. 'Nymans' is a female form that produces red fruits. 'Rubella' is a compact, dome-shaped, male form that has red flowers buds. The buds are conspicuous during winter. 'Veitchii' is a vigorously growing, upright, female form that produces large, bright red berries.

Skimmia x confusa 'Kew Green'

Sophora
Leguminosae

The 50 or so widely distributed species that make up this genus include both deciduous and evergreen trees and shrubs, or herbaceous perennials. They have leaves divided into several to numerous leaflets, and pea-like flowers varying in colour from white to pink, blue or yellow.

The following species are grown principally for their flowers. They require a well-drained soil and a position in full sun.

Sophora japonica

This spreading deciduous tree has glossy dark green leaves, blue-green beneath, with up to 17 leaflets. Fragrant, white, pea-like flowers open in large, pendulous clusters in late summer and early autumn, followed by yellow-brown, persistent pods. It does best in regions with hot summers.

Common name: Japanese pagoda tree
Native range: China
Height: 20 m (65 ft)
Spread: 15 m (50 ft)
Hardiness: Zone 4

Sophora microphylla

This vigorous evergreen shrub or small tree has leaves divided into numerous small, glossy dark green leaflets. The drooping, golden yellow, tubular flowers open in small clusters from late winter to spring. Except in the mildest climates, it is usually best grown against a sunny wall.

Native range: New Zealand, Chile
Height: 6 m (20 ft) or more
Spread: 5 m (16 ft)
Hardiness: Zone 8
Variants: 'Sun King' is bushy and particularly hardy, up to 3 m (10 ft) tall, and grows and flowers well in the open ground.

Sorbaria
Rosaceae

This is a small genus of four species of deciduous, thicket-forming shrubs that spreads by suckers, with leaves divided up into many leaflets. Grown for their foliage and their flowers, they are suitable for any well-drained soil.

Since the following is vigorous, it may need to be restricted unless it has plenty of room to spread.

Sophora microphylla 'Sun King'

Cut down some of the older shoots and reduce the length of the remaining ones in late winter. To restrict its spread, remove some of the suckers.

Sorbaria sorbifolia

This vigorous, suckering shrub forms thickets of upright stems bearing dark green leaves divided up into as many as 25 sharply toothed leaflets. Small, white flowers open in dense, conical clusters, up to 25 cm (10 in) long, in mid- to late summer.

Native range: N Asia
Height: 2 m (6 ft)
Spread: 5 m (16 ft) or more
Hardiness: Zone 2

Sorbus
Rosaceae

The 100 or so species in this genus are deciduous trees and shrubs widely distributed in temperate regions of the northern hemisphere.

The species are very varied in leaf, from toothed to lobed (as in the whitebeams), while others are divided in several to numerous leaflets (as in the rowans or mountain ashes). The small, clustered flowers are usually white and are followed by white to pink, red, orange or yellow fruits. The rowans prefer a moist but well-drained, neutral-to-acid soil; whitebeams are more tolerant and will grow on dry, alkaline soils.

Sorbus alnifolia

This is a conical deciduous tree with a tendency to spread with age. It has dark green, toothed leaves, which turn to shades of orange, red and yellow in autumn. Clusters of small, white flowers open in mid-spring, and these are followed by long-persistent, orange-red fruits. In spite of its common name, this species is closely related to the whitebeams.

Common name: Korean mountain ash
Native range: China, Japan, Korea, Taiwan
Height: 15 m (50 ft)
Spread: 10m (33 ft)
Hardiness: Zone 4

Sorbus aria 'Lutescens'

Sorbus aria

A deciduous tree, conical to broadly columnar in habit, bearing glossy dark green, sharply toothed leaves densely covered beneath in white hairs. Flattened heads of white flowers in late spring are followed by bright red fruits with white speckles.

Common name: Whitebeam
Native range: Europe
Height: 15 m (50 ft)
Spread: 10 m (33 ft)
Hardiness: Zone 5
Variants: 'Lutescens' is the most popular form and has young foliage that is silvery grey.

Sorbus aucuparia

This is a deciduous tree, rounded and spreading in habit when young, bearing dark green leaves divided up into as many as 15 sharply toothed leaflets, sometimes turning yellow or red in autumn. Broad, flattened heads of small, white flowers in late spring are followed by large clusters of bright red fruits, often heavy enough to weigh down the branches.

Common names: Mountain ash, rowan
Native range: Europe, W Asia
Height: 15 m (50 ft)
Spread: 10 m (33 ft)
Hardiness: Zone 3
Variants: 'Aspleniifolia' has leaflets that are, themselves, divided into smaller leaflets at the base. 'Fastigiata' is a very compact form with upright branches bearing deep red fruits in dense clusters. 'Sheerwater Seedling' is a form with a narrow, upright habit.

Sorbus cashmiriana

This is a small, spreading deciduous tree. It has dark green leaves divided up into as many as 21 sharply toothed leaflets. The leaves are blue-green beneath and turn yellow or red in autumn. Clusters of white or pink flowers open in late spring, and these are followed by white, pink-tinged fruits carried on red stalks.

Native range: Himalayas
Height: 8 m (26 ft)
Spread: 8 m (26 ft)
Hardiness: Zone 4

Sorbus commixta

This conical deciduous tree has bright green leaves divided into about 15 taper-pointed leaflets, blue-green beneath, turning yellow to red or purple-red in autumn. Broad, flattened heads of small, white flowers open in late spring, and these are followed by bright orange-red fruits.

Native range: Japan, Korea
Height: 10 m (33 ft)
Spread: 8 m (26 ft)
Hardiness: Zone 5
Variants: The foliage of 'Embley' turn bright orange-red in autumn.

Sorbus hupehensis

This broadly columnar deciduous tree has leaves divided into as many as 17 leaflets, blue-green above and blue-grey beneath. The leaves turn red in autumn. Domed clusters of small, white flowers open in late spring, and these are followed by white fruits, often with a pink flush towards the top.

Native range: China
Height: 10 m (33 ft)
Spread: 8 m (26 ft)
Hardiness: Zone 5

Sorbus intermedia

This is a vigorous, broadly columnar to rounded tree with dark green leaves, grey-green beneath, that are sharply lobed and toothed, more deeply towards the base of the leaf. Dense clusters of small, white flowers open in late spring, followed by broadly egg-shaped, bright red fruits

Common name: Swedish whitebeam
Native range: NW Europe

Sorbus hupehensis

Sorbus vilmorinii

Height: 15 m (50 ft)
Spread: 12 m (40 ft)
Hardiness: Zone 4

Sorbus 'Joseph Rock'

This is a vigorous and deciduous shrub with a broadly columnar habit that produces upright branches. The bright green leaves, divided up into as many as 17 sharply toothed leaflets, turn to colours of orange, red and purple in autumn. Clusters of white flowers open in late spring to early summer, and these are followed by pale yellow, later orange-yellow fruits. It is probably a form of a Chinese species.

Height: 10 m (33 ft)
Spread: 8 m (26 ft)
Hardiness: Zone 6

Sorbus reducta

This is a small, thicket-forming deciduous shrub with upright shoots that spreads by sending out underground stems. The glossy dark green leaves are divided up into as many as 15 leaflets and foliage turns a deep red-purple colour in the autumn. Small clusters of white flowers open in

the late spring, and these are followed by bright pink fruits.

Native range: China
Height: 60 cm (24 in)
Spread: 1 m (3 ft)
Hardiness: Zone 6

Sorbus sargentiana

This broadly columnar to spreading deciduous tree has stout shoots and large, glossy red, sticky buds. The bold, deep green leaves have up to 11 leaflets and turn to orange and red in autumn. Broad, flattened heads of small, white flowers open in early summer, and these are followed by large clusters of small, red fruits.

Native range: China
Height: 10 m (33 ft)
Spread: 10 m (33 ft)
Hardiness: Zone 6

Sorbus thibetica

This vigorous deciduous tree, broadly conical in habit, has bold, dark green leaves densely covered beneath with white hairs. Rather open clusters of

small, white flowers open in late spring to early summer, and these are followed by small, rounded, apple-like fruits, orange or yellow when ripe.

Native range: China, Himalayas
Height: 15 m (50 ft)
Spread: 12 m (40 ft)
Hardiness: Zone 6
Variants: 'John Mitchell' has large, rounded leaves.

Sorbus torminalis

A broadly conical deciduous tree with dark green leaves deeply cut into pointed and toothed lobes, turning yellow, red or purple in autumn. Clusters of white flowers from late spring to early summer are followed by small, russet-brown, speckled fruits.

Common name: Wild service tree
Native range: Europe, North Africa, SW Asia
Height: 15 m (50 ft)
Spread: 10 m (33 ft)
Hardiness: Zone 6

Sorbus vilmorinii

This is a small, spreading deciduous tree of graceful habit, with fern-like leaves divided up into as many as 25 small, glossy green leaflets, grey-green beneath. Clusters of small, white flowers in late spring or early summer are followed by deep red fruits that ripen to pink then white.

Native range: China
Height: 6 m (20 ft)
Spread: 6 m (20 ft)
Hardiness: Zone 6

Sorbus torminalis

Spartium junceum

Spartium
Leguminosae

The single species in this small genus is a deciduous shrub grown for its showy flowers. Suitable for any not-too-rich, well-drained soil, it should be grown in full sun. Able to withstand considerable exposure in mild areas, it can be grown as a specimen or in the border. In colder regions it does well against a sunny wall. Cutting back in spring helps to retain its compact habit.

Spartium junceum

This vigorous deciduous shrub has slender, green, upright shoots bearing small, sparse, dark green leaves. The large, fragrant, golden yellow, pea-like flowers open in clusters at the ends of the shoots over a long period from summer to autumn.

Common name: Spanish broom
Native range: S Europe, N Africa, SW Asia
Height: 3 m (10 ft)
Spread: 2 m (6 ft)
Hardiness: Zone 8

Spiraea
Rosaceae

This genus has about 80 species of deciduous shrubs widely distributed in the temperate regions of the northern hemisphere, and provides numerous ornamental species valuable in gardens.

Grown for their flowers and for their sometimes coloured foliage, these plants are excellent for the border or for ground cover, and look best when planted in groups. They are suitable for any moist but well-drained soil, preferring a sunny position.

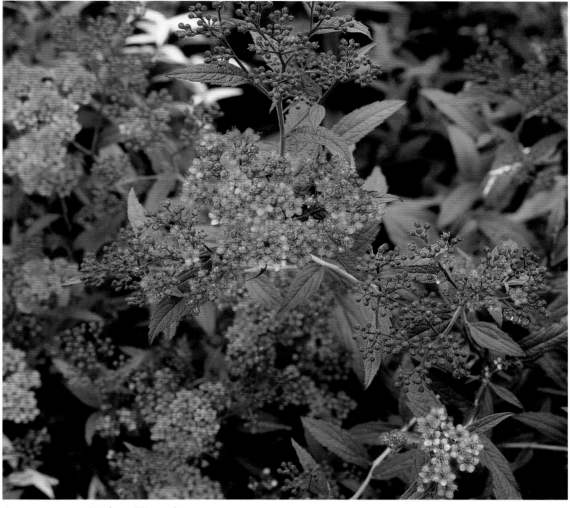

Spiraea japonica 'Anthony Waterer'

Regular pruning and deadheading are beneficial after flowering, and some of the older shoots on mature plants should be cut out. For those flowering from the old shoots early in the year, cut back in summer after flowering. For those flowering on the new shoots late in the year, cut back in early spring before growth restarts.

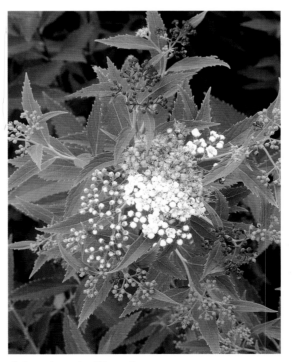

Spiraea japonica 'Genpei'

Spiraea 'Arguta'

This is an old and popular garden-raised hybrid that makes a vigorous deciduous shrub with slender, arching shoots producing bright green leaves. Clusters of small, white flowers are profusely borne along the branches in mid- to late spring from the old shoots.

Common names: Bridal wreath, foam of May
Height: 2 m (6 ft)
Spread: 2.5 m (8 ft)
Hardiness: Zone 4

Spiraea x cinerea 'Grefsheim'

This is an attractive garden-raised hybrid that makes a spreading deciduous shrub with a compact habit. It produces arching shoots bearing slender, blue-green leaves with silky undersurfaces. Dense clusters of small, white flowers open along the branches on the old shoots during mid-spring period.

Height: 1.5 m (5 ft)
Spread: 2 m (6 ft)
Hardiness: Zone 4

Spiraea thunbergii

Spiraea japonica

This is the most popular species in gardens and is grown in a very wide range of different forms. It is a deciduous shrub with upright shoots and dark green, sharply toothed foliage. The leaves are often bronze coloured when young. Broad, flattened heads of small, pink, occasionally white, flowers open on the new shoots in mid- to late summer.

Native range: China, Japan
Height: 1.5 m (5 ft)
Spread: 1.5 m (5 ft)
Hardiness: Zone 4
Variants: 'Albiflora' produces white flowers. 'Anthony Waterer' has very deep pink flowers and leaves that are often marked with white. 'Candlelight' is a compact form with butter yellow young foliage. 'Firelight' has young foliage that is deep orange-red, turning red in autumn, and deep pink flowers. 'Genpei' produces mixed heads of white and pink flowers, and is often grown as 'Shirobana'. 'Gold Mound' is a low-growing, compact form with yellow foliage and pale pink flowers. 'Little Princess' develops into a compact, small mound bearing small heads of deep pink-coloured flowers.

Spiraea nipponica
'Snowmound'

This selection of a Japanese species is among the most popular of the early-flowering spiraeas. It is a vigorously growing, yet compact, rounded shrub producing dark green leaves on graceful, arching shoots. Small, profuse clusters of white flowers open along the branches on the old shoots during the spring.

Stachyurus praecox

Height: 1.5 m (5 ft)
Spread: 2 m (6 ft)
Hardiness: Zone 4

Spiraea thunbergii

This bushy deciduous or semi-evergreen shrub has slender, arching shoots and narrow, pale green leaves. The small clusters of white flowers open on the old shoots before or as the new leaves emerge.

Native range: China
Height: 1.5 m (5 ft)
Spread: 2 m (6 ft)
Hardiness: Zone 4

Spiraea x vanhouttei

This garden-raised hybrid between *S. cantoniensis* and *S. trilobata* makes a vigorous, usually semi-evergreen shrub that develops into a dense clump of upright, arching shoots bearing dark green leaves, blue-green beneath and lobed towards the tip. Profusely borne white flowers in dense clusters open along the branches on the old shoots.

Height: 2 m (6 ft)
Spread: 2.5 m (8 ft)
Hardiness: Zone 3
Variants: 'Pink Ice' has leaves that are heavily mottled with white, and it flowers less freely.

Stachyurus
Stachyuraceae

This small genus of about six species of deciduous and semi-evergreen shrubs are natives of the Himalayas and East Asia. The following is the most popular species, and is grown for its early flowers.

The shrub is suitable for growing in a good, moist but well-drained soil that is rich in organic matter. It can be grown in a border or trained against a wall. Pruning is not usually essential but some of the old shoots of mature plants can be cut back to the base after flowering.

Stachyurus praecox

This is a vigorous deciduous shrub with arching, red-brown shoots and bright green leaves ending in a long, tapered point. Slender, stiffly pendulous spikes form in autumn, opening to pale yellow flowers on the bare shoots before the leaves emerge in late winter or early spring.

Native range: Japan
Height: 3 m (10 ft)
Spread: 4 m (13 ft)
Hardiness: Zone 6

Staphylea
Staphyleaceae

The bladdernuts comprise a genus of some 11 species of deciduous shrubs, sometimes tree-like, with opposite leaves divided into several leaflets.

Grown for their flowers and unusual fruits, the following is suitable for any moist but well-drained soil. It can be grown as a specimen shrub or in a woodland setting. Little pruning is essential but it can be cut back hard in winter if required.

Stewartia pseudocamellia

Staphylea colchica

This deciduous shrub has upright shoots with glossy green leaves divided into three to five leaflets. Clusters of fragrant, white, bell-shaped flowers open at the ends of the shoots in late spring as the young leaves are emerging, followed by pale green, bladder-like fruits divided into two or three lobes.

Native range: Caucasus
Height: 3 m (10 ft)
Spread: 3 m (10 ft)
Hardiness: Zone 6

Stephanandra
Rosaceae

A genus of four species of deciduous shrubs, all natives of East Asia. The following is grown for its foliage, small flowers and attractive winter shoots.

It does best in good, moist, but well-drained soil, and is suitable for a shrub border. To prune, cut some of the old shoots to the base after flowering and reduce the others to strong side shoots.

Stephanandra incisa

This vigorous, clump-forming deciduous shrub of graceful habit spreads by suckers. Its arching, zigzag shoots turn a rich brown in winter, and the deeply lobed and toothed, bright green leaves turn orange-yellow to red in autumn. Clusters of small, greenish-white flowers open during the late spring and early summer.

Native range: Japan, Korea
Height: 2 m (6 ft)
Spread: 3 m (10 ft)
Hardiness: Zone 4
Variants: 'Crispa' is low growing and spreading,

Stewartia pseudocamellia

reaching up to 60 cm (24 in) in height, with deeply cut leaves. It is useful for ground cover.

Stewartia
Theaceae

The nine species making up this genus are deciduous and evergreen trees and shrubs found mainly in East Asia, but with two species in the United States of America. Related to the camellias, the following is grown for its foliage, showy flowers and ornamental bark. It requires a moist but well-drained, lime-free soil rich in organic matter.

Stewartia pseudocamellia

This is a conical to broadly columnar deciduous tree with red-brown bark that peels to leave attractively contrasting patches of cream and pink. The dark green, taper-pointed leaves turn to brilliant shades of orange, yellow and red in the autumn. White, camellia-like flowers, up to about 6 cm (2½ in) across, and with a conspicuous central boss of yellow stamens, open during the summer months.

Native range: Japan
Height: 15 m (50 ft)
Spread: 10 m (33 ft)
Hardiness: Zone 5

Styrax
Styracaceae

This is a genus comprising 100 or more widely distributed species of deciduous and evergreen shrubs and trees, found mainly in the warm regions of the northern hemisphere.

Grown principally for its flowers, the following species requires a moist but well-drained, lime-free soil. It is ideal as a specimen tree in a woodland setting, where it is sheltered from any strong winds by the other trees. Apart from the removal of any dead, diseased or crossing wood, no pruning is usually required.

Styrax japonicus

This is a gracefully spreading deciduous tree, often branching low down, bearing glossy green leaves that turn red or yellow in the autumn. The pendulous, white or pink-tinged, slightly fragrant flowers have conspicuous clusters of yellow stamens in their centres, and they hang along the undersides of the branches in early to mid-summer.

Common name: Japanese snowbell
Native range: China, Japan, Korea
Height: 10 m (33 ft)
Spread: 10 m (33 ft)
Hardiness: Zone 5
Variants: 'Pink Chimes' produces pink flowers.

Symphoricarpos
Caprifoliaceae

This is a genus made up of 17 species of deciduous shrubs with opposite, sometimes lobed leaves. These are densely growing plants, often forming thickets, and they spread by sending out suckers. They are natives mainly of North America, including Mexico, with a single species native to China.

These shrubs are grown for their ornamental fruits and they are suitable for planting in any well-drained soil. They can be used to create low hedges or as groundcover plants. To restrict their growth, they can be cut back as necessary in early spring before the new season's growth starts.

Symphoricarpos x *chenaultii* 'Hancock'

This garden-raised hybrid between S. *microphyllus* and S. *orbiculatus* makes a vigorous, wide-spreading deciduous shrub with dark green,

Styrax japonicus

rounded leaves that are bronze-coloured when young. It is useful for ground cover. Clusters of small, white, inconspicuous flowers open between early and mid-summer, and these are followed by rather sparse, pink fruits.

Height: 1.5 m (5 ft)
Spread: 3 m (10 ft)
Hardiness: Zone 4

Symphoricarpos orbiculatus

This is a bushy deciduous shrub with a spreading habit and with arching branches bearing dark green to blue-green leaves. Small, white or pink-tinged flowers open in clusters in early to mid-summer, and these are followed by small, red-purple, long-persistent fruits. Does best in regions that experience hot summers.

Common names: Coralberry, Indian currant
Native range: United States of America, Mexico
Height: 1.5 m (5 ft)
Spread: 2.5 m (8 ft)
Hardiness: Zone 2
Variants: 'Foliis Variegatis' produces leaves that are conspicuously edged with yellow.

Syringa
Oleaceae

The lilacs are a well-known and popular genus of some 20 species of deciduous shrubs and trees, all with opposite leaves, and are native from East Europe to East Asia.

They are grown for their showy clusters of fragrant flowers, and require a good, well-drained soil, preferably in a sunny position. They require little pruning but they do benefit from dead-heading, particularly when young.

Syringa x *laciniata*

This is a bushy, rounded deciduous shrub of uncertain origin, but is probably a garden-raised hybrid between S. *protolaciniata* and S. *vulgaris*. It is distinct among the commonly grown lilacs in that the leaves are deeply cut into between three and nine narrow lobes. Clusters of fragrant, lilac flowers open in late spring.

Height: 2 m (6 ft)
Spread: 3 m (10 ft)
Hardiness: Zone 7

Syringa meyeri

A compact and bushy deciduous shrub of rounded habit with small, dark green leaves. Dense clusters of fragrant, violet-purple flowers open in the late spring and early summer. This species is mainly represented in gardens by the form described below, which is sometimes grown as *S. velutina*.

Native range: N China
Height: 1.5 m (5 ft)
Spread: 2 m (6 ft)
Hardiness: Zone 3
Variants: 'Palibin' is a very compact, slow-growing form, ideal for the small garden.

Syringa pubescens

This vigorous, upright shrub, sometimes tree-like, has glossy dark green leaves. Large clusters of fragrant flowers, lilac-purple to nearly white, open at the ends of the shoots in late spring. The typical form is rarely seen, and it is mainly represented in gardens by the forms described below.

Native range: N China
Height: 5 m (16 ft)
Spread: 4 m (13 ft)
Hardiness: Zone 4
Variants: subsp. *microphylla* 'Superba' (*S. microphylla* 'Superba') is smaller, up to 2 m (6 ft), and bears profuse, rose-pink flowers in early summer, and intermittently until autumn. subsp. *patula* 'Miss Kim' (*S. patula* 'Miss Kim') is compact, up to about 2 m (6 ft), and has purple-coloured buds opening to ice-blue flowers.

Syringa vulgaris

This, the most commonly grown species, makes a vigorous, large shrub, sometimes tree-like, with broad, heart-shaped leaves ending in a tapered point. The large, conical clusters of very fragrant flowers open in late spring and early summer. Lilac-purple in the typical form, there are many selections with flowers ranging from white to pink, red, blue and purple, and in single or double forms.

Common name: Common lilac
Native range: E Europe
Height: 6 m (20 ft)
Spread: 6 m (20 ft)
Hardiness: Zone 3
Variants: 'Andenken an Ludwig Späth' ('Souvenir de Louis Spaeth') has deep wine-red, single flowers. 'Charles Joly' has deep purple-red, double flowers. 'Katherine Havemeyer' has double, lavender-purple flowers. 'Madame Lemoine' has white, double flowers opening from cream buds. 'Masséna' has clusters of single, red-purple flowers.

Syringa vulgaris 'Masséna'

Syringa x *laciniata*

Tibouchina urvilleana

Tamarix
Tamaricaceae

The tamarisks are a genus of some 50 species of deciduous shrubs, sometimes trees, with feathery, plume-like foliage composed of tiny leaves.

Grown for their graceful habit and small but profuse flowers, they prefer a well-drained soil in full sun. They are an excellent choice for a full coastal exposure, where they will tolerate very dry conditions, but inland they do require more shelter and a moisture-retentive soil. Cut back hard annually to retain a compact habit – *T. ramosissima* in spring, *T. tetrandra* in summer, after flowering.

Tamarix ramosissima

This is a vigorous, spreading deciduous shrub, sometimes tree-like, with long, slender shoots, densely covered in tiny, pointed, pale green leaves. Dense spikes of small, pink flowers open profusely along the new shoots in late summer.

Native range: SE Europe to China
Height: 6 m (20 ft)
Spread: 5 m (16 ft)
Hardiness: Zone 2
Variants: 'Pink Cascade' is very vigorous with rich pink flowers. 'Rubra' has deep pink flowers.

Tamarix tetrandra

This vigorous, spreading shrub or small tree has a graceful habit, with arching, purple-brown shoots and tiny, densely arranged leaves. The slender clusters of small, pale pink flowers open in spring from shoots formed in the previous year.

Native range: SE Europe, SW Asia
Height: 4 m (13 ft)
Spread: 5 m (16 ft)
Hardiness: Zone 5

Telopea
Proteaceae

The four species that make up this small genus of evergreen shrubs or trees are all natives of Australia, including the island state of Tasmania.

The following species is the most commonly grown, principally for its striking flower clusters. It requires a moist but well-drained, lime-free soil in order to thrive. It prefers a sunny position, as long as it is not dry, with its roots shaded from the hottest of the sun.

Telopea truncata

This stoutly branched evergreen shrub has young shoots densely covered in dark brown hairs, and leathery, dark green leaves sometimes toothed or lobed toward the tip. Dense heads, up to 8 cm (3 in) across, of slender, tubular, deep crimson flowers open at the ends of the shoots in early summer.

Common name: Tasmanian waratah
Native range: Tasmania
Height: 4 m (13 ft)
Spread: 3 m (10 ft)
Hardiness: Zone 8

Teucrium
Labiatae

This large genus contains about 300 species of often aromatic herbaceous perennials and shrubs, all with opposite leaves. Species are widely distributed, particularly in the Mediterranean region and Southwest Asia.

The following species is grown for its attractive foliage and its flowers, and it does best in a well-drained soil where it receives full sun. It can be cut back lightly after flowering to retain a compact habit. It is suitable for a border or for growing on a sunny wall in regions where it is not fully hardy.

Teucrium fruticans

This is a compact and vigorous, evergreen shrub with young shoots that are densely covered with white hairs, and bearing aromatic, bright green foliage. The leaves, which are grey-green when young, are white beneath. The lilac-purple, five-lobed flowers open in spikes at the ends of the shoots during summer.

Common name: Shrubby germander
Native range: Mediterranean region
Height: 1 m (3 ft) or more
Spread: 2 m (6 ft)
Hardiness: Zone 8

Tibouchina
Melastomataceae

This is a large genus comprising some 350 species of evergreen shrubs and herbaceous perennials, natives of Mexico and Central and South America.

The following species is grown for its striking flowers but it will survive outside only in the mildest of climates. It is also suitable for training against a wall. Shorten young shoots in spring to encourage a bushy habit.

Tibouchina urvilleana

This vigorous evergreen shrub has stout, four-angled shoots covered in red hairs and softly hairy, prominently three-veined, dark green leaves. The deep violet-purple flowers open over a long period from summer to autumn.

Common name: Glory flower
Native range: Brazil
Height: 3 m (10 ft)
Spread: 2 m (6 ft)
Hardiness: Zone 10

Tilia
Tiliaceae

The limes comprise a genus of some 25 species of deciduous trees that are widely distributed in North America as well as in Europe and Asia. They make handsome specimen trees and they are particularly valued for their habit, foliage and flowers. Some limes also produce coloured winter shoots.

Lime trees are suitable for any well-drained soil that is not too dry. They often respond well to pruning and are commonly pollarded (pruned heavily to reduce the crown and to encourage the production of vigorous shoots) or pleached (kept low by frequent pruning and training the branches to form an interwoven hedge or to grow over a pergola). Those with coloured winter shoots are particularly effective when pleached.

Tilia cordata

This broadly columnar tree has glossy dark green, rounded leaves, blue-green on their undersurfaces, with tufts of brown hair growing from the axils of the leaves. Pendulous clusters of small, pale yellow, fragrant flowers hang from the branches in mid-summer.

Common name: Small-leaved lime
Native range: Europe, W Asia
Height: 30 m (100 ft)
Spread: 15 m (50 ft)
Hardiness: Zone 4
Variants: 'Greenspire' is compact in habit and is broadly conical.

Tilia x euchlora

This deciduous tree is of uncertain origin, possibly a hybrid between *T. cordata* and *T. dasystyla*. It makes a broadly columnar tree with very glossy dark green leaves edged with fine teeth. Pendulous clusters of small, pale yellow, fragrant flowers hang from the branches in mid-summer.

Height: 20 m (65 ft)
Spread: 10 m (33 ft)
Hardiness: Zone 3

Tilia x europaea

This naturally occurring hybrid between *T. cordata* and *T. platyphyllos* is commonly planted in large gardens and or in public spaces. It is a broadly columnar tree with rounded, dark green leaves, paler beneath. It bears pendulous clusters of small, pale yellow, fragrant flowers in mid-summer.

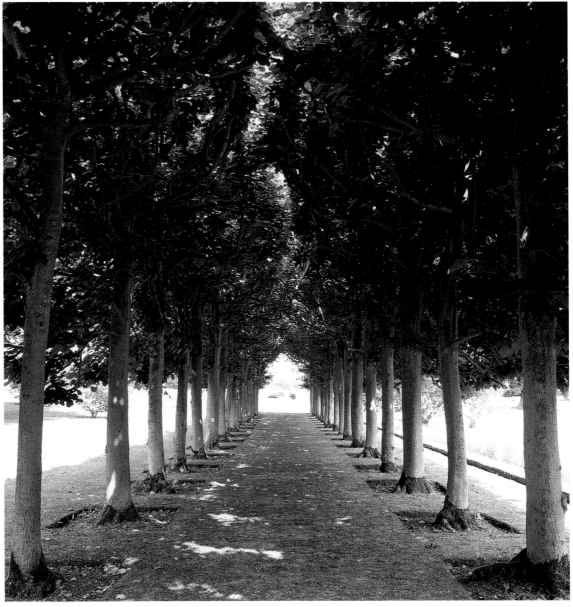

Tilia platyphyllos 'Rubra'

It is often seen with numerous shoots arising from large burrs at the base of the tree.

Common name: Common lime
Native range: Europe
Height: 30 m (100 ft) or more
Spread: 15 m (50 ft)
Hardiness: Zone 3
Variants: 'Wratislaviensis' has attractive foliage that is bright yellow when young.

Tilia platyphyllos

This broadly columnar deciduous tree has rounded, sharply toothed and abruptly pointed, dark green leaves, softly downy beneath, turning yellow in autumn. Clusters of small, fragrant, pale yellow flowers open in early to mid-summer.

Common name: Broad-leaved lime
Native range: Europe, SW Asia
Height: 30 m (100 ft)
Spread: 20 m (65 ft)

Hardiness: Zone 4
Variants: 'Aurea' produces yellow shoots in winter. 'Rubra' has bright red winter shoots.

Tilia tomentosa

This is a vigorously growing, broadly columnar tree with rounded, sharply toothed and sometimes slightly lobed leaves. The leaves, which are dark green above and densely covered in white hairs on their undersurfaces, turn yellow in autumn. Prominent clusters of very fragrant, pale yellow flowers hang down from the shoots in mid- to late summer.

Common name: Silver lime
Native range: SE Europe, SW Asia
Height: 25 m (80 ft)
Spread: 15 m (50 ft)
Hardiness: Zone 4
Variants: 'Petiolaris' (*Tilia* 'Petiolaris'), the weeping silver lime, is a form with gracefully pendulous branches.

Toona
Meliaceae

This is a genus of six species of deciduous and evergreen trees, natives of China, Southeast Asia and northern Australia. Only the following is commonly grown, and it makes a handsome specimen tree. It is suitable for any good, well-drained soil and prefers a position in full sun.

Toona sinensis

This broadly columnar deciduous tree, sometimes spreading by suckers, has stout shoots and bold leaves, up to 60 cm (24 in) or more long, with as many as 30 dark green leaflets that are onion-scented when crushed. Large, pendulous clusters of small, white, fragrant flowers open at the ends of the shoots in mid-summer.

Synonym: *Cedrela sinensis*
Native range: China
Height: 20 m (65 ft)
Spread: 15 m (50 ft)
Hardiness: Zone 5
Variants: 'Flamingo' is slow-growing with brilliant pink young foliage, later creamy white, then green.

Trachycarpus fortunei

Trachycarpus
Palmae

A small genus of six species of evergreen palms, with single or clustered stems and fan-shaped leaves, natives of the Himalayas and East Asia. The following is the most commonly grown species and is the hardiest palm. It makes an excellent specimen tree, and is suitable for any well-drained soil in a sunny position with shelter from strong winds.

Trachycarpus fortunei

This evergreen, single-stemmed palm has a stout trunk densely covered with the fibrous brown remains of old leaf bases. The very large, fan-shaped leaves, up to 1.2 m (4 ft) across, are deeply cut into numerous slender, dark green segments. Massive, drooping clusters of tiny, pale yellow, fragrant flowers open in early summer, males and females on separate plants.

Common names: Chinese windmill palm, fan palm
Native range: China
Height: 10 m (33 ft)
Spread: 3 m (10 ft)
Hardiness: Zone 8

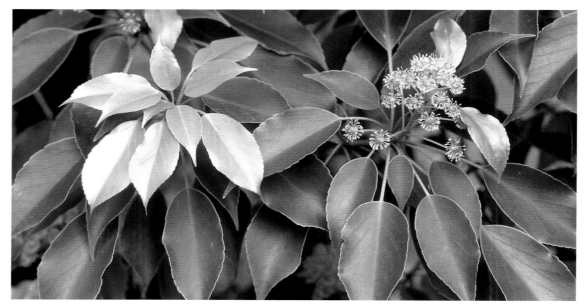

Trochodendron aralioides

Trochodendron
Trochodendraceae

The single species in this genus is an evergreen tree with no obvious close relatives. Handsome in foliage and with unusual flowers, it requires a moist but well-drained, lime-free soil, and does best in a semi-shaded position, sheltered from strong winds perhaps among other trees.

Trochodendron aralioides

This is a broadly columnar evergreen tree, often branching low and shrubby, that is conical when young. The glossy dark green leaves are borne on long, slender stalks, and end in finely tapered points, and leaves are clustered towards the ends of the shoots. Bright green flowers, consisting of a central disc with numerous stamens radiating out, like the spokes of a wheel, are borne in conical clusters in late spring and early summer.

Native range: Japan, Korea, Taiwan
Height: 10 m (33 ft)
Spread: 8 m (26 ft)
Hardiness: Zone 8

Ugni
Myrtaceae

This is a genus made up of about 15 species of evergreen shrubs and trees, natives of South America and all with opposite leaves.

Only the following species is commonly grown, and it is valued for its foliage and flowers as well as its edible fruits. It requires a moist but well-drained soil and does best in areas that experience cool, moist summers and mild winters. Where it thrives, however, it can be used for hedging.

Ugni molinae

This is an evergreen shrub that bears small, dark green, untoothed leaves. The leaves have paler undersurfaces and end in a short, abrupt point. Fragrant, nodding, cup-shaped, pale pink flowers open on slender stalks in the late spring, and these are followed by small, red and aromatic, edible berries.

Synonym: *Myrtus ugni*
Common name: Chilean guava
Native range: Chile
Height: 1.5 m (5 ft)
Spread: 1 m (3 ft)
Hardiness: Zone 9

Ulex
Leguminosae

The gorses are a genus made up of about 20 species of spiny shrubs, natives of Western Europe and North Africa. Leaves are present normally only on young seedlings, and these are replaced by spines as the plants mature.

These shrubs grow best in poor, well-drained soils, in particular sandy soils, and they need a position in full sun. They can be cut back lightly after flowering to retain a compact habit. If plants become leggy, as they do in rich soils, cut them back hard, to within 15 cm (6 in) of the base.

Ulex europaeus

This is a dense, thicket-forming shrub with rigid, green shoots that are formidably armed with

Ulex europaeus 'Flore Pleno'

sharp-pointed, green spines. Masses of bright golden yellow, fragrant, pea-like flowers, up to about 2 cm (¾ in) long, open along the ends of the shoots in mid- to late spring, but sometimes earlier, and often intermittently as well at other times of the year.

Common name: Common gorse
Native range: W Europe
Height: 1.5 m (5 ft)
Spread: 2.5 m (8 ft)
Hardiness: Zone 6
Variants: 'Flore Pleno' produces bright yellow, double flowers.

Ulex gallii

This compact, dwarf shrub has a spreading habit with green shoots bearing sharp-tipped spines. The golden yellow, pea-like flowers, up to 1.5 cm (½ in) long, open from late summer to autumn.

Common name: Dwarf gorse
Native range: W Europe
Height: 1.5 m (5 ft)
Spread: 2 m (6 ft)
Hardiness: Zone 7
Variants: 'Mizen' is a prostrate form with shoots that creep across the ground. It comes into flower in the late summer.

Ulmus
Ulmaceae

This genus is made up of some 45 or so species of elms. They are all deciduous trees and shrubs that are widely distributed in the temperate regions of the northern hemisphere.

While some species of elm are grown for their attractive foliage, others are favoured for their striking bark, but they are all suitable for any well-drained soil. The prevalence of Dutch elm disease has considerably reduced the number and variety of elms that are in cultivation in many parts of the world.

Ulmus x hollandica 'Jacqueline Hillier'

This is a slow-growing and bushy shrub with a rounded habit. It is a compact plant when young, but becomes more open as it matures. The dark green, rough-textured leaves are sharply toothed and neatly arranged in two ranks on both sides of the brown-hairy shoots.

Height: 3 m (10 ft)
Spread: 4 m (13 ft)
Hardiness: Zone 5

Ulmus minor 'Dampieri Aurea'

Vaccinium corymbosum

Ulmus minor

A deciduous tree of broadly columnar habit, with outer shoots that usually droop, and glossy green, rather leathery leaves that turn yellow in autumn. Clusters of tiny flowers, made conspicuous by their red stamens, open on the bare shoots in early spring, followed by pale green, winged fruits.

Common name: Smooth-leaved elm
Native range: Europe, North Africa, SW Asia
Height: 25 m (80 ft)
Spread: 15 m (50 ft)
Hardiness: Zone 5
Variants: 'Dampieri Aurea' is a small, conical tree with golden yellow foliage.

Ulmus parvifolia

A rounded to upright deciduous tree with arching shoots and grey, green and orange-brown flaking bark. The glossy dark green, sharply toothed leaves turn shades of yellow, red or purple in the autumn. Small clusters of tiny red flowers open among the leaves in autumn, and these are followed by small, pale green, winged fruits. It is resistant to Dutch elm disease.

Common name: Chinese elm
Native range: China, Korea, Japan
Height: 15 m (50 ft)
Spread: 12 m (40 ft)
Hardiness: Zone 5

Vaccinium
Ericaceae

This large genus is made up of about 450 species of deciduous and evergreen shrubs, sometimes trees, widely distributed in the northern hemisphere, South Africa and South America.

While some species are grown for their edible fruits, the ornamental types are also grown for their foliage – which, in the deciduous species, often colours in autumn – and their urn-shaped to bell-shaped flowers. They require a moist but well-drained, lime-free and humus-rich soil. Pruning is not usually essential, but cut *V. corymbosum* back in winter to restrict its growth.

Vaccinium corymbosum

This is a vigorous deciduous shrub that forms dense clumps of upright shoots bearing dark green leaves turning to shades of orange, yellow and red in autumn. Small, urn-shaped, white or pink-flushed flowers open in late spring as the young leaves are emerging, and the flowers are followed by edible, blue-black berries.

Common name: Blueberry
Native range: E North America
Height: 2 m (6 ft)
Spread: 2 m (6 ft)
Hardiness: Zone 3

Vaccinium glaucoalbum

This mound-forming evergreen shrub spreads by underground stems and has dark blue-green, leathery leaves, blue-white beneath. Spikes of small, cylindrical, white flowers and blue-white bracts open in late spring and early summer, and these are followed by blue-black, bloomy berries.

Native range: E Himalayas
Height: 1 m (3 ft)
Spread: 2 m (6 ft)
Hardiness: Zone 8

Vaccinium vitis-idaea

A creeping evergreen shrub forming dense mats of glossy dark green, leathery leaves. Clusters of small, bell-shaped, white or pink-tinged flowers open at the ends of the shoots in late spring and early summer, followed by bright red, edible berries.

Common name: Cowberry
Native range: Northern hemisphere
Height: 30 cm (12 in)
Spread: 2 m (6 ft) or more
Hardiness: Zone 2
Variants: 'Koralle' freely produces large fruits.

Viburnum
Caprifoliaceae

This very important genus in gardens has about 150 species of deciduous and evergreen shrubs, sometimes trees, with opposite leaves. They are widely distributed in temperate regions of the northern hemisphere, extending to Southeast Asia and South America.

Viburnums are grown for a range of ornamental features, including their often fragrant flowers, fruits and foliage, which, on the deciduous species, often colours well in autumn. They are suitable for any good, well-drained soil and can be used in the border as specimen shrubs or grown in a woodland setting among other shrubs and trees.

Viburnum betulifolium

This is a vigorous, spreading deciduous shrub that has arching branches bearing dark green, toothed and taper-pointed leaves. Broad, flattened heads of small, white flowers open in the early summer, and these are followed by profuse, small, bright red fruits in nodding clusters.

Native range: China
Height: 4 m (13 ft)
Spread: 5 m (16 ft)
Hardiness: Zone 5

Viburnum x bodnantense

This is a garden-raised hybrid between V. farreri and V. grandiflorum. It makes a stiffly branched shrub of upright habit, becoming more arching

Viburnum betulifolium

Viburnum x bodnantense 'Dawn'

with age, bearing dark green leaves that are bronze coloured when young. The dense clusters of fragrant, tubular, white to pink flowers open on the bare shoots over a long period from the autumn through to early spring. This hybrid is normally grown as one of the selected forms listed below.

Height: 3 m (10 ft)
Spread: 2.5 m (8 ft)
Hardiness: Zone 5
Variants: 'Charles Lamont' has bright pink-coloured flowers. 'Dawn' bears rose-pink flowers that fade with age to a white flushed with pink. 'Deben' produces nearly white flowers that open from pale pink buds.

Viburnum x burkwoodii

This is a garden-raised hybrid between V. carlesii and V. utile that makes a rounded semi-evergreen shrub with glossy dark green leaves, sometimes turning red in autumn. Dense heads of white, very fragrant flowers open in mid- to late spring from pink buds. The flowers are followed by flattened fruits, which ripen from red to black.

Height: 3 m (10 ft)
Spread: 3 m (10 ft)
Hardiness: Zone 5
Variants: 'Anne Russell' is compact with very fragrant flowers. 'Mohawk' has profuse, strongly fragrant, white flowers opening from deep pink

Viburnum x *carlcephalum*

buds. 'Park farm Hybrid' is spreading with large flowers and orange-red autumn colour.

Viburnum x *carlcephalum*

This garden-raised hybrid between *V. carlesii* and *V. macrocephalum* makes a vigorous and stoutly branched, rounded deciduous shrub with broad, dark green leaves that turn red in autumn. The very fragrant, tubular, white flowers flushed with pink open from pink buds in large, domed heads during late spring.

Height: 2.5 m (8 ft)
Spread: 3 m (10 ft)
Hardiness: Zone 5

Viburnum *carlesii*

This very popular species is a deciduous shrub of stiffly branched, rounded habit and with dark green leaves that turn red in autumn. The very fragrant, white to pale pink flowers open from deeper coloured buds in mid- to late spring, sometimes followed by red, later black, fruits. Normally grown as the selected forms listed below.

Native range: Korea
Height: 2 m (6 ft)
Spread: 2 m (6 ft)
Hardiness: Zone 5
Variants: 'Aurora' has pale pink flowers opening from red buds. 'Diana' has red flower buds opening pink, and bronze-tinged young foliage.

Viburnum *davidii*

This evergreen shrub forms a low, spreading mound of compact habit with bold, dark green, conspicuously three-veined leaves. Heads of small, white flowers open in late spring and also at other

Viburnum davidii

times of the year, particularly autumn and winter, followed by showy, egg-shaped, metallic blue fruits. Some plants may be either male or female and both need to be planted to obtain fruits. It makes excellent ground cover in sun or shade.

Native range: China
Height: 1 m (3 ft)
Spread: 2 m (6 ft)
Hardiness: Zone 8

Viburnum x *juddii*

This garden-raised hybrid between *V. carlesii* and the closely related *V. bitchiuense* makes a rounded deciduous shrub with dark green leaves sometimes turning red in autumn. The domed heads of white, very fragrant flowers, flushed with pink, open from pink buds in mid- to late spring.

Height: 2.5 m (8 ft)
Spread: 2.5 m (8 ft)
Hardiness: Zone 4

Viburnum *farreri*

This is a stoutly branched deciduous shrub of upright habit with dark green leaves that are

bronze when young and turn red or purple-red in autumn. Clusters of very fragrant, tubular flowers from pink buds, open to white flushed with pink from late autumn and winter to early spring.

Native range: China
Height: 3 m (10 ft)
Spread: 2.5 m (8 ft)
Hardiness: Zone 5
Variants: 'Candidissimum' has white flowers and foliage that is pale green when young.

Viburnum *opulus*

This is a large, vigorous deciduous shrub with dark green, maple-like, three- to five-lobed leaves that turn orange-yellow to red in autumn. Broad, flattened, lacecap-like heads of white flowers open in the early summer, and these are followed by glossy red fruits.

Common name: Guelder rose
Native range: Europe, North Africa, W and C Asia
Height: 4 m (13 ft)
Spread: 4 m (13 ft)
Hardiness: Zone 3
Variants: 'Aureum' produces foliage that is yellow when young. 'Compactum' is a form with a very

Viburnum tinus 'Eve Price'

Viburnum carlesii 'Diana'

compact habit, growing up to 1.5 m (5 ft) tall. 'Roseum' has rounded heads of large, sterile, white flowers. 'Xanthocarpum' produces yellow fruits.

Viburnum plicatum

This rounded to spreading deciduous shrub has branches often arranged in tiers, with dark green, prominently veined leaves turning red-purple in autumn. Large, flattened, lacecap-like heads of white flowers open on long stalks above the foliage in late spring and early summer, and these are

sometimes followed by small, red fruits. Normally grown as one of the selected forms listed below.

Native range: China, Japan
Height: 3 m (10 ft)
Spread: 5 m (16 ft)
Hardiness: Zone 5
Variants: 'Grandiflorum' has rounded heads of large, sterile flowers but no fruits. 'Lanarth' has lacecap-like heads with very large, sterile flowers but is not free-fruiting. 'Mariesii' has very distinctly layered branches and lacecap-like flowerheads, but few fruits. 'Nanum Semperflorens' is compact and slow growing form, with small flowerheads that are produced over a long period during summer and autumn. 'Pink Beauty' is a striking form with the sterile flowers ageing to deep pink. 'Rowallane' has lacecap-like flowerheads and profusely borne red fruits.

Viburnum rhytidophyllum

This vigorous, large evergreen shrub has stout, scurfy shoots and bold, glossy dark green, leathery leaves, up to 20 cm (8 in) long, conspicuously and deeply veined. Grown mainly for its foliage, it also bears large, domed heads of small, creamy white flowers in late spring and early summer, and these are followed by red fruits that ripen to black.

Native range: China
Height: 5 m (16 ft)
Spread: 5 m (16 ft)
Hardiness: Zone 5

Viburnum sargentii

This is a large deciduous shrub with dark green, three-lobed leaves, bronze when young and turning yellow or red in autumn. Lacecap-like heads up to 10 cm (4 in) across, of white flowers in late spring are followed by bright red fruits.

Native range: NE Asia
Height: 3 m (10 ft)
Spread: 4 m (13 ft)
Hardiness: Zone 4
Variants: 'Onondaga' is a compact and upright shrub with deep maroon young leaves that turn red-purple in autumn. The fertile flowers are red in bud and these contrast with the sterile, white, outer flowers.

Viburnum sieboldii

This large, vigorous deciduous shrub of spreading habit, sometimes tree-like, has bold, glossy dark green, prominently veined leaves. Large clusters of small, tubular, creamy white flowers open in late spring, and these are followed by profuse, persistent, glossy red fruits maturing to black.

Native range: Japan
Height: 6 m (20 ft) or more
Spread: 6 m (20 ft)
Hardiness: Zone 4

Viburnum tinus

This popular and vigorous evergreen shrub of compact habit has rather glossy dark green, usually hairy leaves. The small, white flowers, often tinged pink, open in clusters at the ends of the shoots from pink buds over a long period during the winter and spring, followed by blue-black fruits. It makes an excellent dense screen or hedge.

Common name: Laurustinus
Native range: Mediterranean region
Height: 3 m (10 ft)
Spread: 4 m (13 ft)
Hardiness: Zone 8
Variants: 'Eve Price' is very compact with bright pink buds. 'French White' produces pure white flowers. 'Gwenllian' has profusely borne, pink-tinged flowers, and fruits freely. 'Purpureum' has very dark green leaves that are purple-flushed when young. 'Variegatum' has pale green leaves conspicuously edged with yellow.

Vinca
Apocynaceae

The periwinkles form a small genus of just six species of subshrubs and herbaceous perennials, all with opposite leaves, and slender, trailing or arching shoots.

These plants are suitable for any well-drained soil, as long as it is not too dry, and they make excellent ground cover, whether planted in sun or shade. Flowering is usually best, however, in reasonably bright positions. Cutting back hard in spring can increase their vigour.

Vinca difformis

This is an evergreen subshrub, herbaceous in cold regions, with slender, trailing shoots and bright green leaves up to 8 cm (3 in) long. The pale lilac to nearly white flowers, 4 cm (1½ in) across, with five spreading lobes, open singly along the shoots during late autumn and early winter.

Native range: SW Europe, NW Africa
Height: 30 cm (12 in)
Spread: 3 m (10 ft) or more
Hardiness: Zone 8

Vinca minor 'Atropurpurea'

Variants: 'Jenny Pym' has flowers with deep lilac lobes narrowly edged white and a white centre

Vinca major

This is a vigorous evergreen shrub with arching, slender shoots bearing dark green leaves, up to

Vinca major 'Variegata'

8 cm (3 in) long. Bright blue flowers, up to 4 cm (1½ in) across, with five spreading lobes, are borne singly along upright shoots over a long period from the late spring to early autumn.

Common name: Greater periwinkle
Native range: Mediterranean region
Height: 60 cm (24 in)
Spread: 5 m (16 ft) or more
Hardiness: Zone 6
Variants: 'Maculata' has leaves that are blotched in the centre with yellow-green. 'Oxyloba' produces deep blue flowers with narrow lobes. 'Variegata' bears leaves that are broadly edged with creamy white.

Vinca minor

This vigorous, trailing evergreen shrub forms dense mats of glossy dark green leaves, up to about 5 cm (2 in) long. The five-lobed flowers, about 2.5 cm (1 in) across, in various shades of blue, are produced on the young shoots over a long period from spring to autumn.

Common name: Lesser periwinkle
Native range: Europe, W Asia
Height: 20 cm (8 in)
Spread: 5 m (16 ft) or more
Hardiness: Zone 4
Variants: 'Alba Variegata' produces leaves that are edged with pale yellow and white flowers. 'Argenteovariegata' has leaves edged with creamy white and blue flowers. 'Atropurpurea' has deep violet-purple flowers. 'Aureovariegata' has yellow-edged leaves and blue flowers. 'Azurea Flore Pleno' has sky-blue, double flowers. 'Gertrude Jekyll' has profusely borne white flowers. 'La Grave' has large, azure-blue flowers. 'Multiplex' has double, plum-purple flowers.

Vitex
Verbenaceae

This large genus of 250 or so species of deciduous and evergreen shrubs and trees is widely distributed in warm, mainly tropical regions of the world. They have opposite leaves, which are often divided into several leaflets.

The following is the most frequently cultivated species. It needs a well-drained soil and a position in full sun. In areas where it is not completely hardy it can be grown against a sunny wall. Cut back shoots that have flowered to strong buds in spring.

Vitex agnus-castus

A deciduous shrub of open habit with grey, hairy shoots and dark green, aromatic leaves divided into slender leaflets. Large, branched spikes of fragrant, violet flowers open during early autumn. Flowers best in dry weather after a hot summer.

Common name: Chaste tree
Native range: Mediterranean region to C Asia
Height: 3 m (10 ft)
Spread: 3 m (10 ft)
Hardiness: Zone 7

Weigela 'Bristol Ruby'

Weigela
Caprifoliaceae

The ten species of deciduous shrubs of this genus, all with opposite leaves, are grown for their tubular to bell-shaped, pink to red, yellow, or sometimes white flowers. Suitable for the shrub border, they can be grown in any good, well-drained soil. On mature plants, cut some of the oldest shoots back to the base and shorten shoots that have flowered.

Weigela 'Briant Rubidor'

This garden-raised hybrid makes a deciduous shrub with an upright habit. The leaves are either bright yellow or green edged with yellow, and are up to 8 cm (3 in) long. The clusters of deep red, bell-shaped flowers open in late spring and early summer. It does best with a little shade, as the leaves may burn in full sun.

Synonym: *Weigela* 'Olympiade'
Height: 2.5 m (8 ft)
Spread: 2 m (6 ft)
Hardiness: Zone 5

Weigela 'Bristol Ruby'

This vigorous, garden-raised hybrid of upright habit has dark green leaves. Clusters of rich red, bell-shaped flowers open in late spring and early summer from very dark red buds.

Height: 2.5 m (8 ft)
Spread: 2 m (6 ft)
Hardiness: Zone 5

Weigela florida

This is a deciduous shrub of a compact, rounded, spreading habit with arching shoots and dark green, taper-pointed leaves to 10 cm (4 in) long. Clusters of funnel-shaped, deep pink flowers, pale pink inside, open in late spring to early summer.

Vitex agnus-castus

Xanthoceras sorbifolium

Native range: China, Korea
Height: 2 m (6 ft)
Spread: 2.5 m (8 ft)
Hardiness: Zone 5
Variants: 'Foliis Purpureis' is lower growing and compact, up to 1 m (3 ft) tall, with bronze-purple foliage and purple-pink flowers. 'Variegata' has leaves that are edged with creamy white.

Weigela 'Looymansii Aurea'

This garden-raised hybrid of spreading habit has pale golden yellow young leaves edged with red, later pale green. Clusters of slender, pale pink flowers open in late spring to early summer. Does best given light shade, as it may burn in full sun.

Height: 2 m (6 ft)
Spread: 2 m (6 ft)
Hardiness: Zone 5

Weigela middendorffiana

This is a small, compact shrub with upright shoots and bright green leaves up to 8 cm (3 in) long. Clusters of bell-shaped, pale yellow flowers, often with a conspicuous blotch of deep orange inside, open at the ends of the shoots in the late spring to early summer.

Native range: Japan, N China, Korea
Height: 1.5 m (5 ft)
Spread: 1.5 m (5 ft)
Hardiness: Zone 5

Weigela 'Victoria'

This is a garden-raised hybrid making a deciduous shrub of upright habit with deep bronze-purple leaves growing up to 8 cm (3 in) long. Deep purple-pink, funnel-shaped flowers open in late spring to early summer.

Height: 2 m (6 ft)
Spread: 1.5 m (5 ft)
Hardiness: Zone 5

Xanthoceras
Sapindaceae

The only member of this genus is a deciduous shrub. It is not frequently seen in gardens and is grown for its striking and unusual flowers. It is suitable for any good, well-drained soil and does best in a hot, sunny position. It can be grown in the shrub border or against a warm wall. Pruning is not normally required.

Xanthoceras sorbifolium

A vigorous deciduous shrub, sometimes tree-like, with stout shoots and glossy dark green leaves with up to 17 sharply toothed leaflets. The five-petalled, white flowers, 3 cm (1 in) across, have a yellow-green, later red, blotch in the centre. They open in clusters at the ends of the shoots in late spring.

Native range: China
Height: 5 m (16 ft)
Spread: 4 m (13 ft)
Hardiness: Zone 6

Yucca
Agavaceae

This is a genus of about 40 species of evergreen herbaceous perennials, shrubs and trees natives of the southern United States of America, Mexico and Central America. Grown for their bold foliage and showy flower clusters, they thrive in a well-drained soil and a warm, sunny position. Cut the dead flower stalks back to the base in spring.

Yucca filamentosa

This stemless evergreen shrub spreads by suckers and forms dense clumps of rigid, dark green, sword-shaped leaves up to 75 cm (30 in) long. Pendulous, creamy white flowers, 5 cm (2 in) long, open in summer on spikes up to 1.5 m (5 ft) tall.

Common name: Adam's needle
Native range: SE United States of America
Height: 1.5 m (5 ft)
Spread: 1.5 m (5 ft)
Hardiness: Zone 4
Variants: 'Bright Edge' has leaves edged in yellow. 'Variegata' bears leaves edged with creamy white.

Yucca flaccida

This is a suckering, stemless evergreen shrub resembling Y. *filamentosa* but differing in the slightly shorter, dark green to blue-green leaves, which bend downwards at the end. Pendulous, creamy white flowers, up to 5 cm (2 in) long, open in summer on tall spikes up to 1.5 m (5 ft) high.

Native range: SE United States of America
Height: 1.5 m (5 ft)
Spread: 1.5 m (5 ft)
Hardiness: Zone 4
Variants: 'Golden Sword' has leaves that are banded with yellow in the centre. 'Ivory' produces profuse flowers that are borne horizontally.

Yucca gloriosa

This evergreen shrub has a short, stout, usually unbranched trunk bearing a dense crown of large, rigid, spine-tipped, dark green leaves, up to 60 cm (24 in) long, blue-green when young. Tall spikes of pendulous, creamy white flowers, sometimes flushed red or purple, open in late summer.

Common name: Spanish dagger
Native range: SE United States of America
Height: 2.5 m (8 ft)
Spread: 2 m (6 ft)
Hardiness: Zone 6
Variants: 'Variegata' has leaves edged with yellow.

Yushania
Gramineae

This is a genus of evergreen bamboos, native of East Asia. The following is grown for its foliage and graceful habit, and is suitable for a good, moist but well-drained soil. It will stand exposure and can be planted for shelter, but it will need protection from strong winds in very cold areas. It can be invasive and may need to be restricted at the roots.

Yushania anceps

This is a vigorous evergreen bamboo that spreads quickly by sending out underground stems. The tall, cylindrical canes are purple at first, later turning brownish green, and bear dense clusters of slender, purple branches and glossy bright green leaves, to 10 cm (4 in) long, blue-green beneath.

Yucca gloriosa 'Variegata'

Native range: NW Himalayas
Height: 5 m (16 ft)
Spread: 5 m (16 ft) or more
Hardiness: Zone 8

Zauschneria
Onagraceae

A small genus of four species of deciduous and evergreen, herbaceous perennials and subshrubs, with opposite or alternate leaves, and natives of the western United States of America and northern Mexico. The following is grown for its foliage and its contrasting flowers. It requires a not-too-rich, well-drained soil in full sun, and is suitable for growing in a rock garden or the base of a sunny wall. Cut back to the woody base in spring.

Zauschneria californica

This variable, evergreen, subshrubby perennial forms clumps of upright shoots and spreads by sending out underground stems. It produces slender, green to grey-green leaves and spikes of scarlet, funnel-shaped flowers that open at the ends of the shoots over a long period from summer through to autumn.

Common name: California fuchsia
Native range: California (USA), NW Mexico
Height: 60 cm (24 in)
Spread: 60 cm (24 in)
Hardiness: Zone 8
Variants: 'Dublin' produces profusely borne, bright scarlet flowers and green leaves.

Zelkova
Ulmaceae

This is a genus made up of six species of deciduous trees, grown for their foliage and bark, and natives of southern Europe, the Caucasus and East Asia. The flowers are tiny and inconspicuous, males and females usually separate but borne on the same tree.

They require a good, deep, moist but well-drained soil and they make excellent specimen trees for the larger garden.

Zelkova serrata

This is a spreading deciduous tree producing attractive, smooth, grey bark that flakes as the tree ages. Its dark green, slender-pointed and sharply toothed leaves turn to shades of orange, yellow and red in the autumn. Tiny green flowers open on the young shoots in spring, and these are followed by small, spherical fruits.

Common name: Keaki
Native range: China, Japan, Korea
Height: 15 m (50 ft)
Spread: 15 m (50 ft)
Hardiness: Zone 5

Zenobia
Ericaceae

The single species in this small genus is grown for its attractive foliage and fragrant flowers. It requires a moist but well-drained, acidic soil that is rich in organic matter. It does best given a sunny or lightly shaded position, but it requires more shade in areas where the soil tends to dry out during the summer.

Cut the stems that have flowered back to strong shoots after flowering is over. Cut some of the oldest shoots right back to ground level every year.

Zenobia pulverulenta

This deciduous or semi-evergreen shrub has bloomy, arching shoots and dark green to blue-green leaves that are scalloped at the margins. Nodding, bell-shaped, fragrant, white flowers, up to 1 cm (⅓ in) across, open in clusters towards the ends of the shoots in early to mid-summer.

Native range: SE United States of America
Height: 1.5 m (5 ft)
Spread: 1.5 m (5 ft)
Hardiness: Zone 5

Climbers

The versatility of climbing plants enables them to be grown in virtually any garden situation. Those that are self-clinging, with tendril pads, such as *Parthenocissus*, or with aerial roots, such as *Hedera* (ivy), the climbing hydrangeas and *Campsis*, can be grown on a wall or tree trunk, depending on their requirements for light. Vigorous climbers on a house wall should be kept under control because they can invade loose brickwork and damage guttering.

Other climbers attach themselves by twining their leaf stalks, such as *Clematis*, or stems, such as the honeysuckles (*Lonicera*), or by using tendrils, such as the passion flower (*Passiflora*). If they are grown against a wall, these plants require a suitable support, such as a wire or wooden frame, but they can also be trained into large shrubs or trees or over a pergola or archway. If they are grown over a support, make sure that it is strong enough, as a vigorous climber can be extremely heavy, especially when wet or laden with snow. Choose climbers that are to be grown into a tree or shrub with care, as some, such as *Actinidia deliciosa* and *Clematis montana*, are very vigorous and demand a large tree to act as a support.

Climbers provide a variety of features to delight the gardener, from the striking flowers of *Clematis*, which are often followed by ornamental and long-lasting fruit clusters, to the fragrant flowers of several of the honeysuckles (*Lonicera*) and the showy trumpets of *Campsis*. While many climbers flower in spring and summer, they can be chosen to extend this display throughout the year. The dainty *Clematis cirrhosa* var. *balearica* is particularly useful for blooming between late autumn and early spring. Foliage, too, is an important feature, as in the bold-leaved and variegated *Hedera colchica* 'Dentata Variegata', and the striking autumn colour of *Parthenocissus*.

Actinidia deliciosa 'Hayward'

Actinidia
Actinidiaceae

This genus of some 40 species of deciduous and evergreen climbers with twining shoots are all natives of East Asia. Grown for their foliage, flowers and fruits, they are suitable for good, well-drained soil, flowering best in a sunny position. They can be trained into a tree or some other appropriate support, or grown against a sunny wall.

Except in some forms of *A. deliciosa*, male and female flowers are borne on separate plants and both need to be grown to produce fruit. Cut back to 30 cm (12 in) on planting and tie in the resulting shoots as they grow. Reduce the length of vigorous shoots in early spring.

Actinidia arguta

This vigorous deciduous climber has dark green, finely toothed leaves on red stalks. Clusters of greenish-white, fragrant flowers, 2 cm (¾ in) across, open in early summer, followed by smooth, yellow-green, edible fruits on female plants. Some forms selected for their edible fruits as well as self-fertile forms are sometimes available.

Common name: Tara vine
Native range: E Asia
Height: 10 m (33 ft) or more
Hardiness: Zone 3

Actinidia deliciosa

This is a vigorous deciduous climber with stout, bristly shoots and glossy dark green leaves. Clusters of fragrant, creamy white flowers, 4 cm (1½ in) across, open in early summer, followed on female plants by the familiar bristly skinned, edible fruits. Several forms selected for their fruits as well as self-fertile forms are available. This species has been called *A. chinensis* in gardens.

Common names: Chinese gooseberry, kiwi fruit
Native range: China
Height: 10 m (33 ft) or more
Hardiness: Zone 8
Variants: 'Hayward' is popular for its larger fruits.

Actinidia kolomikta

This deciduous climber has slender shoots and dark green, heart-shaped leaves strikingly blotched with white or pink. Clusters of fragrant, white flowers, up to about 2 cm (¾ in) across, open in the late spring to early summer, and these are followed on female plants by smooth, yellow-green fruits about 2.5 cm (1 in) long. The foliage colour develops best in conditions of bright light.

Native range: China, Japan
Height: 10 m (33 ft) or more
Hardiness: Zone 4

Akebia
Lardizabalaceae

A genus of four species of deciduous and evergreen climbers with slender, twining stems and leaves divided, fan-like, into several leaflets. Grown for its flowers and unusual fruits, the following species needs a good, moist but well-drained soil. Flowering best in full sun, it is suitable for training into a tree or other support or, with support, for growing against a wall. Restrict its growth if necessary by cutting back after flowering.

Akebia quinata

This vigorous, slender-stemmed deciduous or semi-evergreen climber has leaves divided into five leaflets. Emerging bronze, they turn to dark green and can be tinged purple during winter. Pendulous clusters of fragrant, purple flowers in early spring are followed by sausage-shaped, bloomy pods up to 10 cm (4 in) long.

Native range: E Asia
Height: 10 m (33 ft)
Hardiness: Zone 5

Akebia quinata

Ampelopsis
Vitaceae

A genus of about 25 species of deciduous climbers, natives of North America and Asia. Closely related to the grape vines (*Vitis*), they attach themselves to supports by slender tendrils growing from the stems.

They are grown for their often deeply cut leaves and ornamental fruits and they prefer a good, well-drained soil and fruit best if given a sunny position. To restrict their growth, cut them back as necessary in winter.

Ampelopsis brevipedunculata

This vigorous deciduous climber has three- or sometimes five-lobed, dark green leaves, to 15 cm (6 in) long. Clusters of tiny green flowers in summer are followed by striking, bright blue fruits, about 1 cm (⅓ in) across, ripening from yellow and pink.

Native range: E Asia
Height: 6 m (20 ft)
Hardiness: Zone 4
Variants: 'Elegans' has leaves blotched with white and pink and is less vigorous.

Aristolochia
Aristolochiaceae

This genus comprises some 300 species of twining deciduous and evergreen climbers, shrubs and perennial herbs. They are widely distributed and many are found in tropical regions.

Grown for its bold foliage and unusual flowers, the following species does best in a good, well-drained soil. It is suitable for growing over any strong support or into a tree. Cut any weak shoots to the base and train strong shoots on to a support. Restrict growth if necessary by cutting back long shoots in spring or after flowering.

Aristolochia macrophylla

This vigorous deciduous climber has twining shoots and dark green, heart-shaped leaves about 25 cm (10 in) or more long. The unusual siphon-shaped flowers, 4 cm (1½ in) long, are yellow-green with a flared, purple-brown mouth, and are borne singly or in pairs from the shoots in early summer.

Common name: Dutchman's pipe
Native range: E United States of America
Height: 10 m (33 ft)
Hardiness: Zone 4

Ampelopsis brevipedunculata

Berberidopsis
Flacourtiaceae

This genus is made up of two species of evergreen climber, natives of Chile and Australia, but only the following is commonly grown. It needs a moist but well-drained, lime-free soil rich in organic matter, and it generally grows best in the shade.

It prefers areas with cool, moist summers and mild winters, and it can be trained against a shady wall or allowed to scramble over small shrubs.

Berberidopsis corallina

This is a slender-stemmed evergreen or semi-evergreen climber with dark green, spiny margined leaves, up to 10 cm (4 in) long, blue-white beneath. The small, spherical, bright red flowers, up to 1.5 cm (½ in) across, hang from the stems on long, slender shoots, and open over a long period during mid- and late summer.

Common name: Coral plant
Native range: Chile
Height: 5 m (16 ft)
Hardiness: Zone 8

Billardiera
Pittosporaceae

This is a genus of about eight species of evergreen climbers with twining stems, natives of Australia. Only the following species is commonly grown, for its flowers and fruits.

This species requires a moist, well-drained, lime-free soil that is rich in organic matter, and it does best in areas with cool, moist summers and mild winters. It usually needs little pruning.

Billardiera longiflora

This is an evergreen climber with slender, twining shoots bearing narrow, dark green leaves. The slender, tubular, pale yellow-green flowers, up to about 3 cm (1 in) long, open during the summer, and these are followed by rounded, lobed fruits in various colours from deep blue to purple, red, pink or white.

Common name: Climbing blueberry
Native range: Tasmania
Height: 2 m (6 ft)
Hardiness: Zone 8

Celastrus orbiculatus

Campsis
Bignoniaceae

The two species in this genus are deciduous climbers that cling by sending out aerial roots, and are natives of China and the southeast of the United States of America. They have opposite leaves divided, fern-like, into several leaflets.

Cultivated for their showy flowers, they will grow in any well-drained soil. They can be trained over any suitably strong support, such as a pergola, large tree or sunny wall. Train against the support initially as they can take time to attach their roots.

Cut back to 15 cm (6 in) after planting and train the strongest-growing shoots to the desired framework. Once established, prune the side shoots to two or three buds in spring.

Campsis radicans

This vigorous deciduous climber has stout shoots and large, dark green leaves composed of up to 11 sharply toothed leaflets. Clusters of large, trumpet-shaped, bright orange to red flowers, up to 10 cm (4 in) long, open in late summer.

Common name: Trumpet vine
Native range: SE United States of America
Height: 10 m (33 ft) or more
Hardiness: Zone 4
Variants: 'Flava' produces yellow flowers.

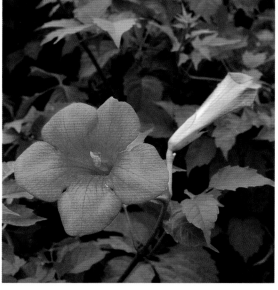

Campsis x tagliabuana 'Madame Galen'

Campsis x *tagliabuana*

This is a garden-raised hybrid between *C. grandiflora* and *C. radicans* that makes a very vigorous deciduous climber clinging by aerial roots, with leaves divided into up to 11 leaflets. Clusters of large, trumpet-shaped flowers open in late summer.

Height: 10 m (33 ft) or more
Hardiness: Zone 5
Variants: 'Madame Galen' is the most popular form with large clusters of bright orange-red flowers up to 8 cm (3 in) long.

Celastrus
Celastraceae

This is a genus of about 30 species of widely distributed deciduous and evergreen shrubs, trees and climbers. The flowers are small and rather inconspicuous but the main attraction is the fruits, which split to reveal coloured seeds. Male and female flowers are usually borne on separate plants; both sexes need to be present for fruiting.

The following species will grow in any well-drained soil and can be trained over any suitably strong support or trained to grow into a tree.

Celastrus orbiculatus

This vigorous deciduous climber has twining stems and bright green leaves turning yellow in autumn. Small clusters of tiny greenish flowers in early summer are followed by yellow, pea-sized fruits. The fruits reveal bright red seeds when they open and have a very striking appearance.

Common name: Chinese bittersweet
Native range: E Asia
Height: 10 m (33 ft) or more
Hardiness: Zone 5

Cissus
Vitaceae

This large genus comprises about 350 species of usually evergreen herbaceous perennials and shrubs, succulents and climbers that are widely distributed, mainly in tropical and subtropical regions of the world.

The following species is grown for its foliage and fruits. It is suitable for any good, moist but well-drained soil, but it will thrive only in mild climates. It can be grown on to a suitable support, or trained against a wall or into a tree. Cut back long shoots as necessary in spring to restrict size.

Cissus striata

This evergreen climber attaches itself to supports by slender tendrils, and has glossy dark green leaves divided into usually five toothed leaflets. Clusters of small, green flowers open in summer, and these are followed by red to purple-red or black berries. Does best where winters are mild.

Common name: Ivy of Uruguay
Native range: Chile, S Brazil
Height: 10 m (33 ft)
Hardiness: Zone 8

Clematis
Ranunculaceae

This is a large genus of about 300 species of climbers, subshrubs and herbaceous perennials, widely distributed, with opposite leaves usually divided into several leaflets. The leaves of climbing species have twining stalks for attaching themselves to supports. Grown mainly for their flowers – the showy part of which is the sepals – they also often produce conspicuous, silky seed heads that can remain an attractive feature for a long period. Petals are absent but some flowers have modified petal-like stamens (staminodes) in their centres.

Grow in good, well-drained soil rich in organic matter, and keep the base of the plant shaded. Cut back deciduous sorts on planting to a pair of buds at about 30 cm (12 in) from the soil.

Prune early-flowering species to restrict growth if necessary in late spring after flowering. Prune early, large-flowered hybrids in early spring by cutting shoots back to a strong bud. Removing flowers once they have faded will encourage a second crop of blooms. Prune late-flowering (from mid-summer) species and hybrids in early spring. Late, large-flowered hybrids, Texensis hybrids and Viticella hybrids can be cut back hard to about 15–20 cm (6–8 in) from the soil.

Clematis 'Abundance'

This late-flowering Viticella hybrid bears profuse, wine-red, slightly nodding flowers, up to about 7 cm (2½ in) across, with centres of golden stamens and deeply veined sepals. Flowering occurs from mid-summer to late autumn.

Height: 2.5 m (8 ft)
Hardiness: Zone 6

Clematis 'Alba Luxurians'

A late-flowering Viticella hybrid with grey-green foliage and white flowers, up to 8 cm (3 in) across, with centres of deep purple stamens, the four sepals flushed green towards their tips. Flowering occurs from mid-summer to early autumn.

Height: 4 m (13 ft)
Hardiness: Zone 6

Clematis alpina

A slender-stemmed deciduous climber with leaves divided into nine sharply toothed leaflets. The nodding, bell-shaped, usually blue flowers, with centres of white staminodes, open on slender stalks in mid- to late spring, followed by silky seed heads.

Clematis 'Alba Luxurians'

Common name: Alpine clematis
Native range: Europe
Height: 2.5 m (8 ft)
Hardiness: Zone 5
Variants: 'Columbine' produces pale grey-blue flowers. 'Constance' has semi-double, deep pink flowers. 'Frankie' bears blue flowers, the staminodes of which are attractively blue-tipped. 'Jacqueline du Pré' produces large, mauve-pink flowers with sepals that are narrowly edged with white. 'Pamela Jackman' has large, rich blue-coloured flowers with outer staminodes that are tinged blue. 'Pink Flamingo' bears profuse, pink, double flowers. 'Ruby' produces deep pink flowers. 'White Columbine' has pure white flowers. 'Willy' bears mauve-pink flowers that are deep pink at the bases of the sepals.

Clematis armandii

This is a vigorous evergreen climber with glossy dark green leaves that are often bronze coloured when young. Leaves are divided into three leathery, prominently veined leaflets. Flowers are fragrant, with four or five sepals, white or pink-tinged, borne in clusters in the early spring. It generally does best in a sheltered position and grows well against a wall.

Native range: China, N Myanmar (Burma), N Vietnam
Height: 10 m (33 ft)
Hardiness: Zone 7

Clematis 'Barbara Jackman'

Variants: 'Apple Blossom' has flowers that are pink in bud. 'Snowdrift' has large, pure white flowers.

Clematis 'Barbara Jackman'

This early, large-flowered hybrid bears mauve-blue flowers, up to 10 cm (4 in) across, with contrasting creamy yellow stamens, each sepal with a central carmine stripe. Flowering occurs in late spring to early summer and again in early autumn.

Height: 3 m (10 ft)
Hardiness: Zone 5

Clematis 'Bees' Jubilee'

This is an early, large-flowered hybrid with deep pink flowers, up to 12 cm (5 in) across, fading to pale pink, with a deeper pink band on each sepal and with a centre of pale brown stamens. Flowering occurs in late spring and early summer and again in early autumn.

Height: 2.5 m (8 ft)
Hardiness: Zone 5

Clematis 'Bill Mackenzie'

This vigorous hybrid between *C. tangutica* and *C. tibetana* subsp. *vernayi* makes a deciduous climber with bright green leaves composed of sharply toothed leaflets. Long-stalked flowers, with four wide-spreading, rather thick, bright yellow sepals, have centres of purple filaments, and flowers open from mid-summer to autumn.

Height: 5m (16 ft)
Hardiness: Zone 5

Clematis campaniflora

This is a vigorous deciduous climber with slender shoots and blue-green leaves with up to 21, usually untoothed, leaflets. The small, widely bell-shaped flowers are pale lilac and open on long, slender stalks in mid- to late summer.

Native range: Portugal, SW Spain
Height: 6 m (20 ft)
Hardiness: Zone 6
Variants: 'Lisboa' has larger, mauve-blue flowers.

Clematis 'Bees' Jubilee'

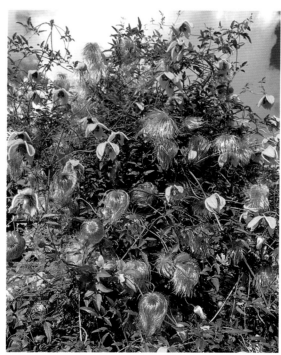

Clematis 'Bill Mackenzie'

Clematis x cartmanii 'Joe'

This garden-raised hybrid between *C. marmoraria* and *C. paniculata* makes a trailing evergreen plant that can be tied in to a suitable support. It produces finely divided, glossy green leaves and masses of white, star-like flowers, up to about 4 cm (1½ in) across, each with six sepals. Flowers are flushed with green in bud and open in early spring.

Height: 1.5 m (5 ft)
Hardiness: Zone 8

Clematis cirrhosa

This is a variable evergreen climber producing slender shoots and glossy dark green leaves. Foliage can vary from undivided to lobed or be divided into three leaflets. Bell-shaped, creamy white, fragrant flowers, up to about 7 cm (2½ in) across, sometimes spotted with purple inside, open from late autumn to early spring, and these are followed by silky seed heads.

Native range: Mediterranean region
Height: 3 m (10 ft)
Hardiness: Zone 7
Variants: var. *balearica* (fern-leaved clematis) has

deeply lobed leaflets that turn a bronze-purple colour in cold weather. 'Freckles' produces flowers that are heavily blotched inside with maroon-purple. 'Wisley Cream' has large, creamy white, unspotted flowers.

Clematis 'Comtesse de Bouchaud'

This late, large-flowered hybrid of vigorous growth bears mauve-pink flowers, up to about 10 cm (4 in) across, with deeper pink veins and centres of bright yellow stamens. It flowers profusely from mid-summer to early autumn.

Height: 4 m (13 ft)
Hardiness: Zone 5

Clematis 'Daniel Deronda'

This is an early, large-flowered hybrid. The strikingly large flowers, which grow up to 20 cm (8 in) across, are violet-blue in colour and have paler-coloured centres and creamy stamens. The plant blooms in the late spring and early summer, and again in early autumn. The flowers produced early in the year are singles or sometimes semi-

Clematis 'Doctor Ruppel'

Clematis cirrhosa var. balearica

doubles, and they are at their most impressive when the plant is given a sunny position.

Height: 3 m (10 ft)
Hardiness: Zone 5

Clematis 'Doctor Ruppel'

An early, large-flowered hybrid with bright pink flowers, a deeper pink band in the centre of each sepal and pale brown stamens. Flowering occurs in late spring and early summer, and again in early autumn. Flowers fade little even in strong sunlight.

Height: 3 m (10 ft)
Hardiness: Zone 5

Clematis 'Duchess of Albany'

A late-flowering Texensis hybrid bearing upright, tulip-shaped, bright pink flowers shading to lilac-pink at the margins of the fleshy sepals, which are striped deeper pink in the centre. Can be grown as a climber or trailing over low shrubs.

Height: 2.5 m (8 ft)
Hardiness: Zone 4

Clematis 'Duchess of Edinburgh'

This is an early, large-flowered hybrid bearing fully double, rosette-like, white flowers, up to about 10 cm (4 in) across, with green shading and centres of yellow stamens. Flowering occurs in the late spring and early summer and again in early autumn. Some of the sepal-like leaves growing below the flowers are often coloured green and mottled with white.

Height: 2.5 m (8 ft)
Hardiness: Zone 5

Clematis x *durandii*

This is a garden-raised hybrid between *C. integrifolia* and *C.* 'Jackmanii'. It makes a stoutly branched deciduous climber bearing glossy green, undivided leaves up to about 15 cm (6 in) in length. The large, deep violet-blue flowers, reaching up to 10 cm (4 in) across, have centres of yellow stamens and open during the summer. It is not a self-clinging climber and so needs to be tied in or staked.

Height: 2.5 m (8 ft)
Hardiness: Zone 5

Clematis 'Elsa Späth'

This is an early, large-flowered hybrid producing flowers coloured an attractive shade of deep lavender-blue. The flowers, which grow up to about 16 cm (6 in) across, have a paler-coloured flush in the centre of each sepal and red stamens. Flowering occurs from the late spring to early summer and again from the late summer to early autumn.

Height: 2.5 m (8 ft)
Hardiness: Zone 5

Clematis 'Ernest Markham'

This late, large-flowered hybrid climber has a vigorous growth pattern and bears rich red-coloured flowers that are up to 10 cm (4 in) across. Each flower has a centre of creamy brown stamens. The blooms start to open in mid-summer and continue through to autumn. If the plant is left unpruned, it will come into flower somewhat earlier – perhaps at the beginning of summer.

Height: 3 m (10 ft)
Hardiness: Zone 5

Clematis 'Duchess of Edinburgh'

Clematis florida 'Sieboldii'

Clematis 'Etoile Rose'

This is a late-flowering Texensis hybrid with nodding, bright rose-pink, bell-shaped flowers, up to 5 cm (2 in) across, with sepals recurving at the tips and edged with silvery pink. Flowering occurs from late summer to autumn.

Height: 3 m (10 ft)
Hardiness: Zone 4

Clematis 'Etoile Violette'

This is a late-flowering Viticella hybrid with profusely borne, nodding, deep purple flowers, up to about 7 cm (2½ in) across, with centres of creamy yellow stamens. Flowering occurs from mid-summer to early autumn.

Height: 3 m (10 ft)
Hardiness: Zone 6

Clematis flammula

A vigorous deciduous climber with bright green leaves divided into three or five, sometimes lobed, leaflets. The large clusters of small, very fragrant, white flowers, 2.5 cm (1 in) across, open from late summer into autumn.

Native range: S Europe, North Africa, SW Asia
Height: 5 m (16 ft)
Hardiness: Zone 6

Clematis florida

This deciduous or semi-evergreen climber has glossy deep green leaves with up to nine leaflets. The strikingly large flowers, 10 cm (4 in) or more across, have up to six creamy white, spreading sepals banded with green on the back, and centres of purple-black stamens. It is normally grown as one of the selections listed below.

Native range: China
Height: 3 m (10 ft)
Hardiness: Zone 8
Variants: 'Flore Pleno' has double flowers, with dense centres of greenish white, petal-like staminodes. 'Sieboldii' has white flowers with contrasting centres of deep purple staminodes.

Clematis 'Gipsy Queen'

This late, large-flowered hybrid bears profuse, deep velvety purple, single flowers, up to about 12 cm (5 in), across with centres of red stamens. It flowers from mid-summer to early autumn.

Clematis 'Henryi'

Height: 4 m (13 ft)
Hardiness: Zone 5

Clematis 'Henryi'

An early, large-flowered hybrid whose creamy white flowers, up to 20 cm (8 in) across, have pointed sepals and centres of dark brown stamens. Flowering occurs in early to mid-summer and again in late summer and early autumn.

Height: 4 m (13 ft)
Hardiness: Zone 5

Clematis 'HF Young'

This is an early, large-flowered hybrid bearing pale blue flowers, up to 20 cm (8 in) across, with overlapping sepals and centres of cream-coloured stamens. Flowering occurs from late spring to early summer and again in early autumn.

Height: 3 m (10 ft)
Hardiness: Zone 5

Clematis 'Huldine'

This is a vigorous, late-flowering hybrid with small, white flowers, about 6 cm (2½ in) across, banded

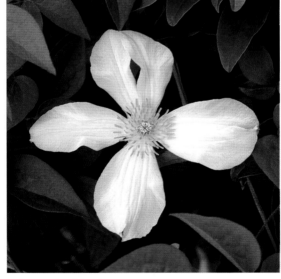

Clematis 'Huldine'

pale pink on the reverse side of the sepals, and with centres of yellow stamens. Flowering occurs from mid-summer to early autumn.

Height: 4 m (13 ft)
Hardiness: Zone 5

Clematis 'Jackmanii'

This is a popular, late, large-flowered hybrid bearing rich, velvety violet-purple, slightly nodding flowers, up to 10 cm (4 in) across, with centres of

yellow-green stamens. Flowering occurs freely from mid-summer through to early autumn.

Height: 4 m (13 ft)
Hardiness: Zone 4

Clematis 'Kermesina'

This is a late-flowering Viticella hybrid bearing freely produced, deep crimson flowers with centres of red-purple stamens. Flowering occurs from mid-summer to early autumn.

Height: 4 m (13 ft)
Hardiness: Zone 4

Clematis 'Lasurstern'

This early, large-flowered hybrid bears single, deep lavender-blue flowers, reaching up to about 20 cm (8 in) or more across, with overlapping and wavy edged sepals and conspicuous centres of creamy coloured stamens. Flowering occurs from late spring through to early summer and again in the early autumn.

Height: 3 m (10 ft)
Hardiness: Zone 5

Clematis 'Little Nell'

This is a late-flowering Viticella hybrid with profusely borne, pale pink flowers, up to 5 cm (2 in) across, with sepals edged pale mauve-pink and centres of green stamens. Flowering occurs from mid-summer to early autumn.

Height: 4 m (13 ft)
Hardiness: Zone 4

Clematis macropetala

This is a slender-stemmed deciduous climber with leaves that are usually divided into nine bright green, sharply toothed leaflets. The nodding, blue to violet-blue flowers, up to about 10 cm (4 in) across, that open in spring and early summer have four spreading sepals and centres composed of numerous petal-like staminodes.

Native range: SE Siberia, Mongolia, N China
Height: 3 m (10 ft)
Hardiness: Zone 5
Variants: 'Ballet Skirt' produces large, deep pink flowers. 'Jan Lindmark' has mauve-pink flowers. 'Lagoon' has large, deep blue flowers. 'Markham's Pink' bears soft pink flowers. 'White Moth' has small, creamy white flowers.

Clematis macropetela 'Jan Lindmark'

Clematis 'Madame Julia Correvon'

Clematis rehderiana

Clematis montana

This is a very popular and an extremely vigorous deciduous climber, and has leaves that are divided into three leaflets. The profusely borne, usually white or pink-flushed, often scented flowers, growing up to about 6 cm (2½ in) across, open in dense clusters in late spring. Many of the plants grown under this name may belong to one of the forms listed below.

Native range: Himalayas to China and Taiwan
Height: 15 m (50 ft)
Hardiness: Zone 6
Variants: 'Alexander' produces creamy white flowers that are very fragrant. The young foliage of 'Broughton Star' is bronze coloured and produces semi-double, dusky pink flowers. var. *grandiflora* has large, white flowers, growing up to about 12 cm (5 in) across. 'Mayleen' bears satin-pink, fragrant flowers and young foliage that is an attractive bronze colour. var. *rubens* produces pink flowers, purple shoots and also has bronze-coloured young foliage. 'Tetrarose' has young foliage that is bronze and bears lilac-pink flowers. 'Vera' has deep pink, fragrant flowers.

Clematis 'Mrs N Thompson'

This early, large-flowered hybrid has a compact growth habit and produces deep violet-purple flowers, reaching up to about 12 cm (5 in) across. The sepals are banded scarlet and the flowers have central clusters of red stamens. Flowering occurs from the late spring to early summer, and again in early autumn.

Height: 2.5 m (8 ft)
Hardiness: Zone 5

Clematis 'Multi Blue'

This is an early, large-flowered hybrid with deep blue-coloured, double flowers, growing to about 10 cm (4 in) or more across. Flower centres have dense clusters of pale to silvery blue, petal-like staminodes. Flowering occurs from the late spring through to early summer, and again in late summer and early autumn.

Height: 2.5 m (8 ft)
Hardiness: Zone 5

Clematis 'Niobe'

This is a late, large-flowered hybrid that produces deep red, single flowers reaching up to about 15 cm (6 in) across. The flowers are very dark and blackish red when they first open, and they have

Clematis 'Madame Julia Correvon'

This is a late-flowering Viticella hybrid bearing freely produced, bright wine red, and widely bell-shaped flowers, reaching up to about13cm (5 in) across. The flowers have strikingly contrasting centres composed of cream stamens and four slightly twisted sepals.

Height: 3 m (10 ft)
Hardiness: Zone 4

Clematis 'Marie Boisselot'

This is an early, large-flowered hybrid of vigorous growth, and bearing pure white flowers, up to 20 cm (8 in) across, composed of overlapping sepals with centres of golden yellow stamens. Flowering occurs from early summer through to early autumn.

Synonym: *Clematis* 'Madame le Coultre'
Height: 3 m (10 ft)
Hardiness: Zone 5

Clematis 'The President'

central clusters of yellow stamens. Flowering occurs from mid-summer through to the early autumn.

Height: 3 m (10 ft)
Hardiness: Zone 5

Clematis 'Perle d'Azur'

This vigorous, late, small-flowered hybrid freely produces slightly nodding, widely bell-shaped, sky-blue flowers, up to about 8 cm (3 in) across, with sepals recurved at the tips, and with pale yellow stamens at their centres. Flowering occurs from mid-summer to early autumn.

Height: 4 m (13 ft)
Hardiness: Zone 5

Clematis rehderiana

A deciduous climber with leaves divided into as many as nine leaflets. The nodding, bell-shaped, pale yellow, cowslip-scented flowers open in large, upright clusters in late summer and early autumn.

Native range: China
Height: 6 m (20 ft)
Hardiness: Zone 6

Clematis spooneri

This is a vigorous, deciduous climber, with young shoots covered in yellowish hairs and dark green leaves divided into three sharply toothed and softly hairy leaflets. White or pink-flushed flowers, reaching up to about 9 cm (3½ in) across, open between the late spring and early summer. This climber has been grown in gardens as *C. chrysocoma*.

Synonyms: *C. chrysocoma* var. *sericea*, *C. montana* var. *sericea*
Native range: China
Height: 8 m (26 ft)
Hardiness: Zone 6

Clematis tangutica

This is a deciduous climber bearing bright green leaves divided into sharply toothed, slender leaflets. The pendulous, yellow-coloured, lantern-shaped flowers have four, slender-pointed sepals. The flowers open on slender stalks in the late summer to autumn, and these are followed by attractive, silky seed pods.

Native range: China
Height: 5 m (16 ft)
Hardiness: Zone 5

Clematis 'The President'

This is an early, large-flowered hybrid that bears rich purple-blue flowers, growing up to about 15 cm (6 in) across. The sepals are silvery beneath and flower centres have clusters of red stamens. Flowering occurs over a long period, from the early summer through to early autumn.

Height: 3 m (10 ft)
Hardiness: Zone 5

Clematis tibetana subsp. vernayi

This vigorous, slender-stemmed deciduous climber has blue-green leaves divided into five to seven or nine untoothed, lobed leaflets. The pendulous, lantern-shaped, yellow flowers, up to about 4 cm (1½ in) long, have very thick sepals and centres of purple-coloured stamens. The flowers are followed by silky seed pods.

Common name: Orange peel clematis
Native range: Nepal, China
Height: 6 m (20 ft)
Hardiness: Zone 6

Clematis x triternata 'Rubromarginata'

This is a vigorous, garden-raised hybrid between *C. flammula* and *C. viticella* that makes a slender-stemmed deciduous climber. The small, profusely borne flowers, up to about 4.5 cm (2 in) across, have four to six slender, red-purple sepals, shading to white at the base, with centres of yellow stamens. It flowers during late summer and autumn, and does best if given a sunny position.

Height: 5 m (16 ft)
Hardiness: Zone 6

Clematis viticella

This is a semi-woody deciduous climber with slender, partially herbaceous shoots and dark green leaves divided into several untoothed leaflets. The nodding, widely bell-shaped, blue-purple to red-purple flowers, up to about 6 cm (2½ in) across, open over a long period from summer to early autumn.

Common name: Virgin's bower
Native range: S Europe, SW Asia
Height: 4 m (13 ft)
Hardiness: Zone 6
Variants: 'Purpurea Plena Elegans' produces fully double, purple-red flowers.

Dregea sinensis

Dregea
Asclepiadaceae

This is a small genus made up of three species of climbers bearing opposite leaves, all natives of the warm regions of the Old World.

The following species is the only one that is generally seen in garden cultivation, and it is grown principally for its attractively fragrant flowers. It is suitable for planting against a warm, sheltered wall and it needs well-drained soil in order to thrive.

Tie young shoots in to a suitable support until they attach themselves naturally by twining. Little pruning is generally needed. However, any dead or damaged wood should be removed in spring, or, if it is necessary to restrict growth, cut stems back after flowering.

Dregea sinensis

This vigorous deciduous climber has heart-shaped, dark green leaves, up to about 10 cm (4 in) long, velvety with hairs beneath. Dense, nodding, long-stalked clusters of small, creamy white and very fragrant, star-shaped flowers spotted with red open in early to mid-summer.

Synonym: *Wattakaka sinensis*
Native range: China
Height: 5 m (16 ft)
Hardiness: Zone 9

Eccremocarpus
Bignoniaceae

This is a small genus of five species of woody or herbaceous climbers that attach themselves by tendrils, and have opposite leaves divided into several leaflets. The following can be grown in any good, well-drained soil in a sunny position. They can be trained over any suitable support or into a tree. Pinching out the tips of the shoots of young plants encourages a bushy habit.

Eccremocarpus scaber

This vigorous, semi-woody evergreen climber has glossy green, fern-like leaves divided into toothed leaflets, and ending in slender, branched tendrils. Clusters of small tubular flowers, up to 2.5 cm (1 in) long, usually orange but sometimes yellow, red or pink, open over a long period from late spring or early summer to autumn.

Common name: Chilean glory flower
Native range: Chile
Height: 5 m (16 ft) or more
Hardiness: Zone 9

Fallopia
Polygonaceae

This genus of seven species of herbaceous perennials and woody climbers is distributed widely in the temperate regions of the northern hemisphere. The following species is grown for its vigorous habit and its small flowers. It will grow in any well-drained soil and is useful for providing quick cover for walls and fences. To restrict growth, cut back, hard if necessary, in early spring.

Fallopia baldschuanica

This is a very vigorous deciduous climber with long, twining shoots bearing bright green, heart-shaped leaves, bronze when young. Clusters of small, white or pink-tinged flowers open over a long period during summer and autumn, followed by small, greenish-white or pink-tinged fruits.

Synonym: *Polygonum baldschuanicum*
Common names: Mile-a-minute, Russian vine
Native range: C Asia to China
Height: 15 m (50 ft)
Hardiness: Zone 4

Hedera
Araliaceae

The ivies are a genus of 12 species of evergreen climbers distributed from western Europe to East Asia. They attach themselves to supports by aerial roots and have two distinct growth phases. In the juvenile phase, the leaves are normally lobed and aerial roots are produced but not flowers or fruits. Plants spread over the ground or climb vigorously in this stage. The adult stage occurs when plants reach or approach the tops of their supports. The plants then become bushy, they do not climb and they start to bear flowers and fruits.

The ivies are useful for growing on a wall or up a tree trunk. They also make good ground cover. They prefer a good, moist but well-drained soil that is rich in organic matter. For ground cover in dense shade, vigorous green-leaved forms are most suitable. Variegated forms colour best in bright positions but should be sheltered from strong, cold winds. Cut them back as necessary in early spring to restrict their growth.

Hedera algeriensis 'Gloire de Marengo'

Hedera hibernica

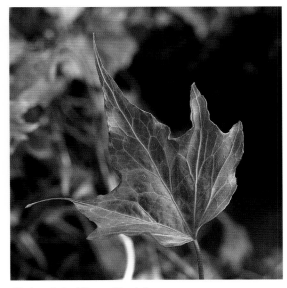

Hedera helix 'Green Ripple'

Hedera algeriensis

This vigorous climber has purple-red shoots and glossy dark green, usually three-lobed leaves, up to 15 or sometimes 20 cm (6–8 in) across, on long, red stalks. It makes excellent ground cover in sun or shade but it is not suitable for colder localities. It is often grown as *H. canariensis*.

Common name: Algerian ivy
Native range: North Africa
Height: 10 m (33 ft) or more

Hardiness: Zone 8
Variants: 'Gloire de Marengo' produces grey-green leaves with margins of creamy white.

Hedera colchica

This is a vigorous climber that produces stout shoots and large, heart-shaped, unlobed or shallowly lobed, leathery, dark green leaves. The leaves sometimes reach as much as 25 cm (10 in) in length. *H. colchica* makes an excellent plant wherever ground cover is required, but it also climbs very vigorously if given support once it has become established.

Common name: Persian ivy
Native range: Caucasus, N Iran
Height: 10 m (33 ft) or more
Hardiness: Zone 7
Variants: 'Dentata' produces large leaves with sparsely toothed margins. 'Dentata Variegata' is similar to 'Dentata' except that its leaves are broadly edged with creamy yellow.

Hedera helix

This vigorous, evergreen climber has dark green leaves often with conspicuous paler veins. The leaves are variable in size and shape, but usually have three to five lobes. This species is mainly grown in gardens as selected forms listed below.

Common name: Common ivy
Native range: Europe
Height: 10 m (33 ft) or more
Hardiness: Zone 4
Variants: 'Adam' has small, shallowly three-lobed, grey-green leaves edged with white. 'Buttercup' produces golden yellow leaves turning yellow-green in shade. 'Caecilia' has strongly wavy edged leaves with a cream margin. 'Erecta' does not climb and produces rigid, upright shoots, up to 1 m (3 ft) in length, bearing small leaves. 'Glacier' has grey-green leaves edged with creamy white. 'Goldchild' has small, bright green leaves that are broadly edged with golden yellow. 'Goldheart' has bright green leaves blotched in the centre with golden yellow. 'Green Ripple' has jaggedly lobed leaves with a long, central lobe. 'Ivalace' produces bright green, shallowly lobed leaves with crisped margins and makes a good groundcover plant. 'Little Diamond' is bushy, up to 30 cm (12 in) tall, with unlobed, grey-green leaves edged creamy white. 'Parsley Crested' has rounded leaves with crimped edges. 'Sagittifolia' has arrow-shaped leaves with slender, pointed lobes. 'Spetchley' is slow growing with very small, dark green leaves.

Hedera hibernica

This is a vigorously growing ivy with broad, usually five-lobed, dark green leaves, up to about 15 cm (6 in) across. It is commonly grown as ground cover, and it is one of the best species for this purpose, thriving even in dense shade. It will also climb vigorously if given support.

Common name: Irish ivy
Native range: W Europe
Height: 10 m (33 ft) or more
Hardiness: Zone 4

Hydrangea
Hydrangeaceae

The climbing species that form a part of this genus make ideal plants for growing against a wall, the side of a house or on the trunk of a large tree. Although they will cling naturally to their support by their aerial roots, they can also be used very effectively as ground cover.

As young plants, they can be slow to attach themselves to their supporting surface, and during this time they can either be tied in until they become established or be allowed to spread across the ground and attach themselves naturally in their own time. If necessary, cut back after flowering to restrict their growth. (*See also chapter Trees, Shrubs and Bamboos.*)

Hydrangea anomala subsp. *petiolaris*

This vigorous deciduous climber has peeling brown bark on older stems, and heart-shaped, glossy green leaves often turning yellow in autumn. Large, flattened, lacecap-like heads of white flowers, up to 25 cm (12 in) across, edged with large sterile flowers open in early summer.

Synonym: *Hydrangea petiolaris*
Common name: Climbing hydrangea
Native range: Japan, South Korea
Height: 15 m (50 ft) or more
Hardiness: Zone 4

Hydrangea seemannii

This is a vigorous evergreen climber with bold, glossy dark green leaves up to 20 cm (8 in) long. The stout stems will creep across the ground and attach themselves to any suitable support, such as a wall or tree trunk. Domed heads of white flowers open from large buds enclosed by conspicuous bracts in summer. Most flowers are small with a few large, sterile flowers on the outside.

Native range: Mexico
Height: 10 m (33 ft) or more
Hardiness: Zone 8

Jasminum
Oleaceae

The climbing species in this genus have twining stems and opposite or alternate leaves that are usually divided into several leaflets. The following species are the ones most frequently seen in

Hydrangea anomala subsp. *petiolaris*

Jasminum officinale 'Argenteovariegatum'

gardens and they are grown principally for their very fragrant flowers.

They are suitable for any good, well-drained soil and they flower best if given a position in full sun. Cut back on planting and then train the resulting shoots over a suitable support, or tie them in against a wall. To restrict their growth, cut back as necessary after flowering. (*See also chapter Trees, Shrubs and Bamboos.*)

Jasminum beesianum

This is a slender-stemmed and twining deciduous or semi-evergreen climber bearing opposite, dark green, undivided leaves, growing up to about 5 cm (2 in) in length. Clusters of small, fragrant, deep red to pink flowers open in late spring to early summer, and these are followed by persistent, glossy black berries.

Native range: China
Height: 5 m (16 ft)
Hardiness: Zone 7

Jasminum officinale

This is a very vigorous deciduous climber producing slender, twining shoots bearing opposite, deep green leaves that are composed of up to nine leaflets. Clusters of white, very fragrant flowers, reaching up to 2 cm (¾ in) across, open at the ends of the shoots over a long period from summer to autumn.

Common name: Common jasmine
Native range: SW Asia to China
Height: 10 m (33 ft) or more
Hardiness: Zone 8
Variants: f. *affine* has flowers tinged with pink. 'Argenteovariegatum' has grey-green leaves edged with creamy white. 'Aureum' has leaves blotched with yellow. 'Fiona Sunrise' has soft yellow foliage. 'Inverleith' has flowers red in bud opening white, red on the back of the lobes.

Jasminum x stephanense

This naturally occurring hybrid, which is also raised in gardens, between *J. beesianum* and *J. officinale*, makes a vigorous, twining deciduous climber. The leaves are opposite and vary from undivided to those with up to five leaflets, and are often edged with creamy yellow and pink when young. Fragrant, pale pink flowers open in early to mid-summer.

Native range: China
Height: 5 m (16 ft)
Hardiness: Zone 8

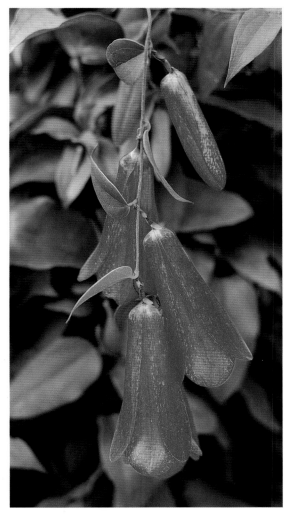

Lapageria rosea

Lapageria
Philesiaceae

The single species in this genus is an evergreen with slender, twining shoots. It is grown for its striking flowers and needs a moist but well-drained, lime-free soil that is rich in organic matter.

At its best in regions with cool, moist summers and mild winters, it generally needs the protection of a shady wall. Little pruning is required, except to remove any dead wood in spring.

Lapageria rosea

This is an evergreen climber that spreads by sending out suckers from the base. It has slender, twining, wiry shoots and rigid, glossy dark green, taper-pointed leaves, growing up to 10 cm (4 in) long. The showy, pendulous, bell-shaped, deep pink flowers, up to 8 cm (3 in) long, open over a long period during summer and autumn.

Common name: Chilean bellflower
Native range: Chile, Argentina
Height: 4 m (13 ft)
Hardiness: Zone 8
Variants: var. *albiflora* produces white flowers.

Lonicera
Caprifoliaceae

Although the honeysuckles contain both shrubs and climbers, it is the climbers that are the best known and most popular in gardens.

They are grown for their usually fragrant flowers, and can be deciduous or evergreen with twining shoots, and they are suitable for any well-drained soil. Honeysuckles can be trained on to any strong support or grown into a tree.

Young plants should be cut back hard on planting and then the resulting shoots tied in to the support. Cut back after flowering if necessary to restrict their growth. (*See also chapter Trees, Shrubs and Bamboos.*)

Lonicera x brownii

This is a garden-raised hybrid between *L. hirsuta* and *L. sempervirens* that makes a deciduous or semi-evergreen climber with blue-green leaves. The uppermost pairs of leaves are joined into a disc around the stem. Whorls of tubular, slightly two-lipped, unscented, orange-red flowers open in late spring and summer.

Common name: Scarlet trumpet honeysuckle
Height: 4 m (13 ft)
Hardiness: Zone 5
Variants: 'Dropmore Scarlet' produces scarlet-coloured flowers over a long period during summer and autumn.

Lonicera caprifolium

This deciduous climber produces deep blue-green leaves, blue-white on their undersurfaces, with the uppermost pairs joined into a disc around the stem. The fragrant flowers are creamy white, flushed with pink on the outside, and open in whorls in the summer. The flowers are followed by orange-red berries.

Common name: Italian honeysuckle
Native range: Europe, W Asia
Height: 6 m (20 ft)
Hardiness: Zone 5

Lonicera x heckrottii

This is a garden-raised hybrid that makes a scrambling deciduous or semi-evergreen shrub with dark green leaves, blue-green on their undersurfaces. The uppermost pairs of leaves are joined to form a disc around the stem. Whorls of fragrant, yellow flowers, flushed with purple-pink on the outside, open in summer and early autumn.

Lonicera x *brownii* 'Dropmore Scarlet'

Height: 4 m (13 ft)
Hardiness: Zone 5
Variants: 'Gold Flame' climbs more vigorously and produces flowers that are more brightly coloured.

Lonicera x italica

This is a garden-raised hybrid between *L. caprifolium* and *L. etrusca* that makes a vigorous deciduous climber with purple-coloured young shoots and dark green leaves, blue-green on their undersurfaces, with the uppermost pairs joined to form a disc around the stem. Whorls of fragrant flowers, purple-pink in bud, open to yellow flushed with red-purple outside during the summer and early autumn. It is sometimes grown as *L.* x *americana*.

Height: 6 m (20 ft)
Hardiness: Zone 6
Variants: 'Harlequin' produces leaves that are edged with creamy white.

Lonicera japonica

This is a very vigorous evergreen climber with dark green, sometimes lobed leaves. The fragrant flowers open white, sometimes purple-flushed, in pairs, and turn deep yellow with age over a long period from late spring or early summer to autumn. The flowers are then followed by black berries.

Common name: Japanese honeysuckle
Native range: China, Japan, Korea
Height: 10 m (33 ft)
Hardiness: Zone 4
Variants: 'Aureoreticulata' has leaves that are veined with yellow. 'Halliana' is very vigorous, with white flowers turning to deep yellow. 'Hall's Prolific' is similar to 'Halliana', but flowers very

Lonicera x *italica*

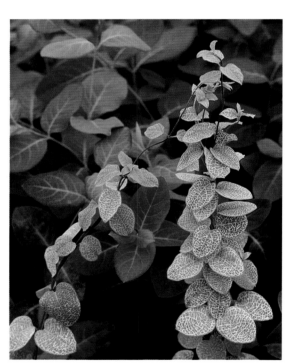

Lonicera japonica 'Aureoreticulata'

profusely. var. *repens* has purple-flushed foliage and flowers tinged purple outside.

Lonicera periclymenum

This is a vigorous deciduous climber with strongly twining shoots and rich green leaves, with blue-green undersurfaces. The flowers are white to yellow, often streaked on the outside with pink, red or red-purple. They are very fragrant and open in dense whorls at the ends of the shoots in mid- to late summer. The flowers are then followed by glossy red, fleshy berries.

Common name: Common honeysuckle
Native range: Europe, North Africa, W Asia
Height: 8 m (26 ft)
Hardiness: Zone 4
Variants: 'Belgica' produces flowers that are reddish-purple on the outside, fading to a yellowish colour. 'Graham Thomas' has creamy white flowers turning to yellow. 'Serotina' produces flowers that are deep red-purple on the outside. 'Sweet Sue' bears very profuse and fragrant white flowers, turning to yellow.

Lonicera x tellmanniana

This garden-raised hybrid between *L. sempervirens* and *L. tragophylla* makes a vigorous deciduous climber with large, bright green leaves, blue-white beneath. The large, unscented flowers have a long, slender tube and are deep yellow, flushed coppery red, opening from late spring to mid-summer.

Height: 5 m (16 ft)
Hardiness: Zone 5

Parthenocissus
Vitaceae

This is a genus comprising about ten species of mostly deciduous climbers, natives of North America, the Himalayas and East Asia. They attach themselves to their support by means of tendrils borne from the shoots, which often end in adhesive discs.

These plants are suitable for any well-drained soil and provide some of the best specimens when a large wall, or similar area, needs covering. In addition, they can also be used for ground cover. To restrict growth, cut them back as necessary in the late autumn.

Parthenocissus henryana

This vigorous deciduous climber attaches itself by means of tendrils ending in adhesive discs. The leaves are divided, fan-like, into three or five, or sometimes seven, leaflets, which are dark green and conspicuously veined in the centre with silver and pink. The leaves turn bright red in autumn.

Native range: China
Height: 10 m (33 ft)
Hardiness: Zone 7

Parthenocissus quinquefolia

This vigorous deciduous climber clings by tendrils ending in adhesive discs. It has bright green leaves divided, fan-like, into five, or sometimes just three, sharply toothed leaflets. The foliage emerges bronze-red and turns brilliant red in early autumn.

Common name: Virginia creeper
Native range: E and C United States of America, Mexico
Height: 15 m (50 ft) or more
Hardiness: Zone 4

Parthenocissus tricuspidata

A vigorous deciduous climber clinging by tendrils ending in adhesive discs. It has bold, glossy dark green leaves, usually three-lobed but sometimes with three leaflets on young plants. It grows rapidly, turning brilliant red and purple in autumn.

Common name: Boston ivy
Native range: Japan, China
Height: 15 m (50 ft) or more
Hardiness: Zone 4
Variants: 'Lowii' has small leaves with deeply cut lobes. 'Veitchii' has leaves turning to deep red-purple in autumn.

Parthenocissus quinquefolia

Passiflora caerulea

Passiflora
Passifloraceae

The passion flowers make up a large genus of some 400 or more species of mainly deciduous and evergreen climbers and, more rarely, herbaceous perennials, shrubs and trees. They are widely distributed, mainly in the tropical regions of South America.

The following is the most reliably hardy species and it is suitable for planting in any reasonably good, well-drained soil. It performs best, however, when trained on a sun-facing wall.

In the spring, cut back the stems to restrict growth and remove any dead wood. Shoots that have flowered should be cut back to two or three buds after the blooms are spent.

Passiflora caerulea

This vigorous evergreen or semi-evergreen climber attaches itself to supports by means of slender, coiling tendrils. It bears deep green leaves, cut nearly to the centre into usually five or seven lobes. The striking, slightly fragrant flowers, 10 cm (4 in) across, are white with a conspicuous corona of white filaments, blue at the tips and deep purple at the base. Flowers open over a long period during summer and autumn and are followed by egg-shaped, orange-yellow fruits, to 5 cm (2 in) long.

Common name: Passion flower
Native range: Brazil
Height: 10 m (33 ft)
Hardiness: Zone 7

Pileostegia
Hydrangeaceae

This is a small genus of four species of evergreen climbers with opposite leaves, natives of East Asia. The following is the most frequently seen species in garden cultivation, and is grown for its bold foliage and attractive flowerheads. It is suitable for any good, well-drained soil and does best grown against a wall or large tree. It will thrive in sun or shade. Prune if necessary in the early spring to restrict its growth.

Pileostegia viburnoides

This is an evergreen climber that attaches itself to supports by aerial roots. It has bold, dark green, leathery leaves up to 15 cm (6 in) long. The broad, flattened clusters, up to 15 cm (6 in) across, of small, creamy white flowers open in late summer and autumn. They resemble those of the climbing hydrangeas but lack the large, sterile flowers.

Native range: India, China, Taiwan
Height: 6 m (20 ft)
Hardiness: Zone 8

Schisandra
Schisandraceae

This genus comprises about 25 species of deciduous and evergreen climbers with twining shoots, natives mainly of East Asia. One species is native to the southeast of the United States of America.

They are grown for their unusual flowers and attractive fruits and prefer a moist but well-drained soil. They can be trained against a wall or other suitable support. Male and female flowers are usually borne on separate plants and both need to be grown in order to produce fruit.

To restrict growth, cut back any very long shoots to a few buds in late winter or early spring. And to encourage vigorous young growth on established plants, cut one of the older shoots back right to the base each year.

Schisandra rubriflora

This deciduous climber has slender, twining shoots, red when young, and dark green leaves, up to about 12 cm (5 in) long, that turn yellow in autumn. Slender-stalked, deep red flowers, about 2.5 cm (1 in) across, open during mid- to late spring, and these are followed on female plants by clusters of red, pea-sized fruits borne on long, red stalks.

Native range: N India, N Myanmar (Burma), China
Height: 6 m (20 ft)
Hardiness: Zone 8

Schizophragma
Hydrangeaceae

This is a small genus of four species of deciduous climbers with opposite leaves, natives of East Asia. They are grown for their showy flowerheads, which, like the climbing hydrangeas, bear large, sterile flowers. Attaching themselves to supports by means of aerial roots, they are suitable for any reasonably good, moist but well-drained soil that is

Solanum crispum 'Glasnevin'

distributed, particularly in the tropical regions of South America.

The following climbing species are cultivated for their showy flowers and they will grow in any good, well-drained soil, but they do best in a sunny position. Train the scrambling shoots over a fence or any other suitable support, or grow them against a wall. To restrict growth, cut back long shoots to a few buds in early spring.

Solanum crispum

This is a vigorous evergreen or semi-evergreen, scrambling shrub bearing dark green, taper-pointed leaves, up to about to 12 cm (5 in) long. The fragrant, blue-purple flowers, reaching about 3 cm (1 in) across, have conspicuous centres of yellow anthers and they open during the summer and early autumn.

Native range: Chile, Peru
Height: 10 m (33 ft)
Hardiness: Zone 8
Variants: 'Glasnevin' flowers over a very long period, sometimes into winter.

Solanum jasminoides

This vigorous evergreen or semi-evergreen climber produces dark green leaves that can be unlobed, lobed or divided into a few separate leaflets. They are borne on slender stalks, which twine around a support. Fragrant, pale blue, star-shaped flowers with centres of yellow anthers open in large clusters during summer and autumn.

Common name: Potato vine
Native range: South America
Height: 6 m (20 ft)
Hardiness: Zone 8
Variants: 'Album' produces white flowers.

rich in organic matter. They can be grown against a wall or the trunk of a large tree. Growth can be restricted by cutting back after flowering.

Schizophragma hydrangeoides

This vigorous deciduous climber has bold, dark green, sharply toothed leaves, up to 15 cm (6 in) long, blue-green beneath. Broad, flattened heads, up to 25 cm (10 in) across, of small, creamy white flowers, each head edged with large, creamy bracts, open in mid-summer.

Native range: Japan
Height: 10 m (33 ft)
Hardiness: Zone 5
Variants: 'Moonlight' has leaves flushed with grey-silver. 'Roseum' has pink-coloured bracts.

Senecio
Compositae

While this large genus contains several cultivated climbing species, most are suitable only for a conservatory. The following, however, can be grown outside in mild areas and requires a well-

drained soil in a sunny, sheltered position. It is suitable for training against a wall or it can also be allowed to scramble through a bushy shrub.

Cut back lightly on planting and reduce shoots by about one-third after flowering. Cut out any dead wood in spring. (*See also chapter Trees, Shrubs and Bamboos.*)

Senecio scandens

This vigorous, scrambling semi-evergreen shrub has long shoots and bears bright green, sharply toothed and often lobed leaves. The bright yellow, daisy-like flowerheads open in large clusters over a long period from autumn until the first hard frosts.

Native range: E Asia
Height: 3 m (10 ft) or more
Hardiness: Zone 9

Solanum
Solanaceae

This is a very large genus made up of as many as 1,400 species of annual and perennial herbaceous plants, shrubs, trees and climbers, very widely

Stauntonia
Lardizabalaceae

This is a genus made up of about 16 species of evergreen climbers. All have twining shoots and leaves that are divided, fan-like, into several individual leaflets.

The following is the most commonly seen species in garden cultivation. Grown for its foliage, flowers and fruits, it requires a good, well-drained soil and a sunny position. It can be trained against a wall or other suitable support, or it will climb into the branches of a tree. Little pruning is needed. Tie in the long shoots as they grow and cut back lightly in early spring.

Stauntonia hexaphylla

This is a vigorous, twining evergreen climber with bold leaves divided in up to seven dark green leaflets. Drooping clusters of white, fragrant flowers, 2 cm (¾ in) across, flushed with violet, open in late summer, and these are followed by egg-shaped, purple fruits up to 5 cm (2 in) long.

Native range: Japan, South Korea
Height: 10 m (33 ft)
Hardiness: Zone 8

Tecoma
Bignoniaceae

A genus of about 12 species of shrubs, trees and scrambling climbers with opposite leaves divided into several leaflets. They are natives from the southern United States to South America, and South Africa. The following is grown for its showy flowers and is suitable for any well-drained soil in full sun. Cut back long shoots in early spring.

Tecoma capensis

This is a vigorous, scrambling evergreen climber with bright green leaves divided into five to nine sharply toothed leaflets. The trumpet-shaped flowers, up to about 7 cm (2½ in) long, are bright orange to red, sometimes yellow, and open in clusters at the ends of the shoots in summer.

Common name: Cape honeysuckle
Native range: S and E Africa
Height: 5 m (16 ft) or more
Hardiness: Zone 10

Trachelospermum
Apocynaceae

This is a genus of some 20 species of twining evergreen climbers with opposite leaves, natives mainly of South Asia but with one species in the southeast of the United States of America.

Suitable for any good, well-drained soil, they are ideal for growing on supports against a wall or over a trellis or pergola.

Trachelospermum asiaticum

This is a vigorous evergreen climber with glossy dark green, often white-veined leaves, up to 5 cm (2 in) long. Very fragrant, five-lobed, creamy white, later yellow flowers, about 2 cm (¾ in) across, open in clusters in mid- to late summer.

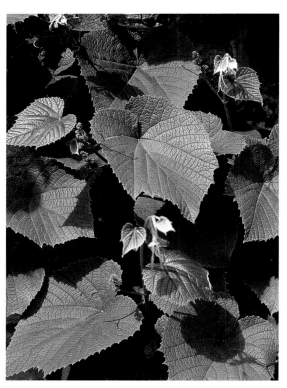

Vitis coignetiae

Native range: Japan, Korea
Height: 5 m (16 ft)
Hardiness: Zone 7

Trachelospermum jasminoides

This vigorous, scrambling evergreen climber has glossy dark green leaves up to 8 cm (3 in) long. The very fragrant flowers, about 2.5 cm (1 in) across, open pure white in small clusters during mid- to late summer and then turn cream with age.

Common name: Confederate jasmine
Native range: China, Japan
Height: 6 m (20 ft)
Hardiness: Zone 8
Variants: 'Variegatum' has leaves that are edged with creamy white. 'Wilsonii' has slender leaves conspicuously veined with white.

Vitis
Vitaceae

This is a genus of about 65 species of deciduous climbers with peeling bark, widely distributed in temperate regions of the northern hemisphere, particularly North America. Attaching themselves to supports with their tendrils, they can be grown in any well-drained soil rich in organic matter.

Many hybrids are grown for their fruits, but the following is the most commonly seen ornamental species, prized for its autumn colour. It is suitable for growing into a large tree or for training on a wall, pergola or other similarly strong support.

Trachelospermum jasminoides 'Variegatum'

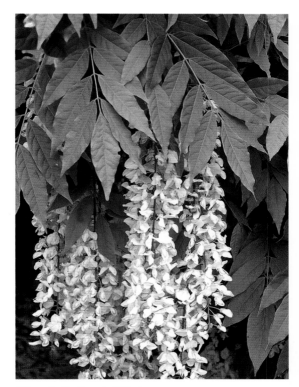

Wisteria floribunda 'Alba'

Vitis coignetiae

This vigorous deciduous climber has stout shoots densely covered with grey hairs when young. The large, shallowly lobed leaves, up to 30 cm (12 in) long, are dark green and deeply veined above and thickly covered with brown hairs beneath. They turn brilliant shades of red in autumn.

Native range: Japan
Height: 20 m (65 ft)
Hardiness: Zone 5

Wisteria
Leguminosae

This genus is made up of five or more species and it contains some of the best known of all the climbers. Natives of East Asia and the southern United States of America, they have deciduous leaves divided into numerous leaflets and showy, pendulous clusters of pea-like flowers. Good, well-drained soil is ideal for them, and they flower best in full sun. They can be trained into a tree, against a wall or over a pergola or similar support. They will also grow as freestanding plants. Generally, plants do not flower when they are young and full blooming is enhanced by correct pruning.

Until they are established, reduce the length of the long shoots in winter and again in summer, training and tying in the resulting shoots to cover the desired space. Once established, cut back the side shoots in summer to about 15 cm (6 in) of a branch, and in winter prune these back again to two or three buds.

Wisteria floribunda 'Multijuga'

Wisteria floribunda

This vigorous deciduous climber has dark green leaves composed of up to 19 leaflets. Slender, pendulous clusters, up to 30 cm (12 in) or more long, of fragrant, purple-blue, pea-like flowers, blotched inside with yellow, open in early summer.

Common name: Japanese wisteria
Native range: Japan
Height: 10 m (33 ft) or more
Hardiness: Zone 5
Variants: 'Alba' produces white flowers. 'Domino' has pale lilac-blue flowers. 'Multijuga' bears very long flower clusters up to 60 cm (24 in) or more in length. 'Rosea' produces bronze young leaves and long clusters of pink-coloured flowers.

Wisteria sinensis

This is a vigorous and popular deciduous climber with dark green leaves divided up into as many as 13 individual leaflets. The foliage is usually bronze when young, and it sometimes turns to yellow in the autumn. Violet-blue, fragrant, pea-like flowers open in compact, pendulous clusters in late spring, and these are followed by attractive, hanging pods with a velvety texture.

Common name: Chinese wisteria
Native range: China
Height: 10 m (33 ft) or more
Hardiness: Zone 5
Variants: 'Alba' is a woody stemmed, large-leaved climber with fragrant, pea-like, white flowers.

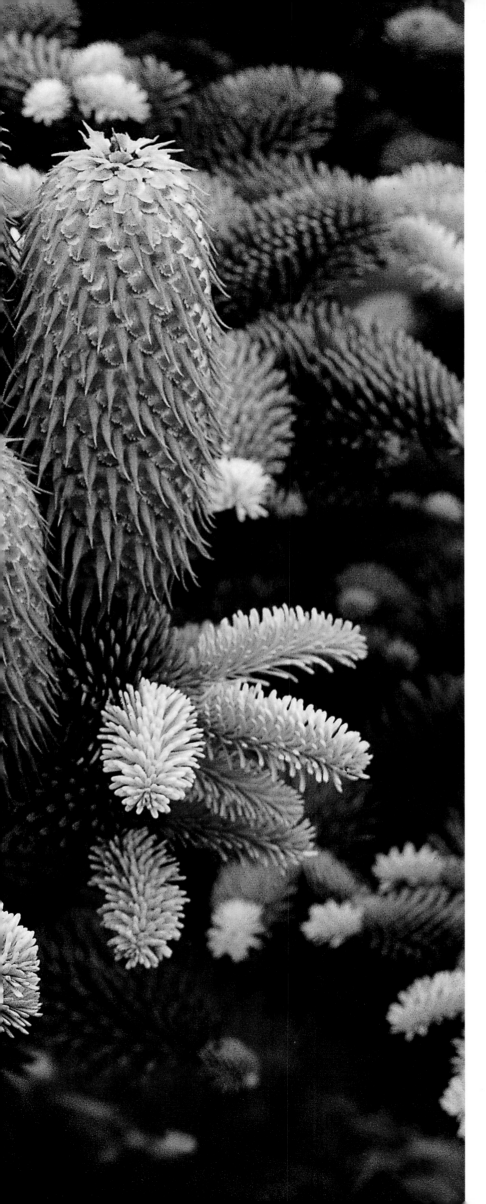

Conifers

Conifers have always had a special place in the garden. Although lacking the striking flowers of many other trees and shrubs, they provide bold contrasts of foliage colour and texture as well as habit. Many conifers grow into large trees and are seen at their best only in larger gardens. Planted as specimen trees, many of them – such as the pines, spruces and silver firs – make prominent focal points of distinctive habit and foliage in the garden landscape.

Large conifers are an excellent choice if you need a windbreak at the edge of your property. The conical habit of such trees as Lawson cypress (*Chamaecyparis lawsoniana*) and western red cedar (*Thuja plicata*) provide a tall, dense screen with enough space between the tops to allow sufficient wind to filter through. Combining different forms with coloured foliage makes the screen as ornamental as it is practical.

In smaller gardens, conifers can also be used for screening and hedging, but they may then need regular trimming to prevent them dominating the scene. Many conifers, however, are suitable for the smallest of positions. Not only are there many species that are naturally low growing, but there is also a large number of dwarf and slow-growing selections of various habits and in colours ranging from silvery blue to bright yellow. These plants often mimic the original large tree, only in miniature form. *Abies lasiocarpa* var. *arizonica* 'Compacta', for example, is at most a small tree, conical in habit, and with striking, silvery foliage, while *Picea glauca* var. *albertiana* 'Conica' makes a dense cone of bright green. In addition to plants such as these, the numerous selections of the cypresses (*Chamaecyparis*) and the prostrate or spreading selections of junipers grown for ground cover, mean that conifers can make a valuable contribution to even the smallest of gardens.

Abies
Pinaceae

The silver firs are a genus of some 50 species of evergreen trees with whorled branches, widely distributed in the northern hemisphere – mainly in temperate regions. Their needle-like, usually bluntly pointed leaves vary from dark green to blue-green and often have blue-white bands of stomata on their undersides. Male and female flowers are borne separately on the same tree, usually only on the upper branches; female flowers are followed by upright cones.

Silver firs mostly prefer a moist but well-drained, lime-free soil, and are best as specimen trees. *A. cephalonica* and *A. pinsapo*, as well as the dwarf forms, will tolerate drier, more alkaline soils.

Abies balsamea

This is a conical tree with grey bark marked with resin-bearing blisters. The bright green needles are often notched at the tip and have two silvery white bands beneath. Flowers open in early summer: male clusters are pendulous and yellow; females upright and purple before turning green and forming brown cones up to 10 cm (4 in) long.

Common name: Balsam fir
Native range: North America
Height: 15 m (50 ft) or more
Spread: 10 m (33 ft) or more
Hardiness: Zone 3
Variants: 'Nana' is a dwarf, rounded bush, up to about 60 cm (24 in) high, with leaves that are densely arranged around the shoots.

Abies cephalonica

A conical tree with glossy dark green, sharp-pointed needles marked with two white bands of stomata beneath. Flowers open in late spring: male clusters are pendulous, red at first opening to yellow; females are upright and green, ripening to a brown cylindrical cone up to 15 cm (6 in) long.

Common name: Greek fir
Native range: Greece
Height: 30 m (100 ft)
Spread: 10 m (33 ft)
Hardiness: Zone 5
Variants: 'Meyer's Dwarf' ('Nana') is a dwarf, bushy form growing up to 2 m (6 ft) tall.

Abies concolor

This is a vigorous, narrowly conical tree with smooth, grey bark that is often marked with resin

Abies concolor 'Compacta'

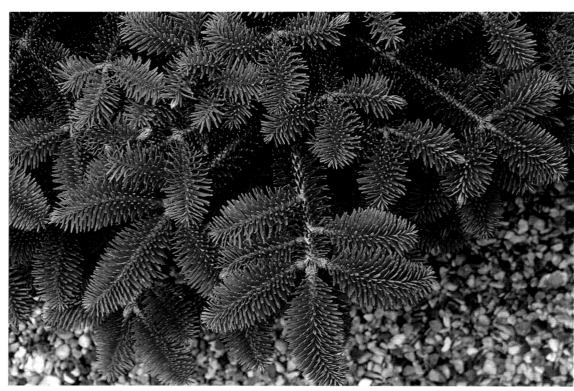

Abies cephalonica 'Meyer's Dwarf'

blisters. The slender, blue-grey, blunt-tipped needles are mostly upswept from the shoots and are a similar colour on both sides. Flowers open in late spring: the male clusters are yellow, pendulous beneath the shoots; the females upright and green, maturing to a green or purple, later brown, cone up to 10 cm (4 in) long.

Common name: Colorado fir
Native range: W United States of America, NW Mexico
Height: 25 m (80 ft) or more
Spread: 15 m (50 ft)
Hardiness: Zone 4
Variants: 'Compacta' is a compact, rounded bush, growing up to about 2.5 m (8 ft) in height.

Abies grandis

A vigorous, conical tree with slender, bright green needles spreading in two ranks either side of the shoots, marked with two white bands beneath. It flowers in late spring: male clusters beneath the shoots, red at first opening yellow; females upright, green, maturing to brown cones 10cm (4 in) long.

Abies concolor 'Compacta'

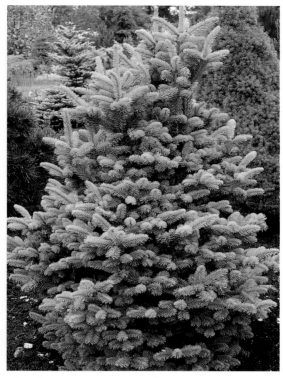

Abies lasiocarpa var. *arizonica* 'Compacta'

their attractively and conspicuously coloured, silvery undersides.

Abies lasiocarpa

This is a conical tree with smooth, grey bark marked with resin blisters. The grey-green, often notched leaves have two white bands beneath. Flowers open in late spring or early summer: male clusters are pendulous, red at first and opening yellow; female flowers are upright and purple, maturing to purple brown cones 10 cm (4 in) long.

Common name: Subalpine fir
Native range: W North America
Height: 25 m (80 ft)
Spread: 10 m (33 ft)
Hardiness: Zone 5
Variants: var. *arizonica* (corkbark fir) has blue-grey foliage and corky bark, and in most areas it is the best form. 'Compacta' is a form of this, making a large, dense shrub or small tree, up to 5 m (16 ft) high, with blue-grey foliage.

Abies nordmanniana

This is a conical tree with lush foliage. The densely arranged needles, notched at the tip, are glossy bright green above with two greenish-white bands beneath. Flowers open in late spring: the males are pendulous and reddish, opening yellow; the females are upright and green, maturing to purple-brown cones up to 15 cm (6 in) long.

Common name: Caucasian fir
Native range: Caucasus, Turkey
Height: 30 m (100 ft)
Spread: 15 m (50 ft)
Hardiness: Zone 4
Variants: 'Golden Spreader' is slow growing and bushy, up to 1.5 m (5 ft), with bright yellow foliage.

Abies koreana

Common name: Giant fir
Native range: W North America
Height: 30 m (100 ft) or more
Spread: 15 m (50 ft)
Hardiness: Zone 6

Abies koreana

This is a conical tree of compact habit with densely arranged, glossy dark green leaves that are a brilliant blue-white colour beneath. The tree flowers in late spring or early summer: the male

clusters are pendulous beneath the shoots and yellow; the female flowers are upright and reddish purple, maturing to purple and then brown cones up to 7.5 cm (3 in) long.

Common name: Korean fir
Native range: South Korea
Height: 10 m (33 ft)
Spread: 5 m (16 ft)
Hardiness: Zone 5
Variants: 'Flava' has yellow-green flowers, maturing into yellow-brown cones. 'Silberlocke' produces leaves that curve upwards and show

Abies pinsapo

This broadly conical tree has rigid, bluntly pointed needles arranged all around its stout shoots. The shoots are grey-green to blue-grey in colour, with white bands displayed on both sides. The flowers open in late spring: males are pendulous and reddish, opening yellow; the female flowers are upright and green, maturing to brown cones up to 15 cm (6 in) long.

Common name: Spanish fir
Native range: S Spain
Height: 25 m (80 ft)
Spread: 15 m (50 ft)
Hardiness: Zone 6
Variants: 'Glauca' has blue-grey foliage.

Abies procera

A narrowly conical tree with blue-green needles, blunt or notched at the tip, with white bands on both sides – more conspicuous below. Flowers open in late spring: males pendulous, red opening to yellow; females upright, red or green, maturing to purple-brown cones 25 cm (10 in) long.

Common name: Noble fir
Native range: NW United States of America
Height: 30 m (100 ft) or more
Spread: 10 m (33 ft)
Hardiness: Zone 5
Variants: Members of the Glauca Group have particularly blue-grey foliage.

Araucaria
Araucariaceae

The 19 species making up this genus of evergreen trees are found in South America, Australia, New Guinea and Norfolk Island. The following is the only species that is hardy in cool, temperate regions. It is suitable for any good, moist but well-drained soil, given a sunny position sheltered from strong winds. It is the hardiest relative of the Wollemi pine (*Wollemia nobilis*).

Araucaria araucana

This is a conical tree when young, with grey, wrinkled bark, but develops a more spreading, rounded head with age. The glossy dark green, spine-tipped and triangular, overlapping leaves, up to 5 cm (2 in) long, densely cover the shoots and persist for many years. Male and female flower clusters grow on separate trees: males cylindrical, green then brown; females rounded, green maturing to brown cones 15 cm (6 in) long.

Common name: Monkey puzzle
Native range: S Chile, S Argentina
Height: 20 m (65 ft) or more
Spread: 10 m (33 ft)
Hardiness: Zone 7

Calocedrus
Cupressaceae

The three species of evergreen trees making up this small genus are natives of the western regions of the United States of America, northern Mexico and Southeast Asia. The following is the only species that is commonly found in garden

Araucaria araucana

cultivation, where it is grown for its characteristic habit. It is suitable for any well-drained soil.

Calocedrus decurrens

A narrowly columnar evergreen tree with red-brown, scaly bark and dark green, aromatic foliage borne in flattened sprays. Tiny, pointed, scale-like leaves densely cover the slender shoots. Male and female flowers are separate on the same tree in spring. Both are small, the females ripening to oblong, yellow-brown cones to 2.5 cm (1 in) long.

Common name: Incense cedar
Native range: W North America
Height: 25 m (80 ft)
Spread: 5 m (16 ft)
Hardiness: Zone 5
Variants: 'Aureovariegata' has foliage that is blotched with yellow.

Araucaria araucana

Cedrus atlantica Glauca Group

Cedrus
Pinaceae

The cedars form a genus of four species of large evergreen trees that are natives of North Africa, Southwest Asia and the Himalayas. They produce two types of foliage: single needles are borne on long shoots; short, slow-growing shoots bear needles in dense whorls. The male flower clusters are often conspicuous above the shoots in autumn, and the small female flowers are followed by barrel-shaped cones.

These trees are suitable for any well-drained soil in a sunny position. However, in their typical forms they are suitable only for large gardens.

Cedrus atlantica

This is a conical tree with ascending branches when young, sometimes spreading as the tree matures. The slender needles, up to about 2.5 cm (1 in) long, are dark green to grey-green or blue-green. Barrel-shaped, purple-brown, later brown cones, up to 8 cm (3 in) long, are borne upright on the branches in autumn.

Common name: Atlas cedar
Native range: Algeria, Morocco
Height: 25 m (80 ft)
Spread: 15 m (50 ft)
Hardiness: Zone 6
Variants: 'Aurea' has golden yellow foliage when young . 'Fastigiata' is a form with a conical habit and with upright branches and blue-grey foliage. Glauca Group (blue atlas cedar) has blue-grey

foliage. 'Glauca Pendula' has this blue-grey foliage as well as weeping branches.

Cedrus deodara

A conical tree with spreading branches and drooping young tips. Bright green to grey-green, slender needles, to 5 cm (2 in) long, are borne in dense whorls. Male flower clusters, upright above the shoots, are purple at first opening yellow in autumn; female flowers are followed by barrel-like, purple-brown cones to 12 cm (5 in) long.

Common name: Deodar
Native range: Afghanistan to W China
Height: 30 m (100 ft)
Spread: 20 m (65 ft)
Hardiness: Zone 7
Variants: 'Aurea' has golden yellow, later yellow-green foliage. 'Feelin' Blue' is shrubby, with grey-blue foliage. 'Golden Horizon' is a form with a low, spreading habit and golden yellow foliage.

Cedrus libani

A conical tree, columnar to spreading with age, with level, tiered branches. The short, dark green to grey-green needles, to 3 cm (1 in) long, are arranged in dense whorls. Flowers open in autumn: males blue-green, opening yellow, upright above the shoots; females maturing to barrel-shaped green cones, to 12 cm (5 in) long, ripening to brown.

Common name: Cedar of Lebanon
Native range: Lebanon, Syria, SW Turkey
Height: 30 m (100 ft)

Spread: 25 m (80 ft)
Hardiness: Zone 5
Variants: 'Sargentii' forms a low mound up to about only 60 cm (24 in) in height.

Cephalotaxus
Cephalotaxaceae

A genus of ten species of evergreen shrubs and trees, natives of the Himalayas to East and Southeast Asia, with needle-like leaves. Male and female flowers are borne on separate plants.

Grown for its habit and foliage, the following is an excellent and tough specimen plant suitable for any good, well-drained soil – in sun or shade.

Cephalotaxus harringtonii

A slow-growing evergreen shrub or spreading tree with red-brown, peeling bark. Slender, blunt-tipped, leathery, dark green needles spread in two ranks, either side of the shoots. The small, creamy white flowers open in spring, males beneath the shoots, females at the tip, followed by fleshy coated seeds, to 2.5 cm (1 in) long, green at first later turning purple-brown.

Common name: Cow tail pine
Native range: Korea, Japan, Taiwan
Height: 6 m (20 ft)
Spread: 6 m (20 ft)
Hardiness: Zone 6
Variants: 'Fastigiata' is compact and narrow, with upright branches, the leaves arranged around the shoots. Can revert, producing spreading branches with normal foliage, which should be removed.

Cephalotaxus harringtonii 'Fastigiata'

Chamaecyparis
Cupressaceae

The cypresses are a genus of six species of evergreen trees, natives of North America and East Asia. The tiny, scale-like leaves are arranged in flattened sprays of aromatic foliage, often marked with white beneath. The spring-opening flowers are small, males and females separate on the same tree. The females are followed by small cones. Juvenile forms may have small, needle-like leaves and no cones. Forms of *C. lawsoniana* are often used for hedging. These should be clipped regularly as necessary between spring and autumn, cutting only into the young shoots.

Chamaecyparis lawsoniana

A narrow, conical tree with flattened, drooping sprays of usually dark green to blue-green aromatic foliage, marked with white beneath. The small flowers open at the tips of the shoots in early spring: males red; females blue-green, maturing to small cones to 1 cm (⅓ in) across.

Common name: Lawson cypress
Native range: W United States of America
Height: 30 m (100 ft) or more
Spread: 8 m (26 ft)
Hardiness: Zone 5
Variants: 'Alumigold' – compact and columnar, to 10 m (33 ft), with bright yellow young foliage. 'Alumii' – columnar, to 15 m (50 ft), with sprays of blue-grey foliage. 'Aurea Densa' – conical, to 2 m (6 ft), with golden yellow foliage. 'Bleu Nantais' – conical and shrubby, to 3 m (10 ft), with silvery blue foliage. 'Broomhill Gold' – bushy and upright, to 8 m (26 ft),with yellow foliage. 'Chilworth Silver' – broadly columnar, to 2.5 m (8 ft), with silvery blue juvenile foliage. 'Columnaris' – compact and narrowly conical, to 10 m (33 ft), with blue-green foliage. 'Ellwoodii' – conical, to 8 m (26 ft), with blue-green juvenile foliage. 'Ellwood's Gold' – similar to 'Ellwoodii', but with yellow-flushed young foliage. 'Erecta Viridis' – upright, to 15 m (50 ft), with bright green foliage. 'Fletcheri' – conical, to 12 m (40 ft), with semi-juvenile grey-green foliage. 'Gimbornii' – rounded bush, to 2 m (6 ft), with blue-green foliage. 'Golden Wonder' – conical, to 5 m (16 ft), with golden yellow foliage. 'Green Globe' – compact, to 45 cm (18 in), with bright green foliage. 'Lane' – conical with golden yellow foliage. 'Minima Glauca' – slow-growing, rounded bush, to 1.5 m (5 ft), with blue-green foliage. 'Pembury Blue' – conical, to 15 m (50 ft), with silvery blue foliage. 'Pygmaea Argentea' – dense and conical, to 2 m (6 ft), with white-tipped foliage. 'Silver Threads' – dwarf, conical form with foliage splashed in silver-white and yellow. 'Snow White' – dwarf and compact with juvenile, white-

Chamaecyparis lawsoniana 'Ellwoodii'

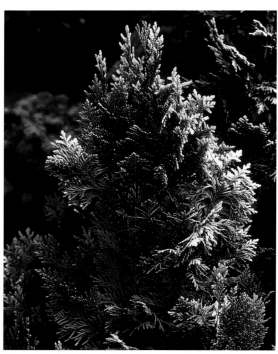

Chamaecyparis lawsoniana 'Pygmaea Argentea'

tipped foliage. 'Summer Snow' – small and bushy shrub, young foliage white in summer, later turning green. 'Wisselii' – narrowly columnar, to 20 m (65 ft), with congested sprays of blue-green foliage.

Chamaecyparis nootkatensis

A conical, evergreen tree with orange-brown peeling bark and pendulous, flattened sprays of dark green foliage. Small flowers open in early spring: males yellow; females blue-green, maturing to a cone about 1 cm (⅓ in) across.

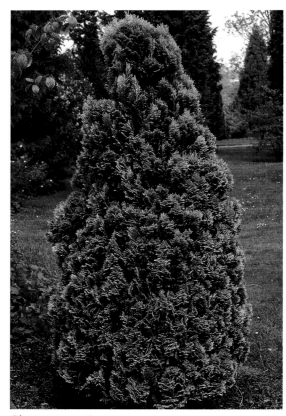

Chamaecyparis lawsoniana 'Aurea Densa'

Native range: NW North America
Height: 25 m (80 ft) or more
Spread: 8 m (26 ft)
Hardiness: Zone 4
Variants: 'Lutea' produces bright yellow foliage that later turns yellow-green in colour. 'Pendula' has very pendulous foliage.

Chamaecyparis obtusa

This is a broadly conical evergreen tree with attractive red-brown bark peeling in strips. The dark green and aromatic foliage has white markings beneath and is borne in flattened sprays. Small flowers open in late winter or early spring: males are yellow tinged with red; females are green at first, then turning brown and maturing to small, brown cones about 1 cm (⅓ in) across. It is mainly grown in gardens as selected forms, many of which are dwarf.

Common name: Hinoki cypress
Native range: Japan
Height: 20 m (65 ft)
Spread: 8 m (26 ft)
Hardiness: Zone 5
Variants: 'Crippsii' – golden yellow foliage. 'Fernspray Gold' – conical, to 3 m (10 ft), with golden bronze, fern-like foliage. 'Kosteri' – makes a dwarf, conical bush, to 1.2 m (4 ft), with dense sprays of bright green foliage. 'Nana Aurea' – a compact and conical plant, to 2 m (6 ft), with yellow foliage. 'Nana Gracilis' – a popular slow-growing dwarf form, to 3 m (10 ft) tall, with dark green foliage. 'Tetragona Aurea' – a small conical

Chamaecyparis obtusa 'Crippsii'

Chamaecyparis pisifera 'Boulevard'

Chamaecyparis pisifera 'Filifera Aurea'

tree, up to 10 m (33 ft) tall, with yellow foliage in four-sided, but not flattened, sprays.

Chamaecyparis pisifera

This is a broadly conical evergreen tree with an open habit and grey to brown bark peeling in thin strips. The glossy green, aromatic foliage is conspicuously marked with white beneath and is borne in flattened sprays. Small flowers open in early spring: male flowers are brown; female flowers green maturing to brown cones about

6 mm (¼ in) across, blue-green when young. It is mainly grown as selected forms.

Common name: Sawara cypress
Native range: Japan
Height: 20 m (65 ft)
Spread: 8 m (26 ft)
Hardiness: Zone 4
Variants: 'Boulevard' is columnar, to 10 m (33 ft), with blue-green juvenile foliage, and prefers moist soil. 'Filifera Aurea' is bushy, to 5 m (16 ft), with golden yellow, thready foliage. 'Nana' is a flat-topped dome of dark green foliage to 60 cm (24 in) high.

Chamaecyparis thyoides

This is a narrowly columnar evergreen tree with grey to red-brown bark peeling in strips. The blue-green to green foliage is borne in small, flattened sprays, marked with white beneath, and it is often speckled with resin above. Its small flowers open in late winter or early spring: males are red; females green, maturing to small, bloomy cones up to 6 mm (¼ in) across.

Common name: White cypress
Native range: E United States of America
Height: 15 m (50 ft)
Spread: 5 m (16 ft)
Hardiness: Zone 4
Variants: 'Andelyensis' is a narrow, conical form growing to 5 m (16 ft). 'Ericoides' is a conical bush, to 2 m (6 ft), with blue-green juvenile foliage turning bronze in winter. 'Rubicon' is compact and upright, to 75 cm (30 in), with grey-green juvenile foliage turning red in winter.

Cryptomeria japonica 'Elegans'

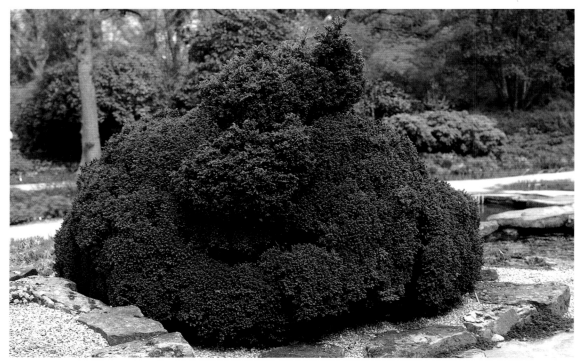

Cryptomeria japonica 'Vilmoriniana'

Cryptomeria
Cupressaceae

The single species that makes up this small genus is a large tree that is grown principally for its attractive habit, foliage and bark, and is suitable for any good, well-drained soil. It does grow to a large size and so is suitable only for larger gardens. However, many smaller selections can be grown in the rock garden or as specimen trees, depending on their eventual size.

Cryptomeria japonica

This is a large evergreen tree with a conical habit and soft orange-brown bark peeling in vertical strips. The taper-pointed, bright green needles are borne pointing forwards all around the slender shoots. The tree's small flowers open in the late winter or early spring: males are yellow-brown in colour and grow in clusters; females are green initially and grow singly at the ends of the shoots, maturing to brown cones up to about 2 cm (¾ in) across.

Common name: Japanese cedar
Native range: China, Japan
Height: 30 m (100 ft)
Spread: 15 m
Hardiness: Zone 5
Variants: 'Bandai-sugi' is a densely branched, slow-growing form, up to about 2 m (6 ft) high, with foliage turning bronze-red in winter. 'Compressa' is a very compact and rounded bush, up to about 60 cm (24 in) in height, with densely arranged upright foliage that turns bronze in

Cryptomeria japonica 'Spiralis'

Cunninghamia lanceolata

shelter from the wind afforded by the surrounding trees. It does best where it receives full sun.

Cunninghamia lanceolata

This conical evergreen tree, with ridged, red-brown bark, becomes increasingly columnar with age. Taper-pointed leaves, up to 6 cm (2½ in) long, spread out either side of the shoots. The leaves are glossy and dark green above and have two greenish-white bands beneath. Flowers open in late spring: the males yellow-brown and in clusters; the females yellow-green and single at the ends of the shoots. Female flowers mature to green, later brown cones up to 4 cm (1½ in) across.

Common name: Chinese fir
Native range: China, Vietnam
Height: 20 m (65 ft)
Spread: 7 m (23 ft)
Hardiness: Zone 7

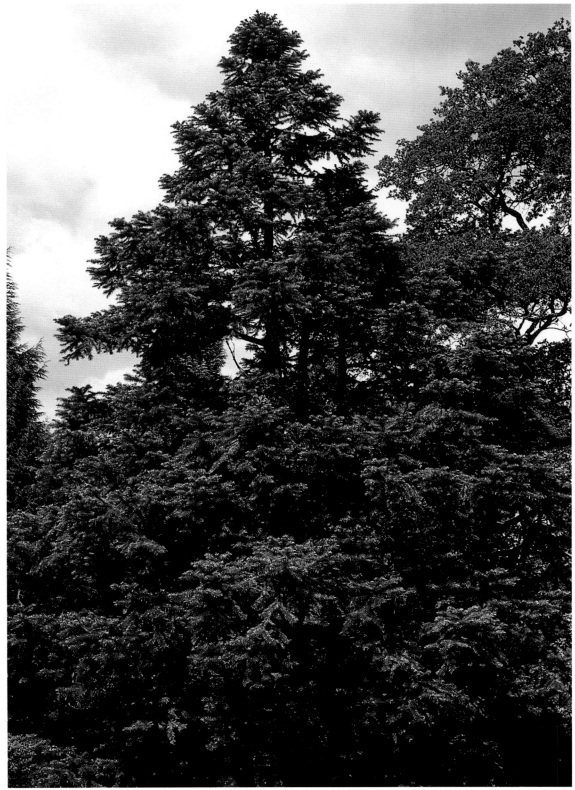

Cunninghamia lanceolata

winter. 'Elegans' is a medium-sized tree, reaching a height of up to 10 m (33 ft) or more, with soft juvenile foliage that is bronze coloured in winter. 'Sekkan-sugi' is a conical form,up to about 10 m (33 ft) in height, and bearing soft creamy coloured foliage. 'Spiralis' is a shrub or small tree, up to about 6 m (20 ft) high, with leaves that are conspicuously twisted around the shoots. 'Vilmoriniana' is a slow-growing form that produces very densely arranged foliage. It eventually develops into a compact, bun-shaped plant, about 60 cm (24 in) in height, and its foliage turns bronze in winter.

Cunninghamia
Cupressaceae

This is a small genus made up of just two species of evergreen trees that are natives of China, Taiwan and Vietnam. The following species is the most frequently seen, mainly in substantial gardens or parks, and it attains its largest size in regions that experience moist summers.

This species requires a moist but well-drained soil and it is usually grown as a specimen tree in a woodland setting, where it benefits from the

x *Cupressocyparis*
Cupressaceae

This is a genus comprising garden-raised hybrids between species of *Chamaecyparis* and *Cupressus*. They are vigorous evergreen trees with tiny, scale-like leaves borne in pendulous, flattened sprays.

The following is the most commonly seen example, planted principally for its habit and fast growth. It is useful as a specimen tree or as a large screen, but is much too vigorous and large for a hedge in small gardens. It needs clipping several times during the summer to keep it under control.

but has brighter yellow foliage. 'Haggerston Grey' is the most commonly grown form, with grey-green foliage, and is usually sold as x *C. leylandii*.

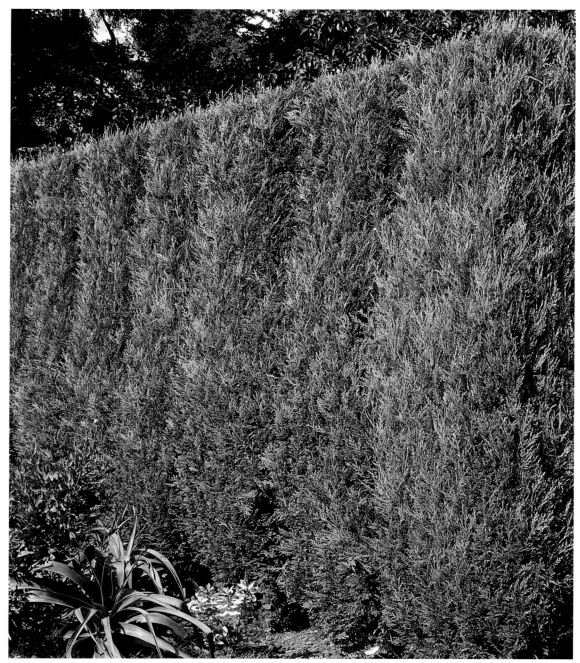

x *Cupressocyparis leylandii* 'Castlewellan'

x *Cupressocyparis leylandii*

This is a garden-raised hybrid between *Chamaecyparis nootkatensis* and *Cupressus macrocarpa* and makes a large and very fast-growing evergreen tree with a columnar habit. The green to blue-green, aromatic foliage is composed of tiny, pointed, scale-like leaves. It produces small flowers that open in the early spring. The male flowers are yellow, while the females are very small and inconspicuous, and are sometimes followed by rounded cones up to 2 cm (¾ in) across.

Common name: Leyland cypress
Height: 30 m (100 ft)
Spread: 6 m (20 ft)
Hardiness: Zone 6
Variants: 'Castlewellan' produces young foliage that is bright yellow but turns more yellow-green with age. 'Gold Rider' is similar to 'Castlewellan',

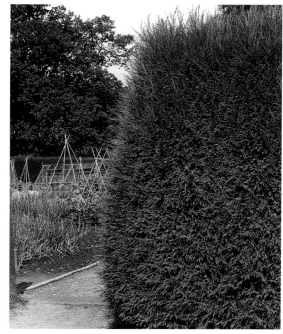

x *Cupressocyparis leylandii*

Cupressus
Cupressaceae

The cypresses make up a widely distributed genus of 17 species of evergreen trees, natives of North and Central America, the Mediterranean region, North Africa, the Himalayas and China. Closely related to *Chamaecyparis*, though not as easy to grow, cypresses have tiny, scale-like leaves that are only occasionally arranged in flattened sprays.

Grown for their habit, foliage and sometimes their attractive bark, they require a well-drained soil and – since not all are fully hardy – they also prefer a position in full sun sheltered from strong winds. Pruning is not necessary and young trees should be securely staked for their first few years until they have put out a securing root system.

Take care in choosing the correct site for a cypress. Young trees tend to establish more successfully than larger, more mature specimens, but they do not tolerate well being transplanted once in the ground.

Cupressus arizonica var. *glabra*

This is a conical evergreen tree with attractive red-brown and red-purple bark that peels in rounded patches. The blue-grey, aromatic foliage is borne in sprays all around the shoots, and the tiny, scale-like leaves feature a spot of white resin on their backs. Small, bright yellow male flowers are often conspicuous in late winter. The green female flowers are followed by rounded cones, up to about 2.5 cm (1 in) across, which can persist for several years.

Synonym: *Cupressus glabra*
Native range: Arizona, USA
Height: 15 m (50 ft)
Spread: 5 m (16 ft)
Hardiness: Zone 7
Variants: 'Blue Ice' has silvery blue foliage.

Cupressus cashmeriana

This is a conical evergreen tree that adopts a more spreading habit as it matures, and features red-brown bark that peels in vertical strips. This is one of the most attractive of the cypresses and is particularly valued for its foliage, which hangs from the shoots in long, flattened, blue-grey sprays. The very small flowers open in the late

Cupressus cashmeriana

Cupressus macrocarpa 'Goldcrest'

autumn to winter. The female flowers are followed by blue-green, later brown, cones, the scales of which finish in hooked points.

Common name: Kashmir cypress
Native range: Bhutan
Height: 10 m (33 ft) or more
Spread: 6 m (20 ft) or more
Hardiness: Zone 9

Cupressus macrocarpa

This is a vigorously growing evergreen tree, dense and conical in shape when young, but becoming spreading and more open with age. The bright green, aromatic foliage – which consists of tiny, scale-like leaves – is borne in dense sprays all around the shoots. The tree's small flowers open in the late spring: male flowers are yellow; females green, followed by rounded, red-brown cones up

to about 4 cm (1½ in) across. Although this species is popular and is commonly found in garden cultivation, it occurs in only a very small region in the wild.

Common name: Monterey cypress
Native range: California, USA
Height: 30 m (100 ft)
Spread: 10 m (33 ft)
Hardiness: Zone 7
Variants: 'Gold Spread' is a low-growing and wide-spreading form, reaching a height of only about 1 m (3 ft), and has golden yellow young foliage. 'Goldcrest' has bright yellow foliage.

Cupressus sempervirens

This is an evergreen tree of variable columnar to spreading, or even pendulous habit. It has dark green foliage arranged all around the shoots and

has little or no scent. The small flowers open in spring: male flowers are yellow-brown; females green, followed by green, later brown cones up to about 4 cm (1½ in) across, and they are slightly longer than they are broad. This species is prone to damage during severe winters and requires a sheltered site.

Common name: Italian cypress
Native range: E Mediterranean region, N Africa, SW Asia
Height: 20 m (65 ft)
Spread: 2 m (6 ft) or more
Hardiness: Zone 7
Variants: Stricta Group is the most commonly seen form in garden cultivation, with trees of a narrowly columnar to narrowly conical habit. Some branches may tend to arch outwards after bearing cones. 'Swane's Gold' is narrowly conical, reaching a height of about 8 m (26 ft), and has yellow foliage.

Ginkgo biloba

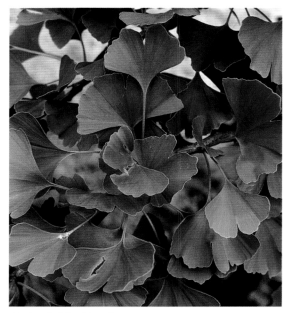

Ginkgo biloba (detail)

Ginkgo biloba

A deciduous, upright and conical tree when young, broadly columnar to rounded with age. The wide, fan-shaped leaves, up to 8 cm (3 in) long, are variously notched, sometimes deeply at the tip, and turn bright yellow in autumn. Small flowers may be borne but only after 20 years or more. This is when pollinated females trees produce edible nuts enclosed in a fleshy, yellow-green and malodorous covering.

Common name: Maidenhair tree
Native range: China
Height: 20 m (65 ft)
Spread: 15 m (50 ft)
Hardiness: Zone 4

Juniperus
Cupressaceae

The junipers are a diverse genus of evergreen shrubs and trees with 54 species widely distributed in the northern hemisphere, and extending to tropical Africa. They bear two types of foliage. All species as seedlings have juvenile foliage composed of needle-like leaves, and some retain this leaf form into maturity. Others have adult foliage, which is composed of tiny, scale-like leaves. Some species can bear both types of foliage. Male and female flowers are normally borne on separate plants, the females followed by berry-like cones.

Junipers will grow in any well-drained soil and prefer a sunny position. They can be used for a variety of purposes – from specimen trees and shrubs, to rock garden plants or as ground cover. As described here, the upper surface of the leaf is that facing the end of the shoot.

Ginkgo
Ginkgoaceae

As is indicated by its appearance, the single species that comprises this genus is not a true conifer, but it is the only living relative of a group of plants once widely distributed in the northern hemisphere. This is the surviving member of a genus that is thought to be in the region of 200 million years old.

Unique among trees for its leaf shape, it is grown for its interesting foliage, which colours in autumn, and is usually planted as a specimen tree. It is suitable for any well-drained soil in full sun, and it is at its best in regions with hot summers. Its tolerance of pollution makes it excellent for cities.

Male and female flowers are borne on separate trees and both are required to produce fruits. The fruits are unpleasantly scented and can be messy when they fall. For this reason, selected male forms are often grown where fruits would prove to be a problem.

Juniperus chinensis

This is a conical evergreen tree with red-brown bark peeling in vertical strips. Foliage is aromatic, and both juvenile and adult forms are usually borne on the same tree. The juvenile foliage consists of sharp-pointed, needle-like leaves banded with blue-white above. Small flowers open in early spring followed, on female plants, by bloomy, berry-like cones to 8 mm (⅓ in) long.

Common name: Chinese juniper
Native range: E Asia
Height: 15 m (50 ft)
Spread: 6 m (20 ft)
Hardiness: Zone 4
Variants: 'Aurea' is a small, narrowly conical tree of compact habit with yellow foliage. 'Blaauw' is shrubby and upright, with grey-blue, mainly adult foliage. 'Blue Alps' is shrubby, to 4 m (13 ft), with steel-blue juvenile foliage. 'Expansa Variegata' is low and spreading, to 1 m (3 ft) tall and 3 m (10 ft) across, with grey-green juvenile foliage blotched creamy white. 'Kaizuka' (Hollywood juniper) is shrubby or a small tree of irregular shape, with bright green adult foliage and profuse, bloomy cones. 'Pyramidalis' is a conical tree with blue-green mainly juvenile foliage.

Juniperus communis

This widely distributed species is very variable in habit – from prostrate to upright, shrubby or tree-like. The aromatic foliage is always juvenile, with sharp-pointed, needle-like leaves marked with a broad white band on the upper surface. Female plants bear small, green, later bloomy then glossy black, berry-like cones to 6 mm (¼ in) long.

Common name: Common juniper
Native range: Northern hemisphere
Height: to 6 m (20 ft)
Spread: to 6 m (20 ft)
Hardiness: Zone 2
Variants: 'Compressa' is dwarf and narrowly conical, to 60 cm (24 in). 'Depressa Aurea' is wide-spreading, to 1 m (3 ft) tall and 3 m (10 ft) across, with golden yellow young foliage. 'Gold Cone' is conical, to 1.2 m (4 ft), with golden foliage. 'Green Carpet' is a creeping form with bright green foliage. 'Hibernica' is narrowly upright, to 5 m (16 ft) tall. 'Repanda' is low and wide-spreading, to 30 cm (12 in) tall, and is good for ground cover. 'Sentinel' is very narrowly upright, to 2 m (6 ft) tall.

Juniperus horizontalis

This is a creeping evergreen shrub with long, trailing shoots, or sometimes with short, upright or arching shoots. The grey-green to blue-green

Juniperus horizontalis 'Wiltonii'

Juniperus chinensis 'Kaizuka'

foliage can be adult or juvenile, or a mixture of both. Female plants bear bloomy cones to 8 mm (⅓ in) long. It is an excellent species for ground cover in a rock garden.

Common name: Creeping juniper
Native range: Canada, N United States of America
Height: 30 cm (12 in)
Spread: 5 m (16 ft) or more
Hardiness: Zone 4
Variants: 'Blue Chip' has bright blue foliage, bronze-tinged in winter. 'Hughes' has silvery blue

Juniperus communis 'Compressa'

foliage. 'Wiltonii' is very low growing with bright blue-green foliage, purple-tinged in winter.

Juniperus x pfitzeriana

This garden-raised hybrid between *J. chinensis* and *J. sabina* makes a wide-spreading evergreen shrub, sometimes tree-like, with arching shoots. It is mainly grown as selected forms, of which there are many. They are invaluable landscape plants as specimens, for mass plantings and for ground

Juniperus sabina 'Tamariscifolia'

Juniperus procumbens 'Nana'

cover. They were originally known in gardens as forms of *J. chinensis* or *J.* x *media*.

Common name: Pfitzer juniper
Height: 3 m (10 ft)
Spread: 5 m (16 ft)
Hardiness: Zone 4
Variants: 'Carbery Gold' is low and wide-spreading with creamy yellow foliage. 'Gold Coast' is compact, to 1 m (3 ft) tall, with golden yellow foliage. 'Mint Julep' has bright green foliage. 'Old Gold' is compact with bronze-yellow foliage. 'Pfitzeriana Aurea' is wide-spreading, to 3 m (6 ft) tall, with golden yellow young foliage. 'Sulphur Spray' is spreading, to 2 m (6 ft) tall, with pale sulphur-yellow foliage. 'Wilhelm Pfitzer' is the form once grown as *J.* x *media* 'Pfitzeriana' and has bright green juvenile and adult foliage.

Juniperus procumbens

This is a low, wide-spreading evergreen shrub with stout, creeping shoots turned up at the ends. The foliage is mainly juvenile with slender, spine-tipped, blue-green leaves with two blue-white bands on the upper surface. Fruit is rarely produced in cultivation, but it makes an excellent groundcover plant.

Native range: S Japan
Height: 45 cm (18 in)
Spread: 3 m (6 ft) or more
Hardiness: Zone 4
Variants: 'Nana' is a compact form producing dense, layered foliage.

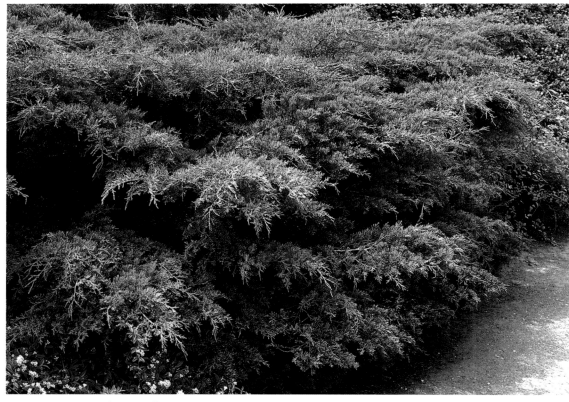

Juniperus virginiana 'Grey Owl'

Juniperus sabina

This is a spreading evergreen shrub featuring attractive red-brown, peeling bark and graceful, arching branches. The aromatic foliage is mainly adult in form, although occasionally there are some sharp-pointed juvenile leaves. In this species, both male and female flowers are sometimes borne on the same plant. It is most frequently grown as selected forms.

Common name: Savin
Native range: Europe to China
Height: 3 m (10 ft)
Spread: 5 m (16 ft)
Hardiness: Zone 3
Variants: 'Tamariscifolia' develops into a low, spreading mound, reaching about 1 m (3 ft) in height, and has the blue-green, mainly juvenile form of foliage.

Juniperus scopulorum

This is a narrowly conical evergreen tree featuring red-brown bark peeling in thin strips. The slightly aromatic foliage is adult in form and varies in colour from grey-green to blue-green. Female plants bear bloomy, blue-black, berry-like cones up to about 6 mm (¼ in) long.

Common name: Rocky mountain juniper
Native range: W North America (Rocky Mountains region)
Height: 15 m (50 ft)
Spread: 4 m (13 ft)
Hardiness: Zone 4
Variants: 'Blue Arrow' is very narrow with silvery blue foliage. 'Skyrocket' is narrow and upright in habit, with blue-grey foliage.

Juniperus squamata

This is an evergreen shrub or tree of very variable habit, and can be found as a creeping, spreading or upright plant. The foliage is all juvenile and is composed of densely arranged, sharp-pointed, needle-like leaves, green banded with silvery white above. Female plants bear blue-black, berry-like cones. It is mainly grown as dwarf selections and is most often seen in the rock garden or is used for ground cover.

Common name: Flaky juniper
Native range: Himalayas, China, Taiwan
Height: to 5 m (16 ft)
Spread: to 5 m (16 ft)
Hardiness: Zone 4
Variants: 'Blue Carpet' is low and spreading in habit, to 30 cm (12 in) tall, with blue-grey foliage. 'Blue Star' makes a dense mound, up to about 45 cm (18 in) high, with silvery blue foliage. 'Holger' is spreading in habit, up to 1 m (3 ft) tall, with blue-grey foliage that is creamy yellow when young. 'Meyeri' is dense and upright, reaching a height of 5 m (16 ft) or more, and has arching shoots and blue-grey foliage.

Juniperus virginiana

This is an evergreen tree of narrowly columnar habit, with red-brown bark peeling in vertical strips. The aromatic, grey-green to deep green foliage consists of both adult, scale-like leaves and juvenile, sharp-pointed, needle-like leaves. Female plants bear bloomy, blue-black, berry-like cones.

Common name: Pencil cedar
Native range: E North America
Height: 15 m (50 ft)
Spread: 5 m (16 ft)
Hardiness: Zone 4

Variants: 'Blue Cloud' is spreading in habit, reaching a height of about 1.5 m (5 ft), with grey-blue foliage. 'Grey Owl' is a vigorous, spreading shrub, up to about 2.5 m (8 ft) tall, with arching shoots and silvery grey foliage.

Larix
Pinaceae

The larches are a genus of deciduous trees with 11 species widely distributed in the northern hemisphere. Like cedars, the larches bear foliage of two types. Long shoots produce single, needle-like leaves arranged spirally, while short shoots produce dense whorls of leaves. Male and female flowers are borne separately on the same tree, the females ripening to a woody, upright cone.

They are suitable for any good, moist but well-drained soil, and they do best if a given a position where they receive full sun.

Larix decidua

This is a conical deciduous tree with spreading branches and drooping branchlets. It bears slender, bright green, needle-like leaves, which open early in the year on yellowish shoots and turn yellow in autumn. The flowers open in early spring as the young foliage emerges. Male flowers are yellow and pendulous, females red, upright above the shoots, maturing to brown, egg-shaped cones up to about 4 cm (1½ in) long.

Common name: European larch
Native range: Europe
Height: 25 m (80 ft) or more
Spread: 10 m (33 ft)
Hardiness: Zone 3

Larix kaempferi

A vigorous, broadly conical deciduous tree with spreading branches. The blue-green, needle-like leaves open early in the year on red-purple shoots and foliage turns yellow to orange in autumn. The flowers open in early spring. Male flowers are yellow and pendulous; females cream to pink or red, upright above the shoots, maturing to brown, rosette-like cones up to 3 cm (1 in) long.

Common name: Japanese larch
Native range: Japan
Height: 25 m (80 ft) or more
Spread: 10 m (33 ft)
Hardiness: Zone 4
Variants: 'Pendula' is a form with conspicuously pendulous branchlets.

Metasequoia glyptostroboides

Metasequoia
Cupressaceae

The single species in this genus is remarkable because it was discovered only very recently – in the 1940s. Before this time it was known only from the fossil record. It is very fast growing and prefers a moist but well-drained soil and a sunny position. Male catkins are usually borne only in regions that experience hot summers.

Metasequoia glyptostroboides

This is a vigorous deciduous tree featuring attractive red-brown bark and a trunk that is deeply fluted at the base when mature. The slender, deep green leaves emerge early in the year and spread out either side of opposite, deciduous shoots. In autumn, the leaves turn yellow to pinkish or red-brown before they fall. Pendulous male catkins open on the shoots in the early spring, and the small female flowers are followed by rounded, green – later brown – cones, up to about 2.5 cm (1 in) across, even if male flowers are not present.

Common name: Dawn redwood
Native range: China
Height: 30 m (100 ft)
Spread: 10 m (33 ft)
Hardiness: Zone 5
Variants: 'Gold Rush' produces golden yellow young foliage.

Picea abies 'Little Gem'

Microbiota
Cupressaceae

The single species in this genus is an evergreen shrub closely related to the junipers. It requires a moist but well-drained soil and a position in full sun. Valued in gardens for its great hardiness and foliage, it can be grown in a rock garden or be mass planted to provide ground cover.

Microbiota decussata

This is a low-growing and wide-spreading evergreen shrub with bright green, aromatic foliage arranged in arching sprays of tiny, scale-like, occasionally needle-like, leaves. Foliage turns bronze in winter. The small cones, to 3 mm (⅛ in) long, resemble those of a juniper, but have woody scales and break open when ripe.

Native range: E Siberia
Height: 30 cm (12 in)
Spread: 3 m (10 ft) or more
Hardiness: Zone 3

Picea
Pinaceae

This is a genus of 34 species of evergreen trees, widely distributed in the northern hemisphere. Needle-like, usually sharply pointed leaves are borne singly on the shoots, and are sometimes marked with white bands beneath. Male and female flowers are borne separately on the same tree: the males usually yellow or red-flushed; the upright females developing into woody cones, pendulous when mature. They require a good, moist but well-drained soil and do best if provided

Picea abies 'Nidiformis'

Picea breweriana

with a sunny position. They will often not grow well on very dry or shallow, chalky soils.

Picea abies

This is a conical evergreen tree with red-brown to grey bark and spreading branches bearing pendulous branchlets. The dark green, four-sided and bluntly pointed needles are densely borne on orange-brown shoots. The flowers open in late spring, the red females maturing to brown cones up to about 15 cm (6 in) long.

Common names: Christmas tree, Norway spruce
Native range: Europe
Height: 30 m (100 ft)
Spread: 8 m (26 ft)
Hardiness: Zone 4
Variants: Numerous, often dwarf forms have been selected. 'Acrocona' is a small, shrubby tree, to 3 m (10 ft), producing cones at the tips of the shoots, even when young. 'Little Gem' is a slow-growing dwarf of a bun-shaped habit. 'Nidiformis' is a low-growing dwarf, to 1.5 m (5 ft), spreading widely.

Picea breweriana

This elegant species is among the most popular of the larger spruces. An evergreen conical tree with spreading branches bearing long, pendulous branchlets, giving a weeping appearance. The flattened, needle-like, dark green leaves are banded with whitish green beneath. The flowers open in late spring, the red females maturing to dark brown cones to 12 cm (5 in) long. This species can be slow to establish and develop its weeping habit.

Common name: Brewer spruce
Native range: W United States of America
Height: 15 m (50 ft)
Spread: 6 m (20 ft)
Hardiness: Zone 5

Picea glauca

A narrowly conical tree with scaly grey-brown bark. The slender, needle-like, blue-green leaves are four-sided and densely arranged on white shoots. The flowers open in spring, the purple-red females followed by pale brown cones to 6 cm (2 in) long. Only the dwarf forms are commonly grown.

Common name: White spruce
Native range: Canada, N United States of America
Height: 20 m 65 ft) or more
Spread: 6 m (20 ft)
Hardiness: Zone 2
Variants: var. *albertiana* (Alberta white spruce) is a form from the Rocky Mountains, which has given

Picea glauca var. *albertiana* 'Conica'

Picea mariana 'Nana'

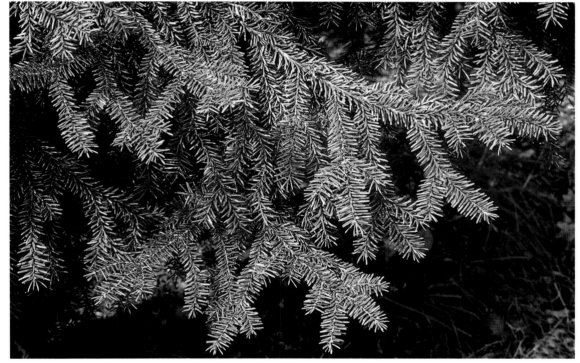
Picea omorika

rise to the following selections: 'Alberta Blue' is compact and conical, to 2 m (6 ft), with striking blue foliage; 'Conica' is compact and conical, to 2 m (6 ft), with green foliage. 'Alberta Globe' is a dwarf, bun-shaped plant of dense, rounded habit. 'J W Daisy's White' is conical with creamy young foliage turning green. 'Laurin' is a slow-growing dwarf of narrowly conical habit with upright branches.

Picea mariana

This is a narrowly conical evergreen tree with grey-brown, flaking bark. The slender, blue-green, four-sided leaves end in a sharp point and are densely borne on yellow-brown shoots. The flowers open in the spring, the red-coloured females maturing to small, red-brown cones up to 4 cm (1½ in) long. It is mainly grown in gardens as the form listed below.

Common name: Black spruce
Native range: Canada, N United States of America
Height: 20 m (65 ft)
Spread: 6 m (20 ft)
Hardiness: Zone 3
Variants: 'Nana' is a dwarf and compact form that makes a dense mound up to 60 cm (24 in) tall.

Picea pungens 'Koster'

Picea pungens 'Globosa'

Picea omorika

This narrowly conical evergreen tree has orange-brown to purple-brown, scaly bark. The slender, glossy dark green leaves are banded with white on the reverse. Flowers are red, opening in late spring, the females maturing to purple-brown cones up to 6 cm (2 in) long. The pendulous branches that make this species so attractive take several years to develop on seedlings.

Common name: Serbian spruce
Native range: Serbia
Height: 20 m (65 ft)
Spread: 5 m (16 ft)
Hardiness: Zone 4
Variants: 'Pendula' resembles mature plants of the typical form, but it develops the desirable, weeping habit from an earlier age.

Pinus armandii

Picea orientalis

This is a narrowly conical tree that becomes columnar with age. The distinctive, four-sided and bluntly pointed, glossy dark green leaves are very short and densely arranged on the shoots. The flowers open in spring: males bright red, opening yellow; females red, maturing to slender, purple, later brown cones up to 10 cm (4 in) long.

Common name: Oriental spruce
Native range: Caucasus, N Turkey
Height: 30 m (100 ft)
Spread: 8 m (26 ft)

Hardiness: Zone 4
Variants: 'Aurea' has strikingly attractive, bright yellow young foliage, which later turns green. 'Skylands' is a slow-growing, small tree, with golden yellow foliage throughout the year.

Picea pungens

This is a conical, evergreen tree with purple-brown, scaly bark and stout shoots. The four-sided, needle-like leaves are rigid and sharply pointed, varying in colour from grey-green to silvery blue. The flowers open in the late spring or early summer: males red,

opening yellow; females green, maturing to pale brown cones up to 10 cm (4 in) long.

Common name: Colorado spruce
Native range: W United States of America
Height: 20 m (65 ft)
Spread: 6 m (20 ft)
Hardiness: Zone 3
Variants: 'Erich Frahm' is a small tree of dense, conical habit, to 10 m (33 ft), with blue foliage. 'Fat Albert' is densely conical, to 5 m (16 ft), with rich blue foliage. 'Globosa' is a dense, rounded bush, to 1.5 m (5 ft), with blue-grey foliage. 'Hoopsii' is conical with densely arranged and

conspicuously blue-white foliage. 'Iseli Fastigiate' has strongly upright branches and steel-blue foliage. 'Koster' is conical with silvery blue foliage.

Pinus
Pinaceae

The pines are a genus of about 120 species of evergreen trees, sometimes shrubs, widely distributed in the northern hemisphere. The needle-like leaves are mainly borne in bundles of two, three or five, and vary in colour from green to blue or blue-green. Male and female flowers are borne separately on the same plant: males yellow; females ripening to cones that may persist for some time. They are generally suitable for any well-drained soil, preferring a sunny position. Those with needles in bundles of five do not grow well on shallow, chalky soils.

Pinus aristata

This is a conical evergreen tree, often branching low, and shrubby in habit. The short, bright green and pointed needles, up to about 4 cm (1½ in) long, are borne in dense bundles of five on stout shoots covered in red hairs, and are marked with conspicuous spots of white resin. Flowers open in early summer, the females ripening to brown cones, up to 10 cm (4 in) long, with prickly scales.

Common name: Bristle-cone pine
Native range: W United States of America
Height: 6 m (20 ft) or more
Spread: 4 m (13 ft) or more
Hardiness: Zone 4

Pinus armandii

This is a broadly conical evergreen tree with smooth, grey bark. The slender, drooping needles, up to 15 cm (6 in) long, are green on the outer surfaces, blue-green on the inner, and are borne in clusters of five. Flowers open in early summer – the females maturing to pendulous cones up to about 20 cm (8 in) in length.

Native range: China, N Myanmar (Burma)
Height: 20 m (65 ft)
Spread: 10 m (33 ft)
Hardiness: Zone 5

Pinus bungeana

This is a conical evergreen tree, often branching low down with several stems, and featuring bark

Pinus aristata

that flakes in conspicuous patches of grey-green and creamy white. Rigid and sharply pointed, dark green leaves, growing up to about 8 cm (3 in) long, are borne in clusters of three. Flowers open in the early summer. The females are red and mature to form small, egg-shaped, brown cones, reaching up to about 6 cm (2 in) in length, with spine-tipped scales.

Common name: Lacebark pine
Native range: China
Height: 15 m (50 ft)
Spread: 10 m (33 ft)
Hardiness: Zone 5

Pinus cembra

This evergreen tree is conical when young and later becomes narrowly columnar, with densely hairy young shoots. The glossy green needles are blue-green on their inner surfaces and are borne in dense bundles of five. Flowers open in late spring to early summer: males red when young; the females red, maturing to form red-brown cones, up to 8 cm (3 in) long, purple-blue when young. The cones contain edible seeds and do not open.

Common names: Arolla pine, Swiss stone pine
Native range: C Europe

Pinus cembra

Height: 20 m (65 ft)
Spread: 6 m (20 ft)
Hardiness: Zone 4
Variants: 'Aurea' ('Aureovariegata') produces yellow-flushed foliage.

Pinus densiflora

This is an evergreen tree that is conical when it is young and becomes increasingly spreading and flat-topped as it matures. Its upper bark has a distinct reddish-brown colour. The slender, dark green needles, up to about 12 cm (5 in) in length, are borne in pairs. The flowers open in the late spring – the females red, maturing to form pale brown cones up to about 5 cm (2 in) in length.

Common name: Japanese red pine
Native range: Japan, Korea, Russian Far East
Height: 15 m (50 ft)
Spread: 12 m (40 ft)
Hardiness: Zone 4
Variants: 'Alice Verkade' makes a dense, bun-shaped dwarf form up to about 60 cm (24 in) high. 'Pendula' grows into a low, wide-spreading mound up to about 1 m (3 ft) in height. 'Umbraculifera' is a slow-growing shrubby form, eventually making a height of about 4 m (13 ft) and with a flattened, spreading head of foliage.

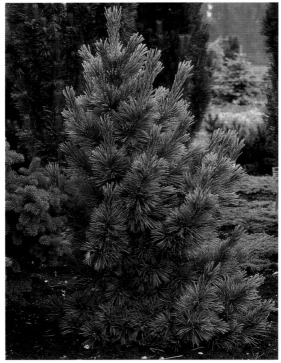

Pinus cembra 'Aurea'

Pinus heldreichii

This is a compact evergreen tree with a conical habit, featuring grey bark that cracks into small, square plates. The rigid, dark green needles are densely borne in pairs. The flowers open in the early summer, the purple-red females maturing

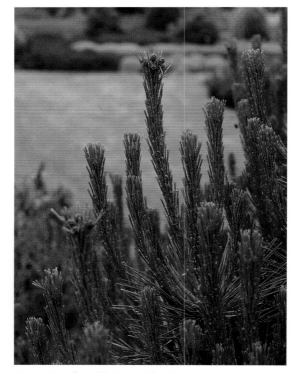

Pinus densiflora 'Umbraculifera'

to form egg-shaped cones, up to about 10 cm (4 in) long, deep blue the first year, yellow-brown when ripe after the second year.

Synonyms: *P. leucodermis*, *P. leucodermis* var. *heldreichii*
Common name: Bosnian pine

Native range: SE Europe
Height: 15 m (50 ft)
Spread: 5 m (16 ft)
Hardiness: Zone 5
Variants: 'Compact Gem' is a slow-growing, dwarf form eventually making 3 m (10 ft) in height.

Pinus mugo

This is an evergreen shrub, more rarely tree-like in habit, of rounded growth and with upright or spreading branches. The dark green, rigid and bluntly pointed leaves are often slightly twisted and are borne in pairs. The flowers open in the early summer, the female flowers followed by brown cones, up to about 6cm (2 in) in length, that are prickly when young.

Common name: Dwarf mountain pine
Native range: Europe
Height: 5 m (16 ft)
Spread: 6 m (20 ft)
Hardiness: Zone 3
Variants: *P. mugo* is very variable when grown from seed and many forms have been selected. 'Gnom' makes a dense, rounded bush up to 2 m (6 ft) tall. 'Humpy' is very slow growing and produces short needles. 'Mops' is a dense, rounded, slow-growing shrub. 'Ophir' is dwarf and rounded in form, making up to 60 cm (24 in) in height, with foliage that turns golden yellow in winter. 'Winter Gold' is a spreading shrub, to 1 m (3 ft) tall, with golden yellow winter foliage.

Pinus nigra

This evergreen tree has nearly black bark and is conical in form when young, becoming columnar as it ages with stout, spreading branches. The rigid, sharp-pointed needles, up to 15 cm (6 in) long, are dark blackish-green and densely borne in pairs. The flowers open in late spring to early summer, the red female flowers maturing to form brown cones up to about 8 cm (3 in) long.

Common names: Austrian pine, black pine
Native range: Europe
Height: 25 m (80 ft)
Spread: 10 m (33 ft)
Hardiness: Zone 4
Variants: 'Hornibrookiana' is a dense, shrubby form, up to 2 m (6 ft), with short needles. subsp. *laricio* (var. *maritima*), the Corsican pine, has more slender branches and grey-green foliage.

Pinus parviflora

This is an evergreen tree, conical when young and becoming broadly columnar to spreading with grey,

Pinus mugo

Pinus heldreichii 'Compact Gem'

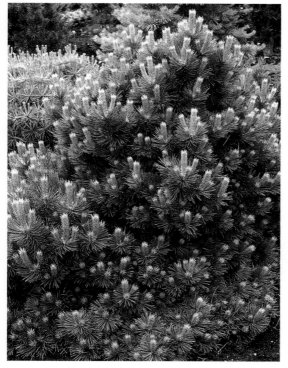

Pinus nigra 'Hornibrookiana'

scaly bark. The slender, slightly twisted needles, up to 6 cm (2 in) long, are green on their outer surfaces, with blue-white insides, and are borne in clusters of five. The flowers open in early summer: males red, opening yellow; females red, maturing to red-brown cones, up to 7 cm (3 in) long, that are green when young.

Common name: Japanese white pine
Native range: Japan
Height: 15 m (50 ft)
Spread: 8 m (26 ft)
Hardiness: Zone 4
Variants: 'Adcock's Dwarf' is slow-growing, up to 2.5 m (8 ft), with dense, blue-green needles.

Pinus parviflora

Pinus sylvestris 'Beuvronensis'

Pinus patula

This very beautiful species makes a rounded evergreen tree that is conical when young, and with thick, red-brown bark. The slender, bright green needles, up to about 20 cm (8 in) or more long, hang in pendulous clusters of three. The flowers open in summer, the females followed by brown cones, up to 10 cm (4 in) long, persisting on the shoots for many years.

Common name: Mexican weeping pine
Native range: Mexico
Height: 15 m (50 ft)
Spread: 10 m (33 ft)
Hardiness: Zone 8

Pinus pumila

This is an upright to spreading evergreen shrub with stout shoots. The bluntly pointed, dark green leaves are blue-white on their inner surfaces and are borne in dense clusters of five. The flowers open in spring: males red-purple in colour; females red when young, maturing to yellow- or red-brown cones up to 6 cm (2 in) long.

Common name: Dwarf Siberian pine
Native range: NE Asia
Height: 5 m (16 ft)
Spread: 4 m (13 ft)
Hardiness: Zone 3
Variants: 'Glauca' produces grey-blue foliage. 'Globe' makes a dense, rounded bush, up to about 2 m (6 ft) across, with grey-blue foliage.

Pinus radiata

This is a vigorous evergreen tree with a broadly conical to columnar habit, and with thick, dark grey bark. The slender, bright green needles, up to 15 cm (6 in) long, are densely borne in clusters of three. The flowers open in early summer, the purple-red females maturing to green, later orange-brown, cones up to 15 cm (6 in) long. The cones persist on the shoots for many years.

Common name: Monterey pine
Native range: California, USA
Height: 30 m (100 ft)
Spread: 10 m (33 ft)
Hardiness: Zone 8

Pinus strobus

This vigorous, conical evergreen tree has smooth, grey bark that becomes fissured with age. The slender, grey-green needles are whitish on their inner surfaces and are borne in clusters of five.

Pinus sylvestris 'Aurea'

Pinus strobus 'Radiata'

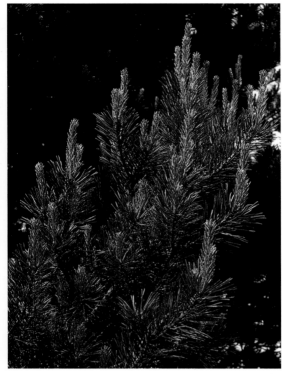

Pinus sylvestris 'Watereri'

The flowers open in early summer, the pink females maturing to slender, curved, pendulous cones, up to about 15 cm (6 in) long, that are often marked with resin.

Common names: Eastern white pine, Weymouth pine
Native range: E North America
Height: 30 m (100 ft)
Spread: 8 m (26 ft)
Hardiness: Zone 3
Variants: 'Radiata' ('Nana') is a dwarf, shrubby form growing up to about 1.5 m (5 ft) in height.

Pinus sylvestris

This is an evergreen tree, conical when young and becoming spreading to domed with age. The bark on the upper trunk is conspicuously orange, while lower down it is purple-grey and flaking. The stout, twisted, blue-green leaves are borne in pairs. The flowers open in late spring to early summer, the red females maturing to green, later brown, cones up to 7 cm (3 in) long.

Common name: Scots pine
Native range: Europe, Asia
Height: 30 m (100 ft)
Spread: 10 m (33 ft)
Hardiness: Zone 3
Variants: 'Aurea' has bright yellow foliage in winter. 'Beuvronensis' is a slow-growing dwarf form, to 1 m (3 ft) tall, with short, blue-grey needles. 'Fastigiata' is narrow with upright branches, to 10 m (33 ft). 'Gold Coin' is dwarf, to 2 m (6 ft), with yellow winter foliage. 'Watereri' is shrubby, to 8 m (26 ft) tall and across, with blue-green foliage.

Platycladus
Cupressaceae

The single species in this genus is closely related to *Thuja* and is better known in gardens under its synonym. Grown for its foliage and attractive cones, it is suitable for any good, well-drained soil. It prefers a position in full sun and if it is planted in cold areas it should be sheltered from strong winds. Useful as a specimen plant or for hedging, it can be trimmed in spring and late summer.

Platycladus orientalis

This is a densely branched evergreen shrub of upright habit, more rarely a tree, with tiny scale-like leaves arranged in vertically held, flattened sprays. The conspicuous cones, up to about 2 cm (¾ in) long, are covered with a blue-white bloom when young and have prominent hooks on the backs of their scales.

Synonym: *Thuja orientalis*
Native range: China, Korea, Russian Far East
Height: 10 m (33 ft)
Spread: 5 m (16 ft)
Hardiness: Zone 6
Variants: 'Aurea Nana' is a dwarf form, to 1.5 m (5 ft), with bright yellow foliage. 'Elegantissima' is narrow and upright, to 5 m (16 ft), with bright yellow young foliage that is yellow-green in summer and bronze in winter. 'Rosedalis' is dwarf, to 1 m (3 ft), with foliage that is creamy yellow when young, bronze-purple in winter.

Podocarpus
Podocarpaceae

This genus of just over 100 species of evergreen trees and shrubs is mainly confined to the warm regions of the southern hemisphere, extending to Central America, Mexico and East Asia. Species are variable in foliage and have male and female flowers on separate plants. The fruit is borne on a flesh-coloured receptacle that is attractive to birds, and is produced only when both male and female plants are present. Plants are suitable for any good, moist but well-drained soil.

Podocarpus nivalis

This is an evergreen shrub that makes a dense mound with leathery yellow-green leaves, to 2 cm (¾ in) long, ending in short points. Male plants bear clusters of small, yellow flowers. Female plants may bear small cones with a fleshy red base.

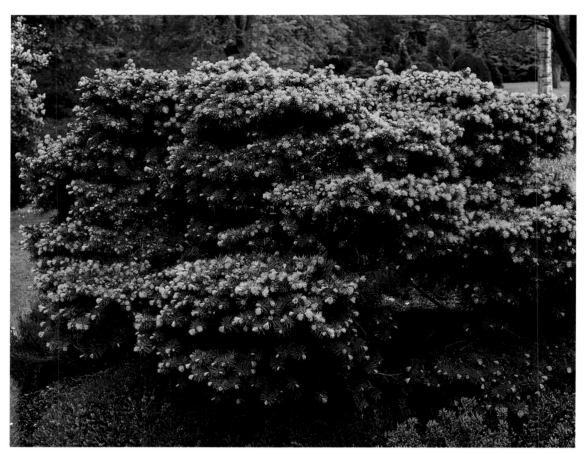

Pseudotsuga menziesii 'Fletcheri'

Common name: Alpine totara
Native range: New Zealand
Height: 1.5 m (5 ft)
Spread: 2 m (6 ft)
Hardiness: Zone 7

Podocarpus salignus

This graceful evergreen tree has a conical habit and red-brown bark peeling in long strips. The slender, glossy green leaves are distinctly curved, up to 10 cm (4 in) long, and are borne on slender, green shoots. Male plants have clusters of small yellow flowers in spring; females, small cones on a fleshy, green to violet base. It is at its best in areas with cool, moist summers and mild winters.

Native range: Chile
Height: 15 m (50 ft)
Spread: 6 m (20 ft)
Hardiness: Zone 8

Pseudolarix
Pinaceae

The single species in this genus is a deciduous tree superficially similar to the larches. Grown for its autumn colour, it requires a good, moist but well-drained, lime-free soil in full sun, and it should be sheltered from the effects of strong winds.

Pseudolarix amabilis

This is a slow-growing, conical deciduous tree with foliage similar to that of the larches. The slender, bright green leaves are borne singly on long shoots and in dense whorls on short side shoots. Leaves turn golden yellow in autumn. Male and female flowers are yellow and are borne separately at the ends of the short shoots in late spring. The egg-shaped cones, to 5 cm (2 in) long, ripen from blue-green to yellow green then brown, breaking up on the tree before they fall.

Common name: Golden larch
Native range: E China
Height: 15 m (50 ft)
Spread: 10 m (33 ft)
Hardiness: Zone 5

Pseudotsuga
Pinaceae

The four species in this small genus are evergreen trees native of western North America, south to Mexico, and East Asia. The following is the only species found commonly in gardens. Frequently grown commercially for forestry, it makes a very large tree, but it has produced a few forms suitable for smaller gardens. Grow in a moist but well-drained, lime-free soil. It reaches its greatest size in areas with high rainfall.

Sequoia sempervirens

Sequoia sempervirens 'Prostrata'

rapid growth rate and final size, this tree is suitable only for large gardens or public spaces.

Sequoia sempervirens

This is a fast-growing, conical, evergreen tree with soft, thick, red-brown bark and spreading branches. The yew-like foliage consists of small, dark green leaves marked with two white bands beneath. The leaves decrease in length towards the end of the shoots. The flowers open in late winter to early spring, males and females separate but on the same tree. The male flowers are yellow-brown; the females green, followed by red-brown cones up to about 3 cm (1 in) in length.

Common name: Coastal redwood
Native range: W United States of America
Height: 30 m (100 ft) or more
Spread: 10 m (33 ft)
Hardiness: Zone 7
Variants: 'Adpressa' is slow growing, up to 10 m (33 ft) or more in height, with white-tipped young foliage. 'Prostrata' is low and spreading, to 1 m (3 ft) high, with broad, blue-green leaves.

Pseudotsuga menziesii

This is a very fast-growing evergreen tree with a conical habit, and producing thick, red-brown bark. The slender, dark green leaves are borne all around the shoots and have two whitish bands beneath. The flowers open in spring, males and females separately but on the same tree: the male flowers are yellow; the females green flushed with pink. The pendulous, red-brown cones that develop are up to about 10 cm (4 in) long, and have characteristic three-pronged bracts emerging from between the scales.

Common name: Douglas fir
Native range: W North America, Mexico
Height: 40 m (130 ft) or more.
Spread: 10 m (33 ft)
Hardiness: Zone 4
Variants: 'Fletcheri' is bushy and spreading, up to 2 m (6 ft) high, with blue-green foliage.

Sciadopitys
Sciadopityaceae

The single species in this genus is the only member of its family, and it is a very distinct and unusual evergreen tree. Grown for its foliage, it is suitable for any good, moist but well-drained, lime-free soil. It makes an excellent specimen tree for a sunny position but is also tolerant of shade.

Sciadopitys verticillata

A densely growing, conical evergreen tree with red-brown bark. It is slow growing when young and often multi-stemmed. The slender, deep green, needle-like leaves, up to 12 cm (5 in) long, are grooved on both sides and arranged in whorls at the ends of the shoots. Male and female flowers are separate on the same tree and open in spring: males yellow-brown; females green maturing to red-brown cones up to 8 cm (3 in) long.

Common name: Japanese umbrella pine
Native range: Japan
Height: 15 m (50 ft)
Spread: 8 m (26 ft)
Hardiness: Zone 5

Sequoia
Cupressaceae

The single species in this small genus is a large evergreen tree grown for its vigorous growth, habit, attractive bark and its foliage. In the wild, trees live to a great age and there is a specimen in California, USA, that is the tallest tree anywhere in the world. In cultivation it is tolerant of a range of conditions, although it does require a good, moist but well-drained soil and a site in full sun. The most rapid growth and largest size are attained in areas with cool, moist summers. Owing to its

Sequoiadendron
Cupressaceae

The single species in this genus is frequently confused with *Sequoia sempervirens*, although the two trees are quite distinct. Despite the fact that it is not generally as tall as *Sequoia*, it reaches a greater girth, and a specimen of this species is the world's most massive tree. In cultivation it will grow in any reasonably good, well-drained soil, but is suitable only for large gardens.

Sequoiadendron giganteum

This very fast-growing, conical evergreen tree has thick, soft, red-brown bark. The downswept branches are clothed with small, sharp-pointed leaves arranged all around the shoots, making the foliage rough to the touch. Separate male and female flowers open in early spring on the same tree. Males are yellow; females green, maturing to barrel-shaped, brown cones up to 8 cm (3 in) long.

Common names: Giant redwood, Wellingtonia
Native range: California, USA
Height: 30 m (100 ft) or more
Spread: 10 m (33 ft)
Hardiness: Zone 6
Variants: 'Glaucum' is narrowly conical with blue-green foliage. 'Pendulum' is slender with main branches hanging vertically.

Sequoiadendron giganteum

Taxodium
Cupressaceae

The two species in this genus – one deciduous, one evergreen – are natives of the southeast of the United States of America through Mexico to Guatemala. The following species has attractive foliage, which colours up in autumn, and it is the only one that is commonly grown.

It prefers a moist, or even wet, lime-free soil and does best in full sun. The cypress 'knees' (woody protuberances growing vertically from the roots) are best produced on moist soils, most prolifically in regions with hot summers.

Taxodium distichum

This is a conical deciduous tree with grey-brown bark, and with a trunk often buttressed and fluted when mature. Two types of leaves are borne: small, scale-like leaves on persistent shoots and slender leaves, to 2 cm (¾ in) long, spreading out either side of deciduous shoots. In autumn, the leaves turn reddish brown and fall with the shoots. The flowers form in autumn but open in spring. Male flowers are yellow-green, held in pendulous catkins. The females are green, and these are followed by rounded, brown cones up to about 3 cm (1 in) across. Cypress knees, up to 1 m (3 ft) tall, may form where conditions are favourable.

Common name: Swamp cypress
Native range: SE United States of America
Height: 30 m (100 ft) or more
Spread: 8 m (26 ft)
Hardiness: Zone 4
Variants: var. *imbricatum* (*T. ascendens*) is a smaller, narrower tree, reaching a height of up to 20 m (65 ft), and has leaves to 1 cm (⅓ in), closely pressed against the upright, deciduous shoots.

Taxus
Taxaceae

The yews form a genus of about ten species of evergreen shrubs and trees that are widely distributed mainly in the temperate regions of the northern hemisphere, extending to Central America and Malaysia.

The following is the most commonly grown species. It is suitable for any well-drained soil, even shallow, chalky soils, and will grow either in sun or shade. The variegated forms colour best if given a bright position. It is a useful plant for hedging and topiary and can be trimmed in both the summer and early autumn. Old plants can be rejuvenated by cutting them back hard in spring.

Taxus baccata

This is a broadly conical, evergreen tree with smooth, purple-brown, flaking bark and dark, blackish green leaves. Small male and female flowers are borne separately on different trees in the spring, but only the pale yellow male flowers are conspicuous in any way. The fruit produced is a single seed partly enclosed in a fleshy, red covering. All parts of the fruit, except the seed coat, are poisonous.

Common name: Common yew
Native range: Europe, N Africa, W Asia
Height: 10 m (33 ft) or more
Spread: 10 m (33 ft)
Hardiness: Zone 6
Variants: 'Fastigiata' (Irish yew) is a female form, narrowly upright when young and with leaves spreading all around the shoots. The tree shape becomes broader with age. 'Fastigiata Aureomarginata' is an upright male form with yellow-edged leaves. 'Repens Aurea' is a low and spreading female form bearing yellow-edged leaves, and it makes attractive ground cover. 'Semperaurea' is male with golden yellow foliage. 'Standishii' is a narrowly upright female form with yellow-edged leaves.

Thuja
Cupressaceae

The five species that make up this genus are all evergreen trees, natives of North America and East Asia. There is one species from China, but this is now extinct in the wild. The trees usually have aromatic foliage composed of tiny scale-like leaves borne in flattened sprays. The small, male and female flowers are borne separately on the same plant.

Thujas do best if given good, moist but well-drained soil and a position where they are sheltered from the effects of strong winds. They are useful as specimen plants, while the dwarf forms are suitable for the rock garden. They can also be used for hedging.

Thuja occidentalis

This is a conically shaped, evergreen tree with a dense habit, and with orange-brown bark that peels in vertical strips. Tiny, scale-like leaves, of a similar colour on both sides, are borne in flattened, aromatic sprays. The flowers open in the spring. The male flowers are red; females yellow-brown, followed by upright cones, up to about 1 cm (⅓ in) long, ripening from a yellow-green colour to brown.

Taxus baccata 'Fastigiata Aureomarginata'

Taxus baccata 'Standishii'

Thuja occidentalis 'Danica'

Common name: White cedar
Native range: E North America
Height: 20 m (65 ft)
Spread: 5 m (16 ft)
Hardiness: Zone 3
Variants: 'Danica' is a compact, rounded, dwarf form with foliage growing in vertical sprays. The leaves turn bronze in winter. 'Hetz Midget' is an extremely compact and slow-growing, rounded bush. 'Holmstrup' is a large, narrowly conical shrub, up to about 4 m (13 ft) in height. 'Rheingold' is a rounded bush, up to 1 m (3 ft), with bronze-yellow foliage that is pinkish when young. 'Smaragd' is a slow-growing, narrowly conical form, to 3 m (10 ft) tall, with bright green foliage. 'Tiny Tim' is a slow-growing dwarf up to 30 cm (12 in) tall. 'Yellow Ribbon' is narrowly conical, to about 3 m (10 ft) tall, with golden yellow foliage.

Thuja plicata

This is a vigorously growing, densely conical evergreen tree with attractive purple-brown bark that peels in vertical strips. Tiny, scale-like leaves are borne in flattened sprays of aromatic foliage marked with white beneath. The flowers open in the spring. The males are reddish black, while the females are yellow-green, followed by small, upright cones, up to about 1 cm (⅓ in) long, ripening from yellow-green to brown.

Common name: Western red cedar
Native range: W North America
Height: 30 m (100 ft)
Spread: 8 m (26 ft)
Hardiness: Zone 5
Variants: 'Atrovirens' produces glossy dark green leaves. 'Aurea' has soft yellow-coloured foliage. 'Rogersii' is a slow-growing form, reaching a height of about 1 m (3 ft), with bronze-yellow foliage. 'Stoneham Gold' is a conical form, up to about 3 m (10 ft) high, with golden yellow young foliage. 'Zebrina' grows vigorously and has foliage banded with yellow and dark green.

Thujopsis
Cupressaceae

The single species that makes up this small genus is an evergreen tree that is grown for its handsome foliage. The tree is suitable for any good, moist but well-drained soil, and it does best if provided with a position in full sun, yet where it is still sheltered from strong winds.

Thujopsis dolabrata

This is a conical evergreen tree with purple-brown bark peeling in vertical strips. The slightly aromatic foliage is borne in broad, flattened sprays composed of small, scale-like, bright green leaves. The leaves are conspicuously marked with large patches of white on their undersurfaces. The small flowers open in the spring. The males are blackish green in colour, while the females are blue-grey, maturing to a brown, bloomy cone, up to 1.2 cm (½ in) long, blue-green when young.

Native range: Japan
Height: 20 m (65 ft)
Spread: 8 m (26 ft)
Hardiness: Zone 5
Variants: 'Aurea' produces young foliage that is flushed with yellow. 'Nana' is a dwarf shrub reaching a maximum height of about 1m (3 ft). 'Variegata' has foliage that is sparsely blotched with white.

Tsuga canadensis 'Jeddeloh'

Thuja plicata 'Rogersii'

Tsuga
Pinaceae

The hemlocks make up a small genus of nine species of graceful, evergreen trees that are natives of North America and East Asia. The following species are those most widely seen in garden cultivation, usually as selected dwarf forms. Male and female flowers are borne separately but on the same tree.

The hemlocks do best if they are provided with a moist but well-drained soil rich in organic matter. They can be grown in sun or shade.

Tsuga canadensis

This is a broadly conical evergreen tree with red-brown bark and bearing slender, flattened leaves that narrow slightly towards their tips. The leaves spread out either side of the shoots and are marked with two white bands on their undersurfaces. The flowers open in the late spring. The males are yellow and the females green, maturing to small, pale brown, pendulous cones up to about 2 cm (¾ in) long.

Common name: Eastern hemlock
Native range: E North America
Height: 25 m (80 ft)
Spread: 10 m (33 ft)
Hardiness: Zone 4
Variants: 'Jeddeloh' is a small bush, up to about 1 m (3 ft) tall, with arching shoots. 'Minuta' is a very compact and slow-growing dwarf form up to about 60 cm (24 in) tall.

Tsuga heterophylla

A conical, evergreen tree with purple-brown bark and dark green leaves with parallel sides and two white bands beneath. The reddish male and female flowers open in spring, the females maturing to pale brown, pendulous cones up to 2 cm (¾ in) long.

Common name: Western hemlock
Native range: W North America
Height: 30 m (100 ft)
Spread: 10 m (33 ft)
Hardiness: Zone 6

Index

(Page numbers in *italics* refer to pages with relevant illustrations.)

299